Leadership for

Special

Education

Administration

A
CASE-BASED
APPROACH

Leadership for
Special
Education
Administration

**A
CASE-BASED
APPROACH**

Mark B. Goor
George Mason University

Harcourt Brace College Publishers

Fort Worth • Philadelphia • San Diego • New York • Orlando • Austin • San Antonio
Toronto • Montreal • London • Sydney • Tokyo

For Eileen
The greatest of life partners

Vice President, Publisher	*Ted Buchholz*
Senior Acquisitions Editor	*Jo-Anne Weaver*
Assistant Editor	*Pam Hatley*
Project Editor	*Elizabeth C. Alvarez*
Production Manager	*Melinda Esco*
Art Director	*Peggy Young*

ISBN: 0-15-501271-1

Library of Congress Catalog Card Number: 94-77141

Address for Editorial Correspondence: Harcourt Brace College Publishers, 301 Commerce Street, Suite 3700, Fort Worth, Texas 76102.

Address for Orders: Harcourt Brace & Company, 6277 Sea Harbor Drive, Orlando, Florida 32887-6777. 1-800-782-4479, or 1-800-433-0001 (in Florida).

Printed in the United States of America

5 6 7 8 9 0 1 2 3 4   016   10 9 8 7 6 5 4 3 2 1

PREFACE

What type of pedagogy can produce both critical thinkers and creative practitioners? *A Nation Prepared: Teachers for the 21st Century* (1989) recommends "teaching cases" as a major focus of instruction. Kowalski (1991) also advises using cases to prepare educational administrators. Case-based pedagogy educates professionals by teaching specialized skills; examining complex, ambiguous situations; encouraging collegial dialogue; and establishing a heuristic for quality service. Recognizing the potential of this method, this textbook employs a case-based approach. Theories, issues, and procedures are presented and followed by cases that demonstrate application of new information and promote reflection of knowledge in practice. In some instances, information is introduced through cases, and students are asked to identify salient issues.

Most cases tell a story which provides enough detail to set a context for specific issues of interest (Grossman, 1992). Four categories are delineated by Shulman (1992): case reports, case studies, case materials, and teaching cases, and each is used in this textbook. *Case reports* are first-person accounts, reporting events and activities as well as interpretations of the experiences. Several interviews take the form of case reports in which administrators describe their jobs and reflect on current issues transforming their roles. *Case studies* throughout the book are third-person portrayals of episodes that use an anthropological reference point; that is, the setting and culture are characterized so readers can understand the context in which decisions are made. *Case materials* include such raw data as letters, work samples, and examples of computer screens. *Teaching cases* are accounts that have been edited to provide dilemmas. Actual or fictitious, they illustrate a point currently not available in local lore. Students read part "A" of the case and then analyze the circumstances and challenges or predict what will happen next. Part "B" presents more information or later developments, and students evaluate their predictions and continue analyzing and proposing solutions. Each case is followed by a section called **Consider This,** which asks readers to apply and reflect on specific concepts or to consider controversial aspects.

CONTENT AND ORGANIZATION

This textbook is designed to prepare educators for today's complex administrative demands by integrating current knowledge with case studies, interviews, and teaching cases. Administrators responsible for special programs are dependent upon a wide spectrum of federal, state, and local systems, as well as a great number of individuals. Accordingly, they must be trained to be facile communicators, effective team builders, proficient managers, and strategic planners. Preparing administrators for these responsibilities requires both practical information about administering programs and heuristics to analyze the problems of leaders in today's schools.

As schools transform to accommodate diversity and prepare students for a new order, it is essential for today's leaders to define the future roles of special educators. The unifying theme of *Leadership for Special Education Administration: A Case-Based Approach* is that administrators of special education can be dynamic leaders during a time of inevitable change. The book advances a paradigm shift from the traditional role of managers concerned with compliance to one of leaders with a new vision: to champion school transformations that result in the best possible outcome for all students. To facilitate the development of leaders with vision, this book offers experiences in analytical problem solving and provides descriptions of innovative programs that exemplify excellence.

Section I, **Responding to Organizational Paradigms,** presents a model for leadership in special education administration within the context of organizational structures and paradigms of schools and government agencies. Chapter 1 describes this model and includes interviews with directors and coordinators from across the country who exemplify leadership that is responding to current challenges. Chapter 2 explores the nature of the change process and how school personnel respond to various attempts to implement change. Chapter 3, special education law, summarizes the overwhelming responsibilities conferred on administrators by the mandates and guidelines of legislation and litigation. Chapter 4, working with government, explores levels of authority, the nature of bureaucracy, and current perceptions of school paradigms. Chapter 5, the final chapter in this section, explores the contemporary system of financing special education programs.

Section II, **Collaborating with Essential Team Members,** portrays the special education administrator as a member of building, district, and community teams. Chapter 6 describes attracting, selecting, and facilitating the growth of quality personnel, advancing the belief that humans are an organization's greatest resource. Chapter 7 proposes that principals are the key to success for special education programs, explaining how building leaders can guarantee success for every learner. Chapter 8 explains how to encourage parents to be partners and advocates and how to deal with those who appear to be adversaries. Chapter 9 examines collaboration in schools and "wraparound" cooperation with outside agencies.

Section III, **Delivering Quality Service in a Changing World,** explores current management issues in a society that continues to confront schools with new demands and opportunities. Chapter 10 provides a thoughtful analysis of the most common direction for educating students with special needs: responsible integration with general education. Chapter 11 addresses another area of growing significance, educating children with special health-care conditions. Chapter 12 deals with the unique characteristics of rural and urban schools and sheds light on the challenges of service delivery for the majority of our nation's students. Numerous applications and the unlimited potential of microcomputers and electronic communication are explored in Chapter 13, technology for special education administrators. Finally, Chapter 14 proposes a model for program evaluation that emphasizes team-based, formative evaluation for today's outcome-based schools.

ENHANCING CASE-BASED LEARNING

The teaching potential of the case-based method may be enhanced by using the following suggestions:

1. Establish a climate for discussion in which students may express views honestly.
2. Encourage students to read and reflect on cases before class so discussion is based on carefully considered positions (Grossman, 1992).
3. After one student has offered an opinion about a case, ask for a different interpretation, demonstrating that there can be more than one perspective and multiple explanations (Schwab, 1969). Commend intellectual disagreement and encourage mutual respect of interpretations and decisions (Kowalski, 1991).

4. Encourage students to discuss with each other rather than make direct comments to the teacher. Reinforce the value of discussing cases as preparation for collegial discourse in the future (Kowalski, 1991).
5. Assist students in examining the values or beliefs underlying the differing interpretations of cases (Kowalski, 1991).
6. Summarize key points regularly throughout the discussion (Grossman, 1992).
7. Examine the conditions in which certain decisions are made in order to determine when to apply principles to future situations (Kowalski, 1991).
8. Probe for clarification and purpose. Students seem able to identify problems but have difficulty isolating elements and defining terms. They will become more effective professionals when they are able to articulate their positions clearly (Richert, 1989).
9. Recognize that not all solutions and interpretations are equally valid. Students need feedback and refocusing to benefit from case-based learning (Grossman, 1992).
10. Encourage students to write their own cases. That will assist students in connecting the case method with their personal experiences (Richert, 1989).

REFERENCES

Carnegie Task Force on Teaching as a Profession. (1989). *A nation prepared: Teachers for the 21st century.* New York: Carnegie Forum on Education and the Economy, Carnegie Corporation.

Grossman, P. L. (1992). Teaching and learning with cases: Unanswered questions. In J. H. Shulman (Ed.), *Case methods in teacher education* (pp. 227–239). New York: Teachers College Press.

Kowalski, T. J. (1991). *Case studies on educational administration.* New York: Longman.

Richert, A. E. (1989, April). *Preparing cases promoting reflection: A case method in teacher education.* Paper presentation at the annual meeting of the American Educational Research Association, San Francisco, CA.

Shulman, L. S. (1992). Toward a pedagogy of cases. In J. H. Shulman (Ed.), *Case methods in teacher education* (pp. 227–239). New York: Teachers College Press.

Schwab, J. J. (1969). *College curriculum and student protest.* Chicago: University of Chicago Press.

ACKNOWLEDGMENTS

I am thankful for the support and helpful feedback received in the preparation of this textbook. Several individuals at Emporia State University provided invaluable assistance: John Schwenn, David Bateman, Tes Mehring, and Festus Obiakor. I appreciated the students enrolled in Administration and Supervision of Special Education who asked questions and suggested changes to the book as it evolved, as well as Ying Chin Chen and Mei Shu Wu, who assisted with research, and Kristy Anderes, who provided her microcomputer expertise. Chapters concerning change, law, government, finance, inclusion, health conditions, technology, and program evaluation were contributed by knowledgeable professionals from across the nation, presenting many valuable perspectives. Thanks also to those who reviewed this book in the manuscript stage: Gerald Wallace of George Mason University, Belinda Skelton of Georgia State University, and James Yates of the University of Texas. Jo-Anne Weaver, Harcourt Brace acquisitions editor, has offered helpful guidance and encouragement throughout the manuscript preparation. This book has also benefited from editorial feedback from Pam Hatley, acquisitions editorial assistant, and Beth Alvarez, project editor, and from the skills of Art Director Peggy Young and Production Manager Melinda Esco. Finally, I acknowledge my parents, who have given me a lifetime of love and pride.

CONTRIBUTORS

David Bateman, PhD, *Director of Sponsored Research,* Emporia State University, Emporia, KS.

Terry Heintz Caldwell, MEd, *Education Consultant,* National Maternal and Child Health Resource Center for Ensuring Adequate Preparation of Providers of Care at Children's Hospital, New Orleans, LA.

K. Kay Cessna, *Supervisor,* Colorado Department of Education, Denver, CO.

Fran Clark, PhD, *Assistant Professor,* College of Education, Wichita State University, Wichita, KS.

Marjory Conners, *Speech/Language Pathologist and Consultant,* Cobb County Public Schools, Marietta, GA.

Sandy Darling, PhD, *Principal,* Clearview Elementary School, Clear Lake, MN.

Bonnie Dye, *Transition Coordinator,* Cobb County Public Schools, Marietta, GA.

Douglas Gill, PhD, *Director of Special Education,* State of Washington, Office of Superintendent of Public Instruction, Olympia, WA.

Nancy Glass, *Director of Children's Services,* United Cerebral Palsy of Queens, New York City, NY.

Jacqueline Harrison, MN, RN, *Program Coordinator,* National Maternal and Child Health Resource Center for Ensuring Adequate Preparation of Providers of Care at Children's Hospital, New Orleans, LA.

Elizabeth B. Hill, EdS, *Special Education Coordinator,* City of Virginia Beach, Virginia Beach, VA.

Maureen Hook, PhD, *Supervisor of Special Education,* Team One, Chesapeake Public Schools, Chesapeake, VA.

Janice Rutledge Janz, MEd, *Special Education Consultant,* National Maternal and Child Health Resource Center for Ensuring Adequate Preparation of Providers of Care at Children's Hospital, New Orleans, LA.

Basil Kessler, *Consultant for Community Transition, Deaf Specialist,* Emporia State University, Emporia, KS.

David E. Kingsley, PhD, *Program Evaluation/Research Specialist,* Southeast Kansas Education Service Center, Topeka, KS.

Frank Kline, PhD, *Assistant Professor,* College of Education, Wichita State University, Wichita, KS.

Diana Larson, *Consultant,* King George, VA.

Steven Mark, *Administrative Coordinator of Special Education,* Los Angeles Unified School District, Los Angeles, CA.

Teresa A. Mehring, PhD, *Associate Dean,* The Teachers College, Emporia State University, Emporia, KS.

Fred Miller, *Director,* Flint Hills Special Education Cooperative, Emporia, KS.

Dick Reed, PhD, *Director of Pupil Services and Special Education,* Cherry Creek Schools, Englewood, CO.

John O. Schwenn, PhD, *Chair, Psychology and Special Education,* The Teachers College, Emporia State University, Emporia, KS.

Giselle Stone, *Program Director,* Cobb County Public Schools, Marietta, GA.

Mary Beth Vautour, *Project Coordinator,* Training School Principals in Special Education Administration, Middletown, CT.

James R. Wheeler, *Executive Director,* Northeast Kansas Education Service Center, Lecompton, KS.

ABOUT THE AUTHOR

Mark B. Goor, PhD, is an assistant professor in the Graduate School of Education at George Mason University. He has been a special education administrator in both public and state institutions. Dr. Goor has been an educator in New York, Colorado, Virginia, Washington, and Kansas. After 18 years in the field, he completed his doctorate at the University of Virginia in the area of special education and leadership/policy studies. Dr. Goor was an adjunct professor at the University of Virginia and James Madison University and assistant professor in the Division of Psychology and Special Education at Emporia State University before accepting his current position. His research and publications have focused on collaboration among general and special educators as well as preparation for educators to accommodate students with special needs. Dr. Goor is associate editor of *Intervention in School and Clinic.* Additionally, he is active in the Council for Exceptional Children and presents regularly at national conferences for several professional organizations. Dr. Goor is a storyteller and has a natural affinity for the case-study approach. He believes that case studies enable teachers and administrators to construct a conceptual framework with which to interpret education and its current challenges.

TABLE OF CONTENTS

SECTION I

RESPONDING TO ORGANIZATIONAL PARADIGMS

Chapter 1

LEADERSHIP

A new generation of leaders is emerging in special education. This leadership has evolved over three decades of dramatic change in special education and as a result of new management paradigms in industry and public schools.

THREE DECADES OF CHANGE

In the 1960s, special education consisted of programs for students with mental retardation and severe disabilities, managed primarily by administrators whose main responsibility was to oversee regular education, federally funded programs, or psychological services. Their titles included director of federal projects, assistant superintendent for instruction, elementary supervisor, or school psychologist. These managers were typically former regular education teachers and principals who had taken the requisite coursework for administrative endorsement. Their knowledge of special education accrued on the job. In some states, school psychologists added to their role description the responsibility for managing a few special classes and coordinating placement of students in residential settings.

Due to the efforts of advocacy groups in the 1960s and early 1970s, landmark legislation in 1975 mandated the provision of a wide array of services for students with disabilities who had been underserved. Because of the enormity and complexity of orchestrating these new services, school districts nationwide hired full-time administrators to establish programs, hire personnel, manage budgets, and respond to legal challenges. These special education administrators were still typically regular education personnel learning to follow federal guidelines and state mandates concerning services for exceptional children. It seemed that their job was to comply with the ever-increasing demands for special programs by hiring as many trained personnel as possible. When the supply of qualified applicants was exhausted, administrators assigned regular classroom teachers to new programs, requiring them to take special education courses over several years through programs springing up in colleges everywhere. Together, teachers and administrators learned about providing special education services.

Several forces changed the direction of education in the 1980s. Research began asking questions about effective instruction. Some investigations questioned the efficacy of new special services that segregated students from regular education peers (Stainback & Stainback, 1990). In response, an emphasis on educating students with disabilities in the mainstream began to emerge. For this to be successful, it became apparent that regular and special educators had to learn to communicate and cooperate (Simpson & Myles, 1993). The face of the American classroom was changing as the population shifted from predominantly Caucasian, non-Hispanic to a kaleidoscope of diverse cultures and languages (Correa & Tulbert, 1991). In addition, parents became more clear in their expectations for improved services for their children and more vocal. Finally, schools began following the lead of business in moving toward site-based management. Education was reorganizing to involve more individuals in decision making, requiring educators to perform new collaborative roles.

In the 1990s, dramatic trends in demography, society, economy, technology, and learning are altering the role of schools in the United States (Hoyle, Fenwich, & Steffy, 1990). Nationwide, 24% of children live below the poverty level, and 60% will live in one-parent families (usually female-headed, low-income households) during their school years. More than 40% of students come from minority backgrounds, and this group speaks 200 languages and dialects. Social trends include a shift in attitude from an emphasis on conformity to an appreciation for diversity. Citizens are calling for reform at schools that do not seem to be producing scholars or skilled workers. Schools are struggling to come to terms with unforeseen demands, including the education of medically fragile children. Industry has become global, demanding the United States redefine its role in world markets and examine what skills students need when exiting school. Students must be prepared for jobs that don't currently exist in engineering, technology, and health fields. Through previously inconceivable technological advances, our society is experiencing an acceleration in the availability of new information and processing capabilities. New "electronic highways" will allow educators and students to access any library and communicate with sister schools around the globe. Interactive video systems expand options for viable learning environments beyond the traditional classroom.

All these forces set the stage for a new definition of special education in a rapidly changing society and educational system. Special education in the 1990s has refocused (a) from emphasizing disabilities to valuing the individual first and attending to the disability second, (b) from providing isolated services to collaborating within schools and integrating all students into the school and community to the greatest extent possible, and (c) from providing effective instructional programs to determining desired life outcomes and planning programs to prepare students for satisfying, independent lives.

As special education evolves, its leadership must evolve, too. More than ever, the special education administrator must be a facile communicator, proficient manager, astute politician, and strategic planner. Successful leaders in special education realize their job is a balancing act—advocating for the best possible services, empowering staff, acknowledging the needs of parents, and collaborating with other administrators. In a time of inevitable change, they must be dynamic leaders with a vision who can champion a school transformation that results in maximal outcomes for all students.

The following interview captures the essence of changes in special education since the mid–1960s. Fred Miller, director of a special education cooperative in central Kansas, has been an administrator since 1966.

A Retrospective: 1966 to the Present

Fred Miller
Director of Flint Hills Special Education Cooperative, Emporia, Kansas

I was trained as a school psychologist in the early 1960s. At that time, it was assumed we would do evaluations and be in charge of special education classes for school districts in which we worked. My training included "road trips" with my adviser to towns around Kansas where we would administer as many as six individual intelligence tests per day to students referred for suspected mental retardation. Then we would write a report and send it to the principal, who decided whether the student qualified for services. Other than our reports, the only paperwork was a half sheet of paper documenting the reason for referral with a line for the teacher and principal to sign. It was not necessary to request permission or even inform parents their child was being evaluated. As a matter of fact, if a child did not qualify for services, it was possible no one would discuss the process with a parent. It a student did qualify, the principal called the parents primarily to arrange transportation to the new class.

In 1966, I began as a school psychologist in Emporia. I was also responsible for three classes of what was termed educable mentally handicapped students and one class for the trainable mentally handicapped. The classes served students up to age 16 (after which they went to the Lyon County Retarded Children's Center). To attend our classes, students had to be toilet trained, verbally communicative, and ambulatory; otherwise, they stayed home. Students who were deaf or blind or who had severe behavior disorders were institutionalized. Speech therapists were organized through a private center. We provided space for two therapists in our schools, and parents transported their children and paid for therapy.

At that time, school psychologists were aware of students who had learning problems other than mental retardation and students who were being expelled from school for inappropriate behavior. We also identified some gifted students. There was no teamwork; school psychologists were the decision makers and offered ideas to classroom teachers for accommodating these exceptional students.

The Kansas Department of Education provided grant funding for innovative programs. In 1968, we offered an innovative summer program for students K–2 with behavior problems. Then, in 1969, we began our elementary Behavior Disorders program, assuming we wouldn't need a secondary-level program because students' problems would be remediated earlier. In 1970, we hired our own speech pathologist to provide no-cost therapy.

In 1974, dramatic changes began. Kansas mandated services for students with developmental disabilities that included learning disabilities, mental retardation, epilepsy, and cerebral palsy. In 1975, all other categories identified in PL 94-142 were to be served. We began to identify large numbers of students and budgeted for scores of positions. However, there were few trained and certified applicants available. General education teachers were assigned to special classes and were asked to take summer courses at the university. Applicants for regular class positions were told there were no openings, but if they would get provisional certification over the summer, we would hire them. At first, three-fourths of our teachers had provisional certifications.

We proposed to consolidate special education services for the surrounding districts to provide cost-effective programs. A state mandate required programs as large as ours to have a designated administrator. Therefore, I took the requisite classes and began as the full-time director of the Flint Hills Special Education Cooperative. Superintendents were pleased to purchase the services because they didn't have the resources or the understanding of the new mandates. As the cooperative grew, it was challenged to hire enough teachers and find sufficient numbers of classrooms. In time, as we were able to train teachers and hire more certified staff, we moved from concern with basic compliance to a focus on quality programs and effective instruction. We opened an instructional materials center and started vocational programs.

Our cooperative was affected by four major trends in the 1980s: increasing parent advocacy, emphasis on mainstreaming, more sophisticated evaluations of program outcomes, and changing student populations. Parents became active supporters of special education programs, participating on advocacy boards and vocalizing concerns to administrators. Parents also demanded the services they thought their children deserved, using due process and litigation procedures. Teachers and parents advocated for students to receive more of their education in mainstream classes. As students' programs were shared by more than one educator, the need for teaming and collaboration skills became evident. Additionally, educators began to ask whether students were being prepared for the realities of postschool life. New thinking regarding outcomes and transition services began to take hold. Finally, as students entered our schools with limited English proficiency and different cultural norms, we were confronted with new questions concerning nonbiased identification and appropriate services for minorities.

My administrative role in the 1990s is now more complex than ever. We are reconceptualizing our services to be more inclusive or at least home-school oriented. Site-based management brings decisions to the school level. Plus, the state has mandated we develop total quality management systems. These new directions have required an aggressive approach to inservice training. We no longer think of inservice as biyearly, obligatory business meetings. Instead, we have large inservice budgets and plan comprehensive training programs.

Kansas is moving away from categorical programs to what our state calls "interrelated," that is, programs that serve all students with mild to moderate disabilities. Emphasis on both younger and older students is also evident as we expand early childhood programs and at the same time develop transition services and community-based programs. Our staffing patterns also have changed; we are hiring more paraprofessionals than ever for early childhood programs and transition services as well as to facilitate inclusion in the regular classroom.

I think it's interesting these trends may signal a new era and the end of our special education cooperative. The original justification for the co-op was to provide cost-effective programs for low-incidence populations. Now, we are preparing educators to accept students with disabilities in their home schools, to accommodate differences in the regular classroom, and to provide quality programs. It will be interesting to see what my role will be in the next few years.

 CONSIDER THIS

1. What major trends have refocused the role of the special education administrator over the past three decades?
2. What preparation would an administrator need for this new focus?
3. Special education cooperatives were originally designed to group students with low-incidence disabilities so that cost-effective programs could be provided in central locations. How might an emphasis on inclusion or home-school service delivery affect the future of cooperative programs?

NEW INDUSTRIAL PARADIGMS

A paradigm is a way of seeing; it is a lens through which individuals experience the world, accepting only what makes sense and filtering out what cannot be explained (Kuhn, 1962). Paradigms are also organizing principles that help individuals or groups to reduce the complexity of experiences to manageable systems for understanding and decision making. For example, the traditional paradigm for industry was: The only way to succeed in a competitive marketplace is for those in authority to make decisions and dictate the actions of workers so that each part of the process is efficiently completed. This translated to a bureaucratic hierarchy in which executives had the exclusive role of seeing the total picture, setting goals, and supervising subordinates to do their small part. Schools accepted this paradigm and built bureaucratic structures in which district goals were developed by administrators, planning was short term, programs were fractionated, and assessment of effectiveness was punitive (Sarason, 1990).

Through the influence of W. Edwards Deming and other persuasive new thinkers in industry, the paradigm shifted to emphasize quality. That is, the quality of products and services is defined by consumers, and achieving quality is the most important factor in experiencing the value of one's work (Audetta & Algozzine, 1992). This new paradigm translated to systems in which all employees participated in formulating a vision for desired outcomes, decisions were made at the level of implementation, and quality control was internal. This new model stressed professional pride, on-going training, and leadership. Schools have noted this transformation in industry and have begun to emulate the new paradigm through such efforts as restructuring districts toward site-based management and focusing on outcome-based education. For schools to be successful in restructuring efforts, they must have exceptional leaders with a new paradigm: Leaders envision a better future, empower all educators to conceptualize maximal outcomes for students, and facilitate collaboration to achieve those outcomes, creating the best possible schools for all children.

LEADERS OF THE 1990s

Five Forces of Leadership

Sergiovanni (1984) characterized educational leaders as individuals who improve schools by bringing about or preserving changes. These leaders have five "forces" available to transform schools into quality-focused organizations: technical, human, educational, symbolic, and cultural. Within these five domains, successful special education leaders of the 1990s approach their assignments in radically different ways than did their predecessors.

Technical forces are derived from sound management procedures. Special education leaders utilize technical forces when they ensure compliance with government monitoring through an efficient record-keeping system that tracks students from prereferral to postgraduation. They develop and administer budgets that allow for change and promote innovation. These administrators are aware of and ready to implement the latest advancement in technology. Special education leaders continually evaluate programs to assess components and compare outcomes with standards.

Human forces involve energizing social and interpersonal resources. Special education leaders focus human forces when they attract, select, hire, and retrain the best possible educators. They recognize they are key players on interdependent teams in schools and communities. They influence decision making by demonstrating the importance of their services, building consensus, and empowering others to do their best. These leaders build trust with teachers and other administrators as well as with parents and community members. They understand how to approach key political figures both on a local level and in higher government positions.

Educational forces are founded on an understanding of curriculum and effective instruction. Administrators can define their role as instructional leaders by maintaining awareness of the current knowledge base and best practices. Through dissemination and implementation of this expertise in carefully developed inservice training programs, these leaders enhance program excellence.

Symbolic forces translate into power through defining values and continually focusing the attention of others on what is important. Successful leaders are public relations experts, promoting visibility of their services to key teachers, administrators, and public audiences. In a time of school transformation, special education leaders demonstrate the significance of their role as consultants and decision makers in reconceptualizing services for all students.

Cultural forces are based on knowledge of the unique characteristics of each environment so that leaders can create a supportive, organic school culture. Special education administrators create such a culture by helping educators reshape beliefs and attitudes toward students with special needs and children from diverse backgrounds.

Visionary Leaders

Successful administrators are adept at employing technological, human, and educational forces. However, these competencies are not enough to induce change in schools; research indicates symbolic and cultural forces are the most powerful aspects of leadership in bringing about educational excellence (Burrello & Zadnick, 1986). Symbolic leaders have a vision and communicate their values and sense of purpose with confidence. Cultural leaders assist the community in experiencing the vision and developing personal meaning. Leaders who use symbolic and cultural forces effectively are confident and respectable, traits that help establish credibility. They clearly communicate plans, thereby clarifying current circumstances and securing commitment to the future. Leaders learn to love change and empower people to be an integral part of the growth process (Peters, 1987).

Barker (1994), a business consultant who assists leaders in examining their organizations, developing a vision for the future, and planning for growth in new directions, says vision should be leader–initiated and communicated in a positive and inspiring way. After articulating the vision, the leader seeks support and consensus from the organization. Based on a shared vision, members of the organization develop a comprehensive and detailed plan for implementation. Peters (1987) asserts leaders must decentralize strategic planning and praise implementers as the heroes of the organization.

Patterson (1993) explains that the greatest barrier to successful leadership is the paradigm "they won't let me." "They" implies a separation between people (i.e., "us" and "them"), and "won't let me" indicates that others decide what I can do. Instead, he proposes action based on openness to five values: participation, diversity, conflict, reflection, and mistakes. Good leaders do more than allow participation, they **encourage active participation** because "we are smarter than they" and because participation results in ownership. Leaders **celebrate diversity**. At one time, success was measured by conformity, but now it is realized that difference of opinion leads to innovation. Leaders **embrace conflict**. Successful administrators create a safe atmosphere in which individuals can resolve conflicts openly in healthy ways. Conflict can spark creative energy and cause organizations to examine inadequacies, resulting in more effective programs. Leaders **value reflection** and take time to reflect. Schools have become too action oriented; that is, efficiency and task completion have overpowered the critical process of examining current practices for improvement. Finally, leaders **learn from mistakes**. Common practice has been to avoid and hide mistakes.

Successful leaders understand that if you did not fall down, you may not have tried very hard. Mistakes are a natural part of growth, and there is much to learn from our errors.

In *A Whack on the Side of the Head,* Von Oech (1990) responds to the cautions leaders hear that block creative thinking and innovative problem solving. Throughout school, students are trained to seek "the right answer." Unfortunately, in complex environments, there are few right answers. Instead, there are potential solutions to consider, and leaders must learn that *the best way to get a good idea is to generate lots of ideas.* Leaders are told to "be logical" and "follow the rules." Yet almost every advancement has been made when leaders *challenge the rules and discover new perspectives.* "Be practical," "don't be foolish," and "mistakes are wasteful" are admonitions that maintain conformity. Creative thinkers *ask "what if," think like fools, and take risks* to arrive at new designs and paradigms.

Principle-Centered Leaders

Covey (1991) has isolated eight characteristics of individuals he believes to be exemplary leaders. He uses the term "principle centered" to refer to leaders who have discovered natural laws that guide them. These laws are like a compass that points the way to right action and inspired interaction with others.

First, Covey writes that these leaders **continually learn**. That is, they seek knowledge and benefit from experience. Second, they are **service oriented**, seeing life as a mission in which their efforts are contributions to others. Next, they **radiate positive energy**. Their attitude is optimistic and enthusiastic. Further, they **believe in people**. They are able to look past the present moment to see potential. This belief in others creates an atmosphere for growth and opportunity.

Principle-centered leaders **lead balanced lives**. They see things on continuums and are able to look at all sides of a situation. They have a healthy sense of humor. These leaders **see life as an adventure**. They look at old things in new ways, plunging into uncharted waters. They savor life. Principle-centered leaders **are synergistic**. They are change catalysts. In negotiations, they separate the problem from the people, knowing a cooperative solution will be greater than any one position or compromise. Finally, they **take time for renewal**. They are active in a variety of spheres, growing intellectually, keeping physically fit, and taking care of their emotional and spiritual needs.

LEVELS OF ADMINISTRATION

Special education administrators provide leadership at many levels with varying amounts of responsibility and complexity. Local school programs may employ **coordinators/supervisors** for a single facet of the program. For example, all school psychologists in a district may be supervised by one individual. These coordinators then report to the **director** or **assistant director of special education** who is responsible for all special education and related services in the district's jurisdiction.

Many schools purchase their special education services from cooperatives or interlocals that pool resources to provide all special services for a few programs for low-incidence disabilities to sparsely populated districts. **Directors of cooperatives** have complex and often difficult-to-define supervisory and financial relationships with school boards, superintendents, and principals. Special education services are also provided by public and private agencies that focus on a particular service or exceptionality. These programs are led by **agency directors**.

At the next level, each state has a **director** and a staff of coordinators or consultants who provide leadership and assure compliance with state regulations. Nationally, there are **directors of federal offices** and coordinating bodies, such as the Office of Special Education and Rehabilitation Services (OSERS) and the National Association of State Directors of Special Education (NASDSE).

The following interviews offer a glimpse into the world of four administrators, from local coordinator to state director, representing diverse regions that include the Northeast, Mid-Atlantic, Midwest, and Northwest. Although their job descriptions vary, the similarity of demands points to a common core of competencies required to lead with excellence. As you read these interviews, identify evidence of the forces of leadership, particularly symbolic/cultural and principle centered.

Local Supervisor
Dr. Maureen Hook
Supervisor of Special Education for Team One, Chesapeake Public Schools, Chesapeake, Virginia

Chesapeake is such a large district that we have divided the schools into regions or teams. We have a director of special education for all of Chesapeake, and area supervisors for each region. I am supervisor of special education services for Team One, which includes several schools and all students who attend programs outside of our district.

I began my career as a special education teacher of students with mental retardation and then taught students with learning disabilities. I decided I would enjoy the challenges of administration and, in 1979, became principal of a small special education school. As our philosophy changed, students returned to their home schools and our program disbanded. Next, I accepted a position as an assistant principal and then as principal of an elementary school. In 1987, I began my present position as special education supervisor.

Administration is exciting. It provides me with a variety of routines, both in the office and in the field, working with parents, teachers, and other administrators. I especially enjoy having an influence on program planning and setting a direction for the future.

About half my day is spent in the office talking on the phone, answering mail, and writing. It's essential that there's a time each day when I can tell people to call me and I'll be there. I do a variety of writing, including reports, summaries of eligibility meetings, new forms, and handbooks. Currently, we're creating a new IEP (Individualized Education Program) format and contributing to our locality's annual plan.

The other half of my day consists of travel and meetings. We have a weekly special education planning session in the central office. As issues arise, I meet with teachers and principals in their schools. I am also a team member of a citywide, multiagency, child and adolescent prescription team. This is an interesting assignment involving collaboration with court personnel, substance abuse agencies, social services, and schools. It will be even more interesting in July when the state changes funding practices and sends money directly to that central team rather than to individual agencies.

Of all my responsibilities, probably the most challenging is dealing with tuition eligibility for students placed outside our district. Like the citywide team, these placements involve cooperating with the court and social services. Each placement is time consuming and complicated. Troubleshooting and maintaining students in these programs means traveling out of the district, and sometimes out of state.

Another challenge is balancing the competing needs of teachers, parents, school board members, and administrators. I feel like I have to answer to a lot of "publics." Change is a slow, frustrating process; it seems we know where we want to go, but getting people to change is another matter. Often, it takes a government agency to mandate a service before I can get a program or delivery model under way. For example, for years we have been proposing programs to assist secondary students with transition into the work force, but it took a federal regulation to establish the services.

One way the supervisors have dealt with the complexity of our job is by developing a yearly time line that assigns certain tasks to a once-a-year rotation. In January, I review IEP planning; in spring, I write the state plan; and in the summer, I develop transportation routes.

Several major forces affect my job. Our district is growing; we are building new schools and hiring 20 to 25 special education teachers each year. Add dealing with normal teacher attrition, and that's a lot of human resource management. Interestingly, new industry in Chesapeake is attracting middle-class, skilled employees, but there is little change in the diversity. The school population remains about 35% minority (mostly African American with a small percentage of people of Hispanic and Asian descent). We are also providing for two previously underserved groups: students with traumatic brain injury and medically fragile children. Although we are growing, we are experiencing the same budgetary constraints as everyone else, having to do more with the same or fewer resources.

There is also a shift from an emphasis on categorical services, such as LD and MR, to programs for students with mild disabilities. And we are definitely moving in the direction of more-inclusive services. This means helping both special and regular educators redefine their jobs. Inservice training has become an important part of my role. We now realize it is essential to upgrade teachers' knowledge and skills to prepare them for change and to maintain effective performance.

When I think about what it takes to do my job well, I'm sure a background in both regular and special education is essential, especially now with more-inclusive models of service delivery. I've had great role models who demonstrated how to develop relationships, motivate teachers, and handle difficult people. Also, university coursework gave me the foundation necessary to make sense of my experiences.

What characteristics are essential for success in special education administration? First, a tolerance for ambiguity. Sometimes it seems things will never change, and at other times everything seems to change so fast that it's difficult to keep up. Another characteristic is an openness to new ideas. For example, teaching techniques for students with severe disabilities have undergone a radical transformation to include community-based instruction and work experience in authentic settings. I think special education administrators have to be task oriented and organized in order to deal with multiple responsibilities. They need good planning and decision-making skills, as well as the ability to communicate clearly and persuasively.

After reflecting, I know why I find my job so rewarding. I can help students who might have been ignored get services in regular schools in their community. I am helping redesign schools to accept differences and provide needed services for everyone. I am part of an exciting movement that's engineering a new social order: We are changing the social fabric of this country to include individuals with disabilities!

 CONSIDER THIS

1. What elements of symbolic/cultural and principle–centered leadership are evident?
2. What impact do shrinking resources have on administrators?
3. What does it mean to you to be part of changing the social fabric of this country to include individuals with disabilities?

Agency Director

Nancy Glass

Director of Children's Services, United Cerebral Palsy of Queens, New York City, New York

I began teaching at United Cerebral Palsy (UCP) 20 years ago. The director who hired me was wonderful, empowering me and encouraging me to take administrative responsibilities. Unfortunately, she left the agency and was replaced by a more bureaucratic administrator. My colleagues thought I could have done a better job, so when the position came open again three years later, they encouraged me to apply. I didn't think I had the necessary skills but felt it was my mission to meet the needs of children with disabilities and their families in the community. Also, I had many ideas about what should be changed and the type of new programs that were needed.

Currently, United Cerebral Palsy of Queens is a year-round program with 150 staff members providing direct services to 300 children and indirect services to children, parents, local schools, and the community. We have a birth-to-5 program, a nursery school that integrates children with CP with children without disabilities, and a program for school-age children. UCP provides staff for Head Start, home-based programs for infants, family-support systems, and case-management services. There's also a center that matches requests for services with appropriate therapists and agencies, or funding sources, as well as a clinic for medical, dental, and psychological care.

Changing demographics have significantly affected our agency and my job. Twenty years ago, our community was predominantly Caucasian, two-parent families with nonworking mothers who had the time and the commitment to support our program and participate in activities. Those parents had the income and health insurance necessary to cope with the challenges of raising a child with a disability. Now, our parents speak many languages and have fewer resources. These parents often don't understand the importance of early intervention, and some are too ashamed to seek services. Many of our students have single, working mothers without personal transportation. Other students live in foster care, which often presents confusing interagency communication problems. Twenty years ago, our parent-training programs provided the information and support necessary for homes to offer maximal learning environments. Now, we struggle to communicate with a diverse clientele. Our parent-support programs help parents obtain health care, handle crises, and learn basic survival techniques.

The challenges of language diversity occupy a lot of my time. When I hire any staff, I must give priority to multilingual applicants. I maintain a list of languages spoken by my staff. New York state has mandated that certain evaluation procedures cannot be merely translated but must be administered in the child's native language. Where do I find a psychologist who speaks Urdu, or a Romanian speech pathologist? Consequently, English-speaking children are processed quickly and receive services immediately, while non-English-speaking children wait months for the appropriate mandated evaluation.

Several staff conflicts related to language have developed. For example, when my paraprofessional who speaks Greek leaves her direct-care duties to interpret at a parent conference, English-speaking staff members have to cover, doing more physical labor. The bilingual workers want more money because of their valued skills, and the unilingual staff members feel they should receive extra-duty pay for increased physical labor.

Managing finances presents another challenge to my administrative role; UCP is a nonprofit, private school. In the face of escalating costs, there is a state freeze on tuition rates. Although my board of directors will give me seed money to start programs, it expects me to secure grants to maintain those programs. Currently, we are expected to generate increased funding for integrated community programs. It is difficult to hire staff, especially therapists, because as a nonprofit agency we can't offer the kind of salaries they could receive in hospitals.

Several other trends affect my job significantly. First, the emphasis on integration into the community and evaluation of the outcomes of these programs has caused us to reevaluate, plan, and redesign programs. Second, an increase in available assistive technology requires extra training for staff and parents. In addition, we seek funding to purchase and disseminate this equipment. Third, we serve an increasing number of health-challenged students. I must provide more rigorous infection-control procedures as well as deal with staff fear.

In a typical day, I spend most of my time meeting with staff, supervisors, and parents. Some of this involves planning, but a lot of time is spent resolving conflicts. Today, I had to deal with complaints about where our buses park, staff morale concerning extra-duty pay, and maintenance staff members who don't feel they should have to clean up around toilets when students "miss." I regularly deal with staff complaints concerning parents who don't adhere to appointment times. When a mother arrived late, the psychologist and speech therapist disagreed over whose schedule would be more disrupted by accommodating this parent. Also, I've been on the telephone with nurses about health issues and with members of the board of directors regarding finances. I have learned that most of the decisions I make have no clear-cut answer, but someone needs to decide, and often it's me. To be successful in this job, one has to be comfortable with seeing more than one perspective, and able to handle conflict and negotiate competing needs.

One of the most rewarding parts of my job has been a growing appreciation for parents' knowledge and opinions. I have learned parents usually know their children best, and we all benefit by being open and accepting of suggestions or criticism.

 CONSIDER THIS

1. What elements of symbolic/cultural and principle-centered leadership are evident?
2. What impact does the language diversity of families served by an agency have on the director's job?
3. What skills are required to meet the administrative demands of a typical day?
4. What must administrators learn to work effectively with parents?

District-Level Director

Dr. Dick Reed

Director of Pupil Services and Special Education, Cherry Creek Schools, Englewood, Colorado

I am responsible for special education and related services in a growing, progressive suburban school district in the greater Denver area. We have 32,000 students (5% annual growth) with 9.4% receiving special education services. Cherry Creek is innovative and committed to site-based decision making.

Over a 24-year period, I worked my way to this position from regular classroom teacher, to team leader, to supervisor, and to director. I see myself as a "third wave" special education administrator. The "first wave" of administrators were advocates, promoting awareness of exceptional students' needs and fighting for services. The "second wave" had the benefit of research and information concerning best practices. They developed innovative models, promoted mainstreaming, and sought effective programming for students with disabilities. The role of the "third wave" administrator has become increasingly more complex. These contemporary administrators realize schools are changing quickly and they must be key players in that metamorphosis. Their job is a balancing act between the needs of students and the realities of a school district in the 1990s. I am constantly in the position of justifying special education services in the context of restructuring, shrinking fiscal resources, and new proposals for integrated service delivery.

My job description has evolved as our office was assigned more responsibility with fewer staff. In addition to special education, we coordinate gifted programs, Chapter 1, school nurses, English as a Second Language classes, and federal programs. At the same time we added responsibilities, our central office was downsized from nine to four administrators.

I guess my major role is dealing with change. I love the challenge, but, frankly, some trends scare me. It seems many parents and educators are quick to embrace new ideas without researching and evaluating the impact on students. Full inclusion is one of those trends that seems to offer many positive outcomes, yet I am concerned. I approve of maintaining students in their home schools to the greatest extent possible. As a matter of fact, we employ more paraprofessionals than ever to assist students, and we have developed an itinerant/consultant model called the "curriculum/behavior specialist" to support inclusive programming. The consultants must be generalists because they have to prepare and support teachers in working with mild through severe disabilities. However, anytime one method of service delivery is proposed for all, I can't agree. Are teachers, students, and parents prepared for the total integration of seriously emotionally disturbed students into the regular classroom? We've come too far in our realization of a continuum of services to accept one model for all.

My role is also changing as the position of the school principal evolves. Building-level administrators are making more special education decisions and must be more knowledgeable concerning the students and the process. As principals take the initiative, my function becomes more consultative and supportive: I develop easy-to-implement systems and provide clear guidelines. Our office has simplified forms and generated a well-organized, accessible special education handbook.

In a typical day, I spend 25% of my time answering mail and phone calls; our office may receive as many as 200 calls daily. I spend approximately 30% of my day in scheduled meetings, including staffings, consultation, planning sessions, and inservice training. At least weekly, I am in contact with our lawyer regarding a parent who is threatening litigation. My function is to mediate, keeping parents satisfied and keeping the school out of court. As a result of parent complaints and educator concerns, I am continuously creating new programs and determining how to pay for those services.

When hiring new staff, our office advertises the position and screens applicants for appropriate certification. The folders are then sent to principals, who work with building-level teams to make hiring decisions. Cherry Creek Schools actively seeks minority applicants; we travel to recruit candidates from Southwest and inner-city universities. However, we have not been too successful, probably because the minority population in our district is low and may not offer the necessary camaraderie teachers need to feel they belong.

My leadership style is proactive, continuously anticipating potential problems. As a member of several teams, I identify areas in which special education is appropriate and assess when I should help regular education retool for handling the challenge. For example, teachers report the "kids are getting tougher." It is my role to help schools determine whether more special services are needed, or whether the schools need to train teachers, offer regular education alternatives, and revamp support or discipline systems.

I am an instructional leader, and in that role I must stay abreast of research and best practices. To do this, I meet monthly with state department consultants, talk regularly with other special education directors, and visit innovative programs. I receive a lot of feedback from parents and advisory boards, attend workshops and conferences, and read professional publications. Finally, I encourage my staff to be creative, and I learn from them.

I want to make it clear that I find my job both demanding and exciting. Sometimes I think I thrive on turmoil, but I enjoy the challenge.

 CONSIDER THIS

1. What elements of symbolic/cultural and principle–centered leadership are evident?
2. How does restructuring affect the job of special education directors?
3. How is the role of an administrator in a school district with educated, assertive parents different from that of an administrator working with a less–informed group of parents?

4. What are some ways administrators stay in touch with the current knowledge base and best practices?
5. What is the role of special education leaders concerning change?

State Director

Dr. Douglas Gill

***Director of Special Education for the State of Washington,
Office of Superintendent of Public Instruction, Olympia, Washington***

I've been the State Director of Special Education for Washington for about a year and a half. I know it will sound removed and bureaucratic when I tell you our three major roles are allocation, regulation, and facilitation. However, within these roles, I have a personal and professional mission: to make a difference in the lives of students with disabilities. On days when the Legislature is wrestling with where to cut to cope with a $2 billion deficit and I'm bombarded with complaints and buried in paperwork, I have to constantly remind myself why I'm doing this job. One way I keep my perspective is to interact with those who are affected by our decisions. It's easy to get overwhelmed by detail and minutia, but we need to remember it's people who are important.

The majority of my workdays involves interactions with people: parents, special education directors, staff, and government officials. I spend a significant percentage of my day talking on the telephone and answering mail. I also attend a lot of meetings and travel around the state. But I do take time each day to reflect on what I'm doing; I think of myself as an "idea person."

Let me explain the three job roles I mentioned. Allocation relates to managing the money. Our section is responsible for distributing state special education dollars, federal flow-through money, and federal discretionary funds. Washington is a "paramount duty" state, which means education is a priority. So if legislators have to cut budgets, they must do their best to preserve education funding. But times are tough; right now, the Legislature is trying to mandate local school districts to bill the federal government for services such as occupational, physical, or speech therapy that could be reimbursed by Medicaid. Our lawmakers believe we can recover $14 million in two years, but it's another example of bureaucratic thinking. The legislators may not realize there will be new paperwork generated and start-up costs for several years before local districts will recover a disappointingly small amount of money (which we hope will not be used to reduce state spending on students with disabilities).

The second job I mentioned is regulation. We are responsible for statewide monitoring of our rules, regulations, and statutes. This translates to managing the compliance of local school districts with state and federal regulations.

The third role is facilitation. We try to encourage promising practices, support state conferences, and manage competitive grants that promote innovation. In some ways, I suppose, it is our job to coordinate public relations.

As our section performs these roles, we strive to be consistent, accountable, and responsive. More important, we see ourselves as proactive. For example, during this time of school reform, many special educators have asked, "What is the response of educational reforms to special education?" Instead, we ask, "What is our (special education) response to school reform?" Although we are shaping the future, we are mindful of the history of special education, remembering that the essential issues should remain unchangeable: individually determined and specially designed education, free and appropriate education, and least restrictive environment. I am excited about the positive gains made by proponents of inclusion, but I remain committed to the notion we must provide a full continuum of options that are individually determined.

There are several issues shaping and influencing special education in Washington today. First is deficit spending. Clearly, there is less money to provide more services. Second, there is a genuine shortage of qualified special educational personnel. Third is the national movement to reform our schools. The real challenge, however, is to balance the promise of reform with the realities of rules and regulations at the federal and state level. Additionally, there is an interplay among these issues. Although some proponents of full inclusion might disagree, I believe in part that the movement for inclusive service delivery rises from the realities of shrinking budgets, a shortage of qualified personnel, and a contemporary atmosphere of school reform. Perhaps inclusion is, in some ways, symptomatic of a much longer-standing issue, that is, concern for the quality of special education services in general.

A fourth issue affecting special education in Washington is the need for better personnel preparation. It is the school's responsibility to provide input to preservice training institutions regarding requirements for effective teaching in today's schools. Then some skills, such as communication and collaboration, need to be reinforced by school districts continually. We, as administrators, have to resist the temptation to say, "We already fixed that," because the environment in which something was "fixed" may have changed.

There are numerous challenges in my role as state special education director. First, there is an incredible amount of input from local schools, parents, federal offices, state advisory councils, and my staff that needs to be assimilated before good decisions can be made. I am constantly figuring out how all the pieces relate to each other in the puzzle.

I should also comment on delegating responsibilities. I try to empower staff to perform all roles. I work with some very competent people who know a lot about the different state functions. It would be easy to rely on them to be the experts so I wouldn't have to be concerned with some areas of operation. But, over the years, I have learned not to delegate a responsibility unless I know something about it. Otherwise, I am not as informed as I should be, and I can't be of assistance to the staff.

The other major challenge, losing perspective, was mentioned earlier. It would be easy to get pulled into the "details vacuum." I strive not to let minutia cloud my perspective. I constantly remind myself that sometimes it is more important to do the right thing than to do things right.

What prepared me for my job? Every experience I've ever had before coming here! When I was younger, I watched how life changed when a family member was disabled. I taught special education fourth graders and high school students, as well as college students at Georgia Southern and the University of Georgia. In addition, every experience with teamwork helped me to do this job better. But most important, I probably grew as a result of feedback from people who were constructive and honest.

I do have some advice for preservice administrators. First, the decision-making process that works for me is to listen, think, then decide. In my job, there is a lot of pressure to make many decisions, often quickly, but I always try to take the time to listen to as much input as possible and then to consider the issue and its ramifications. Second, don't try to do everything. Figure out how things fit contextually and delegate. Third, hire people who have divergent points of view, then empower them, and help them feel what they do is important.

CONSIDER THIS

1. What elements of symbolic/cultural and principle-centered leadership are evident?
2. What balance must administrators seek between the demands of their job and their mission?
3. What does it mean for an administrator to be a proactive leader?
4. What considerations must be involved in delegating responsibilities?

EVALUATING THE INTERVIEWS

Despite the fact these special education administrators hail from New York to Washington; work in urban, suburban, and rural areas; and have responsibilities from supervisor to state director, there are remarkable similarities.

1. Compare the administrators interviewed according to their use of the five forces of leadership. What impact do these forces and characteristics appear to have on the roles these administrators perform?
2. What factors are responsible for differences in their job descriptions?
3. What function did these administrators describe as central to their daily activities?
4. What are their major challenges?
5. What trends and issues are changing their roles?

It is significant to note that each leader said change in schools is inevitable, and that the role of the special education leader is to direct transformation to ensure quality programs for all. The success of the leader can be measured by evaluating his/her vision and assessing the outcomes. Determine whether the administrators interviewed offered evidence of the following indicators of quality schools (Sheider, 1992):

1. Develop common goals through school and community collaboration.
2. Demonstrate a pervasive philosophy that *all* children can learn.
3. Identify barriers and seek solutions.
4. Promote sensitivity to issues of diversity and celebrate individual differences.
5. Use data to evaluate programs and make decisions.
6. Stay current with best practices and provide training opportunities for employees and parents.
7. Regularly assess satisfaction of students, parents, and educators.
8. Measure outcomes by determining whether students are being prepared to be lifelong leaders as well as happy, productive citizens.

Your Turn to Interview

One way to understand the challenges and complex demands of the special education administrator is to conduct your own interview of a director, coordinator, or supervisor. Table 1.1 suggests questions to get a conversation started. Remember, the way to obtain the most information is to use an open-ended

TABLE 1.1
INTERVIEW QUESTIONS

What did you do in education before becoming a special education director?
What interested you in pursuing administration? What is your mission or reason for doing your job?
What is your current job description? What does that mean?
Tell me about a typical day (if there is such a thing).
There are probably challenges that you don't deal with daily but are significant components of your job, such as setting up a budget. I'd like to hear about those.
What are your job priorities? What gets in the way of achieving those priorities?
How do you keep up with changes in the field, such as recent court cases or best practices?
What is most rewarding/frustrating about working with teachers, principals, central office administrators, school board members, parents, or local news agencies?
How has your job changed over the years?
What major forces do you see affecting special education administrators today?
What skills do you think are essential to be successful as a special education administrator?
What advice would you give to someone interested in becoming a special education administrator?

format. For example, "What is the greatest challenge of your job?" or "Tell me about a typical day as a special education director." Follow this with, "That's interesting; I'd like to hear more about . . . " In contrast, a "closed" approach is more likely to result in a brief answer or simple "yes" or "no." For example, "How many teachers do you supervise?" or "Do you like your job?" may yield the unsatisfying answers, "23 teachers" and "I like my job most of the time."

When analyzing the results of your interview, what overall picture developed? What skills did this administrator seem to have? What challenges did he or she face? Were there stories similar to those of the administrators interviewed in this chapter?

Self-Inventory

What are the characteristics of successful leadership? Hoy and Miskel (1987) describe successful leadership as a complex blend of personal characteristics and specific skills, and a match between the individual and the situation. Would you make a good leader? Ask yourself these questions:

1. Can I articulate my personal and professional goals?
2. Do I have the ability to influence others?
3. Do I have a strong drive for responsibility and task completion?
4. Am I original in developing solutions to problems?
5. Am I willing to accept consequences for my decisions?
6. Am I tolerant of frustration?
7. Do I accept change as inevitable?
8. Am I willing to be a team member?
9. Am I willing to empower others to do their job in the way they do it best?
10. Can I handle more than one thing at a time?
11. Am I comfortable knowing a decision must be made even though there is no clear-cut answer?
12. Can I use criticism constructively?

SUMMARY

Special education has evolved over the past three decades from a few programs for children with severe disabilities to a comprehensive, full array of services for all exceptional students. As special education matured and schools experienced escalating demands, a new kind of leadership was essential. Paradigms from industry have shifted focus from top-down authority in efficiency-oriented bureaucracies to participatory management and quality-centered organizations. Education has followed the lead of business and proposed models for contemporary school leadership.

Leaders value competent handling of technological, human, and educational forces. Leaders show they understand the nature of symbolic and cultural leadership by articulating a vision or mission and infusing values, ideals, and principles in their organizations, then assisting all members to create personal meaning for the larger vision. Successful school leaders are open to participation, diversity, conflict, reflection, and mistakes. Principle-centered leaders are lifelong learners, believe in people, and radiate positive energy. They lead balanced lives, see life as an adventure, and take time for renewal.

The interviews in this chapter include representatives from four levels of special education administration and from four regions across the nation. These leaders describe their greatest challenges as accelerated change; shrinking budgets; school restructuring in terms of site-based management and total quality performance accreditation; and reconceptualization of special education services regarding inclusive and noncategorical programming. The student population is changing to include more diversity, limited English proficiency, and health challenges, as well as younger children requiring services and secondary students needing preparation for post-school life. Those interviewed list the characteristics of successful leaders as the ability to communicate a clear mission, listen well, and participate as influential team members. These leaders are proactive, task oriented, and creative problem solvers. They can tolerate ambiguity, appreciate diversity, and thrive on change. As managers, they can write well and generate funds.

Readers are asked to interview an administrator to look for similarities to those interviewed in this chapter. Finally, a self-inventory poses questions current leaders would ask of prospective administrative candidates to determine whether they would be happy and effective leading special education programs in the 1990s.

REFERENCES

Audetta, B., & Algozzine, B. (1992). Free and appropriate education for all students: Total quality and the transformation of American public schools. *RASE, 13*(16), 8–18.

Barker, J. A. (1994). *The power of vision: Discovering the future* (video). Burnsville, MN: Chart House International Learning Corporation.

Burrello, L. C., & Zadnick, D. J. (1986). Critical success factors of special education administrators. *Journal of Special Education, 20*(3), 367–377.

Correa, V., & Tulbert, B. (1991). Teaching culturally diverse students. *Preventing School Failure, 35*(3), 20–25.

Covey, S. R. (1991). *Principle-centered leadership.* New York: Summit Books.

Hoy, W. K., & Miskel, C. G. (1987). *Educational administration: Theory, research, and practice* (3rd ed.). New York: Random House.

Hoyle, J. R., Fenwich, W. E., & Steffy, B. (1990). *Skills for successful school leaders* (2nd ed.). Arlington, VA: American Association of School Administrators.

Kukic, S. (1992, March). *Leadership initiatives.* Panel presentation at the annual international convention of the Learning Disabilities Association, Atlanta, GA.

Kuhn, T. S. (Ed.). (1962). *The structure of scientific revolutions.* Chicago: University of Chicago Press.

Patterson, J. L. (1993). *Leadership for tomorrow's schools.* Alexandria, VA: Association for Supervision and Curriculum Development.

Peters, T. J. (1987). *Thriving on chaos: Handbook for a management revolution.* New York: Knopf/Random House.

Sarason, S. (1990). *The predictable failure of educational reform.* San Francisco: Jossey-Bass.

Sergiovanni, T. (1984). Leadership and excellence in schooling. *Educational Leadership, 41,* 4–20.

Sheider, J. (1992, March). *What is a quality school?* Panel presentation at the annual international convention of the Learning Disabilities Association, Atlanta, GA.

Simpson, R. L., & Myles, B. S. (1993). General education collaboration: A model for successful mainstreaming. In Edward L. Meyen, Glenn A. Vergason, & Richard Whelen (Eds.), *Educating students with mild disabilities* (pp. 49–63). Denver: Love Publishing.

Stainback, W., & Stainback, S. (Eds.). (1990). *Supportive networks for inclusive schools.* Baltimore: Brookes.

Von Oech, R. (1990). *A whack on the side of the head.* New York: Warner Books.

SUGGESTED READINGS

Case in Point. A publication of the Council of Administrators of Special Education, a division of the Council for Exceptional Children, Case Office, 615 16th Street, NW, Albuquerque, NM 87104.

Covey, S. R. (1989). *The seven habits of highly effective people.* New York: Simon and Schuster.

Educational Leadership. A publication of the Association for Supervision and Curriculum Development, 1250 N. Pitt Street, Alexandria, VA 22314-1403.

Senge, P. M. (1990). *The fifth discipline: The art and practice of the learning organization.* New York: Doubleday.

Sergiovanni, T. J. (1990). *Value-added leadership: How to get extraordinary performance in schools.* San Diego: Harcourt Brace Jovanovich.

Chapter 2

LEADERS AND THE CHANGE PROCESS

Frank Kline and Fran Clark

Successful special education leaders create a vision of improved education for students with special needs, communicate that vision to others in the district, and facilitate the changes necessary to bring it to fruition. To effectuate a vision, a leader must have a full understanding of the change process (Fullan, 1982; Fullan & Stiegelbauer, 1991). Although specific aspects of the change process differ based on the innovation being implemented and the demographics of the school district, the basic principles remain the same.

PRINCIPLES AND ASSUMPTIONS OF THE CHANGE PROCESS

An awareness of principles and assumptions concerning the change process is essential. Gene Hall and his colleagues at the University of Texas Research and Development Center on Teacher Education (Hall, 1979; Hord, Rutherford, Huling-Austin, & Hall, 1987) have proposed three principles of change. First, change occurs as a process rather than as a specific event. The decision to adopt a particular innovation is an event that does not immediately result in changed procedures within classrooms and schools; change will occur developmentally over time as teachers and other educational personnel learn and incorporate new procedures, policies, and techniques into their repertoires and apply them in interactions with students, other educators, and parents. Second, change is made by individuals; institutional change can be accomplished only after the individuals implementing the change have incorporated the new techniques into their strategy repertoire and created new patterns of interaction within their daily routines. Third, as the innovation is introduced and implementation is begun, attention must be directed to the personal concerns of the individuals who are implementing the innovation, including management issues, impact upon students, and collaboration with other teachers. Individual differences in response to change, both in the nature and timing of the response, should be expected, and strategies should be developed to support each individual (Hord et al., 1987).

The assumptions people make concerning change affect their approach to change and the success of implementation. Fullan (1982) identified 10 assumptions that he considered "basic to a successful approach to educational change" (p. 91).

1. Assume any significant innovation, if it is to result in change, requires individual implementers to work out their own interpretation.
2. Assume conflict and disagreement are not only inevitable but fundamental to successful change.
3. Assume people need motivation to change (even in directions they desire), but it will be effective only under conditions that allow them to react, to form their own position, to interact with other implementers, to obtain technical assistance, etc.
4. Assume effective change takes time. Substantial changes in educational programs take at least two to three years.
5. Assume you will need a *plan* based on the above assumptions that addresses the factors known to affect implementation.
6. Assume no amount of knowledge will ever make it totally clear what action should be taken.
7. Assume change is a frustrating, discouraging business.
8. Do not assume your version of the change is the one that will be implemented.
9. Do not assume the reason for lack of implementation is outright rejection of the values embodied in the change, or hard-core resistance to all change.
10. Do not expect all or even most people or groups to change.

FOUR PHASES FOR IMPLEMENTING CHANGE

Based on assumptions of the change process and principles of effective staff development procedures, the following sequence for implementing a new program was developed by the University of Kansas Institute for Research in Learning Disabilities (Schumaker & Clark, 1990): (1) needs assessment, (2) initial training, (3) program integration, and (4) institutionalization.

Phase 1: Needs Assessment

Change generally begins as a response to unmet needs. Within a school district, the pressure to change is often the result of dissatisfaction with the current program on the part of one or more groups who hold a stake in it. Regular and special education administrators and teachers, parents, and students all have a vested interest in programs and their outcomes. Recognition that a program is not meeting the students' needs may develop gradually, or it may be a response to feedback such as analyses of test scores, attendance records, or student or program progress reports. Knowledge of new state or federal policies or societal trends may also provide impetus for change.

Once a decision has been made to explore alternatives to the current program, individuals and/or teams must gather information about innovations that have the potential to address the special needs not being met by the current program. Information may be gathered from a variety of sources, such as state departments of education, the federal Office of Special Education Programs, special and regular education administrators and teachers, professional organizations, journals, program developers, and university faculty. Thorough descriptions of the innovative program, its components, and the conditions necessary to implement it, as well as evidence of effectiveness with the target population, are essential to collect. Visitations to sites where the program is in use are generally beneficial.

After the critical information has been gathered, representatives of all stakeholder groups should provide input to the decision makers. An adoption decision should be made, and a written commitment and plan for the implementation of the innovation should be developed. This written document should communicate the vision of the program to be achieved, the benefits to all stakeholders, the potential of the new program, and the conditions necessary to realize this potential. In addition, statements of desired outcomes should be developed. The plan also should specify the tasks to be undertaken to (a) inform all individuals involved in implementation, (b) identify the individuals or groups of individuals who will participate in training and select the type of training needed based on the level of involvement, (c) provide appropriate initial and ongoing training for all individuals, (d) address the personal concerns of the implementers and other stakeholders, (e) provide all materials needed for initial and ongoing implementation, (f) support the implementers during initial and ongoing phases, (g) evaluate training and implementation, as well as the outcomes of the training and implementation, (h) institutionalize the innovation, and (i) address the challenges and problems that may arise.

Phase 2: Initial Training

In this phase, all individuals affected must be prepared for the initiation of the new program. Support and training will be necessary to prepare implementers for ongoing challenges.

Initially, a general overview of the adopted program should be provided for all stakeholders. This overview should be followed by specific training for each group of individuals based on their responsibilities for implementation and the level of impact necessary to enable them to carry out these responsibilities (Joyce & Showers, 1980). For example, some stakeholders may only need to be aware of the general procedures and outcomes of the program; thus, presenting information about the program and describing and modeling aspects of the program may be sufficient. On the other hand, individuals who must apply program components and solve problems that arise during implementation need training techniques with a much higher level of impact, including skill development and ongoing coaching.

Staff developers with expertise in the program model being adopted, the change process, and inservice training techniques will be needed to deliver the training required to achieve full implementation. Training sessions for implementers should include (a) clear descriptions of the program and of the techniques to be used within the program, (b) fluent models and demonstrations of program techniques and components, (c) sufficient opportunities for practice and feedback, (d) attention to implementers' questions and concerns, and (e) opportunities for individuals to set goals and develop plans for their own implementation.

During the initial training sessions, plans should be developed for coaching. Two types of coaching have proven successful. One involves teachers teaming with their peers to observe each other's implementation, to provide encouragement and feedback to one another, and to problem solve (Joyce & Showers, 1982). Coaching of this type has had a positive impact on the success of new techniques. The second form of coaching consists of teacher support teams (groups of five to eight teachers) meeting to discuss the successes and challenges of implementation, share ideas, and discuss and solve problems. Involvement in teacher support teams during implementation has been found to significantly increase the likelihood of success (Kline, Schumaker, & Deshler, 1992).

Phase 3: Program Integration

Following the flurry of activity that surrounds the initial phases of an innovation, attention must be given to integrating components into a cohesive and comprehensive program. Rather than implementing individual elements and components, the philosophy and procedures of the innovation become the focus of the existing program. Teachers learn and implement additional elements as they master the integration of previously learned components. In addition, references to the "new program" decrease as teachers and other stakeholders refine their knowledge and understanding of the program. During this phase, instruction related to the program components is integrated across levels (i.e., elementary, middle, and high school), and teachers work together to develop a scope and sequence of skills at each level.

Phase 4: Institutionalization

In this phase, the district accelerates efforts to become self-sufficient in the use of the model by developing resources to maintain the program without outside assistance. The innovation has now become the established program in the district; district policies and procedures have incorporated the new program and its outcomes. If outside personnel or monetary resources were used during the earlier phases, these resources are gradually reduced, and responsibilities for maintaining the program are transferred to the school district. In-district trainers are in place to ensure continuity in case of staff turnover, and district monies are allocated for maintenance of the program. Teachers continue to share ideas and their personal refinements of the programs with others, and update-training sessions are held as needed. However, in this phase, the innovative program has become the ongoing program, with staff efforts focused on maintaining quality and refining levels of implementation as needed.

The two cases that follow illustrate a school district's efforts to implement two innovative programs. The first is a case study demonstrating the four phases of implementation, and the second is case material exploring the perspectives of individuals affected by the change process.

Implementing Innovations in Wichita, Kansas

Case I: Strategies Intervention Model
Case II: Non-Categorical Programming

Wichita Public Schools serves a medium-sized city with a population of approximately 300,000. Wichita, fairly densely populated within the city limits, is isolated, without the population pressure of a large metropolitan area. There are several manufacturing companies which provide a strong industrial base for an otherwise agricultural (formerly oil-based) economy.

The population is largely conservative and is western in its outlook. It is not uncommon to see businessmen in three-piece suits wearing cowboy boots and hats in the financial district. Although there has been a steady increase in population, and rapid growth in some areas of the city, it has been more than 25 years since a school bond issue has passed. Many schools are crowded and have "temporary portables" that have been in place for more than 20 years.

The district serves approximately 50,000 students. It has seven comprehensive high schools (grades 9–12) plus several topic-centered magnet high schools; 15 comprehensive middle schools (grades 6–8), several of which are topical magnet schools; and more than 80 elementary school attendance centers, 10 of which are magnet schools. Thirty-four percent of students are from diverse racial and cultural backgrounds. The largest subgroup is African American, with Hispanics a close second. Asian populations are third largest, with significant representations from Vietnam, China, and Cambodia. The district provides its informative literature in 18 languages. There are about 6,000 individualized education programs for a great diversity of disabilities and a full range of levels of severity.

Case I: The Long View of Change:
Implementing the Strategies Intervention Model

This case shows a longitudinal view of how innovations are institutionalized. The data were collected in documents used during the institutionalizing of the Strategies Intervention Model (SIM) in Wichita Public Schools (see Ellis, Deshler, Lenz, Schumaker, & Clark, 1991; Deshler & Schumaker, 1986; or Deshler & Schumaker, 1987, for a description of the SIM). The documents are analyzed in chronological order to examine implementation of an innovation over time. Four phases of the institutionalization process (Schumaker & Clark, 1990) are described, including one or two key incidents for each.

General Conditions

The Strategies Intervention Model is a well-researched system designed to prepare teachers to train students to follow specific sequences that enable them to learn, remember, and demonstrate new skills. The impetus for introducing this innovation into the district was a federal research grant written by the senior author and his professors at the University of Kansas during a sabbatical from Wichita Public Schools. Although the grant provided funding to assist in the institutionalization of the SIM, its main thrust was to investigate the dissemination process. The grant was funded, research was completed, and its results have been reported in several publications (e.g., Kline, Deshler, & Schumaker, 1992; Kline, Schumaker, & Deshler, 1991).

The institutionalization of the SIM in Wichita required at least five years, from 1986–1991. From the time initial interest was expressed by the district to the end of the grant, there were several significant changes in administration; that is, there were three directors of special education and four superintendents. The entire administration of the district went through an upheaval and reorganization as a result of these changes. One result of this upheaval that had a significant impact on the project was that the location of the project office moved six times across three different buildings.

The major support for adoption of the SIM was the grant. Federal funding supplied one full-time teacher support position, a part-time secretary, supplies, a limited amount of equipment, technical assistance from the developers of the SIM, and money to hire outside trainers. The district supplied access to the teachers, office space, and other in-kind services.

From a personnel standpoint, the most direct assistance was provided by Frank Kline, who served as the teacher supporter and "change agent." Significant initial encouragement was also provided by all directors of special education and middle-level administrators, who believed in the project from the early stages and provided practical support.

These conditions illustrate two important points. First, changes often occur not as a result of far-sighted planning, but rather as a function of the strengths of the people present, in combination with the opportunities that present themselves. Second, changes do not occur in a vacuum. The entire district does not shut down to allow the training of teachers in special education. Implementation of change often occurs in a milieu of multiple changes. Schools function in a society that seems to worship the new as better and thus experience change continually in many areas.

Phase One of Implementation: Needs Assessment or Adoption

Needs assessment begins with an awareness of the need for change and consideration of potential innovations, and ends with the decision to implement a particular project. From the point of view of the change agent, this was a difficult stage; whether or not the district adopted the SIM was a high-stakes decision for him. The change agent knew the district well, believed this innovation would be helpful to its students and teachers, and had prepared a general training plan for the district. This plan consisted of a gradual implementation in which volunteer teachers would participate in training across the life of the grant. About 20 new teachers would be trained each year so that by the end of the fourth year, about 80 teachers would be trained in at least some elements of the model. This plan offered the advantage of allowing teachers to choose when they would participate in the project.

No formal needs assessment was conducted by the district to determine the need for the innovation. The decision to adopt the SIM was more a result of opportunity, a key factor of which was the availability of a change agent. He had been on sabbatical at the research institution that originated and validated the SIM, so was acquainted with both the district and the innovation. He had significant experience with training in the use of the model and was being mentored by its originators.

The second key factor was the support of outside funding. The research grant that funded training in the SIM as a by-product of the required research supplied the personnel and materials necessary to initiate the training. In addition, it funded release time for teacher training by paying for substitute teachers. Although the decision to assist in the grant application predated the assurance of fiscal support, the district would not commit to the innovation without such support.

In the needs assessment stage identified by Schumaker and Clark (1990), teachers would be included in the decision to adopt by being made aware of the central concepts of the SIM. In this implementation, teachers and students were not included in the decision to adopt the SIM. Their participation in the decision-making process consisted of their personal decisions to participate or not.

Phase Two: Initial Training

Phase Two begins with the first training session, but its conclusion is less well defined. For this project, one semester of detailed planning took place before training began. The trainer took this time to become reacquainted with district policies and staff, and to plan the training and research projects to be completed in the first year. The participants were carefully screened by the change agent and district administrators for potential success.

The initial training stage included acquainting administrators with the SIM, responding to the multiple training concerns of the participants, and adjusting tasks as necessary to assist training. The district provided training material, assisted teachers in modifying the IEPs as necessary, and assisted in the planning and implementation of the training.

Twenty teachers were selected to initiate the use of the SIM. The change agent and supportive administrators believed initial success was crucial because the teachers had not been included in the decision to adopt the SIM. For that reason, the selection of the first teacher participants was critical. Initial success would increase the likelihood that other teachers would make personal decisions to adopt the SIM.

These 20 carefully selected teachers acquired knowledge of several components of the SIM and the skills necessary to implement them. Specifically, the teachers were trained in the use of The Paraphrasing Strategy and The Word Identification Strategy. These elements are often used to introduce teachers to the model.

The students began to have some awareness of the SIM as their teachers introduced the strategies. Out of the 20 teachers selected, 18 were successful in bringing some of their students to the practice stages of the strategies. In total, about 60 students were trained in the two strategies taught the first year. Although this may seem like a small number compared to the number of students for whom the SIM might be appropriate, participants were encouraged to initially teach the strategies to small groups of students they felt might succeed in their first attempt.

Phase Three: Program Integration

The job of the change agent became more complex during the program integration phase. The plan was for gradual implementation over several years. As more training sessions were offered, there were challenges in finding appropriate venues for them, in recruiting new teachers to participate, in finding appropriate times in each year, and in providing significant follow-up activities for each teacher. Some activities became routine, but the increase in the number of participants offset the savings accomplished by the routinization of some tasks.

Although training continued to take a great deal of time, more of the project's time resources were being diverted to the integration of the SIM into the district's overall service plan. This effort at integration can be represented by two activities: defining an appropriate articulation plan for the SIM elements across the years, and defining the appropriate inclusion of specific strategies in student IEPs.

The definition of an articulation plan was necessary so that instruction in elements of the SIM could be communicated from one school to another. As more students began to understand and use elements of the SIM, their geographic and temporal mobility began to have an impact on the receiving teachers. As students moved from elementary to secondary settings, the receiving teachers did not have an accurate set of expectations as to what strategies the students had learned. The IEPs often lagged behind the move, and frequently there were no standard codes in the IEP to describe the materials and approaches that had been used.

To deal with these issues, a committee was formed to obtain and communicate a consensus on which strategies could best be taught at each grade level. The initial definition work was completed during the summer, and the teachers were paid for their work. This is significant because, for the first time, the district committed its own funds to the development of the SIM.

The committee's plan was communicated to all teachers first through a required inservice and then in writing at the beginning of the next year. The teachers on the committee were included in the inservice presentation. The articulation plan was presented to all teachers, even though participation in the training sessions was voluntary and, as yet, incomplete. For those teachers who were still unsure about their participation in learning the model, the money spent and the communication of the plan to all teachers was a strong signal of district support.

The inclusion of the SIM elements in the IEP was the vehicle through which teachers legitimized their teaching of the learning strategies. As one might predict, another committee was formed to represent the teachers and to grapple with the various ethical and logistical issues involved. This committee decided to concentrate on the goals inherent in the SIM and its elements rather than on specific parts. This decision was formalized in a document that listed goals associated with each element of the SIM and with the SIM in general. These goals were distributed to all teachers in a manner similar to the articulation plan.

For the district, the integration phase was characterized by the movement of the SIM into additional special education programs and general education classrooms. Much of the integration effort dealt with the ramifications and implications of districtwide use of the SIM. This movement out of individual classrooms and across the rooms for students with learning disabilities highlighted the commitment made by the district to the SIM as one of the appropriate and important ways in which students with learning disabilities could be taught.

From the teacher's point of view, the integration phase provided opportunities to serve on committees and have significant input into the direction of the SIM. Students began to recognize elements of the SIM as they were being taught, and receiving teachers questioned students about which strategies they had learned.

Phase Four: Program Institutionalization

The institutionalization phase is characterized by a district's commitments to ensure the continuation and development of the SIM. In Wichita, these commitments can be represented by two actions. First, the district created a class for secondary students to accommodate the instruction in elements of the SIM, signaling a systematic approach to the instruction of the strategy. Second, the district created a position funded specifically for support of the model.

This course development involved many decisions, including who could teach the course, who could take the course, how would the course be advertised, and which department would offer the course. Most of these decisions were new for the special education administrators involved; special education courses had been offered as special sections of already existing general education courses. Developing a new course, available exclusively to special education students and taught only by special education teachers, was new. This development process seemed to legitimize the SIM not only for the general education teachers (after all, there was a "real" course) but also for the special education teachers. It was, for them, something new.

Perhaps the most significant event signaling the institutionalization of the SIM was the funding by the district of a teaching position to continue the training work after the external funding was no longer available. The external funding of the project was a double-edged sword. On the one hand, it provided a security that weathered many administration changes, giving the SIM sufficient stability during its early phases to allow it to be nurtured. Also, it specified, to some degree, how the funds would be spent, thus allowing key issues such as access to release time for participating teachers to be established across the life of the grant.

On the other hand, there were always questions in the minds of the participants about the district's commitment to the project. How, and even if, the project would be supported after the grant ran out was a matter of concern. That's why the commitment of funds to the project during the integration phase was so important; it signaled a commitment from the district to the project and to the people involved.

During the last year of the grant, the change agent began to talk to district administrators about the continuation of the project. Records were condensed and provided as evidence supporting the project's value, and two plans for its continuation were developed. Both plans involved funding at least a part-time position to continue the training of teachers in the SIM. No longer bound by the constraints of the grant, the district decided to expand the training to all teachers who wanted it, and a well-trained staff developer was hired. Half of this person's time was to be spent training teachers and developing their use of the SIM, and the other half was assigned to another district project—setting up a computerized IEP for the district. After about a year, it was clear that the computerized IEP was consuming all of the staff developer's time. District administrators decided to assign computerization to someone else. Meanwhile, the original SIM trainer had changed jobs. A new SIM trainer was hired and given responsibility for training in the SIM as well as in collaboration and consultation.

This sequence of events signaled real district commitment to the SIM. First, there was the initial commitment to follow up the external funding with internal fiscal support. There is always competition for the funds that schools have available, so the allocation of half a position along with secretarial support was significant. Second, even though the training did not get the attention it needed because of the computerized IEP, rather than blaming the innovation itself, district administrators recognized the problem and took steps to correct it. Because the results were not up to expectations, it would have been easy for the district to discontinue the training position after the first year of district funding. Instead, the district signaled its commitment to the SIM by changing the conditions so that the program would be more likely to succeed. The administrators recognized that innovations can have problems for two reasons: they are poor innovations, or they are poorly implemented. Four years of success under outside funding made it more difficult to dismiss the innovation and more likely that the administrator in charge could identify the implementation problems.

From the teachers' point of view, the institutionalization phase ensured continued access to valued technical assistance and new innovations. The students saw more and different strategies from the SIM and a more widespread application. This building of commitment, along with the routinization of the use of the innovation, characterizes the institutionalization phase of the change process.

The phases of needs assessment, initial training, integration, and institutionalization include many other elements and incidents besides the ones reported here. These events were selected because they were representative of the phase in which they occurred. Each phase includes many events that, as a whole, characterize the processes and types of decisions involved when innovations are implemented in school districts.

 ## CONSIDER THIS

1. What conditions existed in this setting that promoted or enhanced implementation of change?
2. What conditions or unexpected changes do you think were most challenging for the implementers?
3. Evaluate the time and effort evident in institutionalizing this innovation in terms of the actual outcome.
4. Compare the comprehensiveness of the SIM implementation plan with innovations attempted in your school or district.
5. What principles and assumptions about change from Hall and Fullan are evident in this case study?
6. Reflect on a personal change (e.g., a move in position or geographical location, trying something new in your job, etc.). What events illustrate each phase?

A change from one paradigm to another does not occur all at once. Significant amounts of time are required and numerous challenges need to be met in order to produce the many small changes involved in moving an institution as large as a public school system to a new mode of operation. At its root, each small change must be accomplished by an individual. All change occurs in individuals and only at the rate at which the individual can accept it. The following case materials examine change from several points of view.

Case II: Differences in View: Implementing Non-Categorical Special Education Services

The Scenario

Until this year, special education services in Wichita have been provided through traditional categorical programming. That is, services for students with learning disabilities have been provided in resource and self-contained classrooms exclusively for these students as well as in general education settings using a mainstreaming model or the more recent "class-within-a-class" model. Over a three-year phase-in period, the district plans to move to an "interrelated service delivery model" in which service will be provided to students on the basis of their relationship to the curriculum and without regard to their category of exceptionality. If students need a functional curriculum, they will be educated with other students needing that curriculum regardless of their special education label. This may result in students with learning disabilities, mental retardation, and behavior disorders all receiving services in the same room. It will also result in an increase in the amount of services provided in general education settings.

This year, two of the middle schools and one of the high schools piloted the interrelated service delivery model. Next year, all secondary schools will be required to provide services in an interrelated fashion, and several of the elementary schools will pilot the new model. During the third year of the phase-in, all schools will be required to use the interrelated model.

Interviews

Two teachers, one building-level administrator, and one district-level administrator were interviewed to examine the differences in perspective of educators involved in the change from a categorical services model to an interrelated (non-categorical) service delivery model. All those interviewed were asked the same questions. There are many stakeholders whose voices are not included in this case study. Its purpose is not to provide a balanced or complete view of the change process, nor to evaluate the merits of the specific innovation, but rather to provide a vehicle for understanding the differences that a particular point of view can make in the way a person views an innovation.

The Results

Thirteen questions and a summary characterizing the responses are provided. In general, the teachers' responses are first, followed by those of the building-level and then the district-level administrators.

1. *What is your function in the movement to an interrelated service delivery model?* The teachers' view concerned the "nuts and bolts" of the innovation. They saw themselves as having initiated it in their building, making the necessary adjustments, setting up the schedule, etc. The building-level administrator saw herself as a day-to-day facilitator. This was interpreted to mean she deals with problems as they arise. The district-level administrator saw himself as the person who prepared the district for the innovation. "My role is to set the stage," he said. He spoke of the prerequisites for the innovation and how he had worked to get them in place. His view spanned four to six years; the teachers had a one-year view, and the building-level administrator, who dealt with problems as they arose, had an even shorter view of the innovation.

2. *What is an interrelated classroom?* The difference in viewpoints here centered on whether the respondent was in the school building or at

the district office. All those interviewed spoke of the nature of classrooms in terms of how students were served. They commented on the changes that were made in what students and teachers do on a daily basis. The teachers emphasized the inclusion of students in general education classes, while the building-level administrator emphasized staff cooperation; all, however, focused on the changes in what students and teachers actually do. The district-level administrator, on the other hand, focused on the difference in the placement process. He discussed when to consider the curricular needs and when the category of exceptionality should be considered.

3. *How will your job change?* The teachers saw their workload as increasing. While they acknowledged that some of the perceived increase in work involved having to learn something new, much of it was attributed to having to change their job description. The innovation requires more collaboration with other teachers and a different view of students. The teachers would need to shift their emphasis in instruction from the traditional categorical thrusts, such as behavior for BD, academics for LD, and functional skills for EMH, to a more flexible curriculum.

   The building-level administrator felt that the job would require more cooperation among staff members, herself included. She welcomed this change. She used examples of how discipline would be handled differently, and how the special education teachers would be involved and would assist in the process.

   The district-level administrator said that as the innovation was initiated, rumor control was a big part of his job. He anticipated that as the innovation became established, his job would shift to monitoring its implementation, particularly noting whether students were being placed for administrative convenience or to meet individual needs.

4. *What training/preparation has been/will be provided for participants?* The teachers responded that individually initiated efforts such as university classes, independent studies, and extensive professional readings were the major sources of their preparation. District sources of preparation included participation in district-level committees initiating the change. The teachers said they had received general curricular training in collaboration and consultation, but no training on how to make this change to an interrelated service delivery model.

   The building-level administrator said she received no training or preparation.

   The district-level administrator's response was immediate and direct: "Not enough!" He said the general education staff lacked sufficient training. To him, it seemed to be a grass-roots movement among the special education teachers. He also mentioned getting several prerequisite programs in place. (Interestingly, he cited the starting of the Strategies Intervention Model described earlier as one of the prerequisites.)

5. *Who is involved in implementation?* The teachers listed specific people in their building who were involved in the planning and execution of the model, including the principal and selected teachers. Their strong feeling was that not all general education teachers were suited for working in this model, although they thought the administration seemed to think that all teachers *should* be suited for this work. The teachers interviewed believed that administrators sometimes ignored the individual personalities of the general education teachers involved.

    The building-level administrator initially listed all members of the child study team as implementers. When asked about the involvement of general education teachers, the administrator admitted that there was a fluctuation in the level of success that various teachers experienced in working with models of inclusion.

    The district-level administrator focused on the role of the special education teachers in this change. He felt that if building- and district-level administrators would get out of the way—in terms of scheduling, for example—then the special education teachers would do very well.

6–9. *What was the impetus for change? What do you see as its purpose? What are the benefits/outcomes? What is the impact on the school as a whole?* (Because answers for questions 6, 7, 8, and 9 were similar, responses have been combined.) The teachers, who were more cynical about the reasons for the change, first mentioned reduced cost. Their views of the benefits included a halt to the singling out of special education students, the ability to mediate more effectively between students and general educators, the extension of limited services to both special and general education students, an increase in parent contact, and an expanded view by general education teachers of what special education teachers do.

    The building-level administrator gave general, philosophical answers regarding the change. She listed its benefits as a reduction in the labeling of students and an increase in staff development.

    The district-level administrator listed three reasons for the change: the model better serves students, the state is pushing it, and it's a more efficient way to provide services. His view of the benefits was broader than the other views and included increased collaboration, reduction of staffings, and the exchange of information across special and general education lines. He also cited benefits to the students.

10. *What was your introduction to interrelated service delivery?* One teacher had worked in a rural part of the state where the model was relatively common. It was interesting, however, that each teacher said the other had introduced her to the concept.

    The building-level administrator was not familiar with it before the day it began at her school.

The district-level administrator had worked for its implementation several years ago in a different district. He had the longest experience with it of any of the parties interviewed.

11. *What is your current view of interrelated service delivery?* The teachers' view was focused on what needed to be done that day, or in the next 10 minutes.

The building-level administrator expressed positive feelings about the teacher leading the special education team. She expressed concern, however, that a change of personnel could lead to a rapid deterioration of the program.

The district-level administrator expressed two primary concerns. He questioned whether the building administrators would let the teachers make the key decisions. If principals would empower teachers, he reasoned, things would go much smoother. Additionally, he was concerned that staff members might make their decisions on the basis of administrative convenience rather than students' needs.

12. *What will the interrelated service delivery model look like when it is done?* The teachers stressed the ongoing nature of the change. They felt that certain aspects would become routine, but that the model itself would never be fully implemented. They expressed concern about the district's identification procedures and the impact this had on the service delivery model. This was one area in which they seemed to have a districtwide view.

The building-level administrator thought some changes in staff were necessary to complete the shift to an interrelated model. She expressed concern about losing the special education team leader.

The district-level administrator predicted that when completed, the interrelated service delivery model would place students in rooms "totally on curricular need without regard to disabilities." He was sure more special education students would be served in both general and special education settings by both general and special education staff, and there would be intensive collaboration between all staff members.

13. *Describe how your view of interrelated classrooms has changed as you have become more involved with them.* One teacher quoted another special education teacher who used to say, "I don't 'do' behavior." The person interviewed believed the change to an interrelated service delivery model had helped this teacher broaden her view of the teaching process to accommodate the needs of more students.

The building-level administrator said her view had not changed. She thought there were certain aspects of the model that could be improved, but her overall vision of the model had not changed.

The district-level administrator's view of the model had broadened in the last 10 years. For example, he no longer thought it was necessary to limit the room to two exceptionalities. He was increasingly confident in its ability to meet student needs.

Discussion

There are several general differences in points of view among those interviewed. People are most concerned about, and aware of, that which has a direct impact on their jobs. The teachers provided the most specific information about students, classes, daily schedules, etc. Their focus was centered on this year (if not today), on their building, and on what was happening to the students. The teachers' view of district-level issues focused on the identification of special education students, a procedure that has the greatest impact on their jobs.

The building-level administrator dealt with the staff and the discipline problems in the school; she had equal concern for the staff and students. The district-level administrator conceptualized his role as a leader and demonstrated in his comments a clarity and breadth of vision that extended well beyond the current year and his district. His view extended several years into the past and into the future as well as focused on what happened to district personnel and on the effect on the state.

People interpret change very personally. Their view of change is affected by what they perceive they need to do in relationship to the change. The expectations of one's job provide a particular lens through which to view change. Complex changes involve many people in many roles. They will filter and create that change through the lens of their job and from the reference points of their personality and skills. There is much overlap between points of reference, but to some extent, each person has a unique view.

CONSIDER THIS

1. How does each person's job description impact his or her perspective of any change?
2. How could the various perspectives presented in this case material lead to conflict or misunderstanding? How could these conflicts be avoided?
3. From a philosophical/phenomenological point of view, each person has a personal, subjective, and unique perspective on life. How could this impact the implementation of an innovation?
4. Considering the three points of view presented, what would you recommend to facilitate the implementation of an innovation in a school district?

SUMMARY

Change does not occur all at once. There is a discernible process to change that requires time and effort on the part of many individuals. These processes can be thought of as occurring at the macro or district level, but also at the micro or individual level. The first phase of change is recognition of the need for change. The second phase can be conceived of as the initial change. The new behavior is often mechanical or wooden in its implementation during this phase. The third phase, integration, brings a more fluent use of the innovation. In the fourth phase, there is a fluid use of the innovation across many settings. With the addition of the initial phase of needs assessment, this process can be directly compared to the stages of learning: acquisition, proficiency, and generalization.

The learning of an individual can be used as a metaphor for the adoption of an innovation by a school district. Like an individual learning a new skill, a district's initial implementation of an innovation is often halting and uncertain. Like an individual learning a new skill, a district takes time to achieve a reasonable level of competence. Like an individual learning a new skill, a district can learn from failures through reflection and feedback. Unlike an individual learning a new skill, administrators and others often expect instant change and instant proficiency.

Changes at the district level are, after all, a result of changes at the personal level. A district can encourage change, provide materials, experiences, and conditions that encourage change, and even mandate change, but if the individual doesn't implement the change, or implements the change only half-heartedly, all of the efforts may be in vain. Administrators can write procedures and create forms illustrating how to accomplish the change, but if the people who are to implement the change do not understand or embrace the change at some level, the effort is wasted.

REFERENCES

Deshler, D. D., & Schumaker, J. B. (1986). Learning strategies: An instructional alternative for low-achieving adolescents. *Exceptional Children, 56,* 583–590.

Deshler, D. D., Schumaker, J. B., & Ellis, E. S. (1987). Intervention issues related to the education of adolescents. In J. K. Torgeson & B. L. Wong (Eds.), *Learning disabilities: Some new perspectives.* New York: Academic Press.

Ellis, E. S., Deshler, D. D., Lenz, B. K., Schumaker, J. B., & Clark, F. L. (1991). An instructional model for teaching learning strategies. *Focus on Exceptional Children, 23*(6), 1–24.

Fullan, M. G. (1982). *The meaning of educational change.* New York: Teachers College Press.

Fullan, M. G., & Stiegelbauer, S. (1991). *The new meaning of educational change* (2nd ed.). New York: Teachers College Press.

Hall, G. E. (1979, November). *Using the individual and the innovation as the frame of reference for research on change.* Paper presented at the meeting of the Australia Association for Research in Education, Melbourne, Australia.

Hord, S. M., Rutherford, W. L., Huling-Austin, L., & Hall, G. E. (1987). *Taking charge of change.* Alexandria, VA: Association for Supervision and Curriculum Development.

Joyce, B., & Showers, B. (1982). The coaching of teaching. *Educational Leadership, 40*(1), 4–11.

Joyce, B., & Showers, B. (1980). Improving inservice training: The messages of research. *Educational Leadership, 37,* 379–385.

Kline, F. M., Deshler, D. D., & Schumaker, J. B. (1992). Implementing learning strategies instruction in class settings: A research perspective. In M. Pressley, K. R. Harris, & J. T. Guthrie (Eds.), *Promoting academic competence and literacy in school* (pp. 361–404). San Diego, CA: Academic Press.

Kline, F. M., Schumaker, J. B., & Deshler, D. D. (1991). Development and validation of feedback routines for instructing students with learning disabilities. *Learning Disabilities Quarterly, 14,* 191–207.

Schumaker, J. B., & Clark, F. L. (1990). Achieving implementation of strategy instruction through effective inservice education. *Teacher Education and Special Education, 13*(2), 105–116.

Chapter 3

SPECIAL EDUCATION LAW
David Bateman

Throughout the 19th and mid-20th centuries, children with disabilities were often denied access to a public education. Many parents were told to keep their children home or to send them to residential facilities. Other parents were told that before entering school, their children must have certain basic capabilities, such as using the toilet. The few children with disabilities who were allowed in public schools were often educated in special day schools or in separate classes.

In the mid-20th century, parents and educators began to consider the lack of educational opportunities and the segregation of children with disabilities as inherently harmful. It became apparent that children with disabilities could be taught, that with assistance they could lead productive lives (Scheerenberger, 1983), and that they needed to be integrated more into the mainstream of society. However, the development of free, appropriate public education for children with disabilities required the intervention of the courts—litigation—and the regulation of lawmakers—legislation.

LITIGATION

In 1954, the U.S. Supreme Court issued its decision in *Brown v. Board of Education of Topeka,* and African Americans achieved a milestone in their efforts toward integration. This idea for school integration became a model for many children with disabilities and their families. *Brown* also established that no state could deny an individual "life, liberty, or property, without due process of law . . . and equal protection of the laws." *Brown* was notable for many reasons. It reaffirmed the Constitution as the supreme law of the land, binding throughout the United States, as interpreted by the U.S. Supreme Court; established the entry of the federal government into public education; and showed how the principles of equal protection and due process affect public education.

These important principles from *Brown* drastically changed the education of children with disabilities. Two important court decisions that built upon the principles of *Brown* were *Pennsylvania Association for Retarded Children (PARC) v. Commonwealth of Pennsylvania* (1972) and *Mills v. DC Board of Education* (1973). In the Pennsylvania case, the plaintiffs (PARC) wanted a guarantee that a free education would be provided to all children with mental retardation, even the most severely retarded. Using the principles of equal protection and due process from *Brown,* it was agreed that every child in Pennsylvania not only would be guaranteed a free public education, but also would be provided due process before school authorities could make any substantive change in the child's educational program (Abeson, 1972). In *Mills,* the court ruled that the school district's contention that there was insufficient money was no excuse for failing to provide education, and that students with disabilities had been denied due process rights, again on the principles of *Brown.* Further, the court in *Mills* outlined specific due process procedures. In both cases, the courts stated that education is necessary for success and independence.

LEGISLATION: ANTIDISCRIMINATION LAWS

Rehabilitation Act of 1973

Before 1973, the courts had taken the lead in laying the groundwork for the education of students with disabilities. With the passage of the Rehabilitation Act of 1973 (PL 93–112), legislators moved to the forefront. Commonly referred to as the "Rehab Act," or "Section 504," because of a main provision dealing with individuals with disabilities, this law authorized federal funds for compliance with regulations concerning the education of students with disabilities. The main component of Section 504 of the Rehab Act states:

> No otherwise qualified individual with handicaps shall solely by reasons of her or his handicap, be excluded from the participation in, be denied the benefits of, or be subjected to discrimination under any program or activity receiving Federal financial assistance. (29 U.S.C. Sec. 706)

In addition to students with disabilities, this act protects any person who meets one of three "life-defining" criteria. Any person who "(i) has a physical or mental impairment which substantially limits one or more of such person's major life activities, (ii) has a record of such an impairment, or (iii) is regarded as having such an impairment" (29 U.S.C. Sec 706) is considered under the law to have a disability. For the purposes of Section 504, major life activities include caring for one's self, performing manual tasks, walking, seeing, hearing, speaking, breathing, learning, and working. An important aspect is that individuals who are intentionally and unintentionally discriminated against are protected (Turnbull, 1993). Under Section 504, individuals who have a disability, and therefore might need assistance, qualify for the related services necessary for them to benefit from education. Also, Section 504 has provisions for nondiscriminatory employment.

If students are identified as having a disability under Section 504, schools are obligated to provide accommodations that allow access to an appropriate education, such as providing physical accessibility for students with physical challenges and interpreters for those with a hearing loss. Qualifications for services and procedural safeguards for students are not as clearly defined in Section 504 as they are in later special education laws (PL 94–142 and IDEA). Hence, students may appear to be disabled according to Section 504 but not qualify for special education according to criteria set forth by IDEA, as in the case of students with attention deficits. Consequently, educators are confused about what services should be offered to these students and who is responsible for providing necessary accommodations (Council for Exceptional Children, 1994).

The Americans with Disabilities Act of 1990 (ADA)

Though the Rehab Act was passed in 1973, individuals with disabilities continued to occupy an inferior status in our society and were severely disadvantaged socially, vocationally, economically, and educationally (42 U.S.C. 12101, et seq., Sec. 2[a][6]). Therefore, the law was strengthened through its subsequent amendments and with the passage of the Americans with Disabilities Act (ADA) in 1990 (PL 101-336). The language of ADA is analogous to the language of the Rehab Act in this respect:

> Subject to the provision of this title, no qualified individual with a disability shall by reason of such disability, be excluded from participation in or be denied the benefits of services, programs, or activities of a public entity, or be subjected to discrimination by such entity. (Americans with Disabilities Act of 1990, Section 12132)

The Rehabilitation Act of 1973 and the Americans with Disabilities Act of 1990 are important to children with disabilities because they allow statutory venues for remediation of complaints. This provides individuals with disabilities and their families an avenue through which they can file complaints against public schools. If these complaints are found to be valid, the schools can potentially have all their federal funds terminated. A typical example is a student with a physical disability who does not need special assistance with his schoolwork, but still meets the definition of having a disability under the three-part definition of Section 504 of the Rehab Act. Under Section 504 it would be illegal to discriminate against this child regarding activities, events, or classes. Section 504 and the ADA are broader and more inclusive—providing protection from discrimination for a wider range of conditions—than later special education laws.

The ADA maintains that with the proper support, individuals can attain their goals, and it provides this support by prohibiting discrimination. The ADA strives for "equality of opportunity, full participation, independent living, and economic self-sufficiency" (42 U.S.C. 12101, et seq., Sec. 2[a][8]) for persons with disabilities (Turnbull, Bateman, & Turnbull, 1993). The main purpose of the ADA is to provide civil rights to the 43 million Americans with disabilities who have been unable to fully participate in their communities and receive necessary services. Some have claimed the ADA was developed to prevent businesses from expanding and to wreck small business (Michaels, Nappo, Barrett, Risucci, & Hales, 1993), but its purpose is to promote equal access and freedom for people with disabilities. Others have argued that the ADA extends a contract between individuals with disabilities, their family members, and the government for a lifetime of services and accessibility that starts with special education services received in schools (Turnbull et. al, 1993). Its intent is to open more of society to people with disabilities. It is clear that the ADA will change the norms of society. Individuals with disabilities will be perceived as educable, employable, and able, as well as entitled to and benefiting from education and participation

(Turnbull et. al, 1993). It is hoped that the ADA will transform the physical, attitudinal, and economic barriers that once prevented individuals with disabilities from participating in society. The following case study demonstrates this idea.

Accessibility for *All*

Although Diane had a back brace and used crutches to get around, she was not provided special education services. She was in a regular fifth-grade class and doing very well. Diane enjoyed going to school. She liked her teacher and had many friends. Diane often thought the weekends were too long because she missed her school friends.

The biggest event of the fifth grade was the annual trip to Washington, DC. Every fifth-grade class had made the trip for as long as anyone could remember. Her class had been planning all year for this trip. They were going to stay overnight in a hotel, see the Washington Monument, ride the Metro, and, they hoped, visit their congressman.

One day, Diane came home extremely upset with her teacher and principal; they had told her that she could not go to Washington. They had said that some of the places the class planned to visit would require too much walking for her, it would be hard for her to get on and off the bus, and the steps to the Capitol would be too hard for her to climb.

Diane's parents were incredulous. Despite the problems their daughter sometimes had getting in and out of places, they had done all they could to help her feel that she was the same as other children. They felt she could go anywhere and do whatever she wanted if she wanted it enough. When they asked her if there were other things she was not allowed to do, Diane said she was not allowed to go to the kickball field with her class because it was down a hill. She was not even allowed to go to watch. She also said that when her class did a presentation to the rest of the school, she didn't get to go onto the stage because climbing the steps would have taken her too long.

 CONSIDER THIS

1. What modifications should a school make to ensure access for individuals with physical disabilities and to be in compliance with the Americans with Disabilities Act?
2. For the trip in question, what are the school's options concerning its responsibility to provide accessibility for all students?
3. How can staff members facilitate Diane's participation in physical education, recreation, and performances?

LEGISLATION: SPECIAL EDUCATION LAWS

Education for All Handicapped Children Act (PL 94-142)

With the background of the *PARC* and *Mills* decisions in the early 1970s, Congress realized states were using widely different procedures to provide for the needs of children with disabilities. Many children with disabilities were still not receiving an appropriate education, or, if they were, it was at a substantial monetary cost to the parents. The quality of education was recognized as an important variable for a person with a disability to live and work independently, or at least semi-independently. Congress also realized that it cost more to educate students with disabilities and that some assistance might need to be provided. Additionally, a favorable climate for civil rights existed that provided the right political atmosphere for the enactment of sweeping legislation (Rothstein, 1990). For these reasons, in 1975, Congress passed federal grant legislation to encourage states to adopt appropriate procedures for providing education to children with disabilities between the ages of 3 and 21 (Rothstein, 1990). The states, in turn, were to provide a system for allocating funding to local school districts that complied with the requirements as spelled out in the law and in the implementing regulations. The grant legislation was titled the Education for all Handicapped Children Act, As Amended (PL 94-142).

The most vocal argument against the law was the potential cost of providing services for all children with disabilities. However, the law was not intended to fund the total cost of special education but only to subsidize the state and local education agencies (Turnbull, 1993). When PL 94-142 was initiated, the federal government was to provide up to 45% of the excess cost of providing services for a student in special education. Before 1993, the most it had ever provided was 12%; in 1993, reimbursement was about 8%.

PL 94-142 states that each child with a disability must receive a free, appropriate public education (FAPE). The main components of the law are (a) all children are to be served, (b) there must be procedures for identification, evaluation, and placement, (c) children need to be provided an appropriate education, (d) students should be integrated to the greatest extent possible, (e) decision making must be a shared process, (f) due process procedures need to be followed, (g) related services must be provided, and (h) transition plans are to be developed for when the student leaves school.

Individuals with Disabilities Education Act (IDEA)

In 1990, Congress reauthorized the Education for All Handicapped Children Act in the form of PL 101-476, called the Individuals with Disabilities Education Act (IDEA). The first significant point of the new law was the rewording of its title. In 1975, the law used the term "handicapped children." The new terminology, "individuals with disabilities," reflected the philosophy that the individual should be recognized first and the disability second. Additionally, the new title emphasized the preference for the term "disability" over the label "handicap."

Definition of Disabilities IDEA defines children with disabilities as those with mental retardation, hearing impairment, deafness, speech or language impairment, visual disability, serious emotional disturbance, orthopedic impairment or other health impairment, autism, deaf-blindness, multihandicap, specific learning disabilities, or traumatic brain injury. For these children to be identified under IDEA, they must require special education and related services to receive an appropriate education (Turnbull, 1993). IDEA definitions are not as broad or as inclusive as the definitions put forward by Section 504 of the Rehab Act. For example, an individual who is alcohol dependent could be considered to have a disability under Section 504 (the person either has an impairment, has a record of an impairment, or is regarded as having an impairment) but would not be considered to have a disability under IDEA. This demonstrates that the definitions advanced by IDEA are categorical in nature, while definitions under Section 504 are functional, meeting one of three life-defining criteria. One final point about the differences between IDEA and Section 504: IDEA requires an individualized education program for children with disabilities, while Section 504 does not. Both, however, require an appropriate education. Individualized education plans and appropriate education will be discussed later in greater detail.

All Children The original title for this landmark special education legislation was the Education for *All* Handicapped Children Act (PL 94-142). For too long, children with disabilities had been excluded because they were perceived as not being able to benefit from education or as not being ready for school. Congress wanted to emphasize that no child is to be excluded.

This point was clarified in the 1988 New Hampshire court decision, *Timothy W. v. Rochester School District*. Timothy W. was described as a 13-year-old boy who was blind and deaf, had cerebral palsy, was spastic and was subject to frequent convulsions, lacked carotid tissue, was profoundly retarded, had no communication skills, operated at the brain-stem level, had made no progress in about a year (in fact, he appeared to be regressing), and was unable to benefit from special education services.

The lower court agreed with the decision that he was unable to benefit from special education services. The appeals court reversed the decision, holding that the law was enacted to ensure that *all* children with disabilities would be provided an appropriate public education. It went on to say that "no child, regardless of severity of his or her handicap, is ever again to be subjected to the deplorable state of affairs which existed at the time of the passage of the Act, in which millions of handicapped children received inadequate education or none at all." (*Timothy W. v. Rochester School District,* EHLR 559:480) The law mandates an appropriate education for all children with disabilities, regardless of the level of achievement that such children might attain. Finally, it stated, "the only question left for the school district to determine, in conjunction with the child's parents, is what constitutes an appropriate individualized education program for the handicapped child." (*Timothy W. v. Rochester School District,* EHLR 559:480)

Evaluation, Identification, and Individualized Education Programs

Guaranteeing that all children, regardless of their disability, will be provided an education is of little value unless there are clear and consistent methods for determining how to evaluate, identify, and develop appropriate programs for students in special education. Historically, there have been problems in the testing and placement of children with disabilities, including the use of tests that were not in the child's primary language, failure to measure adaptive behavior, or reliance on a single test as the sole criterion for classification and placement. These inadequate practices resulted in several court cases stipulating correct procedures for the assessment and classification of children with disabilities.

Evaluation Two court cases (*Larry P. v. Riles* and *PASE v. Hannon*) were built upon the constitutional arguments regarding procedures for testing and evaluation that deal mainly with the denial of due process of law and equal treatment. The courts have issued guidelines including (a) all children need to be tested in their primary language, (b) IQ tests alone cannot be used for placement of children into special education programs, (c) unvalidated tests cannot be used, (d) parents must be notified before any testing may be initiated (there are procedures for bypass if parents do not consent to testing), (e) group tests are not to be used for determining eligibility, and (f) adaptive behavior must be taken into account when considering eligibility. Attention to the outcomes of years of case law will provide children with disabilities an appropriate education without denial of due process or equal treatment.

Districts must also implement procedures to screen preschool-age children for disabilities. These procedures can include placing announcements in the newspaper and around town that list dates and locations for screenings to determine eligibility for services before a child enters school at age 5 or 6. School districts must identify the specific nature of the child's disability beginning at age 3 and determine the type and extent of special education and related services required. In addition, it is suggested that school districts provide services for children from birth to age 3.

Identification The evaluation of a child must be an individualized assessment of all areas related to the suspected disability. The determination of whether a child is eligible for special education or related services must be a team decision, with at least one member of the team experienced in the suspected disability category. Parents must be notified of their right to an independent evaluation at public expense if they disagree with the results or procedures of the school district's evaluation. Once the eligibility process is completed, an individualized education program needs to be developed.

In 1994, the Council for Exceptional Children recommended a stronger link between assessment and intervention in a way that shifts the focus from a traditional "categorical" model to a "functional" model. Instead of evaluating students to determine whether they have a qualifiable disability, assessment efforts should be directed toward identification of student competence and instructional need.

With this focus, professionals can move away from a dependence on labels to develop programs that truly meet individual needs.

Determining eligibility for special education is not the only time an extensive evaluation process is required. Because some children have been placed inappropriately in special education and have remained there for the duration of their schooling, the law mandates a three-year, or triennial, evaluation. The entire evaluation process is repeated to ensure that a child still qualifies for special education services, although the Council for Exceptional Children (1994) offers the caveat that not all instruments and procedures administered and carried out in previous evaluations are necessary at the three-year review. Only those assessment practices that ascertain whether the student is receiving appropriate services need to be administered.

Individualized Education Programs As a result of this evaluation, an individualized education program, or plan, (IEP) is developed. An IEP is a document developed by a team of teachers, therapists, and other personnel in a series of meetings. It describes in writing the special education and related services specifically designed to meet the needs of the child. It contains (a) a statement of the child's present level of educational performance, (b) goals and objectives based on this functioning, (c) appropriate objective criteria and evaluation procedures along with schedules for determining, on at least an annual basis, whether instructional objectives are being achieved, (d) who will provide the services, where they will be provided, and the dates and anticipated duration of services, and (e) the related services necessary to reach those goals and objectives and the extent to which they are to be provided.

An IEP is more than a document outlining goals and objectives. It serves as a written commitment by the local education agency (LEA) to provide the specified service. Additionally, the law mandates a review of the progress toward the goals and objectives at least annually. Each goal and objective should be monitored more than annually to provide the student with the best possible education.

An important decision made at the meeting(s) convened to develop the IEP is the determination and description of where services for the child will be provided. The IEP describes the special education placement to be provided (this is *not* decided until the IEP meeting), and it describes the amount and location of the participation with students who do not have disabilities. If a student is not going to have any participation with students without disabilities, detailed documentation is necessary stating why it will not occur, and when it might occur in the future.

The goals and objectives written in the IEP address the areas in which the child will need assistance. IEPs were designed to list and document all special education and related services as well as describe all necessary accommodations to be provided. For many students with disabilities, most, if not all, of their day will be spent in the regular classroom. Any changes and modifications to regular programs need to be listed in the IEP. Typical modifications that should be documented in the IEP include extended time on tests, tape recorders in lecture classes, specified seat arrangements, and additional time for changing classes. It is important to note that when the modifications are written into the IEP, the school system is obligated to provide all modifications and services listed. This also means that LEAs should not write modifications or services they cannot provide. For example, an LEA should not write on all the IEPs of a given class that all students will spend 100% of their time working on a computer, unless enough computers exist for every child to use all the time.

It should be emphasized that the IEP meeting is where placement decisions are made. Often in the course of determining eligibility for services, a student's problem is assigned a label, such as learning disability or mental retardation, and because of this label there is an automatic expectation for placement. Many students with cerebral palsy have been placed in classrooms with other individuals with physical disabilities whether they needed that environment or not; similarly, students with learning disabilities have been placed unnecessarily in self-contained classrooms. The IEP is intended to be completely individualized; the student's placement must be a carefully considered team decision for each individual.

Appropriate Education   Typically, when students were identified as having a certain disability, they were often placed in a specific classroom whether that placement would provide them an "appropriate" education or not. But the term "appropriate" has caused confusion, both before and after the enactment of special education laws. What one parent, supervisor, principal, or teacher finds appropriate, another might deem completely inappropriate. This term has caused the greatest confusion relating to the education of students with disabilities.

For state and local education agencies to receive federal funding for special education programs, they need to document that they are providing an appropriate education for their students with disabilities. The demonstration of an appropriate education is documented through the development of an IEP. The reliance upon the development of an IEP is a method of defining appropriate education through a process definition. In this case, the process definition assumes that if a certain process is followed in the development and implementation of the IEP, then the student should be receiving an acceptable result, presumably an appropriate education (Turnbull, 1993).

The Supreme Court, in *Board of Education v. Rowley* (1982), addressed the issue of appropriate education in its first decision based on the Education for All Handicapped Children Act (PL 94-142). (See "Amy" in *Extraordinary Children: Ordinary Lives* by Martin, 1991). The *Rowley* decision has guided appropriate education decisions since 1982.

In *Rowley,* Amy Rowley was a first-grade student with a profound hearing impairment. Through residual hearing and lip reading she was able to understand only 59% of what transpired in the classroom. Amy was the only child with a hearing impairment in her school. Her parents, who also had hearing impairments, felt she needed an interpreter throughout the school day. The school provided an interpreter for two weeks, and after two weeks the interpreter said he believed he was no longer needed. The parents sued the school because they felt the law was developed to maximize their daughter's potential, not just guarantee her an education.

The Supreme Court held that the law was designed to provide equal access to education for all students with disabilities and was not designed to maximize the benefit of that education. It also reinforced the IEP as the means for controlling the process of determining a child's educational program.

The major principles of appropriate education stem from the *Rowley* decision, though they have been modified slightly over the years. The first principle from the *Rowley* decision is IDEA, which was designed to provide children with disabilities the same basic opportunities for an education offered to children without disabilities (Turnbull, 1993). IDEA set minimum national standards designed to ensure that each student was provided an education, not to ensure that each child reached his or her maximum development.

The second major principle from Rowley is that an appropriate education is based on the use of professional judgment and adherence to a defined process. Specifically, a school system develops an IEP for a student and then makes good-faith efforts to meet the goals and objectives of that program. Questions to be asked in the determination of an appropriate education and the correct process include:

1. Was the child evaluated in a nondiscriminatory fashion?
2. Is everyone certified for the role they are playing in the development and implementation of the IEP?
3. Is the IEP individualized?
4. Are the necessary related services listed?
5. Are all the components of services listed on the IEP being implemented?
6. Is there clear documentation of the level of functioning of the child in comparison to the goals and objectives on the IEP?
7. Is the child receiving some educational benefit from the program that he/she is in?
8. Are all the objectives of the IEP written in behavioral terms?
9. Have the parents or guardians been involved in every step of the development of the IEP?
10. Have the parents or guardians been made aware of their due process rights?
11. Is the student integrated with nondisabled students to the maximum extent possible?
12. If there is no provision for integration, is there a place for future integration with students who are nondisabled?

The important component of the process definition is that it places the burden on the professionals who develop and implement the IEP to demonstrate that it was based on correct information, properly developed and implemented, and properly monitored during its implementation.

The following case study presents a dilemma created by common practices in referral, evaluation, identification, and placement.

Individualizing the Process

George, a third grader with reading problems, was falling farther behind in his class each week. His teacher had used a variety of strategies to help him improve his reading but believed George had more problems than could be addressed in a regular classroom. The teacher referred George for testing to determine eligibility for special education. His mother was told he was being tested to diagnose reading problems.

For many years, Mr. Wilhite had been a resource room teacher of students with learning disabilities. He took pride in his skill in formally assessing students for eligibility in special education. Mr. Wilhite had developed a battery of tests to assess all students referred for learning disabilities. George took the same tests as everyone else and had scores similar to other students receiving LD services. Mr. Wilhite was convinced George was going to be placed in his resource class.

Although the other assessment components had not been completed, Mr. Wilhite told George's mother that George was going to be placed in his resource room for learning disabilities. His mother was confused because she thought George was being tested to assess his reading problem, and she did not want her son in a class for students with learning disabilities. Mr. Wilhite informed her that all students with learning disabilities were placed in his classroom.

 CONSIDER THIS

1. Examine this process in terms of the federal requirements for individualization.
2. What concerns do you have regarding the communication between home and school?
3. When should the decision be made about where to place a student with a disability, and who should make the decision about placement?

Integration

As stated here, students with disabilities need to be educated to the maximum extent possible alongside their nondisabled peers. For many years, the term "mainstreaming" was used as a way of describing circumstances in which special education teachers integrated students with disabilities into general education settings. Note, however, that the term "mainstreaming" does not exist in any legislation; it is a term popularized in special education literature that has influenced much of the debate relating to placement of children with disabilities. PL 94-142 states:

It is the purpose of this Act to assure that all handicapped children have available to them . . . a free appropriate public education which emphasizes special education and related services designed to meet their unique needs. To the maximum extent appropriate, handicapped children, including children in public or private institutions or other care facilities, are educated with children who are not handicapped. (20 U.S.C. Sec. 1401 [b][1]–[5])

There are many arguments for integrating students with disabilities with their general education peers. The legal arguments rest upon the premise that one needs to take the least restrictive steps before taking the more restrictive steps. An analogy might help clarify the concept of the least restrictive alternative: When you get a speeding ticket, you don't expect to receive a life sentence. There are more appropriate, and less aversive, steps that can be taken to help highway patrol officers monitor the speed of motorists. The same is true for children with disabilities. If a child is identified as having a mild speech impairment, the child should not be institutionalized because of the impairment.

The integration of students with disabilities into the general classroom is the area that has provided the most controversy within the field of special education. For many years, when children were identified as having disabilities, they were either excluded from school, or if they attended school, they were placed in a separate building or at least in a separate class. There was little or no possibility for interaction with general education students. After PL 94-142, there was an initiative to mainstream students with disabilities into regular classrooms. This trend was further extended with the debate and discussion around the Regular Education Initiative and with the publishing of a paper by then-Assistant Secretary of Education Madeleine Will titled, *Educating Children With Learning Problems: A Shared Responsibility* (1986).

The emphasis on the integration of children with disabilities into general classrooms is based on several premises. First, children with disabilities are often more alike than different from children who are nondisabled. Second, by integrating children with disabilities into general classrooms there is more emphasis on the individualized nature of the student's needs. No longer can a child receive a label and automatically be placed into a separate special education classroom for students with that label. Third, placement in special education is perceived by some to be a terminal placement; once placed in a separate special education classroom, the student may always remain there. The presumption is that all students will be placed in the regular classroom unless extenuating circumstances prevent such placement, and then every effort must be made to return the student to the regular classroom as rapidly as possible. Finally, there are numerous civil rights arguments relating to the removal from the mainstream of children who are different and the loss of the benefits they could be expected to receive from association with their nondisabled peers.

It is not the intent of this chapter to discuss full inclusion, rather to clarify the law. The law states:

Schools must maintain a continuum of alternative placements such as special classes, resource rooms, and itinerant instruction to meet the needs of the disabled. (34 C.F.R. Sec. 300.551 [1991])

It is often forgotten that the law stipulates services are to follow students; that is, services are to be tailored to the unique needs of the individual in the most appropriate setting. It is not acceptable for students to be assigned only those services that have been designated for a particular disability or those programs that are available or convenient. Just because a student is labeled TMR does not mean the student has to be placed in a self-contained classroom when a partial-day program for EMR or a resource room might be more suited for that child. The school district needs to have available a continuum of services, including everything between the regular classroom and hospital-type settings.

In 1993, the federal Third Circuit Court of Appeals ruled in favor of parents who sought full inclusion in a regular classroom for their 8-year-old with Down syndrome (*Oberti v. Board of Education*). The school district argued that the student would make the greatest academic gains in a special education program. The court advanced the following three standards for considering whether a student can be educated satisfactorily in the general education program: (1) The school district must demonstrate that reasonable efforts have been made to accommodate the child in the general classroom. (2) Supplementary aids and services must be implemented to confer benefit from education in the general classroom. (3) The negative effects of the child's inclusion in the general classroom must be considered (Order for Full Inclusion, 1993).

A District-Level Response

Responding to the national and state debate surrounding the inclusion of students with disabilities into the regular classroom and recent interpretations from court cases regarding education in the general classroom, a school district disbanded its self-contained classrooms. During the summer before the inclusion in the general classroom of these formerly self-contained students, the school system offered inservice training programs on topics such as curriculum-based assessment, collaboration, management in the classroom, and working with a paraprofessional. In the fall, students with disabilities were placed in general education classes most of the time. Special education teachers provided consultation to general education teachers, and more paraprofessionals were available to assist in the regular classroom.

Some of the students with disabilities were clearly benefiting from the education they were receiving in the regular classroom. Although the school system had provided inservices about inclusion, it became quickly evident that many general education teachers were unprepared to teach students with disabilities. Additionally, for some students, education in the regular classroom was not an appropriate setting. Several parents complained that their children with disabilities had received a better education in the self-contained classroom. At the same time, some parents of nondisabled children complained that too much time was being spent on the students with disabilities at the expense of their children's education.

CONSIDER THIS

1. To what issues was the school system responding?
2. What preparations for change might have enhanced the new approach to special education service delivery?
3. How should the school administrators handle parental dissatisfaction with a systematic change?
4. How will the guarantee of an individualized education program for all special education students be realized in the current setting?

Historically, parents have been shut out of the decision-making process because it was assumed they were the cause of the child's disability (e.g., Bruno Bettleheim and autism), or they were thought to be ignorant of their children's educational needs. Realizing that parents or guardians have essential information about their children, legislators outlined provisions in PL 94-142 to ensure parent participation in the special education process. Procedures were enumerated for notification, access to records, consultation, and participation in advisory panels.

Shared decision making involves parents in the protection of their minor sons and daughters. It protects the rights of students in that it ensures there is someone involved in the process who has a long-term interest in the children's well-being. Additionally, what affects the student with a disability also affects the parents; therefore, parents are important stakeholders.

IDEA states that parents need to be aware of, and consent to, every step of the process. This includes the initial evaluation, the eligibility meeting, the development of the IEP, annual reviews, and the triennial evaluation process. Parents also need access to all the records kept on their child and to receive assurance that information about their son or daughter (or about them) will be kept confidential.

The provisions of Part H, the early childhood amendments to PL 94-142, have additional requirements for parent involvement. Under the requirements for Part H, school systems must establish a public awareness campaign, a comprehensive Child Find program, and a central director of information. School systems also have an obligation to work with families when the child is identified as needing special education services. Early childhood personnel should begin working with families as soon as possible after the child is born, thereby providing the child as much assistance as possible before entering school.

Part H also calls for the development of an individualized family services plan (IFSP). Similar to the development of the IEP, the IFSP includes a heavy family component because there is realization that families play a vital role in the development and nurturing of the child. Working with the family to help it meet the needs of its family member can be accomplished either through training family members to carry out specific duties or through collaborating with them to determine the best methods for working with the disabled person. The IFSP is more than just an IEP with a family twist, though; it is a multidisciplinary document designed to enhance a child's development and minimize delays, and to enhance the family's capacity to meet a child's needs.

Another important component of Part H is the realization that one service provider (schools) does not have to be the sole discipline providing for the child with a disability and his or her family members. Multiple agencies must work together to provide a combination of approaches and interventions.

Due Process

One main component of the law for children with disabilities is the opportunity for parental decision making on all the levels affecting their child's eligibility for special education services (Rothstein, 1990). If parents or guardians disapprove of the methods used for determining eligibility and educational programming or disapprove of the resulting decisions, due process procedures allow for interested parties to challenge the school system. Due process protection comes from the 5th and 14th amendments of the U.S. Constitution, in that ". . . no person shall be deprived of life, liberty, or property without due process of law." As Turnbull (1993) noted, "due process means that no child with a disability can be deprived of an education without the opportunity of exercising the right to protest what happens to him or her (p. 207)."

The requirements of due process procedures expand on the basics outlined in the *Mills* (1972) case. As a result of this case, the DC Board of Education was ordered to locate all children with disabilities and advise them of their right to an education. *Mills* also outlined the rights to an appropriate education at public expense. PL 94-142 expanded the constitutional guarantees of *Mills* to include specifics regarding the form of notices along with the content of and procedures for a hearing.

Appropriate notification is one key element of procedural due process. The law is very specific about requirements relating to notice. The law requires written notice before the schools can: (1) propose to initiate or change, or (2) refuse to initiate or change the identification, evaluation, or educational placement of the child or the provision of an appropriate education (20 U.S.C. Sec. 1415 [b][1][C]). The schools also must convey the details of the proposed action and the reasons for it. The law does not stipulate how to convey the written information to families who cannot read, although it is expected that the information will be conveyed to a family in its primary language.

Next, parents may request a due process hearing if they are not happy with any or all aspects of the procedures or the education of their child. The purpose of the due process hearing is to resolve differences of opinion between parents and school officials regarding the education, placement, or services for the child with a disability. If the parents request a hearing, it must be conducted by a hearing officer who is independent of the local school board. The hearing must be conducted at a time and place suitable to the parents. The parents must be notified of free or low-cost legal assistance. There is also an expectation that the hearing will be conducted within a reasonable time after the request.

Finally, there are specific procedures that must be used in a due process hearing. These include procedures for the presentation of evidence, confrontation relating to this evidence, cross-examination, and the attendance of witnesses. At the parents' request, the hearing may be either closed or open to the public. If the court rules in favor of the parents, all costs are paid for by the school system. If not, parents incur the costs of their attorney.

While the outcome of the hearing is pending, the student remains in the current educational placement, which explains the need to expedite the hearing. This is known as the "stay-put" rule. Variations of this rule can occur only if the child is a danger to himself or others.

As one might ascertain, because one side "wins" and the other "loses," a due process hearing tends to be an antagonistic process. It usually ends with both parties unhappy about the results or feeling they received less than they wanted. It is a legal procedure, and like other legal procedures, there are challenges with the process. Due process hearings require an enormous amount of energy, time, and money. Despite these challenges, due process procedures are an invaluable means of ensuring an appropriate education and the participation of parents in the education of their children (Turnbull, Turnbull, & Strickland, 1979; Budoff, 1981).

Instead of due process hearings, more individuals and school systems are using another form of resolution called mediation. Mediation involves the use of less formal, less adversarial, more negotiated-settlement meetings for resolving disputes (U.S. Department of Education, 1984). In mediation, one or more neutral third parties usually are brought in to hear the issues and find an acceptable solution. There has been a significant increase in the number of cases using mediation. This also might be seen as a verification that due process hearings are taxing on all involved.

Due Process

Cory had always had problems in school. He was diagnosed in first grade as having a learning disability and began receiving services from a special education teacher in a resource room. In fourth grade, Cory did poorly on his first report card and complained that school was too hard. His parents felt he was not getting sufficient special attention and therefore not making progress. They had him retested at their own expense at a private agency. The results of the retesting confirmed for the parents their perception that Cory was not receiving an appropriate education. He was not making progress, and indications of a learning disability were even more pronounced than in the earlier school assessment.

The parents presented the report to the school system and requested a change of placement to a self-contained program. A committee met with the parents and agreed that, according to the testing, Cory was not making much progress, but committee members argued that a self-contained classroom was too restrictive in this case. The parents were very upset. They felt they had spent a lot of money for nothing and that something needed to be done. They contacted their lawyer, and the lawyer called the school system to request a due process hearing regarding Cory's placement.

The principal contacted the special education director, and the staff began collecting the necessary information for a due process hearing. The requisite paperwork included the child's school history, clear documentation on identification of the child's condition, description of the programs and/or services being proposed to meet the child's educational needs, anecdotal notes, and a chronology of contacts with the parents. With this information, administrators were able to build a case for keeping Cory in the resource setting.

 CONSIDER THIS

1. What steps might be proposed as an alternative to a due process hearing?
2. What types of evidence should be collected in preparation for a due process hearing?
3. What should the special education administrator do to prepare for a due process hearing?
4. What should the special education administrator to do prepare others for a due process hearing?

Transition

When the Education for All Handicapped Children Act (PL 94-142) was implemented, there was no mention of transition or the need for transition services for students with disabilities. The original intent of PL 94-142 was to provide access to school for students with disabilities; it did not consider issues of postschool life for these individuals. This lack of policy initiatives occurred despite the knowledge that vocational training and transition services are a necessary part of the education of students with disabilities (Brolin, 1988).

In 1984, transition from school to work for students with disabilities became a major priority for the Office of Special Education and Rehabilitative Services (OSERS) (Will, 1986). Many people who had never thought of transition as a function of special education now had at least heard about the need for transition services. Concurrently, initiatives were presented by the federal government for supported employment (Will, 1986). These initiatives stressed that students with disabilities could potentially move into employment that was integrated into the community rather than provided in a sheltered workshop or work activity center (Moon, Goodall, Barcus, & Brooke, 1986; Rusch & Hughes, 1990; Wehman & Moon, 1988).

Three main factors brought about the changes in transition services for students with disabilities: the lessons of history, the realization that students with disabilities were leaving a free, appropriate public education and entering a system where there are no mandates, and the realization that students educated in special education were not achieving desired outcomes.

The definition of transition services, as defined in IDEA, is a coordinated set of activities for a student, designed within an outcome-oriented process that promotes movement from school to postschool activities, including postsecondary education, vocational training, integrated employment (including supported employment), continuing and adult education, adult services, independent living, and community participation. (20 U.S.C. 1401 [a][19])

Beyond High School

Tricia had received services for learning disabilities in a self-contained class during her elementary and middle-school years. When she got to high school, she received resource services for only one period a day from the special education teacher. She was proud to be in regular classes with other students, and her parents were proud of the work she did. In fact, Tricia did so well she graduated with her friends. Her delighted parents had a big party and invited all her friends.

Six months after graduation, Tricia was spending most of her time sitting at home watching television. She had attempted to find a job, but was unable to find one. Tricia had received no training in how to look for a job, how to fill out a job application, how to interview, or even how to work with a boss.

Her parents were shocked. They had been so proud of their daughter, and now all she could do was baby-sit or cut grass.

 CONSIDER THIS

1. What should have been done in school to prepare Tricia for postschool life?
2. What responsibility does the school have for formulating transition goals and developing a program for students?

Related Services

So far, we have dealt with the services and rights that are an integral part of the educational needs of students with disabilities. In addition to the educational services, there are other services the child might need to benefit from special education. These are called related services. Related services include:

"transportation, and such . . . other supportive services (including speech pathology and audiology), psychological services, physical and occupational therapy, recreation, including therapeutic recreation and social work services, and medical and counseling services, including rehabilitation counseling, (except that such medical services shall be for diagnostic and evaluation purposes only) as may be required to assist a child with a disability to benefit from special education, and includes the early identification and assessment of disabling conditions in children." (20 U.S.C. Sec. 1401 [17])

The rationale for school systems providing related services was reiterated by the Supreme Court decision in *Irving Independent School District v. Tatro* (1984). To keep in perspective the obligation to provide services that relate to both the health and educational needs of students with disabilities and to minimize the educators' concerns that providing related services will incur a burden, the court clarified several conditions that must be met before services are provided. First, to be entitled to related services, a child must be eligible for special education services. Unfortunately, there are students who might benefit from these related services, but because they are not eligible for special education, they cannot receive related services. In the absence of this eligibility, the student does not qualify for related services. Second, only those services necessary to help a child benefit from special education must be provided, regardless of how easily a school nurse or layperson could furnish them. For example, if a particular medication or treatment may appropriately be administered to a child other than during the school day, a school is not required to provide a nurse to administer it. Third, the regulations state that medical services must be provided only if they can be performed by a nurse or other qualified person, not if they must be performed by a physician.

Just as classroom placement is individually determined for the child with a disability, the need for related services should be determined in the same manner and listed on the IEP. Once they are delineated on the IEP, the school system is obligated to provide them, regardless of whether they are currently available.

SUMMARY

In 1972, litigation against the state of Pennsylvania enlisted court support to ensure equal protection and due process rights regarding education for individuals with mental retardation. Further court cases clarified the rights of all individuals with disabilities to free, appropriate public education. In 1973, federal legislators passed the Rehabilitation Act of 1973, offering protection of individuals with disabilities from discrimination and setting forth guidelines for access to education, employment, and public services. In landmark legislation the following year, the basic laws of special education were outlined in PL 94–142. In 1990, the Americans with Disabilities Act extended the rights of individuals with disabilities, previously available only in federal and state sectors, to the private sector. Additionally that year, PL 94–142 was reauthorized, enhanced, and renamed the Individuals with Disabilities Education Act (IDEA).

According to federal law, all children, without exception, must be offered an appropriate education. Identification, evaluation, and placement must be nonbiased and individually determined based on the specific needs of the child. Parent involvement is required in all phases of the assessment, placement procedures, and decision-making process. Each child is to have a written individualized education program that describes all services to be provided and is binding on the school system. Students must be educated in the least restrictive environment to the greatest extent possible. Recent interpretations of this requirement have resulted in the inclusion of many students with all levels of severity of disabilities into general education environments.

PL 94-142 requires schools to screen children of preschool age and older for disabilities. Early childhood services include more parental involvement and coordination of many support services. IDEA provides a new focus at the other end of the age range, with requirements that schools actively prepare students with disabilities for transition into postschool life.

Federal laws for children with disabilities also delineate due process rights to ensure that parents can contest decisions they believe are not in their child's best interest. In addition to receiving special education services, individuals identified as handicapped for school purposes become eligible for related services, such as transportation or physical therapy.

REFERENCES

Abeson, A. (1972). Movement and momentum: Government and the education of handicapped children. *Exceptional Children, 39,* 63–66.

Americans with Disabilities Act, PL 101-336. (July 26, 1990). 42 U.S.C. 12101, et seq. *Federal Register, 56*(144), 35544–35756.

Board of Education v. Rowley, 458 U.S. 176, 102 S. Ct 3034, 73 L.Ed., 2d 690 (1982).

Brolin, D.E. (1988). *Vocational preparation of citizens with mental retardation.* Columbus, OH: Merrill.

Brown v. Board of Education of Topeka, Kansas, 347 U.S. 483 (1954).

Budoff, M. (1981). Special education appeals hearing: Are they fair and are they helping? *Exceptional Education Quarterly,* 37–48.

Council for Exceptional Children (1994). *Issues in the implementation of IDEA.* Reston, VA: Department of Public Policy.

Education for All Handicapped Children Act, As Amended, Public Law 94-142 (20 U.S.C. Sec. 1401 [b][1]–[5]).

Individuals with Disabilities Education Act, PL 101-476, 20 U.S.C. Sec. 1401 et. seq.

Irving Independent School District v. Tatro, 468 U.S. 883 (1984).

Larry P. v. Riles, 343 F. Supp. 1306, aff'd., 502 F.2d 963, *further proceedings,* 495 F. Supp. 926, aff'd., 502 F.2d 693 (9th Cir. 1984).

Martin, R. (1991). *Extraordinary children: Ordinary lives.* Champaign, IL: Research Press.

Michaels, C., Nappo, P., Barrett, K., Risucci, D.A., & Hales, C.W. (1993). Provisions of reasonable accommodation: What do employers think? In P. Wehman (Ed.), *The ADA mandate for social change* (pp. 89–115). Baltimore, MD: Paul H. Brookes Publishing Co.

Mills v. DC Board of Education, 348 F. Supp. 86 (D.D.C. 1972).

Moon, M. S., Goodall, D., Barcus, J. M., & Brooke, V. (1986). *The supported work model of competitive employment for citizens with severe handicaps: A guide for trainers.* Richmond, VA: Rehabilitation Research and Training Center, Virginia Commonwealth University.

Oberti v. Board of Education of the Borough of Clementon School District, 801 F. Supp. 1392 (D.N.J. 1992), 19 IDELR 423, _____ F.2d _____ (3rd Cir. 1993), 19 IDELR 908, 2:40n; 4-20n-21n, 23n, 29n, 44n-45n, 47, 79.

Order for full inclusion upheld on appeal. (1993, July). *Individuals with Disabilities Education Law Report, 19*(19), 129, 131.

Parents in Action in Special Education (PASE) v. Hannon, 506 F. Supp. 831 (N.D.Ill. 1980).

Pennsylvania Association for Retarded Children (PARC) v. Commonwealth of Pennsylvania, 334 F. Supp. 1257 (E.D. Pa. 1971) 343 F. Supp. 279 (E.D. Pa. 1972).

The Rehabilitation Act of 1973 (PL 93-112). 29 U.S.C. Section 794.

Rothstein, L. F. (1990). *Special education law.* White Plains, NY: Longman Publishing Company.

Rusch, F. R., & Hughes, C. (1990). Historical overview of supported employment. In F. R. Rusch (Ed.), *Supported employment models, methods, and issues* (pp. 5–14). Sycamore, IL: Sycamore Publishing Company.

Scheerenberger, R. C. (1983). *A history of mental retardation.* Baltimore, MD: Paul H. Brookes Publishing Co.

Timothy W. v. Rochester School District, Education for the Handicapped Law Reporter DEC. 559:480 (D.N.H. 1988).

Turnbull, H. R. (1993). *Free appropriate public education: The law and children with disabilities* (4th. ed.). Denver: Love Publishing.

Turnbull, H. R., Bateman, D. F., & Turnbull, A. P. (1993). Family empowerment. In P. Wehman (Ed.), *The ADA mandate for social change* (pp. 157–174). Baltimore, MD: Paul H. Brookes Publishing Company.

Turnbull, H. R., Turnbull, A. P., & Strickland, B. (1979). Procedural due process: The two-edged sword that the untrained should not unsheath. *Boston University Journal of Education* (Summer), 40–59.

U.S. Department of Education (1984). *Sixth annual report to Congress.* Washington, DC: U.S. Government Printing Office.

Wehman, P., & Moon, M. S. (Eds.) (1988). *Vocational rehabilitation and supported employment.* Baltimore, MD: Paul H. Brookes Publishing Company.

Will, M. C. (1986). Educating children with learning problems: A shared responsibility. *Exceptional Children, 52,* 411–416.

Chapter 4

WORKING WITH GOVERNMENT: LEADING WHILE RESPONDING WITHIN THE LARGER SYSTEM

K. Kay Cessna

Special education administrators have the primary authority and responsibility for ensuring that the laws pertaining to exceptional children are implemented in their jurisdiction. Local directors of special education have a unique role; they function as executives when developing and coordinating services in their schools, yet they are inherently middle managers on a chain of command. They make decisions and direct the activities of subordinates, while at the same time following the directives of their superiors.

The simultaneous roles of executive and subordinate are not as contradictory as they might first appear. Rather, they might be viewed as if they were Russian nesting (Matryoshka) dolls. These sets consist of five to ten dolls, each painted differently, but with the same colors and design theme. The dolls are constructed so that smaller ones fit inside or "nest" in larger ones; each doll is unique and autonomous while still fitting into the larger set.

In the same manner, special education directors are executives who create designs and make decisions resulting in a program unique to their district. Activities might include designing a staff development initiative, arranging with principals for program space in buildings, authorizing expenditures on tests and materials, hiring professionals, and negotiating with parents. At the same time, this executive role "nests" within the subordinate role. That is, all decisions must fit within the boundaries of laws, rules, policies, and guidelines established by any number of agencies that are "larger" or farther up the chain of command. For example, staff development initiatives and space discussions must fit into the district's calendar and facilities plan. Expenditures for materials and the hiring of staff must be aligned with state reimbursement procedures. Parent negotiations must comply with federal due process guidelines.

As a middle manager, the special education director must understand policies and laws that come from farther up the chain of command and translate them down the chain into effective programs for children. An individual director's ability to create responsive programs in the executive role is directly related to the informal and functional authority the director accrues from performing the subordinate role well. Special education directors can provide leadership to their own district or cooperative while at the same time influence and respond to persons and agencies up the chain of command.

LEVELS OF GOVERNMENT

To effect this delicate form of leadership, it is necessary to recognize and understand the three levels of government that have an impact on special education. Local, state, and federal levels of government create the context within which a special education director operates.

Local Government

Within the local community, individuals are elected or appointed to a local board of education to set educational policy for the school district. This board hires a superintendent (in some states, superintendents are elected) to implement its policy decisions, and the superintendent in turn creates a management team to assist in this endeavor. Frequently, directors of special education serve on superintendents' central management teams. If the district is fairly large, there may be one or more assistant superintendents. In that case, the director may report to one of the assistant superintendents and may not be a member of the superintendent's management team, or one of the assistant superintendents may function as director of special education and pupil services.

Most states have intermediate school organizations or cooperatives, governed similarly to local school agencies, which coordinate specific efforts or programs involving several districts. This is especially helpful when several small, isolated districts cannot provide specific services alone or when there are functions that local schools could accomplish more effectively and efficiently through cooperation with other districts. Special education is frequently one of the programs districts consider to be most effectively and efficiently implemented through a cooperative. Special education intermediate agencies have a variety of names, such as "special districts," "regionalized agencies," "special education cooperatives," or "board of cooperative services" (Sage & Burrello, 1986). Requirements for district participation in an intermediate unit vary from state to state, with participation mandatory in some, voluntary in others.

Intermediate units or cooperatives are governed by a board typically composed of superintendents of the member districts. This board usually hires a director for the cooperative to implement its policy decisions. If the cooperative is large and responsible for a number of programs, the director of the cooperative may hire a special education director. Cooperatives present a special challenge for local directors of special education. Superintendents function as policy makers on the cooperative's board, but within the directives of their own local board. The number of stakeholders (or supervisors) who must be kept informed and brought to agreement on each initiative increases with each additional district.

Regardless of the organizational structure, local and intermediate school boards make the educational policy decisions, and the superintendent is charged with implementing them. The director of special education is responsible to the superintendent for carrying out local board decisions related to programs for students with disabilities. In this capacity, local directors ensure that free, appropriate public education is provided to all exceptional individuals. Beyond mere compliance with the law, this administrator must aspire to develop quality programs through visionary, long-range planning and staff development (Audetta & Algozzine, 1992).

Local school administration is the first step up the chain of command, providing parameters that local directors must function within when designing local systems.

Suggestions for working within local government parameters:
- Keep close to the chain of command in order to influence decisions, receive information more quickly, and understand the rationale for decisions.
- Interact on a regular basis with those on the leadership team. This provides an opportunity, often informal, for keeping leadership apprised of your current thinking and initiatives.
- Present proposals so that special education efforts are consistent with larger, district initiatives. In this way, special education begins to be viewed as an integral part of the system rather than as a mandated program operating independently.
- Avoid using the law as the primary reason for action. Providing an educational rationale for initiatives lets your co-workers know the values underlying the law.

The following case poses a challenge faced by a special education director attempting to work within a local education system.

Outcome-Based Education for All?

Sharon Stone has been director of special education for two years in a medium-size school district in which she reports to the assistant superintendent for support services. Stone prides herself on staying current with the latest innovations in service delivery and has been able to generate enthusiasm and movement in her staff toward creative program improvement.

Last summer, the entire central management team attended a training program designed to assist school administrators in creating performance-based systems. Sharon Stone saw the possibilities and immediately formed committees within her staff to explore issues specific to outcome-based education for students with special needs. She wanted to ensure that her staff was prepared to advocate for the use of an outcome-based model for all students.

Liz Carter, the assistant superintendent for curriculum and instruction, also returned from the training program with a plan. However, she was determined that students with disabilities were not to be included in the districtwide testing programs and that the special education staff would develop its own outcome-based system to provide for its students' unique needs. Carter formed three districtwide outcome-based education task forces of primary, intermediate, and secondary general educators, refusing to allow special educators to participate on these teams.

CONSIDER THIS

1. Compare the philosophies that have brought these two administrators to opposite positions on outcome-based education for students with disabilities.
2. How should Sharon Stone approach this controversy within this local structure?

State Government

At the state level, governance and educational policy are addressed by the legislature and the state board or department of education. The state legislature is composed of elected members who create laws to guide the development of educational policy for the entire state. In the past, educational legislation was usually limited to major categorical initiatives or addressed indirectly through budget and funding decisions. Over the last decade, however, many state legislatures have become more actively involved in directing the development of educational policy through sweeping school reform legislation. In addition, governors, who have traditionally implemented legislative mandates, are taking a more active role in initiating educational policy. Currently, many states are reviewing policies and procedures, resulting in major revision and reorganization.

All states have a board of education composed of representative individuals, either elected or appointed. A chief school officer, sometimes called the state superintendent of education, also may be either elected or appointed. The key function of this state officer is to implement legislation and policies developed by the state legislature and school board. Professionals are employed as consultants to assist the chief state school officer in administering programs and implementing policy initiatives. An additional role of the state special education agency is to be a resource to the legislature concerning the needs of exceptional students (Meyen, 1988).

States vary in the organization of their departments of education. Most have a special education section or unit administered by a state director of special education. Recently, however, some state departments have reorganized to reflect the more integrated, transdisciplinary approaches recommended for local school districts. In these organizations, persons with special education expertise may be assigned to other offices within the department of education.

Traditional relationships between governing bodies and their offices have undergone considerable scrutiny in the last decade. In the past, state boards tended to set educational policy and direction, then expected chief state school officers to implement them. Similarly, legislatures provided the funds, intending for governors to coordinate efforts and implement programs. Inherent in this arrangement was a balance of power with clearly defined roles. Currently, these arrangements are being questioned by legislators, governors, boards of education, and chief state school officers, all of whom have a valid and keen interest in establishing educational policy for the state.

The state department is the second step up the chain of command in providing yet further parameters that local directors must function within when designing their local systems.

State Department of Education and Local District Relationship

State departments of education employ individuals, sometimes called consultants, to assist and monitor the activities of local schools. These consultants typically view local directors of special education as their primary clients. This is a logical approach, since these consultants are responsible for ensuring implementation of state laws regarding programs for students with disabilities, and the implementation of those laws in a school district is the responsibility of the local director of special education.

State departments provide leadership to local schools and perform two regulatory functions: ensurance of compliance with the laws, and distribution of funds. Department personnel are organized to offer services determined to be most effective in supporting these functions. While some state departments may focus only on compliance and funding, more progressive departments seek to provide leadership and offer a wider variety of services. Leadership with support is more in alignment with current reform efforts, which revolve around the principle of decentralization of decision making and professional empowerment. New systems of on-site management will be ineffective as long as decisions, standards, and accountability are centrally controlled (Fishkin, 1993). The variation in support systems available is a reflection of the differences in philosophies of the various state departments and the individual consultants who work there. For example, one state may determine that the best way to ensure compliance for the correct development of individualized education programs (IEP) is to offer training statewide so that all service providers receive the same information. Another state department may decide that having a standard, computerized IEP form will better ensure compliance.

State departments ensure compliance with special education laws through a system of approving comprehensive plans and performing on-site monitoring visits. Each local director is required to submit a comprehensive plan detailing how the school district proposes to implement state and federal special education laws. Some states now allow local districts to adopt the state plan as their comprehensive plan, saving duplication of effort. State agencies establish rules and regulations for the approval of local agencies' comprehensive plans (Meyen, 1988). State officials evaluate local plans and, if the plans are approved, on-site monitoring visits are conducted to determine whether the policies and procedures outlined in the district's plan are being implemented. Distribution of funds is typically contingent on the successful completion of both requirements (Sage

& Burrello, 1986). In most states, the submission of the comprehensive plan and on-site monitoring visits occur on a regular cycle.

State departments of education also play a significant role in the interpretation and application of legislation. The state director of special education is responsible for the development of the rules and regulations outlining more specifically how the state laws are to be implemented. Although procedures vary among states, there is a formal process for the development and adoption of these rules. This includes formal hearings on rules before they are adopted by the state board of education. Once the state board adopts the rules, they have the impact of law.

Suggestions for working within state government parameters:
- Develop the local comprehensive plan in a manner that simultaneously creates districtwide discussion of special education and accomplishes strategic planning.
- Use your approaching on-site monitoring visit to motivate your staff to ensure that all assessment reports and other paperwork are current. Use the on-site visit as a deadline.
- Work with the state director during the development of state rules and regulations to determine which issues should be included in the rules and which should be included in local comprehensive plans. Issues that tend to be ongoing and important enough to carry the weight of law should be included in the rules and regulations. On the other hand, some procedures may change with shifting demographics and situations, and these should be addressed in the local comprehensive plan, where changes are more easily accomplished.
- Be strategic in opening the laws or the rules and regulations for amendment. Once the laws or the rules and regulations are opened, all sections are subject to amendment, not just the section you might be interested in altering. Opening a law demands political astuteness and careful planning.
- Build liaisons with your state special education consultants. They share the goal of providing good services to students within the mandates of state and federal laws. They can become valuable resources in working effectively with this level of government.

The following case presents a dilemma faced by a new director addressing local concerns in the context of state regulations.

New Director Faces Impending Compliance Visit

David Manning became special education director of Melrose last school year after serving as a school psychologist for 12 years. The former administrator, Jack Sparks, had been director of special education since the district began offering services 18 years ago. At the time Sparks assumed the directorship, it was necessary for special education administrators to be demanding and employ aggressive tactics to obtain services; Sparks was very effective in this approach. Unfortunately, rather than developing new strategies or interpersonal skills, he continued to use his aggressive style long after it served any purpose. The resulting problems aroused animosity from the superintendent toward not only the director, but also the entire special education program.

The superintendent's frustration culminated last year in the removal of Sparks and the appointment of Manning as special education director. The superintendent's first directive was to reduce the special education budget by 15%. As a result, new teachers could not be hired, and some resource teachers' caseloads approached 30, even though state regulations mandate caseloads of no more than 18. Morale was at an all-time low when Manning was notified that his district was scheduled for its regular on-site monitoring visit in six months.

 CONSIDER THIS

1. What are the new director's most apparent problems and which is of most concern?
2. How could Manning use the approaching on-site visit to his advantage?

Federal Government

Samuel Kirk, best known for his instrumental work in the field of learning disabilities, explained that although local and state governments have the primary responsibility for education, special education would still be in its primitive stages if not for federal leadership in research and professional preparation (Harris & Kirk, 1993). At the federal level, Congress creates laws, the executive branch implements them, and the judicial branch interprets their meaning and determines whether they and their practice are constitutional.

Congress creates laws that guide the development of educational policy for the nation and its territories. As with state legislatures, federal laws enacted by Congress usually are limited to major categorical initiatives or addressed indirectly through budget and funding decisions. Categorical initiatives are legislative efforts to respond to a specific group or "category" of persons for whom the current system has not been effective. The passage of PL 94-142 in 1975 is an example of a major categorical initiative.

Individual legislators may have supported new laws for students with disabilities as a way to provide financial assistance to states under pressure to dramatically expand services (Lynn, 1983). However, the real hope was that new laws would initiate a change in philosophy so that schools would be more accepting of students with significant differences. Unfortunately, federal initiatives and court actions were met with resistance at both the state and local level as individuals who would be responsible for implementation in the schools realized the magnitude of the proposed changes (Sarason & Doris, 1978). Federal legislation has resulted in increased services for students with disabilities and better preparation of special education personnel. At the same time, however, serious problems have emerged because funding has never been adequate, schools have focused on procedural safeguards instead of substantive change, and general educators have resisted modification because they were not prepared for their new role in mainstreaming (Sage & Burrello, 1986).

During the 1980s, major reports, including *A Nation at Risk: The Imperative for Education Reform* (1983) and *A Nation Prepared: Teachers for the 21st Century* (1986), questioned the adequacy of education. These have helped spur both the legislative and executive branches to become more active in creating laws and setting educational policy as outlined in the documents *America 2000: An Educational Strategy* (1991) and *Goals 2000: Educate America* (1993), which proposed six goals for our nation's educational system. Eisner (1992) states that federal efforts to reform education overemphasize competition, measurement, and the education-work relationship, which distracts educators from tackling the structural problems of schools and generates cynicism and passive resistance in overworked teachers. There is a tendency among local school officials and parents to interpret federal intervention as an imposition from a distant bureaucracy that generally proposes unrealistic and unworkable practices (Goldberg, 1986).

The executive branch implements mandates established by the Congress through the development of regulations (Sage & Burrello, 1986). The ideal is that the executive branch translates the intent of the law into rules, regulations, or guidelines that ensure its implementation. Within the executive branch is the federal Department of Education, which has a number of assistant secretaries, each with responsibilities for some aspect of federal education functions. Programs for individuals with disabilities are the responsibility of the Assistant Secretary for the Office of Special Education and Rehabilitation Services (OSERS). OSERS enforces the implementation of federal special education laws and serves as a resource to legislators regarding issues of exceptional individuals. One branch of OSERS is the Office of Special Education Programs (OSEP), which is charged with the implementation of the Individuals with Disabilities Education Act (IDEA). OSEP administers federal funds to state and local education agencies and provides leadership in stimulating research and personnel training (Meyen, 1988).

OSEP consultants have a monitoring process allowing them to ensure that the legislative mandates of IDEA are being met. OSEP requires each state to submit a plan detailing how it intends to ensure the implementation of IDEA. State plans are submitted on a regular cycle and must be approved before funding provided by IDEA will be sent to the state for distribution to local districts. After approving the state plan, OSEP consultants make an on-site visit to determine whether the policies and procedures outlined in the state plan are being implemented.

OSEP consultants are responsible for ensuring implementation of federal laws regarding programs for students with disabilities. They consider state department of education personnel to be their primary clients because they are responsible for ensuring the implementation of laws in their jurisdiction. Although local directors have little interaction with OSEP, OSEP is the third step up the chain of command that provides parameters within which directors must function when designing their local systems.

Suggestions for working within federal government parameters:
- Stay informed on current OSERS and OSEP policy considerations and provide input. The *Federal Register* contains notices of impending policy decisions and invites comments. To comment, write or call either office.
- Local directors should provide state directors with data showing the impact on local districts of current or proposed federal policies. State directors can collaborate with each other to create a stronger coalition on important issues.
- Use the power and regulations of each level to get the most out of all levels.

PRAGMATICS, POLITICS, AND POLICY

Rarely are special education administrators presented with simple decisions requiring only an application of the appropriate regulation. More often, administrators are confronted with dilemmas necessitating a knowledge of applicable policy as well as an awareness of the politics involved and a sense of the reality of pragmatic issues.

Pragmatic concerns involve decisions in which administrators must consider practical matters such as the availability of resources or the actual ability to provide what is required. Directors are involved in pragmatics when they decide who will attend staffings at the high school level. Ideally, all decisions personify the organization's vision and understanding of best practices. In this case, it would be ideal to have all of a student's classroom teachers at staffings so that everyone truly understood the individualized education plan developed. However, the administrator might decide it is unrealistic or impossible to release that many teachers at the same time. The director may decide, pragmatically, that counselors will attend staffings and then communicate the information to all teachers.

Politics involves individuals or groups attempting to influence the direction of the organization to reflect their own interests or their perception of the organization's interests. Political systems usually operate outside the formal structures for decision making and employ personal pressure or group lobbying. For example, special education administrators may find themselves in politically difficult situations when dealing with teachers or parents who have connections with important community leaders or school board members. Another example is the political influence public schools have used to block any federal funding for private schools.

Policy making is determining objectives that will guide the decision making within an organization about its resources of people, money, authority, and materials (Hoy & Miskel, 1991). Policy provides broad criteria for action and shapes the character of the organization. For instance, a special education director might develop a policy that parents are equal partners in the education of their children. This policy will serve as criteria in making decisions throughout the special education program. Specifically, it might be used to determine whether it is appropriate for parents to serve on school and district task forces and then to decide whether to include parents in workshops on effective team functioning.

At the state and federal government levels, pragmatics, politics, and policy are intricately interrelated in the following case study.

Policy, Politics, and Pragmatics:

Colorado's Definition of Seriously Emotionally Disturbed

In June 1990, the Colorado Legislature changed the label for students who qualified for services as a result of emotional or behavioral disorders. Before the change, students were identified as having a "significantly identifiable emotional or behavioral disorder" (SIEBD). House Bill 90-1137 removed the term "behavioral" from SIEBD and redefined this category as "significantly identifiable emotional disorder" (SIED). Policy, politics, and pragmatics each played an important role in this definition change, and their impacts wove together in complex ways to create unexpected results.

Before 1989, there were a number of pragmatic concerns related to students typically identified as SIEBD. First, directors of special education had a practical concern related to the increasing cost of private placements for identified students. Many believed that some students identified for special education were troubled, but not necessarily disabled. These directors reasoned that if "behavior" was eliminated from the definition, students who were defiant and delinquent would no longer be eligible for special education, and the schools would not have to bear the costs of their placements. Second, principals expressed concern that they were hampered in responding to increasing gang activity and violence in the schools, because many of the students involved were protected from expulsion by special education due process. They, too, felt that changing the definition would prevent inappropriate identification of "bully" kids. Principals would then be able to keep their schools safe, because they would be able to expel those students who were no longer identified. The third pragmatic concern was raised by special education staff, who felt increasingly impotent as students' needs had become more intense and complex, especially citing the difficulty of teaching defiant and aggressive students. The staff reasoned that because special education services were not effective for these students, and because these students made programs ineffective for other students, students with behavior disorders should not be eligible for services.

These three sets of pragmatic concerns coalesced into significant pressures to create a new policy regarding who should qualify for SIEBD. Previously, state policy had reflected a paradigm that emotional and behavioral problems are different faces of the same problem, and therefore students with either should be eligible for services. If the paradigm shifted to view students with behavior problems as not deserving special help, legislation would need to be enacted to guide policy development. The result was a major lobbying effort that persuaded several legislators to draft new laws that would result in a policy change. Lobbyists stated rationales for the change: First, Colorado's definition for SIEBD should be more consistent with the federal definition, which excludes students who are socially maladjusted from qualifying for special education services under the heading of emotional disturbance. Second, conduct disorders are social maladjustments, and the defiant, dangerous students in question obviously have conduct disorders. Therefore, these students should not be eligible for special services and due process protection.

Although there was considerable lobbying regarding a possible definition change, it did not result in any proposed legislation. Then, the political process was activated by what appeared to be a totally unrelated pragmatic issue. Colorado had not yet mandated early childhood services, and 1989 was the last year to pass such legislation if the state were to avoid losing federal funding. Legislators were hesitant to pass new taxes in Colorado's recessive economy, but also did not wish to be seen as unsupportive of early intervention for infants with disabilities. The Joint Budget Committee of the Colorado Legislature conjectured that by reducing the number of students who formerly qualified for special education services because of behavior problems, enough additional money could be freed to fund the preschool programs. As a result, legislation was proposed and passed to remove behavioral disorders from the SIEBD label and to use the new term SIED.

 ## CONSIDER THIS

1. Compare the pragmatic and political forces involved in this new legislation.
2. Did the new definition result in a true policy change?
3. What other options might have been considered to address the pragmatic concerns?
4. Why were students labeled SIEBD especially vulnerable to the political pressures, whereas early childhood programs were not?
5. What impact will this new legislation have on the local directors of special education in Colorado?

SPECIAL EDUCATION DIRECTORS AS TRANSLATORS

The multiple layers of authority within which the local special education director must work may appear overwhelming, if not stifling. Interestingly, the actual situation is quite the opposite. Positions of middle management often hold the potential for significant power within the system. The location of the position in the chain of command is the key.

In complex systems there are three central functions: developing, translating, and implementing policies. Setting direction and developing policy usually occur through some legislative or rule-making process. Persons at all levels of authority spend a significant amount of time fulfilling this role. Interpreting and translating policy into implementation procedures and programs is the second function. Here, persons take policies developed by the first group and translate them into practices for a third group to implement. The third function is implementation and day-to-day application of the translated policy. Teachers and support staff perform this function.

The first function, policy making, is essential because it provides a common vision. For instance, most special educators agree with the concept of a free, appropriate public education. However, any vision is just a "good idea" unless it becomes reality. The third function, implementation, is the ultimate goal of the organization, but unless delivery is systematic and coordinated it will lack strength and may dissipate over time. For example, many professionals no longer agree that segregated programs are appropriate, and the ensuing debate has resulted in uneven services in some districts. Of the three functions, the second, the role of translator, holds the most potential for positively influencing the system. Describing and defining the form a concept will take in becoming a reality is an awesome and creative responsibility. This is the function special education directors provide.

If directors are to access the potential power of their position, they must appreciate that their role is defined by the interaction of legal compliance (authority) with delivery of services (implementation). There is much in the system encouraging directors to view their job as helping the district "stay in compliance." Accepting this perspective would result in the director's position becoming merely an extension of the authority system. At the same time, it would be equally limiting to view the job as just "creating good programs." This approach would result in simply augmenting the implementer's role through the director's position.

Potency is achieved through a combination of the two views. The director's task becomes designing the best programs possible within the parameters of the law. This requires creative interpretations on occasion. For example, a director might choose to support early intervention by interpreting school psychologists' participation on teacher assistance teams as permissible under the law because the director sees their participation as part of Child Find. Designing the best possible programs also assumes that traditional definitions of good programming will need to be questioned and stretched. In essence, programs will need to be redesigned to include the visions and values expressed in the law.

Two administrative activities that exemplify the role of translator are writing a comprehensive local plan and preparing for the state on-site evaluation visit. The local comprehensive plan must translate state and federal law into school district policies and procedures. In this document, the director describes how the district defines and complies with such legal requirements as education in the least restrictive environment, providing transitional services, and handling complaints. To prepare for on-site compliance visits, special education directors must translate for the staff the intent of the process, defusing the fear and anger toward "the state" while explaining that it is a cyclical opportunity for self-examination. The director should prepare central office administrators for interviews concerning delivery of services, prompt teachers months ahead to ensure paperwork is up to date, and direct clerical staff in order to facilitate the collection of documents while heeding confidentiality procedures.

Functioning as a translator forces directors to become comfortable with ambiguity. When involved in a creative endeavor, there are no clear answers. There are only the best solutions at this time for a specific situation. However, comfort with ambiguity in no way implies that directors do not have a clear vision for what they are attempting to achieve. In fact, if they are to perform effectively as translators, directors must have defined their personal philosophy regarding the education of student with disabilities and have clear goals for the program (Sarason, 1990).

Goals are important to leaders for two reasons. First, goals serve as criteria for decision making, helping to maintain focus. For example, a director might ask whether providing staff development to general educators in behavior management would lead the district toward its goal. If it does, pursue it. If not, forgo it in order to avoid diffusing efforts toward goals. Second, clear goals allow the director to be proactive in a job that by its very nature is often reactive because it involves crisis management. It is even possible for crisis management to be proactive if all decisions, even those made in crisis situations, are consistent with goals. In this manner, every decision becomes a part, however small, of movement toward the established goal.

SURVIVING AND THRIVING IN BUREAUCRACIES

If directors are to accomplish goals for special education programming within the context of school and government organizations, it is helpful for them to understand organizational structure. Almost all modern organizations contain elements of bureaucratic structure. Bureaucracies developed in response to industrialization in which goods became mass produced and managers saw a need to organize large groups of workers to achieve common goals in an efficient and dependable manner (Blau & Scott, 1962). Industrial bureaucracies provided the organizational model for governments and schools as we know them.

While bureaucracies have served well for a long time, many people are finding it increasingly difficult to function within such systems. Societal challenges addressed today seem to demand more fluid or organic organizations; that is, they must be more flexible, responsive, and continuously evolving. Special education directors feel the need for organic structures as children's needs become more complex, forcing schools to restructure in order to be responsive and effective. Yet, the rules and regulations of special education laws and the levels of government involved in implementing them appear to be the very personification of bureaucracy. If special education directors are to accomplish the mandates within bureaucratic decision-making structures, it is essential that they have a basic understanding of bureaucracies, allowing them to use the elements of the bureaucracy to their advantage.

The classic analysis of bureaucracy is provided by Max Weber (Scott, 1981). In his 1947 seminal work, Weber identified the five characteristics of bureaucracy as division of labor and specialization, impersonal orientation, hierarchy of authority, rules and regulations, and career orientation.

Division of Labor and Specialization

Weber defined the division of labor and specialization to mean "the regular activities required for the purposes of the bureaucratically governed structure are distributed in a fixed way as official duties" (Gerth & Mills, 1946, p. 196). When tasks are too complex to be accomplished by one individual, they are divided among several people, each of whom then becomes expert and knowledgeable in completing his or her specific duty. Production increases as a result of each individual's increased skill at his or her assigned task.

In government agencies, only the office that specializes in a specific need can respond in that situation. As government grows larger, it specializes more, resulting in increased frustration on the part of those attempting to access the services.

Local directors of special education will experience this frustration when attempting to communicate with higher levels of authority. Three possible strategies for addressing this difficulty are (1) asking for direction from others who interact with state or federal offices, (2) cultivating one person at each level who can serve as an information source and provide direction to appropriate offices at that level, and (3) if several offices must be called, making note of the persons contacted and the responsibilities of their office. In this way, a personal directory of offices and responsibilities can be created for future use.

Division of labor and specialization is easily seen in schools and is based primarily on curriculum (math, science, and so forth) and level (elementary or secondary). Special education might be viewed as the ultimate in specialization, where the instructional task is subdivided once again by disability. Specialization has facilitated the development of a comprehensive knowledge base in each of these areas.

Directors of special education have the responsibility for hiring personnel with certification to serve in each area of specialization. Sometimes this approach is too confining to meet the needs of students. A director may wish to create more flexibility by listing all areas of expertise each specialist is expected to have and then identifying the areas of overlapping skills. This would allow the hiring of a different configuration of personnel while still ensuring the skills were available in the district.

Division of labor and specialization also holds the possibility of creating boredom. Tasks that are done repeatedly, even if they are highly technical, contain the possibility of becoming tedious, frequently resulting in reduced productivity as well as a lower quality of work. Varying job responsibilities and encouraging special educators to schedule a semester of team teaching with a general educator are strategies that might assist in applying specialized skills in new, invigorating ways.

Impersonal Orientation

The atmosphere in a bureaucracy should provide "the dominance of a spirit of formalistic impersonality, *sine ira et studio,* without hatred or passion, and hence without affection or enthusiasm," according to Weber (1947, p. 331). Such an impersonal orientation was intended to encourage employees to make decisions based on facts (that which can be proven scientifically) and not feelings or values. The primary benefit of an impersonal environment is the assurance of equality of treatment through rational decision making.

Both government and schools have responded to the current litigious orientation and increased pressure for accountability in our society by retreating to a more impersonal, rational approach because it is more easily defended. This is especially true of special education. For instance, it is not acceptable to simply report on the IEP that the teacher thinks the student has made good gains during the year. Progress must be recorded in measurable objectives that can be scientifically proven.

The impersonal orientation inherent in bureaucracies affects directors of special education in their ability to work effectively with people in authority and subordinates. When functioning in their executive role, directors design impersonal systems that are objective and fair, then communicate them to everyone. However, they may wish to use their discretion when applying the system to an individual in a specific instance. This approach allows the director to function more humanely within the protection of the bureaucracy. Strategies that special education directors might use to counteract the effects of the impersonal system include organizing staffing teams so that members provide support to one another, asking various professionals to chair an important committee, and sending personal notes of recognition.

It is equally important to remember the impersonal orientation of bureaucracies when working up through the levels of authority. Directors may become frustrated when seeking assistance at the district, state, or federal level, feeling there is an unwillingness to understand their unique situation or to problem-solve with them. The best strategy is to prepare before these situations occur by cultivating a relationship with at least one person at each level of authority.

Hierarchy of Authority

Weber (1947) maintains that offices are arranged in a hierarchical fashion in bureaucracies where "each lower office is under the control and supervision of a higher one" (p. 330). The primary benefit of a hierarchy of authority is to assure compliance with directives from superiors in order to accomplish the various tasks critical to the organization. Hierarchy is probably the most pervasive characteristic of modern organizations.

Hierarchies are pervasive in government and schools. As a subordinate working through the various levels of government, it is critical to follow the chain of command. It is not always easy to know the appropriate chain of command; however, the additional time used to determine hierarchical relationships is time well spent. It should be standard practice to conclude each conversation by asking whether there are any other persons who should be informed and, if so, who should contact them.

The hierarchy of school districts consists of the superintendent at the top, with assistants, directors, principals, and teachers at successively lower levels, culminating with the student at the bottom. Knowledge of the bureaucracy provides critical information regarding the relative power to ensure directives will be followed. This knowledge is especially important for directors of special education. The law holds them responsible for some actions they often do not have the authority to ensure will be followed. In short, they often have responsibility without authority. It is prudent to mitigate this situation by negotiating for the line of authority necessary to ensure mandates in the law are met. It is equally important for directors to have an awareness of those above them on the organizational chart. People in any of these positions can rescind or reorient directives made by the special education director.

The hierarchy of authority often carries a hidden cost in discouraging effective communication through either distortion or blockage of communication. Subordinates tend to communicate only those things that reflect well on them or that they believe their supervisors want to hear (Blau & Scott, 1962). One of the most effective techniques directors can employ is to communicate honestly and admit their mistakes.

Rules and Regulations

Weber (1947) states that every bureaucracy has a "consistent system of abstract rules which have normally been intentionally established. Furthermore, administration of law is held to consist in the application of these rules to particular cases" (p. 330). These rule systems usually cover the rights and duties of each position and how they relate to other positions in the hierarchy. In this manner, the rules and regulations serve an impersonal coordination function for the bureaucracy. The primary benefit of rules and regulations is to provide continuity of operations through ensuring the uniformity and stability of various employee actions.

In addition to creating uniformity and stability in the system, rules have several other functions. First, they serve to make operating procedures more explicit by explaining employee obligations, reducing the ambiguity often left after a verbal command, providing a system of communication to direct performance in various roles, and reducing the need to repeat routine orders. Second, they serve as a buffer between administration and employees because they are not personal and are applied equally to everyone. Third, they serve to legitimatize punishment because the rules provide warnings about behaviors that invite sanctions.

However, the very rules that foster organizational uniformity and stability can also contribute to organizational rigidity, resulting in a means/end inversion in relationship to the goal of the organization. When rules are applied rigidly, people often lose their ability to adjust, and such conformity may interfere with achieving the original intent of the rules. The dysfunction reaches it zenith when employees begin to see the implementation of the rules as the end, rather than as a means of reaching the organization's goals. At this point, goal displacement has occurred, and the organization is effectively gridlocked.

Hoy and Miskel (1991) propose that educational administrators maximize the positive use of rules and avoid the negative consequences. One strategy for accomplishing this is to continually ask whether each rule is good for the children, and if it is, how can it be followed within the context of the laws. This effectively models the value that the rules and regulations addressing special education are critically important, but they are, after all, only the means and not the end.

Directors of special education are part of the larger hierarchy of rules that includes state laws regarding students with disabilities and IDEA. Within that hierarchy, the local director's responsibility is to carry out the rules and regulations as they apply to "particular cases"; in this instance, individual children. The director accomplishes this by developing a system within which subordinates operate to ensure that special education services will be available and delivered consistently. Continuity of operation makes it possible for students to have their IEPs implemented regardless of which school they attend or which service provider is assigned to them.

It would appear that rules and regulations are handed down the chain of command and there is little interaction; however, special education directors can influence rules and regulations. When rules and regulations are being developed and adopted, it is important to provide input, and when the implementation of rules and regulations is questioned, directors should carefully consider what questions are asked and of whom.

Systems for implementation of rules and regulations should be devised to facilitate the effective planning and delivery of services. A good system should never add tasks solely for the maintenance of the system nor make the accomplishment of required functions more cumbersome than necessary. Additionally, the system should be designed so that the director becomes personally involved with only a few situations in which the rules are more difficult to apply. This is a proactive time-management strategy assisting directors to utilize their time most productively.

Career Orientation

Weber's fifth characteristic of bureaucratic organizations is career orientation in which "there is a system of promotion according to seniority, achievement, or both. Promotion is dependent on the judgment of superiors" (1947, p. 334). People in bureaucracies know their employment is based on technical skills, and employees with special skills are protected from arbitrary dismissal or denial of promotion. The primary benefit of a career orientation is the fostering of loyalty to the organization through protection.

Special education directors must be aware of the impact of career orientation upon the chain of command. Specialists at each level often have been in their position for some time. These individuals know their specific area well but may not have general information. Directors can reduce their frustration when communicating with these specialists by expecting it to take several phone calls or letters to determine who has the desired expertise or power. Unfortunately, the protections against dismissal inherent in a bureaucracy may allow employees to meet only the letter of their job description and still continue in employment. Despite one's frustration with this reality, a respectful, friendly demeanor usually brings a more helpful response. With care, the director can foster working relationships that expedite the delivery of services to students.

This characteristic also has implications for directors in their executive role. The quality of programs for students is directly related to the expertise of the special education teacher. Because special education teachers are protected from arbitrary dismissal, it may be difficult to dislodge an ineffective teacher. Therefore, it is worthwhile to spend the time necessary to obtain the highest quality of personnel when hiring. Additionally, because staff members have a career orientation, it is critical to provide ongoing, professional development opportunities.

The most serious criticism of the bureaucratic model is its lack of attention to the informal structures within the organizations. A complete understanding of the dynamics of any organization involves knowledge of the informal as well as the formal structures. The informal include those rules, groupings, leaders, and sanctioning systems that have no official recognition, but have emerged spontaneously as members of the group interact with one another in carrying out their various responsibilities. This creates a lasting culture and can have a positive or negative effect on members' behavior and ultimately on the organization's ability to meet goals. Often it evolves to circumvent formal structures. This is not always negative. For instance, communication may be necessary, but impossible, through formal channels. At this point, the informal organization of the grapevine can effectively accomplish what cannot be achieved formally. Directors are encouraged to recognize the existence of the informal organization and refrain from attempting to eliminate or suppress it. Judicious use of both the formal and informal structures of government results in increased effectiveness.

When working in the context of the larger bureaucratic system, directors need to be aware of the positive as well as the negative aspects of the system and work to increase the positive and decrease the negative. Because the structure of schools is so bureaucratically complex, yet informally organic, directors of special education have a difficult role both as middle managers and as leaders of multidimensional organizations.

NOTIONS OF BUREAUCRACY REVISITED

Professional Bureaucracies

An analysis of school systems would reveal characteristics common to bureaucratic organizations; however, a different frame of reference may assist in understanding other dimensions of schools not explained by classical bureaucratic models. Mintzberg (1979) differentiated "machine bureaucracies" from "professional bureaucracies." Machine bureaucracies do simple work and produce items in a way that can be rationalized and systematized into precise, routine tasks. In comparison, professional bureaucracies do complex work involving individual cases and are uncertain as to the application of general principles. Simple work is controlled through rules and regulations, whereas complex work is controlled through professionalism.

Schools can be conceptualized as professional bureaucracies in which individuals are trained to do complex tasks in interdependent environments. Based on this conceptualization, educators will be successful if they work well independently with students but also share resources such as facilities and materials. Unfortunately, the public expects schools to conform to the institutionalized image of machine bureaucracies, legitimizing the institution as efficient (Hampton, 1991; Weick, 1982). So, although schools are professional organizations, they may be managed as if they are machine bureaucracies. One of the most difficult aspects of the machine/professional dichotomy is that machine bureaucracies require workers to conform, yet conformity is the nemesis of professional integrity. Educators must feel the freedom to create and innovate to meet the unique needs of their students. Possibly the most effective way for schools to operate is to create a formal appearance of a machine bureaucracy through symbols and ceremonies, while developing informal structures that support the demands of complex, client-centered work (Skrtic, 1988).

Paradigms and Paradigm Shifts

School organizations can also be analyzed from a cultural reference point, that is, based on the principle that realities are socially constructed. Ravetz (1971) explained that knowledge is bound by culture, place, and time. What is understood by any group is a reflection of the beliefs of its society in a certain environment at a specific time. The culture of a school can be viewed as the manifestation of current societal beliefs. This is radically different from earlier concepts of bureaucracies. Bureaucracies were understood to be closed systems, self-contained and isolated. From a cultural reference point, systems are open, which means an organization engages in interaction with the environment and is changed as a result.

One way to appreciate the power of the cultural reference point is to explore the concept of paradigms and paradigm shifts. According to Kuhn (1962), a paradigm is a way of seeing that explains what exists, how it is organized, and how it behaves. A paradigm is also a lens through which individuals see the world, filtering out what we do not understand or what does not fit (Skrtic, 1988). Organizations such as governments and schools have paradigms that guide their perceptions, policies, and procedures. For example, using a paradigm from industry, the goal of manufacturing is to produce identical goods of similar quality. Analogously, using an educational paradigm, schools are for students who perform within certain boundaries of behavior and ability. Based on this paradigm, educators believed that students who did not fall within these parameters did not belong. Policies and procedures developed in alignment with this belief.

A paradigm shift is a break with traditional or old ways of thinking and valuing (Covey, 1989). For individuals and organizations to perceive events or circumstances in a new way, a paradigm shift is necessary. If groups confront information that does not fit their paradigm, they resist change until they develop new ways of seeing.

The passage of PL 94-142 and its effect on schools can be examined through a cultural reference or paradigm model. In the early 1970s, a new cultural understanding was emerging regarding civil rights, specifically that equal access and due process rights were for all classes of people. Based on this new paradigm, advocates for children with disabilities observed schools were not providing education to all children. These advocates exerted powerful influence on federal legislators to mandate services and due process protection for exceptional students. PL 94-142 was a landmark bill and appeared to herald a new day in education. To accept this legislation, however, educators had to experience a paradigm shift. PL 94-142 presented a new paradigm: It was intended to be the end of mass-production schooling and "the beginning of an era of respect for and nurture of each student as a unique and ultimately valuable individual" (Skrtic, 1988, p. 514). If the schools had been ready for a paradigm shift, individualized education for all children would have become the norm. Instead, the message of PL 94-142 confronted the old paradigm of sort and segregate, and, rather than changing education, the new law of special education became an "add-on" to schools as they had always been. Hence, many educators see special education rules and procedures as additional hassles.

People Change Schools

Schools have been remarkably resistant to change and improvement, but some schools have changed, and there are some effective schools. Weick (1985) explains that although schools are bureaucratic organizations, they are underorganized and ambiguity prevails. In loosely structured settings, "confident, persistent, forceful people" can tighten up the system, defining the environment according to new paradigms that include their "values, presumptions, expectations, and commitments" (Skrtic, 1988, p. 513).

Effective schools are led by excellent people who create a culture or paradigm that says people matter most (Clark, Lotto, & Astuto, 1984). People organizations are not bureaucracies, they are adhocracies in which leaders create organizations that are effective, adaptable, and responsive. In adhocracies, people are reinforced for being problem solvers. In this capacity, they identify what does not work and examine the prevailing paradigm, opening it to new values (Skrtic, 1988).

To create schools that educate and support all learners, leaders must understand school organizations and the nature of paradigms. Although schools seem to be bureaucratic organizations, people make a difference, and change is a result of shifting beliefs to prepare for new ways of seeing and serving our children and youth. True progress results from loosening our paradigms, exploring divergent paths, and discovering new paradigms.

SUMMARY

Special education administrators are responsible for ensuring implementation of local, state, and federal regulations regarding education for exceptional children. Local directors are essentially middle managers who are executives in their districts but subordinates to state and federal authorities.

Each level of government has a structure in which elected or appointed boards hire chief officers who in turn create management teams. In local agencies and intermediate (cooperative) units, administrators work within local structures to ensure free, appropriate public education to all exceptional children and youth by developing quality programs and monitoring their delivery. At the state level, legislators pass laws and the state board of education establishes policies. The chief state school officer, backed by a department or division, monitors the delivery of services and provides funding to local districts throughout the state. The federal government has been responsible for major legislative initiatives that have increased the availability and range of services for students with disabilities. The function of the federal level is to ensure that each state has a plan to provide education and due process protection for all identified children and youth. The operation of government agencies is a fascinating, although often frustrating, interaction of pragmatics, politics, and policies.

In most organizations, policies are developed, translated, and implemented. The role of the special education director can be conceptualized as a translator. This offers power to individuals with the vision to do more than comply with mandates; special education directors can translate rules and regulations into quality, innovative programming to meet individual needs.

Most government and school organizations exhibit characteristics of bureaucracies, including division of labor and specialization, impersonal orientation, hierarchy of authority, rules and regulations, and career orientation. Criticisms of bureaucracies abound and are well founded. However, bureaucratic organization has allowed the mobilization of large numbers of people in a reasonably efficient manner to achieve goals. When bureaucratic organizations are successful, it is because they are tight procedurally but loose conceptually (Peters & Waterman, 1982). That is, individuals focus only on doing their assigned part while upper-level managers deal with the larger vision. Understanding the positive and negative aspects of bureaucracies will help special education administrators accomplish their functions more efficiently and with less frustration.

Some organizational analysts have examined school systems and determined that schools are professional bureaucracies in which individuals do complex tasks independently. Unfortunately, schools are often managed as if they were machine bureaucracies in which teachers are expected to "manufacture" identical products. Other theorists describe schools as open systems that interact with the environment, engendering beliefs that are culturally bound. These analysts demonstrate how paradigms affect the way schools accept and reject new ideas. Finally, some authors have explained that effective schools may actually be underorganized institutions in which strong leaders wisely use the loose structure to create cultures of new values and expectations. Further, schools distinguished as having excellent programs may actually be adhocracies in which people are empowered to be problem solvers, creating exceptional programs through a commitment to respect all students and provide for their individual needs.

REFERENCES

Audetta, B., & Algozzine, B. (1992). Free and appropriate education for all students: Total quality and the transformation of American Public Education. *RASE, 13*(6), 8–18.

Blau, P. M., & Scott, W. R. (1962). *Formal organizations: a comparative approach.* 28–29. San Francisco: Chandler.

Carnegie Forum on Education and Economy. Task Force on Teaching as a Profession. (1986). *A nation prepared: Teachers for the 21st century.* Washington, DC: The Forum.

Clark, D. L., Lotto, L. S., & Astuto, T. A. (1984). Effective schools and school improvement: A comparative analysis of two lines of inquiry. *Educational Administration Quarterly, 20*(3), 41–68.

Covey, S. R. (1989). *The seven habits of highly effective people.* New York: Simon and Schuster.

Eisner, E. W. (1992). The federal reform of schools: Looking for the silver bullet. *Phi Delta Kappan, 73*(9), 722–23.

Fishkin, A. S. (1993). Reforming special education. Paper presentation at *Rural America: Where all the innovations begin.* Savannah, GA, March 11-13 (ERIC document reproduction service #ED 358 985).

Gerth, H. H., & Mills, C. I. (Eds.). (1946). *Max Weber: Essays in sociology.* New York: Oxford University Press.

Goldberg, S. S. (1986). Implementing legal change in the schools: Recent research and comments. *Planning and Changing, 17*(4), 209–215.

Hampton, E. (1991). A not-so-modest proposal: The fate of special education. *British Columbia Journal of Special Education, 15*(2), 127–36.

Harris, G. A., & Kirk, W. D. (Eds.). (1993). *The foundations of special education: Selected papers and speeches of Samuel Kirk.* Reston, VA: Council for Exceptional Children.

Hoy, W. K., & Miskel, C. G. (1991). *Educational administration: Theory, research, and practice.* New York: McGraw-Hill.

Kuhn, T. S. (Ed.) (1962). *The structure of scientific revolutions.* Chicago: University of Chicago Press.

Lynn, L. E. (1983). The emerging system for educating handicapped children. *Policy Studies Review, 2*(1), 35–43.

Meyen, E. L. (1988). A commentary on special education. In E. L. Meyen & T. M. Skrtic (Eds.), *Exceptional Children and Youth* (3rd ed.) (pp. 3–48). Denver, CO: Love Publishing.

Mintzberg, H. (1979). *The structuring of organizations.* Englewood Cliffs, NJ: Prentice-Hall.

Peters, T. J., & Waterman, R. H., Jr. (1982). *In search of excellence.* New York: Warner Books.

Ravetz, J. R. (1971). *Scientific knowledge and its social problems.* Oxford, England: Clarendon Press.

Sage, D. D., & Burrello, L. C. (1986). *Policy and management in special education.* Englewood Cliffs, NJ: Prentice-Hall.

Sarason, S. B., & Doris, J. (1978). Mainstreaming: Dilemmas, opposition, opportunities. In M. C. Reynolds (Ed.), *Futures of education for exceptional children: Emerging structures.* Reston, VA: Council for Exceptional Children.

Sarason, S. B. (1990). *The predictable failure of educational reform.* San Francisco: Jossey-Bass.

Scott, W. R. (1981). *Organizations: Rational, natural, and open systems.* Englewood Cliffs, NJ: Prentice-Hall.

Skrtic, T. M. (1988). The organizational context of special education. In E. L. Meyen & T. M. Skrtic (Eds.), *Exceptional Children and Youth* (3rd ed.) (pp. 479–517). Denver, CO: Love Publishing.

U.S. Department of Education. The National Commission on Excellence in Education. (1983). *A nation at risk: The imperative for educational reform.* Washington, DC: U.S. Government Printing Office (ED1.2:N21).

U.S. Department of Education. (1991). *America 2000: An educational strategy.* Washington, DC: Author.

U.S. Department of Education. (1993). *Goals 2000: Educate America.* Washington, DC: Author.

Weber, M. (1947). *The theory of social and economic organizations.* Talcott Parsons (Ed.), A. M. Henderson & Talcott Parsons (trans.). New York: Free Press.

Weick, K. E. (1982, June). Administering education in loosely coupled schools. *Phi Delta Kappan.* 673–676.

Weick, K. E. (1985). Sources of order in underorganized systems: Themes in recent organizational theory. In Y. S. Lincoln (Ed.), *Organization theory and inquiry: The paradigm revolution* (pp. 106-138). Beverly Hills, CA: Sage.

Chapter 5

WHO CONTROLS THE PURSE STRINGS CONTROLS THE PROGRAMS

John O. Schwenn

Leaders who control funding have the power to enforce their own political agendas; changes in special education have been influenced and mandated by the money suppliers (Bernstein, 1993). Historically, one can see the visions of those holding the purse strings. Residential facilities were expanded and improved during the '60s because states received federal monies to develop what were considered, at that time, to be great institutional programs. Then, these segregated facilities were reduced or closed as support was more available for developing self-contained classes in regular education schools. In the late '60s and early '70s, special education cooperatives pooled the resources of local education agencies to provide services to low–incidence populations when the capital was supplied for their formation. During the '70s and '80s, mainstreaming was thrust to the forefront as funding was available to local education agencies (LEA) that placed students with special needs in regular programs for at least part of the day. Today, many states are providing financial incentives for more inclusive programs for all students; consequently, these settings are proliferating while resource programs are decreasing in popularity.

The federal government mandates local education agencies to provide a full array of comprehensive special services for students identified as having a disability that affects school performance. Both federal and state sources funnel money into local programs through various funding distribution formulas based on factors such as the number of students identified as disabled, the number of special education professionals employed, or the excess cost of educating students with special needs above what is spent for general education students. Local special education administrators must learn to access available federal and state funds plus locate any additional money necessary to provide special services. It is essential for special education administrators to know how to deal with the financial policies and procedures of their state (Weisenstein & Pelz, 1986).

SOURCES OF REVENUE

According to PL 94-142, the federal government was to pay the excess cost of educating students with special needs. However, the maximum amount reimbursed has never been above 12% of program cost. Federal flow-through money is provided to states to reimburse local education agencies for the excess cost of educating students who are identified and placed in special education programs. Of this federal money, at least 75% must go to local education agencies. State administration costs can be up to 5%. The remaining 20% is discretionary money and can be used by the state for grants to districts to implement innovative programs or solve problems; additional flow-through monies for local education agencies; or special projects the state deems necessary, such as evaluation, teacher recruitment/retention activities, or development of management information systems. Because the federal government is unwilling to pay for the total excess cost of educating students with special needs, state funds and the local property tax base provide the remainder of the funding.

Types of Revenue

Crowner (1985) discusses eight types of revenue and their restrictions. They are:

1. **Continuing Funds.** These funds tend to be stable and can be relied upon to support long-term services, but funding may fluctuate from year to year. State funding of basic education is continuing.
2. **Noncontinuing Funds.** These are short-term funds frequently used to remedy a problem or meet a specific need. Items generating long-term benefits such as equipment or facilities should be funded in this manner. Grants frequently are used for such needs and rarely last more than three years. Districts should not use these monies for essential services that will have to end when the revenue is no longer available.
3. **Targeted Funds.** Specific items are earmarked for this funding. These can include specific programs (e.g., transition), classifications of students (e.g., secondary learning disabilities), categories of personnel (e.g., paraprofessionals), or equipment (e.g., computers). Money must be spent only on the targeted items.
4. **Discretionary Funds.** Discretionary funds may be used for any activity considered relevant to the objectives the funding source sets forth.
5. **Inside Formula Funds.** When one funding source provides monies for services, the costs must be deducted from a request for reimbursement from a second source. Districts use inside formula funds to distribute financial support to various programs.
6. **Outside Formula Funds.** Revenues received from outside sources are used to pay for services, personnel, or equipment. Two sources cannot, however, be used to pay for the same item.

7. **Matching Funds.** The agency receiving money under matching funds must provide a preestablished portion of the cost of the funded program. In some cases, "in-kind" contributions (e.g., services, facilities, staff, and/or equipment) may be used.
8. **Mixed Funds.** Two or more of the above-mentioned funds constitute mixed funds.

CALCULATING COSTS OF SPECIAL EDUCATION SERVICES

Federal regulations must be followed in funding special education programs. Each state develops policies and procedures to reimburse local education agencies for additional costs incurred in providing a free, appropriate education for *all* students with disabilities. Additionally, states monitor local education agencies to ensure LEAs are not using funds inappropriately or overclassifying or misclassifying students (Schoppmeyer, 1984).

Determining the costs of special education is elusive and varies not only from state to state but also from district to district. According to Bernstein (1993), a major funding issue is defining "special education," including determining its boundaries. For example, is special education financially responsible for assessing all students or is it accountable only for assessment of those ultimately labeled? In some states and local education agencies, school psychologists are assigned to special education, while in others, a fee for each assessment is charged to special education. Must services be provided in a resource room or self-contained classroom with support staff to qualify as special education, or do services provided in the regular classroom also count? Is adaptive physical education a special service, a regular service, or does it depend upon each individualized education program (IEP) and what transpires in the physical education class? Answers to questions such as these define special education and must be considered by policy-makers in each state and district.

Cost and reimbursement are related but easily confused concepts. **Cost** is the market value of an item or service (Bernstein, 1993). For example, Jose, a student with a severe hearing loss, needs a phonic ear that costs $1,950 to purchase or $75 per month to lease. **Reimbursement** is the amount of money the Plum Hill School District will receive toward the cost of items or services purchased. The state provides an **allocation** or **reimbursement** that may, but generally does not, cover the cost to the district. If the state reimburses Plum Hill 85% of the expenditure, the district would be reimbursed either $1657.50 for the purchase of the phonic ear or $63.75 per month for leasing. However, in many states, limits or ceilings are placed on how much is reimbursed. In this case, the state may reimburse Plum Hill only the cost of a phonic ear up to $750. Additionally, there is the confounding variable of inflation. Items purchased during one fiscal year are likely to cost more during future fiscal years. The special education administrator must structure the budget to accommodate annual inflation (Bernstein, 1993).

Allowable costs are amounts approved for reimbursement by the state for designated services and resources. Some incurred costs are not approved and thus are less likely to be reported. Therefore, submitted figures represent only approximate expenditures but do not necessarily reflect what is actually spent for special education (Bernstein, 1993). Providing services for which school districts will not be reimbursed poses a practical and ethical dilemma for administrators. Money spent, but not refunded, must come from other sources.

Direct cost is the amount necessary to fund special education programs, including all special services personnel and resources but excluding what is provided for all general education students. These additional costs are referred to as **excess costs.** The excess cost of providing a service to one child could be $35,000 and include the salary and benefits of one teacher plus supplies and materials. However, the excess cost for a second child might be only $400 for additional materials. If the state's financial system provides $3,000 per child identified as requiring special education services, districts may readily develop programs for high-incidence populations, such as learning disabilities, but there is an insufficient incentive to create expensive special services for low-incidence disabilities, such as profound hearing losses. This is especially a challenge in rural areas, where it is highly unlikely any one low-incidence category will include more than a few students.

Several options are available to special education administrators to provide costly services to small populations. Some states provide extra monies for low-incidence disabilities. Local schools can join a cooperative with other rural districts in the geographic area: all students in need of the same service could then be sent to one school. However, at this point, transportation becomes an issue, as long-distance busing is tiring for students and expensive. Some districts have developed an itinerant model in which teachers travel to serve students in their home school or at least a nearby school. This reduces contact hours per week and generally requires paraprofessionals in all school sites to carry out programs planned by the itinerant teacher.

Historically, **relative costs** have been defined by the disability label. Bernstein (1993) explains that these costs do not reflect the additional complications of severity or level of placements that have evolved over the years. Nor do they take into account the fact that the costs of regular programs vary, and therefore marginal costs will also vary. Thus, districts are not generating the same amount of money to support similar programs. Further, the belief that more funds are required to serve severely involved students is often unsupported. In actuality, a student with a mild disability may need a large number of support services to fully function in a general education classroom. For Maria, who has a behavior disorder, this includes a special education teacher as well as a paraprofessional for mainstream class, a speech/language therapist, and a special time-out area. In comparison, Alicia, a child with a severe disability, needs only the services of one special education professional in a self-contained classroom of eight students. The cost might actually be less for Alicia. The following case compares three students with the same disability but widely divergent special needs and consequent costs.

Relative Costs for Newport School District

The cost of educating students with the same disability can vary tremendously. No predetermined cost guidelines can guarantee that the needs of individuals or the requirements of a local education agency will be met. For example, Sam is a student with cerebral palsy in rural Newport School District. Sam entered the school district after having been provided excellent preschool services, including parent training. As a result, with Sam's parents supporting him at home, the regular education teacher is able to offer appropriate instruction within the general classroom. The only additional expense to the district is a once-a-month consultation visit from a physical therapist.

Another student, Phyllis, also has cerebral palsy. When she entered Newport School District, her needs included intensive specialized training from a speech pathologist and a physical therapist. For this small district, these services must be contracted. The speech therapist comes weekly, and the physical therapist comes once every other week to train a paraprofessional to work with Phyllis. It is more expensive to educate Phyllis than Sam.

Ming-Shu, a third child with cerebral palsy, incurs much higher expenses. Ming-Shu is in a wheelchair and requires specialized equipment. Although the school is generally accessible, there are structural barriers in his classroom that make remodeling necessary, and assistive equipment must also be provided to meet his needs. In addition, Newport School District has to purchase a wheelchair-adapted bus to transport him to and from school.

Students with the same disability label may cost an LEA minimal additional funds or an extraordinary amount of money. Further, disability conditions are *not* distributed equally throughout school districts. Some local agencies will have a plethora of expensive challenges while others might have relatively few (Schoppmeyer, 1984).

 CONSIDER THIS

Choose another disability category, such as visual impairment, and describe how services might vary for children with this same disability but different individual needs.

SYSTEMS OF DISTRIBUTING THE FUNDS

Numerous formulas exist to provide reimbursement for special education programming. Since special education is expensive, most systems provide a mechanism for advanced funding so that local education agencies can meet their expenditures. Weisenstein and Pelz (1986) caution schools not to (1) **supplant** or use federal funds in place of basic state allocations to all students or (2) **double dip** by charging more than one source for the same service.

Excess-Cost Reimbursement

The concept of **excess cost** arises from the philosophy that LEAs are responsible for the education of *all* students, but that the state or federal government is responsible for the additional or excess cost of educating students with specific needs or disabilities that makes their education so expensive (Bernstein, 1993). The cost is usually limited to specified amounts and categories of disability. Colorado, Maryland, New Hampshire, North Dakota, Oregon, Pennsylvania, and Rhode Island use excess-cost reimbursement systems (Thompson, Wood, & Honeyman, 1994).

Excess Costs for Lakewood School District

In Lakewood School District, $3,500 is reimbursed for each regular education child. The class of 10 students with severe mental retardation costs $60,000. The state reimburses the district the difference between the total classroom cost of $60,000 and the income it generates under regular education of $35,000. This reimbursed difference, or excess cost, is $25,000 for 10 students.

CONSIDER THIS

The term "excess" may have the negative connotation of unnecessary or excessive. How would a special education leader explain disproportionate funding for students?

Unit Reimbursement

The **unit** system counts personnel or resources necessary to serve a designated group of children. These reimbursement systems calculate numbers of teachers, paraprofessionals, administrators, classes, offices, materials and supplies, janitorial services, transportation, and utilities. The specified unit enumerates ratios of staff to student, such as 15:1 for professional staff, 250:1 for administration, and 75:1 for transportation. States frequently utilize different pupil-teacher ratios for each disability level. Each unit then results in a funding level (Bernstein, 1993). Some systems pay all expenses while others pay percentages (Schoppmeyer, 1984). Some states that use unit reimbursement are Alabama, Alaska, California, Kansas, Kentucky, Louisiana, Mississippi, and Missouri (Thompson et al., 1994).

Unit Cost at Henderson School District

The cost of educating a class of 10 special education students in Henderson School District is $60,000. By the unit reimbursement system, Henderson is reimbursed for its expenses or $60,000. This simple system may work with regular education and probably worked well in times past with self-contained classrooms and fewer related services. However, today's special education programs are complex, and calculating unit cost is no longer simple.

 CONSIDER THIS

1. What issues may be present concerning unit reimbursement for services for low-incidence disabilities in rural areas?
2. What questions come to mind concerning unit reimbursement in a continuum of services?
3. How might a district use unit reimbursement for full-inclusion programming?

Weight Reimbursement

Weighted formulas began during periods of high inflation. The cost of special education is calculated as a multiple of regular education. The cost of regular education is given as 1.0. Various disabilities are assigned values greater than 1.0 commensurate with the theoretical additional cost of personnel and resources. For example, students with learning disabilities might cost 1.8 times as much as those in the general education program. Thus, the local education agency is reimbursed on the basis of 1.8 times the reimbursement for regular students (Mayer, 1982). Other values might be higher, such as 2.5 for educable mental retardation, 3.0 for trainable mental retardation, 3.5 for behavior disorders, and 4.0 for severe and profoundly disabled. The cost for regular education is determined, and then special education reimbursement is calculated according to the number of students in each disability category multiplied by the weight. For example, the cost of regular education is $4,000 per student. For students with a learning disability (1.8 weighted value) we multiply $4,000 by 1.8 to get a weighted amount of $7,200. If the local education agency has 93 students with learning disabilities, the weighted amount would be multiplied by 93 to get $669,600 (1.8 × $4,000 × 93 = $669,600). States using weighted reimbursement include Arizona, Arkansas, Delaware, Florida, Georgia, Indiana, Iowa, Massachusetts, New Jersey, New Mexico, Oklahoma, South Carolina, Tennessee, Texas, Utah, and West Virginia (Thompson et al., 1994).

Weighted Formula for Bridgewater School District

Bridgewater School District has the same $60,000 cost for a class of 10 but uses the weighted formula. The weight assigned to each student with special needs is 1.5. The cost for a regular education student is $4,000 per year, so the special education student generates $6,000 per year ($4,000 × 1.5 = $6,000). This class of 10 then yields $60,000 (10 × $6,000).

 CONSIDER THIS

1. Much of the cost of special education services is designated for personnel, which is compatible with the weighted formulas. However, other costs are less consistent. For example, major expenditures for specified equipment may need to be made only one time, such as mats for occupational therapy. How can administrators plan for these yearly variables?
2. Use of the weighted formula indicates that students within each category cost the same to educate. This may not be a problem if it costs less to provide for these students, but what can an administrator do to provide individualized programs that cost far more than reimbursement?
3. When funding is tied to labeling students, schools are encouraged to label in order to receive reimbursement. Many professionals believe the labels used for determining the formulas stigmatize students with special needs. How could weighted formulas continue to be used but not be based on labels?
4. The weighted system is based on an average cost and does not reflect actual need. This may be unfair to both large and small districts. What problems will rural districts have? What problems will large, urban districts have?
5. Districts may attempt to avoid providing appropriate services for expensive, low-incidence disabilities. How can districts be encouraged or supported to provide these services?

Actual Cost

In an **actual cost** system, local education agencies are reimbursed for all or a portion of approved, total costs. Approved reimbursements could include salaries of teachers, paraprofessionals, and related services; fringe benefits; transportation; and materials, equipment, and books. Most states impose a ceiling on the approved expenditures. This ceiling frequently varies from one year to the next. Hawaii reimburses using a "full-funding" formula, as shown in Table 5.1 (Thompson et al., 1994).

TABLE 5.1
ACTUAL COST FOR HANAMA BAY SCHOOLS

The state reimburses the Hanama Bay local education unit at 80% of the total expenditures. The 10-student special education class has the following expenses:

Teacher Salary	$30,000
Paraprofessional	$12,000
Benefits	$10,000
Materials	$ 6,500
Books	$ 2,500
Janitor/Utilities	$ 4,500
Overhead	$ 9,500
Total	$75,000

Because the state reimburses expenses at 80%, Hanama Bay receives $60,000.

 ## CONSIDER THIS

> Some expenses may be excessively high for particular geographic areas in which states set ceilings for reimbursement and therefore fund only a small portion of the bill. For example, in a rural area, it may be difficult to find an occupational therapist as required by a student's IEP. There are expenses for travel from another community plus a salary. What system might be developed for accommodating excessive costs? How might money be generated when a wheelchair needs to be adapted so that a student can successfully use assistive technology, and the state will reimburse only a fraction of the cost?

According to Bernstein (1993), a problem with actual cost is that it is "an after-the-fact system" (p. 116). That is, before the money can be requested, it has to already be spent. If estimates for future needs can be predicted and advances forwarded, administrators may be more comfortable but still wary of spending monies not already in hand. This system requires "an elaborate set of accounting standards, a reasonable level of accounting oversight, and an extraordinary amount of expensive recordkeeping" (p. 116).

Personnel Reimbursement

Some states reimburse local education agencies for the number of **personnel** employed. Certified personnel include teachers, speech and language therapists, school psychologists, art therapists, and other professional support staff. Classified staff includes paraprofessionals and clerical personnel. Frequently, local education agencies must obtain advanced approval to employ staff. States may compensate local education agencies at a flat dollar amount for the professional staff. The salaries of classified staff members may be reimbursed at a flat rate or at percentages of the salary (Bernstein, 1993). Other operating expenses for the classroom are not reimbursed (Schoppmeyer, 1984).

Personnel Formula for Atwood School District

With the personnel formula, the state reimburses Atwood School District the full salary of the classroom teacher ($30,000), the paraprofessional ($12,000) and their benefits ($10,000), plus $8,000 for the shared occupational therapist working in this classroom and in a neighboring district, for a total of $60,000.

 CONSIDER THIS

1. Today, special education no longer consists solely of a teacher in a self-contained classroom. Related and support services are a significant portion of the cost of special education. As more full-inclusion classrooms evolve, the relationships will continue to change. How can the special education administrator convince the legislature to fund these important services?
2. When a formula considers personnel only, new technology may be ignored. What system might be developed to encourage the use of technology in a personnel-reimbursement state?

Fixed Sum Reimbursement

When reimbursement is based on a specified amount for each student, the disability, severity, and type of service form the basis of the **fixed sum** reimbursement. For example, the cost of educating a student with severe behavior disorders in Victoria is $6,000. The state reimburses this school district $60,000 for the entire class of 10 students.

Problems in using the fixed sum formula include (a) the formula is based on historical data, (b) cost-of-living adjustments may not be related to the costs of the program, and (c) funds are distributed according to disability labels (Bernstein, 1993).

CONSIDER THIS

What problems might be anticipated with this type of funding formula?

Service Funding

In contrast to fixed sum reimbursement, **service funding** would reimburse only the services the child needs as determined by the IEP committee, not as prescribed by a child's label. In this approach, costs are attached to services. Districts can be reimbursed for what they actually provide, which allows them to offer what each child needs.

Service Funding for Artesia Unified School District

Artesia Unified School District has 10 students who need services in a self-contained setting. This group is composed of seven students with behavior disorders, one with a severe learning disability, and two with mental retardation. Rather than funding the one class based on 10 students with behavior disorders, the state reimburses the district for services needed by each student. In this case, the state reimbursed Artesia $6,000 for each student whose IEP states the need for a self-contained class.

In addition, the school is reimbursed for other services specific to two of the students. Jason has the label "mental retardation" and, according to his IEP, requires occupational therapy. This generates an additional $1,200 for these services. Violeta, who has severe learning disabilities, receives weekly speech therapy for which the district receives $800. No other student requires these services, so the district is reimbursed only for occupational and speech therapies for these two students.

CONSIDER THIS

1. What apparent advantages and disadvantages would service funding present?
2. How would service funding affect inclusive programming?

Combination of Reimbursement Systems

Although states are categorized as having one type of funding, reimbursement typically is provided to local school districts through a *combination of methods and unit counts.* For example, special education administrators might receive funding based on a combination of partial salary reimbursement for certified teachers and special education paraprofessionals, money for transportation costs, fixed sums for numbers of pupils with IEPs, and targeted funding for special education preschool enrollment.

 ## CONSIDER THIS

1. Which distribution formulas are more likely to encourage appropriate services?
2. Which distribution formulas are more likely to promote innovative programming?
3. As districts move toward full inclusion, does it make sense to have separate financing for special education and general education?

UNEXPECTED EXPENSES

Invariably, unexpected expenses create havoc with the best-planned budget. Special education administrators must be prepared for litigation, for students who enroll during the year, or for events causing already-enrolled students to need new services. Additionally, as students with severe disabilities return to local schools from segregated environments, new support services must be developed, provided, and funded.

Due process procedures alone can cost $10,000 or more. Some districts may need to include a line item in their budget for legal fees. In a Wisconsin case, parents of a child in a coma requested transportation by ambulance with a nurse from the hospital to the school three days a week for full inclusion in the regular classroom. The school district may not have planned for this level of expense nor built contingency plans into the budget. Another student enrolled in the high school was involved in a serious car accident resulting in traumatic brain injury. The district paid for tutoring during hospitalization. When he returned to school, the student needed the services of a physical therapist and weekly transportation to a rehabilitation hospital. When interactive television becomes available, teachers and paraprofessionals can be trained to provide the student with the necessary therapeutic exercises through long-distance learning, but the cost is $80 per hour. In cases reported across the country, parents are requesting greater inclusion of their children, necessitating the hiring of paraprofessionals to support these students in general education classes.

SAVING MONEY

Rural districts tend to have higher costs in providing services than urban districts. Transportation barriers, minimal professional resources, and small numbers of students in a category all contribute to the excess cost of educating students with special needs (Helge, 1984). Some rural local education agencies form cooperatives to meet their needs. "Special education administrators must capitalize on the inherent rural attributes of 'community spirit' and 'helping others'" (O'Connor & Rotatori, 1987, pp. 57–58), such as sharing resources and encouraging volunteers, to help meet the needs of special students. For example, all districts need to assess students with the best possible instruments. However, some assessment devices are expensive and seldom used. In this case, several districts could purchase the instrument together and share it (Harris & Schultz, 1986).

Technology may also provide cost-effective ways to communicate and to train personnel. Many rural districts are taking advantage of expanded communication technology. Administrators can interact via electronic mail. Once the fiber optics lines are in place, the local education agency can hook up with any other link in the world. One innovative use is interactive long-distance learning. Experts or trainers in areas such as speech control, physical movement, or occupational therapy can watch as the services are being performed, then instruct the district personnel in appropriate methods. Depending on the system, more than one site can be served at a time.

ADDITIONAL SOURCES OF FUNDING

The administrator who understands federal, state, and local funding as well as grants and business partnerships can locate additional resources (Weisenstein & Pelz, 1986). Medicaid/Medicare and grants offer additional sources of funding.

Medicaid/Medicare Reimbursement

The **Medicaid** and **Medicare** programs, created by the Social Security Act, are a source of funding for certain special services. The Medicare Catastrophic Coverage Act of 1988 allows states to pay for medical services that are provided to children with disabilities who are eligible. To get this coverage, the service must be included in the individualized education program (IEP) or the individual family service plan (IFSP) (Turnbull, 1993). By combining funds from IDEA for special education personnel with funds from Medicaid and Medicare, districts may be able to afford otherwise costly special education and related services such as physical therapy, occupational therapy, medical evaluations, speech pathology, and audiology.

Medicaid/Medicare Funds for
Culpeper School District

Felisha was born with multiple disabilities and is now ready to enter the Culpeper School District. Medical documents indicate that she might need special services because of physical disabilities. A school psychologist employed by the district was qualified to assess her level of mental retardation, but no employee of the district was qualified to evaluate her medical needs. Medicaid/Medicare funds were used to pay for the medical evaluation to determine district medical responsibilities. The IEP committee used this information to determine that Felisha needed physical therapy, which was written into her IEP.

CONSIDER THIS

Additional funds may be funneled into special education programs to provide related services. However, this will increase pressure on health-care dollars. How might government officials respond to schools fully utilizing this source of funding?

IDEA, *Title VI Part B Grants*

After the required amount of **Title VI Part B** funds is distributed among the districts and state-level administration funds are used, some states earmark the remaining Part B funds for grants to local education agencies to encourage innovative programs. Local education agencies can apply for a grant to solve a unique problem or to implement an experimental program.

Some school districts have written Title VI Part B grants proposing innovative programs that would increase parent participation or collaboration with local mental health services. Others have used grant money to develop intensive reading-tutor programs in response to decreasing reading scores.

CONSIDER THIS

What are some problems local districts are experiencing that grant money might help resolve?

Grant Writing

Grant writing allows the special education administrator to solve problems by obtaining additional funds for creative, innovative, and experimental programs. Although writing grants is time consuming, once the process is understood, it is straightforward and relatively simple. Guidelines for state, federal, and private funding sources vary. However, generally, the grant is submitted through a proposal describing the project to a panel of reviewers. The following suggestions may facilitate the process of writing grants and result in more successful proposals (Deaton, 1989; Graduate Studies and Research, 1993; Zimet, 1993).

Procedure To produce successful grants, administrators investigate sponsors and clarify the purpose of the grants, develop goals and budgets, include all required elements and supportive data, and obtain critical feedback on content and writing.

1. Government agencies are major sources of grants. Foundations and corporations are also important sources. Do your homework. Before writing your proposal, it is to your advantage to know as much about your source as possible.
2. Government agencies publish Requests for Proposals (RFP), which include deadlines. Grants must be submitted by this date or they will not be considered. Foundations also have deadlines but may not be as strict.
3. Once a deadline is established, a time line should be constructed for the completion of each phase of writing the grant.
4. Contact the grant sponsor early to discuss the components of the grant. Ask about preferences regarding length, complexity, budget detail, statistical support, and personal contact before submitting the proposal.
5. Sponsors will provide guidelines that must be meticulously followed. Develop a checklist of the criteria and specifications before you begin to write. If you are unclear about items in the guidelines, call the sponsor's program officer for clarification. Do not make suppositions.
6. Clearly match the project to the sponsor's objectives and priorities.
7. Obtain critical feedback concerning your project idea from several associates before writing a full-scale proposal.
8. A good rule of thumb is to use as few writers as possible. Committee writing does not always work well. However, if you choose a committee approach, divide the tasks. One individual can oversee and coordinate all efforts. Others should be responsible for reviewing the current literature or gathering pertinent information, such as demographic data. Finally, one person should write and edit the proposal.
9. A logical sequence in planning the project and writing the proposal must be maintained. Most sponsors list segments to be included. Write your proposal in this order. Each section should flow logically from the preceding section.
10. Federal and state RFPs tell how many points will be awarded to various components of the proposal. Allocate pages for each segment by

considering the potential points the reviewer can award each area. Stay within advised page limits.

11. Establish needs only for which you intend to create a solution.

12. Set goals to meet your needs. Write clear, measurable, and evaluation-based objectives for each goal. Outline several activities for each objective. Establish a reasonable time line for achieving goals. The budget should be planned to cover all activities listed.

13. If budget limits are not indicated, discuss this with the funding source. Ask, "We are thinking of requesting X dollars. Is this appropriate?"

14. Write a budget and include a narrative explaining why each item is needed. Include "donated," "requested," and "in-kind" columns in your budget.

15. Most grants require letters of support and other supporting documents such as vitae. These may take time to gather, so begin early.

16. The first draft should be written for accuracy, clarity, and sequence. Anticipate possible pitfalls and criticisms. These should be addressed directly in the proposal. Be thorough and do not assume the reviewer will know anything about the project or investigator beyond what is stated in the proposal.

17. Be sure an associate with a sharp eye edits your drafts. Your own errors are difficult to find, and you may not have expressed your ideas clearly. This person should look for grammatical errors, incorrect punctuation, inconsistencies in logic, unjustified budget items, undefined or confusing terms, unsupported arguments, unfounded assumptions, weak documentation, and ways to improve the overall proposal. A person outside your field must be able to understand your project.

18. All blanks on state and federal applications should be filled out. Write N/A (Not Applicable) if appropriate.

19. Grants will need the signatures of specified people. Allow enough lead time to gather signatures.

Content The grant should demonstrate convincingly that the proposed program is a perfect match between sponsors and agency. In addition, the packet should include evidence of research, staff expertise, and well-developed programs models.

1. Begin the proposal with the most important point concerning what you hope to achieve.

2. Indicate why the funding source is the most appropriate source for this project.

3. Emphasize how the client benefits from your work and why the project should be funded **now**.

4. Quote enabling legislation, a foundation founder's words, or a foundation's or corporation's annual report to show how your project fits the intent of the grant-making organization.

5. Stress the innovative nature, timeliness, and significance of your project.

6. Demonstrate knowledge of current literature in the field. Include recent sources and be sure to include them in a reference list.

7. Demonstrate the expertise and capability of those implementing the objectives of the grant and the appropriateness for your local education agency to undertake this project.
8. Include your plan for funding your project after the grant period ends.
9. Write clearly and concisely, including all necessary information without extra verbiage.
10. Watch gender, ethnicity, and educational status references. Do not offend anyone.
11. Explain all acronyms and abbreviations.
12. Subdivide your proposal with **bold headings** that make sense.
13. <u>Underline</u> to bring attention to key words and phrases.
14. Use wide margins for reviewer's notes and visual attractiveness.
15. Use models or visual symbols to demonstrate your ideas. For example, a symbol for a four-step program could be a square with each corner representing a step and each side representing the relationship between the steps.
16. Illustrate points with graphs, charts, and maps whenever possible. These will stand out from the narrative.
17. Include endorsement letters and additional supportive material in the appendices. Putting supportive material in the appendices rather than in the body of the proposal generally improves readability.
18. Prepare a table of contents for proposals of 10 or more pages.

WHAT WILL FUTURE FUNDING STRUCTURES LOOK LIKE?

Characteristics of Systems

For funding systems to meet the changing needs of school districts, Bernstein (1993, p. 105) says they must be:

- **Comprehensive**—supporting the full range of programs deemed desirable
- **Flexible**—permitting programs to adapt to changing needs, encourage efficiencies whenever possible, and incorporate new programs and changing prices without requiring a reformulation of the entire system
- **Equitable**—providing funds so that resources are allocated according to needs
- **Simple**—helping to permit everyone to understand what is being funded and why, as well as minimizing the costs of implementing the system
- **Compatible**—complementing the regular education financial system so that special programs can be integrated with regular education programs.

ISSUES FOR CONSIDERATION

The Council for Exceptional Children, Department of Public Policy (1994) has delineated several major issues regarding financing that are arising as IDEA goes through the process of reauthorization.

1. Currently, Part B funds are allocated according to the number of children served. This system evolved to encourage states to identify greater numbers of students for special education programs. In contrast, the proposed argument is that the allocation formula should neither promote, nor discourage, special education services and should be funded solely on the state's population.

2. Separate placements receive more funding than placements in inclusive classrooms. A change promoting the more equal distribution of monies will support the national effort toward education within the regular classroom. A negative side effect is the possible reduction in a full range of placement options.

3. Although Part B was designed for federal funding of 40% of expenditures, actual funding never exceeded 12%. It has been proposed that federal funds not be used for general funding but for specific activities. While this could result in more restructuring of schools, it also could bring chaos to states and districts that rely on current funding.

4. A "schoolwide" discretionary program allowing for experimentation and innovation could benefit special education students through schoolwide instructional improvement programs, including the promotion of inclusive schools and reducing barriers in coordinating separate federal programs. Numerous concerns regarding this approach include the necessity of a visible audit trail; the need for full implementation of IEPs; the maintenance of accountability mechanisms; the inclusion of parents, advocates, and professionals; the appropriate preparation of all persons; and the match of state/local dollars to special education funds to make the schoolwide effort feasible.

5. Part B funds should be used to expand services to include prevention and at-risk students. Monies should also go to prereferral interventions. This proposal is based on the effectiveness and efficiency of intervening before a problem becomes severe enough for identification. General education, special education, and other support programs could be coordinated. Some argue that interventions for at-risk students should not be considered until Part B is fully funded.

6. More emphasis needs to be placed on the improvement of student performance in addition to the guarantee of a free, appropriate education. This is in tandem with national education standards.

The Center for Special Education Finance (1994) reports that 28 states are considering major reform in special education funding. Of the 19 states using pupil-weighted funding systems, 13 are considering reform; of 9 states utilizing resource-based systems, 6 are changing; of the 14 states employing a system based on the percentage of actual allowable costs, 7 are looking at the reform; and of the 8 states participating in a system where each school receives a flat amount of funding for each special student or special education unit, 2 are working on new formats. These changes will encourage some practices while discouraging others. It is therefore imperative that states develop and maintain systems that meet their policy and program objectives.

Block Funding

Block funding or **flat grants** are large, undifferentiated sums of money used to cover the costs of a variety of programs. At this time, many states are experimenting with providing block grants for local schools, allowing individual districts to determine how best to meet the unique needs of their students with learning challenges. One typical formula for block grants is based on the estimate that the average school provides special services to 10% of the population for mild to moderate disabilities and an additional 2% for more severe challenges. According to this formula, the state supplies reimbursement for 10% of the student count at a higher level than for general education students and an additional 2% at a still higher level for the more severe population. Using this model, a school with 5,000 students would receive additional funding to provide services to 500 students with mild to moderate disabilities and to 100 students with severe/profound disabilities. The school district may choose how to use the money to serve the needs of its population considering its resources, community characteristics, and geographical environment. Nevada and North Carolina use a flat grant system of reimbursement (Thompson et al., 1994).

Block Grant for Battle Mountain Unified School District

The state provides Battle Mountain Unified School District with an overall block grant of $1,250,000. The district uses $60,000 from this grant to cover special education and compensatory services for the class of 10 students with behavior disorders.

CONSIDER THIS

1. In what creative ways might a school provide special services if it were freed from the confines of labeling and able to designate types of programs?
2. What abuses might occur within a block funding format?

DEVELOPING A BUDGET

Developing a budget means projecting income and allocating resources over a period of time. Budgets are based on such factors as estimates of enrollment, average daily attendance, state and local allowances for all students, funding formulas (as already described), federal entitlements (based upon formulas), competitive grants, special revenues for such items as transportation, and tuition from other districts. Yearly budget periods are based on either the calendar year or the fiscal year. The calendar year begins Jan. 1 and ends Dec. 31. Schools frequently use the fiscal year, July 1 through June 30. The federal government's fiscal year runs from Oct. 1 through Sept. 30 (Schoppmeyer, 1984).

To formulate a budget, the administrator divides service components into specific programs or segments of programs so that funds can be spent and traced to program results. Current funding is based on categorical areas but is tied to the specific program funded. Each funded area, by disability or service, has its own budget and includes such items as personnel, instruction, supplies, and maintenance. Schoppmeyer (1984) indicates the budget should be developed on the basis of costs reflecting actual needs, not on income estimates, which are then spread around.

Schoppmeyer (1984) lists relevant factors that must be considered before the budget can be developed:

1. An estimate needs to be made of the number of children in each disability category. Using numbers from the previous year, an estimate is made of the number of students in high-incidence categories. Low-incidence disabilities can be more easily counted, especially in lower-enrollment districts, while high-enrollment districts utilize averages over the years.

2. These estimates in each category are used to calculate Full Time Equivalents (FTE) by multiplying the number of students by the percent of time in services. For example, a child with a disability spending a half day in a resource program is listed as a .5 FTE for the special education program.

3. School, classroom, and equipment needs must be identified. Included in this cost should be new equipment and repairs to existing equipment.

4. Pupil-teacher ratios must be calculated according to state regulations or best practice. This determines personnel costs.

5. The necessary number of paraprofessionals, based on previous needs and state guidelines, can be estimated.

6. Reimbursement to external agencies providing services to the district must also be estimated.

7. Transportation costs for special needs students must be calculated. This includes the cost and maintenance of vehicles, fuel, and drivers.

8. Minor remodeling of existing facilities may need to be done to make them totally accessible for certain students.

9. The costs of screening, referrals, and full assessments must be accounted for and prorated among the various categories.

10. The salary and fringe benefits of the special education administrators should also be prorated among the various categories.

11. Contingency funds for necessary but unforeseen expenses should also be included.

Developing a Budget

Administrators typically collect data and enter them on a spreadsheet. Practice developing a budget using the data presented in Table 5.2 and the sample budget worksheet, Figure 5.1.

You are the special education administrator for Springfield School District. The district has 150 special education students with the following labels and placements:

1. To begin your budget, determine your FTE expected revenue. Self-contained students count as 1 FTE. Communication impairment is counted as .2 FTE. Your district counts full inclusion the same as resource help at .5 FTE. For example, 70 students with learning disabilities in resource and inclusive programs count as 35 FTE. Each FTE special education student generates $5,000 for excess cost reimbursement. This amount is your total, expected revenue.

Personnel Costs

2. Based on the number of students in Springfield, you need to determine the number of teachers needed. State guidelines indicate the number of students each special education teacher is allowed to teach. This is generally based on the disability label and severity. To compute this budget, calculate 15 students with high-incidence disabilities per teacher and 10 students with low-incidence disabilities per teacher.

3. Paraprofessionals have to be hired. Your state guidelines indicate minimum numbers of required paraprofessionals. You may, however, hire more than the minimum. For every 15 students in resource programs and for every 10 in self-contained classrooms, 1 paraprofessional should be hired. In addition, the IEPs of students with behavior disorders in inclusive classrooms require paraprofessionals, as do 2 of the educable mentally retarded and 2 of the students with learning disabilities.

4. Two drivers are needed for the buses carrying students with physical disabilities.

5. Salaries for you (the special education administrator) and your secretary have to be paid.

6. The IEPs of 15 students list related services personnel. Six students need the services of an art therapist, 2 of a physical therapist, and 7 of an occupational therapist. A full-time related service provider serves 20 students.

7. The law requires transition services for all special education students. The transition coordinator is included in the special education budget and receives a 10% administrative salary supplement.

To keep your budget simple, each full-time employee in a particular category will have the same salary. This, of course, will not be the case in a real

TABLE 5.2
DATA FOR BUDGET SPREADSHEET

Category	Number of Students	Placement
Learning Disabilities	70	35 resource 35 inclusion
Behavior Disorders	15	8 resource 5 self-contained 2 inclusion
Communication Impairment	35	30 pull-out 5 inclusion
Educable Mentally Retarded	10	7 resource 3 inclusion
Trainable Mentally Retarded	5	3 self-contained 2 resource
Physically Handicapped	5	5 transportation only
Autistic	5	5 self-contained (2 from out-of-district paying tuition)
Severely Multiply Disabled	3	3 self-contained
Blind	1	1 placed out-of-district
Deaf	1	1 placed out-of-district

district. For Springfield, the salaries and fringe benefits that must be budgeted are listed in Table 5.3.

Out-of-District Tuition
  8. Two out-of-district students with autism are educated in your district, for which the district receives $12,000 each.
  9. The district is charged $10,000 tuition for the student who is blind to be educated at the state school.
  10. The district is charged $8,000 tuition for the student who is deaf to attend the state school.

Transportation Costs
  11. Additional transportation costs are sometimes incurred by special education programs. These include the costs of special vehicles, maintenance, fuel, and drivers. Springfield covers the average cost of transportation per pupil. In this case, the excess cost for the two drivers' salaries and fringe benefits is charged to special education.

Assessment
  12. In Springfield, school psychologists are included in special education. The district employs two full-time school psychologists and hires out-

FIGURE 5.1
SAMPLE BUDGET WORKSHEET

FTE Revenue	LD	BD	CI	EMR	TMR	PHYS	AUT	S/P	B	D	OTHER	TOTAL
# students												
x 4,000												
Personnel:												
# teachers needed												
salary												
benefits												
# paraprofessionals												
salary												
benefits												
support/related												
salary												
benefits												
administrator												
salary												
benefits												
secretary												
salary												
benefits												
out-of-district tuition												
transportation												
equipment/supplies												
contracted services												
contingency fund												

Total FTE expected revenue _____

Total expenditures _____

Difference (less) _____

TABLE 5.3
PERSONNEL COSTS

Personnel	Salaries	Fringe Benefits
Teachers	$28,000	$ 7,000
Paraprofessionals	$14,000	$ 3,500
School Psychologists	$30,000	$ 7,500
Speech Pathologists	$28,000	$ 7,000
Art Therapists	$29,000	$ 7,250
Occupational Therapists	$31,000	$ 7,750
Physical Therapists	$31,000	$ 7,750
Bus Drivers	$ 4,500	$ 1,125
Administrators	$42,000	$10,500
Secretaries	$18,000	$ 4,500

side psychometrists to conduct screening. The cost for screening is $75 per child. Last year, 55 students were screened for special education.

13. A new intelligence test has been required by your state. The price of each test is $1,100. You need a minimum of two. In addition, six other assessment devices need updating at a total cost of $1,200.

Materials and Supplies
14. Materials and supplies for students with special needs must be purchased. The average cost per child per disability is shown in Table 5.4:

TABLE 5.4
AVERAGE COST PER CHILD FOR MATERIALS AND SUPPLIES

Disability	Average Cost
Learning Disabilities	$150
Behavior Disorders	$325
Speech/Language	$ 20
Educable Mentally Retarded	$175
Trainable Mentally Retarded	$250
Physically Handicapped	$100
Autistic	$750
Severely Multiply Disabled	$700

Contingency Funds
15. Unforeseen expenses do arise. A contingency fund is therefore necessary. Title VI Part B of IDEA is a major source of contingency funds (Schoppmeyer, 1984). As long as the carryover amount does not exceed the federal flow-through funds in the district, the Title VI Part B funds can be carried over from one fiscal year to the next.

SUMMARY

Legislators can influence the development or the demise of programs by directing funding. The federal government mandates local school districts to offer comprehensive special education services, yet it has never provided full reimbursement. Revenue for special education comes from the federal, state, and local government as well as from business partnerships.

Determining the cost of special services is complex and varies among states and local agencies. There is a variety of formulas used to reimburse schools for money spent to educate exceptional students. Each method of disbursing funds has benefits and liabilities.

Special education administrators seek procedures that save money. Creative leaders also look to government and business grants to obtain additional funds. Administrators must learn to develop budgets that support a full array of comprehensive special services.

REFERENCES

Bernstein, C. D. (1993). Financing the educational delivery system. In J. I. Goodlad & T. C. Lovitt (Eds.), *Integrating general and special education*. New York: Merrill.

Center for Special Education Finance (1994). Most states considering funding reform. *The Special Educator, 9*(11), 162.

Council for Exceptional Children (1994). *Issues in the implementation of IDEA*. Reston, VA: Department of Public Policy.

Crowner, T. T. (1985). A taxonomy of special education finance. *Exceptional Children, 51,* 503–508.

Deaton, W. L. (1989, November). A systematic approach to winning grants. Presentation at the annual meeting of the Mid-South Educational Research Association. Little Rock, AR.

Graduate Studies and Research (1993). *Horizons, 5,*(2). Emporia State University: Author.

Harris, W. J., & Schultz, P. N. P. (1986). *The special resource program*. Prospect Heights, IL: Waveland Press.

Helge, D. (1984). Technologies as rural special education problem-solvers. *Exceptional Children, 50,* 313–324.

Mayer, C. L. (1982). *Educational administration and special education: A handbook for school administrators*. Boston: Allyn & Bacon.

O'Conner, N. M., & Rotatori, A. F. (1987). Providing for rural special education needs. In A. F. Rotatori, M. M. Banbury, & R. A. Fox (Eds.), *Issues in special education*. Mountain View, CA: Mayfield.

Schoppmeyer, M. W. (1984). Finance and budgeting. In R. S. Podemski, B. J. Price, T. E. C. Smith, & G. E. Marsh (Eds.), *Comprehensive administration of special education*. Rockville, MD: Aspen.

Thompson, D. C., Wood, R. C., & Honeyman, D. S. (1994). *Fiscal leadership for schools: Concepts and practices*. New York: Longman.

Turnbull III, H. R. (1993). *Free appropriate public education. The law and children with disabilities*. (4th ed.) Denver: Love Publishing.

Weisenstein, G. R., & Pelz, R. (1986). *Administrator's desk reference on special education*. Rockville, MD: Aspen.

Zimet, E. (1993). Grant writing techniques for K–12 funding. *T. H. E. Journal, 21*(4), 109–112.

SECTION II

COLLABORATING WITH ESSENTIAL TEAM MEMBERS

Chapter 6

ATTRACTING, SELECTING, AND FACILITATING THE GROWTH OF QUALITY SPECIAL EDUCATORS

The success of education is primarily the result of attracting the best possible personnel, encouraging their performance, facilitating their growth, and ensuring satisfaction in their placement. At one time, personnel management meant recruiting and selecting qualified staff as well as handling problems such as disputes over salary and benefits. More recently, the title "personnel director" has been replaced by "human resource manager" to reflect a broader understanding of the importance of people as a major resource of an organization. The primary purpose of the human resource manager is to develop human potential by assisting personnel to be more productive and satisfied with their work. The new role is more service-oriented and stresses proactive rather than reactive approaches to personal and professional development.

FOUR FUNCTIONS

Castetter (1986) delineates the four functions of the human resource manager as: (a) to attract, develop, retain, and motivate personnel, (b) to assist individuals to achieve standards of performance, (c) to maximize career development of personnel, and (d) to reconcile individual and organizational differences. Personnel functions for special education staff are typically divided among the central office human resources manager, the building principal, and the special education administrators. Often, the special education director serves as consultant to the human resource manager and the principal for all four human resource management functions.

The first personnel function concerns **attracting, developing, retaining, and motivating individuals.** The special education director generally participates in the employee selection process as a member of a selection team. Human resource managers generate pools of qualified applicants from which principals, special education administrators, and other educators choose applicants to interview and hire. The first case in this chapter addresses many of the steps and decisions to be made when hiring special educators.

Because personnel vary in their expectations, temperament, attitude, and skills (Castetter, 1986), special education administrators need to perform various roles in assisting educators to **achieve standards of performance.** Typically, principals take the primary responsibility for supervising and evaluating the staff in their building, asking special education administrators to provide input into the process (Zadnick, 1992). This input may concern instruction or may be feedback regarding activities specific to special education, such as completing individualized education programs, maintaining records of parent contacts, or coordinating triennial reviews. Although the roles of special educators vary considerably from those of general educators, the same instruments are typically used to evaluate both (Zadnick, 1992). Evaluation tools should be responsive to differences in educators' job expectations and should be based on valid measures of performance.

In the area of **maximizing career development of personnel,** the special education director may again perform many roles. A separate inservice training agenda may be provided for special education personnel. Special education administrators may also be part of a task force to develop a more comprehensive program for all teachers in the district. These task forces work to design staff development programs that foster authentic personal engagement and ownership of learning (Lee, 1993) as well as promote ongoing professional growth (Sadowski, 1993). "Education is a profession which requires continuing renewal of members to retain and increase its vigor and artistry" (Hunter, 1993, p. 42). Currently there is an emphasis on staff development that engenders reflective educators (Langer & Colton, 1994). Special education administrators can encourage inservice training formats that promote flexible and thoughtful teacher behavior because reflective teachers are better prepared for students with special needs. These teachers should be equipped to utilize a circle of inquiry: experiment, observe and collect meaningful data, analyze and interpret findings, hypothesize on the results, and experiment again (Sparks & Simmons, 1989).

The fourth function of human resource managers, **reconciling individual and organization differences,** translates into assisting teachers to follow guidelines and find satisfaction working in the school and district. When special educators experience job-related difficulties, special education administrators have to determine whether the issues are special education-related, such as advocating for the most appropriate inclusive program or assessing the appropriateness of a referral for multidisciplinary evaluation. It is the role of the special education administrator to support the teacher in furthering special education in the schools. There are times when special educators feel alone in a general education environment and need the support of their administrator in professional or personal issues. Administrators who are successful in resolving disputes have learned to examine their own values, patterns, strengths, and weaknesses, which allows them to observe with a minimum of judgment and make thoughtful decisions (Ellis & Macrina, 1994). They have realized there is no condition without problems, and their role is to facilitate cooperation, creativity, and shared responsibility.

In this chapter, three cases are presented to illustrate human resource management issues related to special education administration. The first is a teaching case that details the process of writing a position description, selecting the best candidate for the job, and proposing an individual staff-development program. The second examines peer review, an alternative to the traditional supervision procedure, which is designed to support teachers and promote teacher retention. The third raises intriguing questions about evaluation of special education administrators, such as "who are the customers of special education administrators and how do we obtain their feedback?"

The following teaching case will provide the reader with an opportunity to write a position description and vacancy opening, establish a selection process, and design an individual staff-development program.

Replacing Mrs. Lopez

The setting is a moderate-sized, Southwestern suburb within a 30-minute drive of a large multiethnic city. The population is growing as new homes are built primarily for commuters to the central city. The majority of the community is Caucasian non-Hispanic, although 25% of school-age children are Hispanic and Native American. Last year, more than 50% of the students in 3 of the 10 kindergarten classes had limited English proficiency. In response, the district hired a teacher to coordinate English as a Second Language programs. Demand for special education services has increased dramatically as multidisciplinary teams have found more students than ever eligible for learning disability and behavior disorder services. Additionally, in the past two years service delivery models have changed as the special education director, school psychologists, and a few teachers have advocated for more collaborative teaming as well as coteaching formats.

Mrs. Lopez is a special education teacher at Fillmore Elementary School, the largest elementary building, which houses 500 students and four special education programs. In April, she notified the special education director that her husband had been transferred to another city and she would be moving at the end of the school year. The special education director began the process of hiring a replacement by notifying the human resource administrator that Mrs. Lopez intended to leave.

The following position description was on file:

Elementary Special Education Resource Room Teacher. Primary responsibility is to teach students with learning and behavior difficulties in a resource room setting. Also responsible for testing students referred for special education evaluation and participating in multidisciplinary team meetings as well as writing reports and individualized education programs.

CONSIDER THIS

Given the description of the school district and school population, as well as current trends toward collaboration and inclusive programming, what might be added to this position description to more aptly describe the job?

Position Description

The special education director decided the present position description was inadequate, and that it would be best to interview Mrs. Lopez so she could describe the actual requirements of her job. Mrs. Lopez described a typical day and some weekly responsibilities as follows:

"Several mornings each week before classes begin, I meet with teachers to discuss student progress and to plan lessons I will help teach in regular classrooms. About half of my day is spent in regular classrooms assisting individual students or teaching small groups. The other half involves teaching students who come to my resource room, evaluating students as part of their multidisciplinary team assessment, writing reports, communicating with parents, and consulting with teachers. Many afternoons after students leave are spent in meetings with parents, teams of teachers, and occasionally the principal or school psychologist. I feel like I have a lot of bosses; I guess the principal most often sees what I do, but perhaps the special education director better understands what I do. I've liked my job, but frankly I thought I was hired to teach students, yet sometimes I feel I work more with teachers, parents, psychologists, and administrators. And then there are the kids. They seem to be getting worse, coming from broken homes. My limited Spanish background isn't enough to communicate with many of my students' parents. And I don't understand the Native American families at all."

CONSIDER THIS

1. Based on the interview with Mrs. Lopez, rewrite the position description to address new emphases.
2. Identify the supervisor and reporting systems.
3. What unique talents/characteristics should this teacher possess in order to succeed?
4. After interviewing Mrs. Lopez, it occurs to the special education director that there are other key players in the selection process. Who else should have input into this teacher's job description? What questions would you ask others to help them develop a list of desirable skills and characteristics for the new teacher?

Recruitment Process

Typically, personnel directors have developed policy and procedures for coordinating searches. Their offices generate a pool of qualified applicants from which special education directors and principals select interview candidates. Recruiting begins with identifying characteristics of desirable applicants and then determining the best sources for these candidates. Contacting college and university placement offices usually results in applicants with limited experience but with the latest training; advertisements in newspapers, professional journals, and booths at conferences may yield more experienced applicants.

Every effort must be made to recruit candidates from minority backgrounds to represent the diversity of the community and to offer a wide range of role models. Affirmative Action procedures require that efforts to recruit protected classes be documented. In addition, human resource managers develop procedures to evaluate the success of their efforts in assembling the best possible pool of applicants.

CONSIDER THIS

The human resource administrator was impressed with the special education director's thorough and insightful approach to rewriting the position description. The vacancy announcement must next be sent to colleges, newsletters, and journals. In 50 words or less, describe the community, school, position, and desired qualifications.

Selection

Prospective candidates complete application forms and submit a variety of supporting documents, such as letters of reference, transcripts, evidence of certification, and writing samples. Personnel clerks make folders for this material and notify applicants it has been received. The personnel director screens the completed folders to establish the best possible pool of applicants.

At the same time, the special education director and principal designate a committee to select the individual for the job. The committee delineates the criteria it will use to compare candidates' folders in order to identify a few top individuals. Next, the committee develops a list of interview questions that will allow candidates to (a) share their backgrounds, (b) discuss their strengths and weaknesses, (c) explain their ideas concerning instruction, discipline, motivation, and evaluation, (d) explore their thoughts regarding working with peers and parents, and (e) state their professional goals.

CONSIDER THIS

1. What supporting documents do you think are important to request during the application process?

2. Who should be on the committee to select a special education teacher?
3. Develop a list of the criteria you would use to select interview candidates. Is experience essential? What attitudes or skills do you value most?
4. Write a set of interview questions based on the list in the previous paragraph. Ask a teacher to answer these questions in order to determine whether your interview questions will assess what you are interested in learning about candidates.

Interviewing

It was decided that the selection committee should consist of the special education director, principal, and two teachers (one special education and one general education) from Fillmore Elementary. Committee members reviewed 12 folders according to their criteria and selected two applicants for interviews. Both teachers interviewed were excellent, and the committee had difficulty choosing between the two. Each candidate is summarized below:

Michelle is a Caucasian, non-Hispanic female in her early 30s. She has a master's degree in special education and 4 years of experience teaching students with learning disabilities in a suburban school in Texas. Her husband was recently transferred to the city near Fillmore Elementary, and her family will move to the suburb in July. She has two children in school. Michelle presented her ideas about teaching and classroom management in an impressive way. Her references describe her as organized and caring. Teachers reported she was easy to work with, and her parent involvement program was very successful. Michelle has had experience with collaborative teaming and had just begun experimenting with coteaching. She was guarded in her opinion of collaboration, saying there was a lot to learn before special education teachers could work well in other teachers' classrooms.

Adrianna is a Hispanic female in her early 20s. After graduation, she could not find a job as a teacher, so she accepted a job as a paraprofessional, assisting students with physical disabilities. For the past 2 years, she worked and took courses toward a master's in special education; by taking night and summer classes, she will be able to finish in December or May. Adrianna grew up in a city and feels excited about the idea of teaching a diverse population of students. She has great ideas and can hardly wait to get started in her own classroom. Also, Adrianna has done extensive research on collaboration and coteaching. She believes it to be the most promising instructional format ever conceived. Adrianna's references are glowing with only small reservations. She is described as enthusiastic and creative but somewhat unstructured. The students all loved her and wanted to be one of her students.

CONSIDER THIS

Make a list of each candidate's strengths and weaknesses. Compare this list with the position description. Which candidate would you choose and why?

ORIENTATION AND STAFF DEVELOPMENT

Recruiting and selecting the best candidate for a position is an important beginning. However, once an individual accepts a job, another realm of human resource management begins. It is essential that new employees meet important staff and learn critical information concerning their new district, new school, and specific position. Successful orientation speeds acclimation and helps new employees feel they belong. Employees who understand what is expected of them and who feel they belong are more likely to be satisfied, be prepared to perform the tasks required of them, and remain in their job longer (Rebore, 1991).

Personnel vary in temperament, attitudes, preparation, experience, expectations, skills, and values. Through inservice programs, human resource managers can help personnel to grow and work together in order to achieve the purposes of the system. Sage and Burrello (1986) state there are four consistent trends in inservice education. First, we are moving away from a compensatory view to a complementary view. That is, instead of focusing on weaknesses, staff development could build areas of strength or expertise. Second, inservice training is seen as continuous. Formerly, inservice programs consisted of discrete workshops arranged to expose everyone to a current idea or to skills administrators determined were lacking in the faculty. Third, inservice programs have become complex. Large portions of budgets are set aside to arrange a variety of options and opportunities. Fourth, there has been a shift in control from central office to task force/teacher involvement.

At the beginning of employment, teachers should confer with their supervisors about areas in which they would like to grow or areas in which they feel they need help. In this way, a program of staff development could be tailored to the individual needs of new teachers. Possibly a mentor or peer support could be established, or release time to observe other teachers or programs or to attend workshops could be arranged.

CONSIDER THIS

1. What type of orientation is essential for teachers when they begin working in a school district and new school?

2. What activities could help new teachers become oriented to district procedures and school routines?
3. Both candidates interviewed would benefit from personalized inservice training programs. Imagine discussing the personal and professional goals of each candidate. What ideas do you have for individualized orientation/inservice programs for Michelle and Adrianna?

SUPERVISION AND EVALUATION

Educational administrators frequently have difficulty separating supervision from evaluation functions (Zadnick, 1992). Supervision is usually based on a helping relationship and is designed to improve performance and increase satisfaction. In contrast, evaluation is directed at determining status in terms of continuing employment (Sage & Burrello, 1986) and program effectiveness. Because most administrators are required to perform both functions, and because helping and judging are generally incompatible, it is no wonder administrators struggle with being supportive while enforcing school guidelines.

Analogously, teachers and administrators may find it difficult to trust those who supervise them and who are also responsible for evaluating their performance. However, effective supervision relies on a strong supervisory relationship built on trust and communication. Therefore, the first step in any supervisory process is building a quality relationship.

Zadnick (1992) stresses supervisory practices (a) based on written policy and procedures, (b) provided by trained administrators, and (c) utilizing tools supported by research. The most common form of instructional supervision is called clinical supervision. This approach typically follows a systematic procedure of conferencing, gathering data, giving feedback, and maintaining continuous contact.

Recently, there has been a recognition of the potential for peers to provide a supplement to supervision in the form of orientation for new teachers (Cheney, Krajewski, & Combs, 1992) as well as continuous opportunities for professional growth (Williamson & Russell, 1990). In this model, new teachers participate in what is generally called induction programs with mentor teachers who guide them through a series of predictable stages of novice-teacher maturation. Teachers who have participated in these programs have demonstrated greater confidence and clarity of educational philosophy along with more willingness to be observed and receive feedback than teachers who have not been involved in an induction process (Cheney et al., 1992).

Peer coaching, as described in the case study by Dye, Stone, and Conners (see below), involves educators supporting, observing, and providing helpful feedback to their peers. The peer coaching process facilitates better instruction by training teachers how to observe, analyze, and solve problems. It also fosters an acceptance of responsibility for personal growth as well as for the quality performance of peers (Dye & Stone, 1992).

The practice of peer coaching has been advocated for more than 20 years and is referred to by such names as teaching clinic (Dowling, 1983), peer clinical supervision (McFaul & Cooper, 1984), and peer group review (Dowling, 1987). Research has demonstrated that the teaching clinic was similar to supervision in its use of clinical verbal behaviors (Dowling, 1983), and many teachers preferred the teaching clinic to traditional supervision. Teachers perceived supervisors to be superiors and therefore were less likely to ask supervisors, rather than peers, for suggestions. Additionally, the teaching clinic proved to be more flexible than the typical supervisory relationship (Dowling, 1987). Leggett and Hoyle (1987) stated that peer coaching provided the continuous follow-up teachers needed to implement new ideas after professional-development activities.

A cautionary view of peer clinical supervision was expressed by McFaul and Cooper (1984). They found most peer teachers were able to execute the format, but not thoroughly. Preobservation conferences were conducted cursorily, insufficient data were presented, and when an issue was raised, participants proposed simplistic solutions to complex problems. Additionally, teachers appeared to honor an unwritten agreement that no one would be made uncomfortable during the process.

Peer coaching is in sync with current models of adult learning. Roy (1987) stresses that learning in children involves forming new ideas and skills, while adult learning consists of transforming already learned behaviors. Adult learners are achievement oriented and expect to be successful. They do not want to waste time, and so they demand relevancy and immediate application. Croteau and Richardson (1987) also point out that adults learn best when they are confident they can meet the challenge; the support of peer coaches can enhance that confidence. The following case study examines implementation of a peer coaching model called peer group review.

Peer Group Review

Bonnie Dye, Giselle Stone, and Marjory Conners

Cobb County School District is the 36th-largest school system in the United States, located in Marietta, Ga., across the Chattahoochee River from Atlanta. It is the largest school system in Georgia, with 72,000 students in 12 high schools, 17 middle schools, and 54 elementary schools.

The peer model was introduced in 1987 when the special education department chose to implement the Learning Strategies Curriculum from the University of Kansas as a component of the Study Skills Interrelated Course. The curriculum required extensive training and a strong commitment on the part of the teachers. It was proposed that a peer coaching model might provide the ongoing support needed to implement and maintain the Learning Strategies Curriculum. Peer coaching involves teachers helping teachers, and is based on the premise that the best way to improve instruction is to receive assistance from someone in a similar situation. It teaches skills and boosts confidence as well as encourages friendship, support, and understanding.

The peer model is sometimes called peer coaching because of its similarity to the skills used by a good athletics coach. The peer model (a) encourages personal goal setting, (b) breaks complex skills into small units that can be learned, (c) allows for guided practice and corrective feedback, (d) encourages independent practice, and (e) praises and rewards as well as reassures and supports where appropriate. In the Cobb County model shown in Figure 6.1, the peer coaching was called Peer Group Review and consisted of support groups of three or four coaching teams (CT), each with two or three teachers who observed each other.

The peer review process consists of a prelesson conference, an observation, and a feedback session. During the preconference, teachers may identify problem areas, such as the need for ideas to help students having difficulty learning math skills or following classroom expectations. Then, individual goals are set. Observers may choose to use a formal instrument or collect a wide range of data. Following the observation, the observed teacher receives feedback from the coaching team and the support group. Monthly meetings provide a structure for the peer review process. Table 6.1 gives an example of the results of a peer group review for a high school teacher. The written feedback delineates areas of strengths and weaknesses, then documents strategies the teacher might choose to implement.

To begin, the Cobb County School District scheduled two full-day training sessions for the instruction of the Learning Strategies Curriculum, followed by monthly three-hour support group meetings (teachers were released from 2:00 to 3:00 and paid extra for 3:00 to 5:00). In the first support meetings, teachers made commitments, set goals, divided into coaching teams, and established an observation schedule. Just like any other innovative idea,

FIGURE 6.1
PEER COACHING MODEL

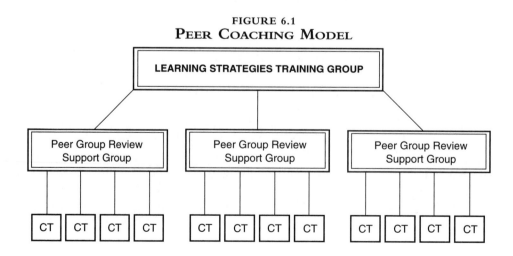

TABLE 6.1
PEER GROUP REVIEW
FOR A HIGH SCHOOL TEACHER

In Attendance: **Demonstration Teacher:**

Bonnie   Joyce
Bob
Brenda
Karen
Sharon
Joyce
Roy
Caroline

Areas of Strength:

1. Teacher used visuals to demonstrate the concept of kinetic energy.
2. Teacher used appropriate wait time when seeking answers to questions she had asked the class.
3. Teacher quickly got students involved in the lesson by making individual assignments.
4. Teacher repeated students' answers when it was important for the entire class to get the answer to the question.
5. The teacher made sure that all students recorded the measurements that would work in the experiment.
6. Students were allowed to move from one activity to the next.
7. Student asked to go to the restroom. Without disrupting the instruction, the teacher indicated that the answer was no.
8. Teacher rephrased questions when the students did not understand the original questions.
9. The students actively participated in the lesson.
10. The teacher had the students work together in groups.

Areas of Concern:

1. The teacher asked most questions to the entire class without choosing a specific student to respond.
2. During transition time, some students had not completed their assignments.
3. Samantha passed a note during class.
4. Several unsolicited responses from Jamie. Some were negatively focused to other students in the class.
5. Students talked while the teacher wrote on the board.
6. Students had difficulty moving around the classroom.
7. Demonstration was difficult for some students to see.
8. Some students seemed unclear about the directions for the assignment.

TABLE 6.1 *(Continued)*

Strategies:

1. Call on some students by name in a random manner rather than directing all questions to the class in general.
2. Time movement so that the lesson stops and then begins again rather than moving while some students are still working.
3. Teacher or paraprofessional could move around the classroom and stay in a closer proximity to students to monitor behavior such as passing notes.
4. Redirect questions to Jamie when another student has answered. This will make him listen to the other answers and, it is hoped, limit negative comments, since he often does not appear able to make a better response than the student he is critiquing. The teacher could also use response cards to limit the number of times Jamie is allowed to speak out or answer questions.
5. Delegate a student recorder to place answers to experiment questions on the board.
6. Teacher could possibly elevate demonstrations to table top, have students in the back of the room stand, place desks in a circle or move students to floor level by removing desks to ensure that all students are able to see the demonstration of the experiments.
7. Teacher could ask one or more students to restate her directions until she feels that everyone clearly understands them.

coaching took time to implement well. The first few observations were difficult, but once a bond was struck between individuals, coaching took off in a positive direction.

Two teachers, Colleen and Margaret, provide an example of the dynamics of peer coaching. After 18 years, Colleen was considered a master teacher. She had taught in a variety of systems nationwide and for the Department of Defense. Colleen had joined the Cobb County staff two years before being asked to be part of the peer model. She was a delightful peer, the type of teacher who was capable of making a difference in students' and teachers' lives. As a resource teacher in a team teaching model, she was able to help teachers change their instructional style and modify assessment procedures, all the while thinking it was their own idea. Unfortunately, over 2 years her attitude had deteriorated. She began to act frustrated and angry, complaining of excessive amounts of paperwork, preparation time, and testing responsibilities.

Margaret, who had an art degree, was idealistic and ready to save the world, but she was unable to find a job as an art teacher. She was told she would have a better chance if she changed fields and applied for a provisional certificate to teach special education. Margaret saw this as a challenge and proceeded with gusto. To bolster her initiation into special education, she joined the peer model, thrilled about the opportunity to learn from "the masters," as she put it.

At the first meeting, Margaret requested she be paired with Colleen, realizing that Colleen had a wealth of experience and could assist her in becoming a better teacher. Flattered by Margaret's interest and quest for knowledge, Colleen agreed to be her coaching partner. For Colleen, this was the boost she needed to renew her spirit. Colleen shared everything she could, and Margaret kept asking for more.

Colleen was selected by her peers as "Teacher of the Year." Through peer coaching, her entire attitude changed. She became empowered again, seeing the value of her knowledge; through sharing her expertise, she found a renewed sense of meaning. Margaret gained a great deal of confidence. She learned and perfected techniques far beyond what might be expected of a novice teacher and avoided common pitfalls because she was walking in another's footsteps. Colleen predicted that one day Margaret would be selected "Teacher of the Year" and she would share in the joy of that success.

In a related field, using a different version of the model, speech/language pathologists from Cobb County participated in a total of 14 peer groups over a 5-year period. These therapists worked in clinic, hospital, and school settings and varied in number of years of experience. The peer review format focused on 15-minute video recordings of students or groups for whom speech pathologists had requested professional peer input. Each peer review session began with a discussion of the impact of the previous session. Next, the demonstration teacher introduced the video by describing the student to be viewed and requesting specific information. During viewing of the videotape, everyone made notes and then formulated ideas in writing concerning the student. In turn, each peer presented one idea which was written onto a flip chart. Ideas were presented until everyone had finished, then the collective list was examined by the group. Recommendations for intervention were made. Finally, the group evaluated the effectiveness of the group interaction.

Over the years, the therapists learned to improve the peer review process. It was determined that the process was most successful with the continuity of one leader and one leadership style, using a speech/language pathologist, not a supervisor, as leader. Leaders learned to address uncomfortable concerns even though it might create tension or upset peers. Most peers became supportive of this leadership role and counted on the leader to keep the group functioning smoothly.

In the opinion of supervisors, many speech/language pathologists who had done an average job before peer group review improved their therapy skills and increased their interest in working with other therapists on department projects. Unfortunately, some therapists who entered the peer process with minimal skills exited with little improvement, usually because their attitude and inability to function in a group kept them from learning.

Before peer group review, speech/language pathologists typically complained of isolation in public schools. The process offered a chance to meet with other professionals and created a forum to publicly test philosophies and ideas. The peer group offered reassurance that their attempts to grow were valued. In addition, the opportunity to be experts enhanced self-esteem.

When challenged by a teacher, administrator, or parent, group members who had learned to present their ideas to peers felt more confident in asserting their professional opinion to others.

In job settings which seem increasingly more paperwork- and due process-oriented, the peer group review reminded professionals that students and effective practices should be the focus of their activities. Participants improved analytic and problem-solving abilities as well as increased feelings of professional responsibility for the quality of peers' work. Unexpected benefits included groups that cultivated specific areas of interest and developed consistency across the school district in such areas as eligibility criteria and severity ratings.

Because speech/language pathology is not frequently an area of the building administrator's expertise, principals were appreciative of the supervision offered by peer group review. The program coordinator of speech/language pathologists participated in the groups, increasing the number of contacts and providing the opportunity to observe all the therapists more equally. Coordinators were better able to identify strengths and weaknesses in the staff as a whole. Additionally, therapists reported being more comfortable in asking for help because of the atmosphere created through the peer review.

Although peer group review proved to be a valuable process, some resistance was encountered by the Cobb County groups. Many experienced therapists, especially those who seemed to need the process most, chose not to participate. There were also cases in which the coordinator determined that certain members were not benefitting from the process or were sabotaging the group's efforts with negative and distracting behaviors. Coordinators sometimes became discouraged because it took so much time to establish effective working groups. Because of this initial resistance, coordinators had to be willing to advocate for the peer review and enforce the procedural guidelines. Success required commitment to the process, patience, and perseverance.

 ## CONSIDER THIS

1. What benefits might peer group review have over conventional supervisory practices?
2. What concerns might supervisors raise related to peer group review?
3. What type of training would educators need to participate effectively in this process?
4. How would you motivate educators to participate in peer group review?
5. Should teachers be required to be part of a peer review process?
6. What are the pros and cons of using videotaping for the peer review process?

EVALUATION OF SPECIAL EDUCATION ADMINISTRATORS

The third case in this chapter poses questions related to performance evaluation of special education administrators. Evaluation of employee performance is based on the collection of data regarding the way individuals perform the various tasks of their assignments. These data may be the result of an examination of files, observations, or reports from individuals who work with the administrators. One innovative school district has decided to apply practices from business and industry by utilizing feedback from individuals served by the administrators as part of the employee performance evaluation.

Using Customer Satisfaction as a Component of Employee Performance Evaluation
Elizabeth B. Hill

Virginia Beach is the second-largest school division in the state of Virginia, with a student population of approximately 80,000 and a reputation of educational excellence. Geographically it is the largest city in the state, sprawled over 310 square miles. It is a relatively wealthy community largely because of the large tourism industry. The school system has recently suffered through a series of leadership crises at the superintendency level. The current superintendent was hired to restore the reputation of excellence and bring Virginia Beach into the forefront of the restructuring movement. Subsequently, the middle- and upper-management staff was reduced, and decision making was decentralized. As part of these changes, the office of special education was reorganized.

Traditionally, special education coordinators "policed" federal regulations for the school system and made most of the programming decisions for students with special needs. Responsibilities were delegated among the coordinators on the basis of such categories as learning disabilities, behavioral disorders, and mental retardation. In an attempt to serve as facilitators and resource personnel for the special and general education classes in our schools, this role is changing. Under the current structure, each coordinator is assigned a set of schools from one attendance zone, which typically includes one or two high schools, one or two middle schools, and five to seven elementary schools.

I first heard about customer satisfaction as a component of performance evaluation during the interview process for special education coordinator. A panel of other coordinators introduced the concept and asked who I thought my customers were and how I would address their needs. At that time, I said my customers would be special education students and their parents; meeting their needs seemed a natural part of the coordinator role. However, the concept of customer satisfaction proved to be much more complex and controversial than was first apparent.

Using customer satisfaction to evaluate employee performance has its conceptual framework in the literature of business management (Demming, 1986; Lawler, 1992; Peters & Waterman, 1982). Companies striving to improve their productivity, and ultimately their profits, found that putting the customer first was a successful tactic. Although success in education is more difficult to measure than productivity and profits, and the learning process is infinitely less tangible than the production process, educators have reasoned that these principles could be effectively applied to schools. Initially, a task force of coordinators from several central office departments met to determine who were the customers of central office personnel and how their satisfaction could be measured in a meaningful, equitable way. Our representative to that task force presented the first draft of the customer survey to the special education coordinators for our reactions and input, then it was returned to the task force for further fine-tuning. (See Figure 6.2.)

FIGURE 6.2
SAMPLE CLIENT SURVEY

DEPARTMENT OF INSTRUCTIONAL SUPPORT SERVICES
Office of Special Education Services

CLIENT SURVEY

Virginia Beach City Public Schools

FIGURE 6.2 *(Continued)*

DEPARTMENT OF INSTRUCTIONAL SUPPORT SERVICES
Office of Special Education Services

School: _____

Coordinator: _____

Date: _____

Because we value your opinion, please take a moment to complete this brief questionnaire and return it to the Department of Instructional Support Services. This will enable us to continue to offer the best service possible.

1. Kind of service provided:
   _____ a. In-service programs
   _____ b. Training/Workshops
   _____ c. Classroom assistance
   _____ d. Information
   _____ e. Delivery of materials
   _____ f. Administrative assistance
   _____ g. Assistance with school-based initiative
   _____ h. Assistance with division-wide initiative
   _____ i. New teacher assistance
   _____ j. Curriculum development
   _____ k. Other (Please specify)

2. The service from this coordinator was appropriate for the situation.
Strongly Agree ❑ Agree ❑ Disagree ❑ Strongly Disagree ❑ No response ❑

3. The service from this coordinator was delivered as I expected it to be.
Strongly Agree ❑ Agree ❑ Disagree ❑ Strongly Disagree ❑ No response ❑

4. I would recommend this coordinator's service to a colleague.
Strongly Agree ❑ Agree ❑ Disagree ❑ Strongly Disagree ❑ No response ❑

5. I would rate the overall service from this coordinator as
Outstanding ❑ Excellent ❑ Good ❑ Satisfactory ❑ Unsatisfactory ❑

Comments:

Please return to: Dr. K. Edwin Brown, Assistant Superintendent
Department of Instructional Support Services

The following dialogue from that meeting illustrates the concerns of special education coordinators but is also indicative of feedback from other central office personnel regarding the use of customer satisfaction as a component of employee evaluation.

James: *Every time we provide a service, any service, in one of our schools, we're supposed to give everyone involved one of these surveys?*

Charles (our representative): *Right. They send the completed surveys to the assistant superintendent, who compiles the feedback and sends the surveys to our director, who passes them back to us. We use the feedback to adjust our service to the schools and hopefully improve our overall performance.*

Sarah: *So the goal is improved performance, not to compile data for hiring, firing, or promotion decisions?*

Charles: *Well, I'm not sure.*

Sheila: *It would seem pretty naive of us to assume that these surveys won't be used against us if they're negative.*

John: *How can they not be negative? Every time we go to a school to troubleshoot a conflict, someone will be dissatisfied! When it comes to difficulty with state and federal regulations, someone always feels like a loser.*

Joanne: *He's right. Even if we are only "reminding" parents and building administrators of the federal regulations, rather than enforcing these regulations, everyone blames us.*

James: *Wait a minute! What's to stop someone from only giving out surveys to the people involved who are satisfied? If our jobs are on the line, even the most ethical of us will have trouble asking an obviously dissatisfied customer to send his opinion to the assistant superintendent.*

Sarah: *What about the annoyance factor? If I were an assistant principal or a teacher, I would get pretty tired of filling out these surveys. Couldn't that affect our ratings, too?*

John: *Sure it could. I think I'd feel pretty foolish handing out these surveys to the same people several times a week. It feels demeaning, too.*

Joanne: *Not only that, has anyone noticed these surveys are anonymous? What would stop someone from giving us a bad rating just because they didn't like us or were generally negative about special education?*

James: *I think parents should be able to send in an anonymous survey, but building administrators are just as much our peers as our customers. They should be required to sign their names as a professional courtesy and to make them accountable for their opinions.*

Sarah: *Not only accountable but meaningful. If improved performance is really the goal, we should know who says what.*

Charles: *I got the feeling there is a general perception people won't say what they really feel if they have to sign their name.*

Joanne: *Exactly my point. How unprofessional is that? If anyone is going to send a rating to the assistant superintendent about someone's professional performance, they should be responsible enough to sign their name!*

Phoebe: *I just thought of another problem. What if a coordinator, for whatever reason, doesn't provide services at all? You know, answers questions but never goes to the school much, can't make it to*

	meetings, doesn't make the extra effort. No one can register a complaint if no one gives them a survey to fill out.
Sarah:	*What if we give out surveys, but the customers don't bother to fill them out? That coordinator's data will look the same as the data for the coordinator who doesn't do anything.*
Joanne:	*I bet it's more likely disgruntled customers will fill out the surveys than those who are generally satisfied. How can our performance be evaluated on data that could be so skewed?*
James:	*Even worse, what if a school doesn't want our services? If they feel confident to handle special education issues on their own, the coordinators will be twiddling their thumbs. We're not supposed to force ourselves on a school.*
Charles:	*My guess is the coordinators in the other departments will be even more worried about that issue. At least special education is an area most people feel less than confident about, unless they've received special training.*
John:	*I bet there are more assistant principals and principals who have received special education training than you might think.*
Sarah:	*We sound pretty negative about this whole idea. There must be some good points, too.*
Joanne:	*I think most professionals could embrace customer satisfaction as a concept. I feel positive about receiving feedback, and I think most of us want to do the best possible job. It's just this instrument and its application seem flawed.*
Sheila:	*I don't think we can guess how this survey is going to work. We're going to have to try it and work out the bugs as we go along.*
James:	*Will we be given the opportunity to fine-tune this process on an ongoing basis?*
Charles:	*As far as I know, we will.*

CONSIDER THIS

1. Who are the customers of special education administrators?
2. What type of feedback would you be interested in receiving from customers?
3. How should data from customer satisfaction be used in performance evaluation?
4. How would you design a customer feedback system that would address some of the concerns expressed by these coordinators?
5. What are the potential benefits to the employee and the system of using customer feedback data?

SUMMARY

The title "human resources manager" has replaced "personnel administrator" to reflect a greater awareness that the success of an organization is primarily the result of the quality of its employees and how well they are supported in performing their jobs. The field now realizes that the process of attracting, selecting, and retaining superior candidates requires thoughtful planning, group decisions, new-teacher induction, and continuous support. Successful personal and professional development programs are ongoing, multifaceted, and designed to involve individuals in their own growth process.

Supervision and evaluation are complicated, interwoven administrative functions. Supervision is seen more in terms of building relationships to improve performance and increase job satisfaction, whereas evaluation determines status and rates performance. The evaluation process raises concerns and questions among teachers and administrators. Innovative models of new-teacher induction and peer coaching offer exciting possibilities for facilitating growth and supporting teachers during challenging times.

REFERENCES

Castetter, W. B. (1986). *The personnel function in educational administration* (4th ed.). New York: Macmillan.

Cheney, C. O., Krajewski, J., & Combs, M. (1992). Understanding the first-year teacher: Implications for induction programs. *Teacher Education and Special Education, 15*(1), 18–24.

Croteau, J. M., & Richardson, T. (1987, February). Helping teachers become effective trainers. *The Developer,* 6–7.

Demming, W. E. (1986). *Out of the crisis.* Cambridge, MA: M.I.T. Center for Advanced Engineering Study.

Dowling, S. A. (1983). An analysis of conventional and teaching clinical supervision. *The Clinical Supervisor, 1*(4), 15–29.

Dowling, S. A. (1987). Teaching clinic conference participants interaction. *The Journal of Communication Disorders, 20,* 119–128.

Dye, B., & Stone, G. A. (1992, March). *Techniques for teacher retention: Peer review enhances collaboration.* Paper presented at conference of the Learning Disabilities Association, Atlanta, GA.

Ellis, A., & Macrina, A. N. (1994). Reflection and self-appraisal in preparing new principals. *Journal of Staff Development, 15*(1), 10–15.

Hunter, M. (1993). Education as a profession. *Journal of Staff Development, 14*(3), 42–44.

Langer, G. M., & Colton, A. B. (1994). Reflective decision-making: The cornerstone of school reform. *Journal of Staff Development, 15*(1), 2–7.

Lawler, E. E. (1992). *The ultimate advantage: Creating the high-involvement organization.* San Francisco: Jossey-Bass.

Lee, G. V. (1993). New images of school leadership: Implications for professional development. *Journal of Staff Development, 14*(1), 2–5.

Leggett, D., & Hoyle, S. (1987). Peer coaching: One district's experience in using teachers as staff developers. *Journal of Staff Development, 8*(1), 16–20.

McFaul, S. A., & Cooper, J. M. (1984). Peer clinical supervision: Theory vs. reality. *Educational Leadership, 41*(7), 4–11.

Peters, T. J., & Waterman, R. A. (1982). *In search of excellence: Lessons from America's best companies.* New York: Harper & Row.

Rebore, W. (1991). *Personnel administration in education: A management approach* (3rd ed.). Englewood Cliffs, NJ: Prentice-Hall.

Roy, P. (1987, February). A consumer's guide to selecting staff development consultants. *The Developer,* 1–9.

Sage, D. D., & Burrello, L. C. (1986). *Policy and management in special education.* Englewood Cliffs, NJ: Prentice-Hall.

Sadowski, L. L. (1993). Staff development 101 for administrators: Alternatives for thirteen management myths. *Journal of Staff Development, 14*(3), 46–51.

Sparks, G. M., & Simmons, J. M. (1989). Inquiry-oriented staff development: Using research as a source of tools, not rules. In S. Caldwell (Ed.), *Staff development: A handbook of effective practices* (pp. 126–139). Oxford, OH: National Staff Development Council.

Williamson, L. S., & Russell, D. S. (1990). Peer coaching as a follow up to training. *Journal of Staff Development, 11*(2), 2–4.

Zadnick, D. (1992). Instructional supervision in special education: Integrating teacher effectiveness research into model supervisory practices. *Case Research Committee information packet*. Bloomington, IN: Indiana University.

SUGGESTED READINGS

Killion, J. P., & Lanzerotte, J. K. (1992). Is the grass greener on the other side? Discoveries about training in business and industry. *Journal of Staff Development, 13*(4), 6–10.

Kolenko, C. L., & Schrup, M. G. (1986). Inservice education: Staff development. *Case Research Committee information packet*. Bloomington, IN: Indiana University.

Merseth, K. K. (1992). First aid for first-year teachers. *Phi Delta Kappan, 26*(7), 678–683.

Chapter 7

COLLABORATIVE PRINCIPALS ARE THE KEY

Of the key variables associated with effective schools, educational leadership has been ranked No. 1 (Kirner, Vautour, & Vautour, 1993; McLaughlin & Kienas, 1989). Principals play a critical leadership role in implementing and managing all programs in their schools (Mirsky, 1988). The atmosphere encountered just by walking into a school is almost always a direct reflection of the school's principal. Building administrators shape instructional practice; as a matter of fact, the best predictor of a program's success is the principal's attitude toward it (Kirner et al., 1993). This is particularly true in the administration of special education programs. Principals' attitudes toward special education and the concern expressed for the needs of exceptional children influence the success of special programs (Burrello, Schrup, & Barnett, 1992; Leibfried, 1984).

Negative attitudes, role confusion, and lack of preparation hamper the administration of special education in school buildings. Principals may resent that students with disabilities require disproportionately large amounts of time and resources, and believe these students should be educated in other, more segregated environments. There may be confusion regarding the role of principals and the role of special education administration in the management of programs for exceptional children (Crossland, Fox, & Baker, 1982). In addition, principals often feel unprepared for the unique responsibilities of managing special education programs.

In response to concerns that principals need more training to lead special education programs, staff development models have emerged across the country (CASE, 1992; Kirner et al., 1993; Lindsey, 1986; McLaughlin & Kienas, 1989). Many of these staff development programs utilize tenets of adult learning, such as the need for locally determined training content, ongoing peer support, and feedback on attempted application of learning (Merriam & Caffarella, 1991). Some utilize a trainer-of-trainers model in which principals presented with new perspectives on special education leadership share what they've learned with other administrators (Lindsey, 1986). Each of these training programs has identified essential skills and requisite knowledge for building administrators to be successful in providing leadership for special education programs.

ESSENTIAL SKILLS AND REQUISITE KNOWLEDGE

Seven training issues have been identified by Kirner et al. (1993): (a) trends and historical perspectives of special education, (b) federal laws and state statutes,

(c) team building and coordination between general and special education, (d) communication and organizational structures that enhance cooperation, (e) leadership styles that facilitate change, (f) appropriate instructional learning environments for students with disabilities, and (g) integration into society and inclusion of students with disabilities in public schools. Burrello, Schrup, and Barnett (1992) delineate additional specific administrative skills which include monitoring special education procedures, scheduling, allocating resources, dealing with behavior management/suspension problems, developing staff inservice training, and providing physical accessibility. Other authors stress that principals must understand the impact a child with disabilities has on a family, learn to evaluate special education teachers, become knowledgeable about due process procedures, and learn how to develop teacher assistance teams (Abernathy & Stile, 1983; McInerney & Swenson, 1988; O'Reilly & Squires, 1985).

Principals who provide exceptional leadership for special needs students collaborate with educators and parents as coequal team members, establishing mutual goals and solving problems to design and support innovative programs that meet the unique needs of children. Building administrators who facilitate learning for all students in this manner can be called **collaborative principals.** Collaborative principals embrace a philosophy that values differences and models advocacy for individual rights and appropriate services. Such building leaders facilitate the development of a rapport between general and special educators. Collaborative principals advocate that special education is a vital component of the total system and gain support for the fact that equal opportunities for special education require unequal resources (Burrello et al., 1992).

The following case study explores the thoughts of a principal as he prepares for a change in which the education and accommodation of special education students will have a significant impact on the total school program.

Junior High to Middle School

Mary Beth Vautour

Project Coordinator, Training School Principals in Special Education Administration, Middletown, Conn.

Phil Johnson had worked long and hard to bring about change at Griswold Junior High School. Largely due to his leadership, today was the unveiling of the school's new name; from now on he would be principal of Griswold Middle School. Three intensive years of planning and staff development had gone into this effort. At first, some staff members were reluctant, but now they seemed to be excited about the concept of middle school education.

Though Phil should have been particularly pleased with this celebration, he was actually preoccupied with a memo that had just arrived on his desk from the district director of special education. A decision had been made to move toward inclusion of all special education students in their neighborhood schools. Phil and his staff would have to increase efforts to accommodate already enrolled special education students in the general classroom. Additionally, it meant the school could expect to receive 8 to 10 new students with fairly significant disabilities.

In anticipation of the impact of this new development, Phil jotted down these questions about a program that would integrate middle school organization, new school district initiatives, and concerns regarding inclusion:

1. There are already designated planning periods and common team meetings for teachers to create interdisciplinary units. How can a schedule be reconstructed to accommodate weekly meetings to discuss special education issues?
2. There are four special education teachers and six teams. What system or configuration would enhance the education of students with special needs?
3. Does the learning strategies/study skills course offered to all students fit the needs of special education students?
4. How can the physical education department be encouraged to include the recreational, noncompetitive athletic activities that best accommodate special needs students?
5. How will the guidance department provide appropriate services for special education students in a school that now espouses a student-adviser program using classroom teachers? Will the teachers be comfortable working with special education students in this capacity?
6. The board of education was promised a model that would guarantee success for all students through the use of such techniques as mastery learning, cooperative learning, individually guided experiences, and multisensory approaches. Now, with the move to inclusive programming, can we deliver?

CONSIDER THIS

1. Based on the type of questions Phil asked, what is his attitude toward special education?
2. How might the inclusive programming of special education students affect the implementation of the proposed model?
3. What should Phil's next step be?

CHARACTERISTICS OF SPECIAL LEADERS

In addition to developing the necessary competencies to manage special education programs, such as assigning resources and monitoring referral procedures, leaders of special education must demonstrate a set of distinctive characteristics

(Bank Street, 1982). These characteristics are attributes or distinguishing qualities, such as patience or charisma.

Principals who lead special education programs most effectively are empathetic, recognizing the impact of disabilities on individuals, their parents, and those who teach them (Bank Street, 1982). These administrators are often described as having integrity, honesty, adaptability, creativity, imagination, openness, self-awareness, and a sense of humor. Special education programs need collaborative principals who have a personal and professional commitment to students *and* teachers. Finally, they are agents of change, working for renewal for themselves and their organizations.

COMPETING INTERESTS

In the role of symbolic and cultural leaders, principals are the most visible, and ultimate, authority in the school. As such, principals interpret and implement district policy, assuming responsibility for the legal and ethical issues of the whole school program while maintaining an excellent and safe educational environment. It is often necessary for principals to advocate for a program or an individual in the face of the bureaucracy. However, principals represent many groups, some of which have competing interests; these leaders find they must maintain marginal roles, taking care not to align with any one interest group (Brennan & Brennan, 1988).

Sometimes events happen quickly and must be resolved without time for reflection. Therefore, collaborative principals have plans of action in place for difficult situations in which quick decisions must be made. For example, students identified as needing special services in another school district arrive in school without their IEPs, or students with IEPs break rules that would normally result in expulsion. The competing concerns of protecting the legal rights of exceptional students while maintaining a safe school are addressed in the following case study.

Dangerous Weapons
Mary Beth Vautour

Elm Grove Senior High is an inner-city school in Elksville, a community of 250,000; like most inner-city schools, it has its share of violence. Two months ago, gang warfare erupted, and there was a drive-by shooting in front of the school, killing an innocent freshman.

As a result of the violence, the board of education met to adopt stringent policies concerning the possession or use of weapons or other dangerous instruments on school property. To demonstrate their concern, the board decided that students found in possession of weapons or dangerous instruments would be expelled.

Jason is a student with learning disabilities at Elm Grove. He has had a difficult time fitting in with the other students over the last three years. Jason has on occasion demonstrated poor judgment by following some of the more rebellious students at the school. Despite these minor problems, staff and administrators view him as a well-meaning student.

One morning, Jason was in an auto mechanics class with Todd, Chris, and Ned. Todd was in possession of an M-80 firecracker. He displayed it in the presence of the teacher, Mr. Jeffers, and made some crack about detonating it in the back of the school lot after class. Mr. Jeffers told Todd to put the M-80 away and take it home. Todd, Chris, and Ned showed Jason the M-80 and challenged him to set if off in the ceiling of the boys bathroom. Todd explained how the M-80 could be set off by placing the fuse next to a lit cigarette so that no one would be near when it exploded. After considerable taunting, Jason took the dare and set the M-80 to explode in the boys lavatory. Luke entered the bathroom at the moment the M-80 exploded, and the blast threw him to the floor. When the assistant principal found Luke, he was sitting on the floor, dazed, with blood seeping out of his left ear.

Luke was rushed to the emergency room of the nearest hospital. It was determined he had an 85% loss of hearing in his left ear and a 75% loss in his right ear. Though it was too early to tell, the attending physician was concerned there would be some permanent loss.

An investigation quickly uncovered what had happened. By the close of the next day, the principal had discerned the roles that Jason, Todd, Chris, and Ned had played in the incident. Additionally, students volunteered that Mr. Jeffers had seen the explosive but had not confiscated it.

 CONSIDER THIS

1. How should the principal deal with Todd, Chris, and Ned?
2. Jason has an IEP for learning disabilities services. Do you think this behavior is related to his disability? If so, how should the matter be handled?
3. How should the principal address Mr. Jeffers' role in the incident?

Principals become involved in a variety of complex and competing issues. The following case study begins a dialogue proposing the right of high school students with disabilities to be educated alongside their age-appropriate peers, while considering the reality of teacher readiness and instructional relevance.

Parent Request for Inclusion

Mrs. Karr, the geometry teacher, was intrigued by the request for her to attend the IEP meeting for Jimmy Tolliver. She hadn't been involved in a planning session for a special education student before and wondered how it worked. Mr. Roth, the assistant principal generally responsible for special programs, was alerted by Ms. Marcino, the special education teacher, to be sure to attend Jimmy's IEP meeting because the parents had some new ideas for next year's program.

Jimmy, an 18-year-old student at Lincoln High School in central Massachusetts, has received special education services since he was 4. Over the years, Jimmy has consistently scored in the lower 50s on the WISC-R. Although he has a short attention span and limited language skills, he is cooperative and tries his best to please his teachers. His current school program includes a community-based, work-study program in the afternoon in which he is learning job skills at a commercial laundry.

The IEP meeting was attended by Jimmy, his parents, the special education teacher, the principal, the school psychologist, the work-study coordinator, and the geometry teacher. Jimmy's parents expressed how pleased they were with Jimmy's progress in general, and his success in the work-study program in particular. His teacher and work-study coordinator concurred. Jimmy's parents said they had been reading about inclusive programming and recently talked with a special education advocate who was surprised that Jimmy hadn't been more involved in general education classes. Ms. Marcino responded that it has seemed most appropriate for Jimmy to receive the majority of his instruction in the special education classroom, and all through school, he has been involved with PE and special activities as planned at the annual IEP meeting.

Jimmy's mother turned to him and asked whether he'd like to be in classes with students his age who aren't in special education. Jimmy said he'd like to make more friends. Turning to the principal, Mrs. Tolliver stressed the importance of students Jimmy's age being around peers who act like teen-agers and talk like teen-agers. Further, Mr. Tolliver said, he had heard what an excellent teacher Mrs. Karr is for math, and also emphasized how much Jimmy has always enjoyed shapes and geometric things. (Mrs. Karr began to be concerned where this conversation was headed.) As Mrs. Karr suspected, Mr. Tolliver proposed that Jimmy's schedule for the next school year include spending one period each day in a geometry class. The parent contended it would be good for Jimmy socially; besides, the advocate said, teachers can adapt the curriculum to be more functional.

Mrs. Karr began to reason with the parents that students taking geometry have all had algebra and many of them do not pass. Mr. Tolliver said he didn't expect for Jimmy to take the same tests as everyone else because he would be doing different things. "Like what?" Mrs. Karr asked. Ms. Marcino interceded and explained that if the IEP committee decided this was the best program for Jimmy, then that is what he would do, and Ms. Marcino would consult with Mrs. Karr in developing an adapted curriculum. (Ms. Marcino, however, began to sweat because she was not strong in math.) Mrs. Karr embarked on a barrage of questions: "You mean you can just place anyone in my class if you want? I don't know anything about special education students; how am I supposed to develop a program for him? Is someone going to help me with him in class? What is he supposed to learn? Who is responsible for his grade? Is he going to get geometry credit for this? What do I say to the other students who all have to learn the prescribed curriculum?" Mrs. Karr took a deep breath, turned to the assistant principal, and pleaded, "Say something."

 CONSIDER THIS

1. What should the assistant principal say at this point?
2. What are the competing issues?
3. Given the nature of content-driven high school courses, should parents advocate for more-inclusive programming for their adolescent children? Why or why not?
4. If the geometry teacher refuses to cooperate, what should the principal do?

ACTIVE INVOLVEMENT

Building administrators have so many responsibilities that they frequently delegate special education functions to designees (Mirsky, 1988) such as school psychologists or counselors. However, the research is clear that for special education programs to be successful, principals must be actively involved in special education programming, from preparing teachers to ensuring service excellence (O'Reilly & Squires, 1985; Mirsky, 1988; Salisbury & Smith, 1991). (See Table 7.1.)

Assessing the Environment

Successful principals assess the school climate and learning environment to identify strengths and weaknesses of the overall program. It is essential for principals to ensure the physical accessibility of classrooms and activity areas. Environmental factors such as teacher–student relationships and appropriate curriculum/instructional modification affect the achievement of students with difficulties (Fuchs, Fernstrom, Scott, Fuchs, & Vandemeer, 1994). Principals can promote staff awareness of how the environment affects students and then encourage the necessary modifications.

Reshaping Attitudes

Helping reshape beliefs and attitudes is the most important function collaborative principals can perform in preparing teachers to work with students who experience difficulty in learning (Hixson, 1993). There are three components to reshaping attitudes: (a) restructuring the knowledge base, (b) expanding professional exposure and experience, and (c) focusing on learning outcomes rather

TABLE 7.1
COLLABORATIVE PRINCIPAL'S RESPONSIBILITIES AS A LEADER OF SPECIAL EDUCATION

1. Assess the environment.
2. Reshape beliefs and attitudes.
3. Hire teachers who are open to collaborative teaming and inclusive programming.
4. Promote change and encourage innovative solutions to instructional challenges.
5. Encourage parent participation.
6. Establish teacher assistance teams.
7. Encourage interventions before or as an alternative to special education referrals.
8. Monitor assessment activities.
9. Participate in eligibility decisions.
10. Select general education teachers who provide exceptional students with an environment conducive to learning.
11. Plan for students who are not eligible.
12. Provide input for individualized education programs.
13. Support integration of students with disabilities into general education classes and activities.
14. Coordinate schedules and provide resources that facilitate the participation of students with disabilities in all school activities.
15. Include special education teachers on schoolwide and districtwide committees.

than instructional activities (Hixson, 1993). First, educators need to learn new knowledge in a safe environment. Teachers can reexamine their old beliefs in light of new facts. Second, educators must have the opportunity to experience other professionals who have applied the new knowledge. Teachers will learn best when they can see others positively engaged in innovative instruction. Third, teachers must learn to be researchers and reflective practitioners. For the last two decades, teacher training has focused on strategies and effective instruction. It is now time to assess whether these teaching practices have resulted in improved outcomes, focusing more on whether the child learns and less on how effective a particular activity promises to be.

Promoting change takes time and patience. Agents of change help people define what they want, develop plans, identify obstacles, solve problems, and implement ideas (Ellis, 1992).

Prereferral and Assessment Activities

Collaborative principals who promote educational excellence take an active role in the process in which teachers request help with students before referring them for special education evaluation (Mirsky, 1988). McInerney and Swenson (1988) advise principals to organize prereferral committees or teacher assistance teams (TAT) designed to support teachers and encourage interventions as an alternative to referral for special education. Unless principals advocate for alternatives to direct referral, prereferral activities become a perfunctory step in the inevitable path to evaluation for special education (Lombardi et al., 1990). Collaborative principals encourage TATs to generate appropriate interventions, document the results of implementing these strategies, and hold follow-up meetings to assess the effectiveness of the prescribed interventions. It is also recommended that principals check records and observe students when teachers express specific concerns (Mirsky, 1988).

If students are assessed by the multidisciplinary team for special education eligibility, collaborative principals are actively involved in providing support and monitoring the process (McInerney & Swenson, 1988). The building administrator's involvement gives legitimacy to the process. Such principals question the appropriateness of the tests used and challenge assumptions apparent in discussions. Additionally, involvement in the eligibility process allows the principal to learn about students who are not found eligible for special education services, thereby providing an opportunity to participate in generating appropriate alternative programming or strategies.

Language and Minority Issues

By the year 2000, one-third of school-age children will be African American, Hispanic, or Asian American (Shea & Bauer, 1994). Principals must be aware of the special challenges posed by students from these backgrounds concerning accurate identification of disabilities and appropriate educational programming. Behaviors considered to be acceptable within some neighborhoods are labeled dysfunctional or disabled in another environment. Principals must guard against the overidentification of students of color or children from low socioeconomic backgrounds by encouraging the use of nonbiased, functional assessments of students. The Council for Children with Behavior Disorders (CCBD) (1987) suggests that evaluations focus on learning models rather than medical models. Learning assessment models emphasize searching for effective strategies and modifications, recording all efforts toward remediation and accommodation, and fostering an ecological approach in which responsibility for learning is shared by the school, student, and family.

Students from nondominant culture families and neighborhoods present additional challenges concerning language. These students may use nonstandard English or may have limited English proficiency. There is a great deal of confusion over whether these students have lower abilities because they speak differently and are frequently confused during standard English instruction (Hunt & Marshall, 1994). Further, students with limited English proficiency and documented disabilities require special programming and well-trained teachers to meet their needs. Principals must be vigilant in ensuring fair assessment practices, encouraging cultural sensitivity, and developing appropriate programming for these growing populations.

Appropriate Referrals?

In response to citizen complaints regarding substandard facilities and inadequate resources in some of the poorer neighborhoods of Fairview City Schools, the school board reorganized the elementary program into K–3 and 4–6 buildings and began busing across town. As a result, teachers and principals who formerly worked with primarily Caucasian non-Hispanic, middle-class students confronted new challenges. During the first year in these schools, referrals for speech and other special education services tripled.

When the special education director saw the first wave of referrals from Woodward Elementary, she called the principal to arrange a conference. At that meeting, the director pointed to four referrals for speech based on dialect difficulties/language deficiencies, three for the reading problems of students who spoke limited English, and two for minority students' behavior problems. The director said, "I can only conclude your staff is unprepared for working with a diverse population of students, and you assume special education is responsible for addressing all students' problems."

The principal was stunned at first and then responded, "I don't know where to begin. The teachers are exasperated, demanding I do something about these 'new' students who are not prepared to learn. Because we have such faith in our special educators, we immediately turned to them for assistance." The special education director questioned, "Was it actually faith in our abilities or were you just used to our taking care of all students who didn't fit the mold?"

CONSIDER THIS

1. What issues must be confronted regarding dialect and speech referrals, limited English proficiency as it relates to learning difficulties, and referrals for behavior problems of minority students?
2. What is the role of special education in this setting?
3. How might the principal direct the school committee that considers teacher concerns about individual students before referral for special education evaluation?
4. What leadership does the staff need at this time?

Designing Programs

After the meeting to determine eligibility, the next time a principal can assert an influence is while attending the individualized education program (IEP) meeting (O'Reilly & Squires, 1985). First, collaborative principals ensure the IEP is tailored specifically for the individual and not pigeonholed according to whatever special classes are available in that school. Second, a significant component of the IEP is the statement describing the least restrictive environment for the student. Principals who advocate whole-student development actively support integration of identified students into general education classes. There are several ways to support the responsible integration of students with special needs: (a) provide time and funds for teachers to learn the necessary skills to teach special needs students, (b) facilitate teaming and collaborative teaching, (c) encourage innovative programs, (d) provide incentives for educators who actively include students with disabilities (Salisbury & Smith, 1991), and (e) carefully select mainstream teachers (Wong, Kauffman, & Lloyd, 1991). The compatibility between teacher attitude/skill and individual student characteristics is essential. The following case study explores an issue related to teacher selection.

Which Teacher?

Julia has received special education services since preschool for developmental delays. Beginning with kindergarten, her IEP outlined a program of a half day in the general education classroom and a half day of specialized instruction in speech and language, social skills, fine and gross motor skills, and preacademics. Similar individualized programs were written during the next 3 years with half-day participation in grades one, two, and three. Julia showed remarkable progress in speech and social skills, as well as demonstrating a good grasp of beginning academic skills.

At the end of Julia's third-grade year, her special education teacher, Mrs. Marcus, set a date for an IEP meeting with Julia's mother. Mrs. Marcus was proud of Julia's progress and anticipated discussing an increase in Julia's participation in the general education classroom for the next year. After school that day, Mrs. Marcus went to talk with Mr. Nanos, the fourth-grade teacher who has worked best with special students. She found him in his room with the usual creative chaos of setting up a new learning center and putting the best of the day's work on the "I'm proud" bulletin board.

Mrs. Marcus greeted him and explained she was trying to set up a program for Julia for next year. Before she could even finish, Mr. Nanos whirled around to confront her, saying rather emphatically to "Ask Mai" (Ms. Mai Kim, the other fourth-grade teacher). He was already aware of six special students to be included in his classroom, one of whom was the infamous Carlos, an aggressive boy with serious behavior problems. As far as he knew, Mai had no special students this year, and no one had asked her about working with any next year.

Mrs. Marcus was shocked by this response. She and Mr. Nanos had a good working relationship. Mrs. Marcus sat down and apologized; she hadn't realized how next year was stacking up. But, she argued, Mai Kim had really high expectations; she was great with most kids but didn't work well with students who had low ability. It just wasn't a good match for Julia. Mr. Nanos apologized for his abrupt response but stood his ground. "Is it fair to me and the students in my class that we have all the special students because I'm good with them, and no one asks Mai because she won't cooperate?" he asked.

CONSIDER THIS

1. What are the issues involved in selecting general classroom teachers for including students with special needs?
2. Should students be placed with a teacher who is unwilling or unprepared to deal with special populations?
3. What compensation/arrangements could a principal propose if it is determined that one teacher's classroom is a more appropriate placement for most students with disabilities?
4. What is the principal's role in this dilemma regarding staff supervision, teacher equity, and advocacy for inclusive programming?

Representing Special Education

Once principals develop sensitivity to the impact of exceptionalities and the commitment to serving special needs students, there is a variety of additional ways building leaders can facilitate a superior education for all. When interviewing applicants for general education positions, collaborative principals seek to hire individuals who are prepared to teach children with special needs. Building administrators should also be involved with interviewing special education candidates, asking whether these individuals are prepared to work collaboratively with general educators.

Marino (1984) explains other ways principals can ensure that the interests of special students are represented. They can appoint special education teachers to all building- and district-level teams. Building administrators can optimize conditions by coordinating nonacademic services with the special student in mind, such as bus schedules that accommodate the whole school day. Principals also assign space in schools, remaining cognizant of the needs of special students. Additionally, as in the following case study, they must determine the involvement of special students in schoolwide and districtwide achievement testing.

Reporting Special Scores
Mary Beth Vautour

Many states nationwide administer mastery tests to students at regular intervals, such as grades 4, 6, 8, and 10. These tests evaluate students' progress toward specific competencies and determine whether instructional programs are preparing students adequately. Under one state's policy, all students are expected to take the test, with two exceptions. Students in bilingual programs who have been enrolled for less than two years are exempt, and some special education students are exempted by the decision of the child study team, as indicated by documentation on their individualized education programs (IEP).

In that state, a recent memorandum has come from the commissioner of education's office expressing concern over the high percentage of special education exemptions noted on the mastery tests, particularly in the more affluent districts. It seems that local superintendents concerned over poor scores actively seek to exclude from testing potentially low-scoring special education students.

At Moser Middle School, an eighth-grade student, Susan, has received special education assistance in an LD resource room for 5 years. Even though Susan is not performing completely at grade level, her resource teacher thinks she is ready for gradual dismissal from the program. As a measure of success, Mrs. Libby, the resource teacher, requested that Susan's IEP be modified to allow her to take the state mastery test.

The building principal is aware that the superintendent has expressed concern over low eighth-grade mastery test scores. As a matter of fact, the effectiveness of the middle school academic program will be measured in part by the overall performance of students on this test.

 ## CONSIDER THIS

1. What realistic and ethical pressures confront this principal concerning who takes the state mastery test?
2. How should the principal respond to Mrs. Libby's plan to include Susan in the state mastery test?
3. What policy should be developed concerning the inclusion/exemption of students with disabilities in taking standardized group tests?

Leadership Can Transform a School

Christensen (1991) described the 10 leadership behaviors of effective principals as: (a) ask the right questions, (b) clarify the mission, (c) build consensus, (d) articulate visions, (e) focus the organization, (f) think strategically, (g) live the question, (h) empower the process and the people, (i) get things moving, and (j) feel comfortable with innovations and ambiguity. The following case study depicts an elementary school with an exceptional building leader. While reading the study, decide whether the principal of Clearview Elementary School displays Christensen's 10 leadership behaviors.

Success for Every Learner

Sandy Darling
Principal of Clearview Elementary School, Clear Lake, Minn.

Clearview Elementary School, surrounded by cornfields and pumpkin patches and bordering a national forest, serves 600 students from several rural Minnesota communities. Over the door of the school, a colorful banner declares "Success for Every Learner." Inside, classroom walls have been removed and most desks are gone. Children work primarily at tables in multiage groups, and there are two or more adults in every area. All classes have computers, and additional technology is available on carts for specific units (thanks to a school-community partnership with IBM). The media center is an extension of the classrooms, buzzing with research and activities.

All teachers are assigned to multigrade teams, including special education and Chapter I teachers and teachers aides. This also means that students with special needs are assigned to a team rather than to a special education or remedial teacher. Because the staff at Clearview believes *all* students have unique learning needs, each student has a personalized learning plan developed by teachers and the child's parents. The plan outlines the student's needs and consequent goals for the year. Periodically, teachers check personalized learning plans for mastery of skills and set new goals with the parents. If students have not achieved their goals, teams seek creative ways to help, giving them "another turn to learn."

Parents truly are partners in this school. All task forces, including the leadership team, consist of teachers *and* parents. When listening to participants of these meetings, it is often difficult to distinguish professional educators from parents.

Was Clearview Elementary School always this picture of collaborative learning and collegiality? No. From 1987 to 1991, it had four principals. During the fourth year, dissatisfied teachers sent the school board a long list of complaints. In response, central office administrators searched for an individual with an exceptional understanding of leadership, someone to help the staff work together. In 1991, Dr. Sandy Darling was hired as principal.

Before the new school year began, Dr. Darling met with the teachers and asked whether they would be willing to develop a new concept for serving all the children of the community. It would take hard work and mean letting go of old beliefs. The teachers weren't sure what they might be getting into, but, hoping for a positive change, they agreed.

The new principal wrote a successful state grant to become a pilot site for outcome-based education. The goals of the grant were to develop computerized personalized learning plans for all students and to implement multiple instructional strategies that would expand opportunities for students to learn, such as flexible grouping, nonlabeling, cooperative learning, and parent involvement. The grant asked for money to provide teacher release time and resources for training.

During the first year, Dr. Darling organized inservice training for teachers and parents to develop interpersonal and group process skills as well as to gain the knowledge necessary to reconceptualize education. The principal emphasized that people and communication skills were the essential elements in successful change and effective teamwork. The staff and parents had to learn to appreciate differences, understand how to work with various styles of communication, resolve conflicts, and develop leadership skills. Inservice programs also addressed outcome-based education, integrated curriculum, developmentally appropriate instruction, and inclusive programming.

At the end of the year, the entire staff and a group of actively involved parents attended a three-day retreat to develop a five-year plan. They explored beliefs, articulated a mission, and outlined a plan. Because the staff and parents felt they owned the mission and plan, they were excited about the new concepts. When school board members questioned the plan, the parents said, in no uncertain terms, that this program was what they wanted, and it received approval.

Hurriedly that summer, staff and parents met to develop specific plans for year-one implementation, and Dr. Darling scurried to get the technology ready for the personalized learning plans. The principal was aware that staff and parents would need time to meet regularly throughout the year to plan and resolve problems. She proposed a new schedule using "banked time," in which extra time was added to each school day so that for one day each month, students had a day off and staff and parents had a workday. In addition, the schedule included daily common planning periods for groups of four to five teachers. Instead of weekly faculty meetings, a daily bulletin communicated information that would have been given out at those meetings. Then, during the time normally spent in faculty meetings, multigrade teams, mixed teams, and the leadership team collaborated on current and future issues.

Clearview had to apply for a waiver from the state to utilize special personnel in a nontraditional way. The school received the designated complement of special education and Chapter I teachers for the number of identified students. At that point, it became the goal of the staff and parents to provide for the individual needs of all learners without labeling children. The state department of education and the school district have agreed to continue funding the same number of special education teachers even though it appears Clearview has fewer identified special students each year.

The leadership provided by Dr. Darling has been the pivotal element in the successful restructuring effort. She said, "I perceive myself as a change agent and a member of the team. It isn't *my* program, it's *our* program. If I left today, there's a blueprint the rest of the staff can follow. I help staff stretch as far as they can. I say, 'Tell me where you want to go, and I'll help you get there.'

"When we embarked on the new adventure, we experienced a lot of fear. It was like the feeling of being between the trapezes. You have to let go of one to get to the other, but then you are in midair with none of the security of what you had and not quite anything else to grab on to, either. The special education teachers experienced a sense of loss when their role changed, and they didn't know what they were supposed to do. The general education teachers felt an increase of responsibility without the necessary training. Inclusion and teaming were so new, teachers found they didn't know enough about what to expect to plan ahead more than one day. They spent time rethinking their role as teachers and reevaluating traditional teaching strategies. More than once, I think my staff wanted to tie rocks to my feet and throw me in the lake.

"It's not always comfortable; we are different. Teachers at other schools heard that sometimes our staff members spend hours after school working on new challenges and expressed concern that I require my staff to work inordinately long hours, evenings and weekends included. But, *I* didn't ask them to stay. They met on their own because it was their program, not mine, and they wanted it to work!"

At the end of the first year, the Clearview staff and the faculty from a local university evaluated the new program, reviewing the strategic plan, conducting structured interviews with teachers, parents, and students, and administering the Woodcock-Johnson Psycho-Educational Battery to selected students. "The results were favorable and we felt good about what we are doing," Dr. Darling said. "Let me give you another measure of success. At the end of last year, our teachers heard we would be teaching a student with autism this year. In response, they asked for books and articles about educating these students to assist in preparing an individualized program.

"Change is cultural transformation. You have to confront old beliefs to change them. For example, an old belief is students with disabilities are better off in specialized settings taught by specialists. But, special education and remedial teachers aren't the only ones who can instruct exceptional children successfully. Our staff now believes that all kids belong, and we celebrate our differences."

 CONSIDER THIS

1. Sergiovanni (1987) says that principals should articulate a mission and communicate values, then allow staffwide discretion in how those values are to be manifested. In your opinion, did Dr. Darling follow this prescription?
2. Which of the 10 leadership behaviors proposed by Christensen did this principal use?
3. What are the potential benefits/problems with using special educators in nontraditional ways?
4. What assumptions and principles of change are evident here?

SUMMARY

Collaborative principals are the key to success for special education. Because of the significance of the building administrator's role in leading special programs, many states and organizations have developed principal-training programs. These staff development programs stress that principals need to understand the impact of disabilities on individuals, their parents, and their teachers. Principals must also be aware of special education laws, regulations, and procedures. When building administrators model positive attitudes toward individuals with disabilities and the integration of exceptional students into general classroom environments, students with special needs are more likely to succeed. In the role of leaders, collaborative principals promote change, facilitate planning and implementation, and ensure program excellence. Their involvement in prereferral, referral, assessment, and individualized programming is essential for the success of special education. Collaborative principals also provide the leadership necessary to restructure schools so that general, special, and remedial teachers, as well as parents, work in cooperative teams and collegial environments to serve all students better.

REFERENCES

Abernathy, S. M., & Stile, S. W. (1983). *Special education needs of regular education administrators.* Paper presentation at the annual meeting of the Rocky Mountain Educational Research Association, Tucson, AZ, November. (ERIC Document Reproduction Service No. ED 238 177)

Bank Street College of Education (1982). *The school principal and special education: Basic functions for principals who have special education programs in their schools with competencies needed to perform the role.* Guide produced by the Office of Special Education and Rehabilitative Services. (ERIC Document Reproduction Service No. ED 228 781)

Brennan, A. D. H., & Brennan, R. J. (1988). The principal, ethics, and special education decisions. *NASSP Bulletin, 72*(512), 16–19.

Burrello, L. C., Schrup, M. G., & Barnett, B. G. (1992). *The principal as the special education leader.* Bloomington, IN: University of Indiana, Department of Educational Leadership and Policy Studies.

CASE Research Committee and National Academy of the Principalship (1992). *Collaborative leadership development: Instructors packet.* Bloomington, IN: University of Indiana, Department of Educational Leadership and Policy Studies.

Christensen, D. (1991). What is the role of leadership in school restructuring? *Kansas Education, 6*(2), 4–5.

Crossland, C. L., Fox, B. J., & Baker, R. (1982). Differential perceptions of role responsibilities among professionals in public schools. *Exceptional Children, 48,* 535–538.

Council for Children with Behavior Disorders. (1987). Position paper on definition and identification of students with behavior disorders. *Behavioral Disorders, 12*(1), 9–19.

Ellis, S. S. (1992). Principals as staff developers: Systematic change in an elementary school. *Journal of Staff Development, 13*(4), 54–56.

Fuchs, D., Fernstrom, P., Scott, S., Fuchs, L., & Vandemeer, L. (1994). A process for mainstreaming: Classroom ecological inventory. *Teaching Exceptional Children, 25*(3), 11–15.

Hixson, J. (1993). Staff development and the urban school: Attitudes, beliefs, and student success. *Journal of Staff Development, 14*(2), 48–50.

Hunt, N., & Marshall, K. (1994). *Exceptional children and youth.* Boston: Houghton Mifflin.

Kirner, M., Vautour, J. A. C., & Vautour, M. B. (1993, April). *Enhancing instructional programs within the schools: Training school principals in special education administration.* Paper presentation at the international conference of Learning Disabilities Association, San Francisco, CA.

Lindsey, B. (1986, November). *PRIDE: Principals, resources, information, and direction for excellence in special education.* Paper presented at the annual meeting of the National Council of States Inservice Education, Nashville, TN. (ERIC Document Reproduction Service No. ED 277 123)

Lombardi, T. P. et al. (1990). *Special education and students at risk: Findings from a national study.* Paper presented at the annual conference of The Council for Exceptional Children, Toronto, Canada, April 23–27. (ERIC Document Reproduction Service No. ED 320 311)

Marino, R. P. (1984). *Secondary public school principals' self-ratings of their competency to administer special education programs.* Master's thesis, Slippery Rock University, Slippery Rock, PA. (ERIC Document Reproduction Service No. ED 246 588)

McInerney, W., & Swenson, S. (1988). The principal's role in the multi-disciplinary assessment team. *NASSP Bulletin, 72*(512), 88–94.

McLaughlin, M. J., & Kienas, K. (1989). The administrators' roundtable: A model for increasing the leadership of elementary school principals in special education. *International Journal of Disability, Development, and Education, 36*(2), 107–16.

Merriam, S. B., & Caffarella, R. S. (1991). *Learning in adulthood.* San Francisco: Jossey-Bass.

Mirsky, P. S. (1988). *The implementation of consultation strategies to improve communication between special educators and teachers, principals, and parents at the elementary level.* Practicum, Nova University, Fort Lauderdale, FL. (ERIC Document Reproduction Service No. ED 294 669)

O'Reilly, R. C., & Squires, S. K. (1985). *Special education in-service for metro area school administrators.* Nebraska University, Omaha. (ERIC Document Reproduction Service No. ED 288 311)

Salisbury, C., & Smith, B. J. (1991). The least restrictive environment: Understanding the options. *Principal, 71*(1), 24–25, 27.

Shea, T. M., & Bauer, A. M. (1994). *Learners with disabilities: A social system approach.* Madison, WI: Brown & Benchmark.

Wong, K. L. H., Kauffman, J. M., & Lloyd, J. W. (1991). Choices for integration: Selecting teachers for mainstreamed students with emotional or behavioral disorders. *Intervention in School and Clinic, 27,* 108–115.

SUGGESTED READINGS

Leibfried, M. (1984). Improving one's attitude toward special education programs: The principal's role is instrumental. *NASSP Bulletin, 68*(475), 110–13.

Sergiovanni, T. V. (1987). The theoretical basis for cultural leadership. In *Leadership: Examining the Elusive,* L. T. Sheive & M. B. Schoenheit (Eds.). Washington, DC: Association for Supervision and Curriculum Development.

Chapter 8

PARENTS AS PARTNERS, ADVOCATES, AND ADVERSARIES

The nature of the relationship between parents and education professionals has undergone substantial change in recent years. Parents have joined the system as partners and policy-makers (Vosler-Hunter & Hanson, 1992) and have challenged the system as advocates and adversaries (Dobbs, Primm, & Primm, 1991). There is a growing awareness that involved parents can powerfully affect the outcome of their children's education. School districts across the country are directing efforts toward the goal of building and maintaining relationships within their school communities that foster openness, honesty, and cooperation between parents and school personnel (Lewis, Marine, & Van Horn, 1991).

Before the enactment of Public Law 94-142, educators typically made the important decisions concerning identification, placement, and program evaluation, and parents trusted their expertise. But this special education law enfranchised parents to become active participants in making decisions regarding their children's special education programming. In addition, special education laws include provisions for dispute resolution and due process procedures if there is a disagreement between parents and school personnel (Garfunkel, 1986).

The fiscal, personnel, curricular, and disciplinary management of schools has been the responsibility of professional educators. Any change in the direction of parent control will naturally meet resistance from those in power. Many parents of children with exceptional needs also may resist parent-school partnerships because of competing personal needs, lack of awareness, or inadequate skills to participate effectively in educational decision-making. If parent partnerships are to be successful, both school personnel and parents must be willing to grow.

PARTNERS AND POLICY-MAKERS

School personnel initiate the partnership process by accepting parents as partners and encouraging them to be active participants in their children's education. Too often parents are seen as the source of the problem or merely paper-signers (Turnbull & Turnbull, 1986). Instead, educators can recognize their students as interdependent parts of larger systems, including families and communities (Winton, 1986). Working on only one part of a system is not as effective as approaching change from many directions. To facilitate progress, educators working with students will also seek to understand and influence the other major contributors in the children's social systems. This calls for educators gaining awareness of social context such as cultural norms, socioeconomic status, family structures, and support systems.

No one design or single method of communication will always be successful with all parents. Most schools making strides in parent involvement began by working to understand how, when, and why parents were hard to reach. Then systems were modified to accommodate the qualities, characteristics, and needs of these families (D'Angelo & Adler, 1991).

Parents also must prepare for the multifaceted role of active participant in their children's education (Vosler-Hunter & Hanson, 1992). First, parents should gain an understanding of their rights. They will require encouragement to feel like respected partners in the education of their children. Second, parents need to learn about the opportunities for active involvement beyond meetings, conferences with teachers, and home support of their children. For example, a significant way for parents to become involved is as members of advisory boards.

Parents who choose to become advisory board members need to learn a few basic skills and attitudes. They need to understand the importance of regular attendance, because presence can be power. They also need patience, tenacity, a sense of humor, resiliency (expect some rejection), optimism, assertiveness, and a willingness to set realistic expectations and compromise when appropriate (Vosler-Hunter & Hanson, 1992).

In addition to being partners, parents can be policy-makers. Those who choose this activity need more sophisticated skills. They learn to trust their expertise as parents, gain support from other parents, become willing to take risks, and maintain objectivity. Effective parent policy-makers must become good public speakers and learn group process skills, such as rules of order, to achieve their objectives (Vosler-Hunter & Hanson, 1992).

There is growing evidence that taking extra care in fashioning and maintaining channels of communication between schools and families has many dividends. Educators can learn from the wisdom of parents who have lived with exceptional children. Students benefit from consistency of goals at home and school. Parents learn skills for behavior management and academic support.

A variety of programs has evolved in schools nationwide to encourage parent participation. When developing a parent participation program, five guidelines or "effectiveness indicators" should be considered (Lewis, Marine, & Van Horn, 1991): (a) The program promotes effective two-way communication and collaboration between parents and teachers, (b) It teaches methods for parents to actively support their children's learning in partnership with the school staff, (c) Educational staff provides ongoing support for parents, (d) Parents are involved in program improvement efforts, and (e) Ongoing parent training programs are offered.

SEVEN PARENT INVOLVEMENT PROGRAMS

Seven successful parent involvement programs will be presented. Some are designed to meet a few specific needs, while others attempt to address a multitude of concerns. Each should be evaluated to determine whether it meets the designated needs and fosters increased parent participation in the education of their children.

Parent Involvement Programs for Migrant Families

Children of migrant families may be among the most vulnerable of our nation's at-risk students (Salend, 1990). Their life-style is characterized by high mobility, poor housing, limited health care, and irregular school attendance. Further, these families often have limited English proficiency and a history of school failure. In spite of these barriers, schools are learning how to educate students from migrant families. An integral part of this education is parent involvement.

Federal money is available to fund migrant education programs. This funding requires the establishment of parent advisory committees to involve these parents in determining the educational needs of their children. These advisory committees contribute to the development of programs, evaluate program effectiveness, and suggest revisions to improve educational services to migrant students.

The barriers to parent participation include long working hours, child care needs, and language and cultural differences. For example, parents may want to be involved in the education of their children, but they cannot leave younger siblings in order to attend meetings. And, their cultural beliefs dictate that school authorities know best.

Successful parent involvement in a migrant education program will include realistic accommodations, multifaceted attempts at communication, and programs tailored to the real needs of these families. Realistic accommodations consist of providing child care and transportation to meetings. An awareness of harvesting schedules permits teachers to schedule meetings at times when parents are more likely to attend. Conferences can be held and materials can be distributed at the local community center.

To accommodate the complications of communicating with migrant families, some schools have established a migrant education center where parents can receive information from multilingual staff and through printed materials in several languages. If a center cannot be established, an individual may be hired to coordinate efforts for educating migrant children. These coordinators visit the community and work within the framework of this life-style. Successful programs also enlist the support of key figures in the migrant community such as crew chiefs or religious leaders. Other times, programs recruit bilingual peers who are more familiar with the education process.

The migrant population has unique needs. Educators working with these families must strive to understand how cultural and linguistic differences, as well as working conditions, affect attitudes and communication. Professionals may also want to develop materials that help these parents learn ways to interact with their children that promote school success. Parent information or training might address stimulation for children, effective discipline, child development, and enhancement of self-esteem. Schools may also cooperate with social services and community agencies to develop adult education programs for learning to speak English and obtaining a high school equivalency diploma or job training. Additionally, migrant parents can be taught to facilitate the school process by keeping accurate records of school and medical information.

Shifting the Balance of Power for African-American Parents

Our nation's teaching force continues to be almost 90% Caucasian from Eurocentric backgrounds, while the demographics of classrooms have changed dramatically and are now composed of large populations of minority students, including African Americans (Obiakor, 1995). It is clear that partnerships with parents of special education students are essential to the children's success; unfortunately, the majority of teachers are not typically well-prepared to create the necessary partnerships with African-American parents. Eurocentric teachers often harbor assumptions that disempower these parents, including: African-American parents are apathetic, they are the source of problems, and individuals from minority groups are inferior. Teachers with these assumptions believe only educators have wisdom and motivation, while parents do not have this wisdom or are not interested in making important contributions to their children's education. Therefore, these educators seek to reserve the power to make instructional decisions (Harry, 1992).

For African-American parents to become an integral part of their children's education, teachers must be willing to shift the current balance of power and offer new roles to parents. First, parents should become **members of the assessment team** from the beginning. By the time most minority parents are invited to be part of the identification process, critical decisions have been made and the power of the school has been established. Instead, beginning with the first concern, teachers, speech pathologists, and psychologists can seek the input of parents as experts on their children and the culture in which they are growing up. Parents may help explain history, language, behavior, and beliefs and how these affect their children. In this role, parents are **presenters of reports.** When these reports are entered into the records, the role of the parents is legitimized.

To increase participation of African-American parents in meetings, schedules and personal needs must be accommodated. Successful programs schedule conferences during evening hours as well as provide transportation and child care.

It is essential for schools to recruit African-American parents as **policymakers.** School-based advisory teams should include parents who represent all groups proportionately. Administrators can form advisory teams and support parents to feel a part of the process while assisting educators to share power. The parent groups can advise administrators and teachers concerning the needs of special students and their families. In addition, these advisory groups can initiate activities as **parent-to-parent supporters.** Research indicates that two reasons for low participation of African-American parents are feelings of alienation and low awareness of rights and procedures. As advisers and advocates, African-American parents may invite other parents to participate and provide basic information on legal rights and due process procedures. The goal of all efforts toward greater parent partnership with African-American parents is to enlist them as integral, competent members of their children's educational team.

Disability Awareness Program Run by Parents

Although the legal and organizational barriers to education in the mainstream had been eliminated, several Minnesota parents were concerned that their children with disabilities still had one more obstacle to success in the mainstream: the negative attitudes of general education classmates (Binkard, 1985). These parents belonged to an advocacy organization called PACER, whose philosophy was that parents of children with disabilities could be trained to make positive contributions to their children's education. PACER parents reasoned that the way to change negative attitudes was to present information regarding disabilities to general education students, and to encourage teachers to explore with their classes information and attitudes concerning the integration of students with disabilities. A group of PACER parents developed "Count Me In" (CMI), a disabilities awareness program to be presented in schools by the parents of children with disabilities. PACER decided that puppets offered a medium that would capture students' interest. Children with cerebral palsy and mental retardation were typically depicted by the commercially produced puppets. Puppets also represented peers without disabilities who asked questions and interacted with the other characters. As the program grew and requests for the use of the puppets increased, CMI participants began making their own puppets.

PACER parents developed scripts of realistic but lively dialogue encompassing family situations, emotions, and sports activities. At first, the program was aimed at preschool and grade school students, then scripts were developed for secondary school students. Presentations vary from 45 minutes for younger children to an hour for high school students; each disability is the subject of a 7- to 10-minute script.

The CMI staff applied for and received funding to train additional volunteers who could present programs in communities across the state. A network developed throughout Minnesota that has provided programs to more than 50,000 students. During the third year, the CMI staff attracted new audiences of recreational, mental health, and medical professionals as well as members of the business community.

Teachers responding to follow-up evaluations strongly agreed that students have gained knowledge about disabilities and developed more positive attitudes about individual differences. Teachers have also responded that, as a result of the program and suggestions for further activities, all classes have participated in discussions, read books, and/or watched films concerning individuals with disabilities. In addition, teachers have said that CMI and its follow-up activities have truly facilitated the inclusion of students with disabilities into their classroom because mainstream peers have become more socially and emotionally receptive.

Together We Can Make a Difference

McAllen, Texas, has a commitment to parent involvement. Over the past seven years, it has developed a model parent participation program with the philosophy, "All children can learn, and together we can make a difference." The parent involvement staff has grown from one coordinator for the Chapter I program to a districtwide effort, employing five parent coordinators and several federally funded community aides. This clearly demonstrates that parent participation is an integral part of the operation of the entire school district (D'Angelo & Adler, 1991).

Each building hires a facilitator to assist with instructional leadership, freeing the principal to spend more time with parents and parent activities. In addition, each school has at least one community partner who provides resources to support school programs; more than 200 businesses contribute to the district in this way.

Five options exist for parents to become participants in their children's education: (a) learning through parent education programs, (b) facilitating school/home and home/school communication, (c) volunteering for school projects, (d) helping their children at home, and (e) participating in the Parent-Teacher Organization (PTO). To accommodate the large Hispanic and migrant population, parent coordinators and assistants are either bilingual or are making efforts to become bilingual. Handbooks are printed in both English and Spanish.

Each principal is responsible for the design and direction of his/her parent involvement program. Innovative activities include: (a) a PTO that trains parents and other volunteers to run programs that build self-esteem, (b) several schools that have set aside space for parents and volunteers to meet, (c) schools that provide child care and, in some cases, transportation for evening meetings, (d) parent liaisons who visit families new to the community, (e) teachers at the junior high who have two planning periods a day so that they can meet with or visit parents, and (f) in some schools, principals who teach classes while teachers conduct home visits.

Parent Communication Network

Administrators of South Bend Community Schools, in Indiana, wanted to develop a genuine communication process among parents, teachers, and administrators. In 1982, they began to establish a parent network within the district that would (a) provide an avenue for genuine communication between home and school, (b) identify the needs and concerns of parents concerning their child's education, (c) generate positive public support for the schools, and (d) identify community resources for both home and school (Lewis, Marine, & Van Horn, 1991).

The Parent Communication Network began at the school level and then added two districtwide levels. Each school publicized meeting dates. There were to be at least four meetings a year. Summaries of the discussions and decisions were published in school newspapers.

After each school had established a local committee, a district-level committee was formed. It included one representative from each elementary school, two from each secondary school, and the principals of each school. Summaries of each meeting were sent to the local schools. In addition, a third committee consisting of parent representatives from each school and district-level administrators was formed, with the superintendent acting as meeting chair. This group was to provide parents with access to the superintendent to discuss community and districtwide concerns.

Parents, teachers, and administrators have expressed appreciation for the opportunity to hold ongoing dialogue. Maintaining formal and informal communication between home and community has ensured a better understanding of the goals parents and educators have for their students. Based on this understanding, parents and educators can support each other in reaching optimal outcomes for children and youth.

Panel for Parents

Educators in West Lyon Community School District (Inwood, Iowa) expressed concern that multidisciplinary team meetings were often overwhelming experiences for parents. Each meeting seemed to be a race against time;

parents did not have the opportunity to ask important questions or talk meaningfully with teachers. In response, resource room teachers and support staff developed a program that would supply information and emotional support to parents, include parents in the resource room program by fostering their understanding of their children's needs, and provide a means for parents to share their knowledge and concerns with the school and other parents (Hallenbeck & Beernink, 1989).

At the beginning of the first school year, parents were invited to a dinner, panel discussion, and question/answer session. The panel included a professor from the university, parents of children with learning disabilities, and a college student who formerly had been enrolled in the resource room program. Rather than giving a formal presentation, panelists talked about their personal experiences.

For the question/answer session, participants were assigned to small groups led by parents and graduates. Group leaders met an hour before the dinner to receive lists of suggested discussion topics and review guidelines for leading a group.

The question-and-answer session proved so helpful that parents recommended the following year that students in grades 6–12 be included in small-group discussions after the panel presentation. In subsequent years, general education students and their teachers, as well as administrators and school board members, were invited.

Attendance was more than 80%. Evidently, many needs were met by these dinner sessions. The high rate of attendance may also be attributed to sending registration forms three weeks before the meeting and making follow-up phone calls for nonreturned forms.

In addition to the dinner at the beginning of the year, two or three less elaborate meetings were scheduled each school year. The other gatherings included guest speakers, videos of special education topics, transition meetings for juniors and seniors, and a panel of parents discussing current issues.

Feedback from parents, students, teachers, and administrators has been exceptionally positive. The reputation of these meetings has spread to surrounding school districts, which have begun to implement similar programs.

Attribution Training for Parents

Attribution theory states that people who do not believe they have the ability to influence outcomes are more likely to avoid cognitive challenges than individuals who feel their effort affects their lives. Children acquire these beliefs from failure experiences in combination with feedback from parents and teachers regarding their abilities, as well as from watching significant adults model confidence or helplessness. Research indicates that mothers of students with learning disabilities tend to attribute their child's successes more to luck than ability, whereas they attribute failures more to lack of ability than luck (Dohrn, Bryan, & Bryan, 1993).

Based upon these findings, a private day school for students with learning disabilities offered parents the opportunity to participate in a weekly training program to learn attribution feedback to enhance their children's self-esteem. Each weekly session consisted of three parts: a short training lesson, time to practice new skills with their children, and a feedback/discussion session. The program taught the parents to respond to children's successes with statements concerning ability and effort such as, "You're getting really smart at subtracting because you're working hard." In contrast, the parents were taught to respond to failure with a suggestion for the use of another strategy. For example, when a child was unsuccessful, the parent might say, "This problem is hard; try to say aloud the steps you need to do to solve it." In addition, parents were given a family math activities program and trained in how to use each activity.

After each short training session, mothers worked with their children doing math activities for 20 minutes with the goal of applying their newly learned attribution/strategy feedback skills. Immediately after the mother-child work sessions, trainers offered feedback, and mothers had the opportunity to discuss their progress.

This program demonstrated that parents can be taught to assist their children with academic tasks, but more important, parents can learn to give feedback that enhances their children's self-esteem. As a result of this program, children of attribution-trained mothers were more likely to attribute their success to ability and their failure to lack of effort, which has the effect of building self-confidence over time. In addition, parents' attitudes toward their children became more positive.

 CONSIDER THIS

1. Evaluate each of the seven parent involvement programs according to the five "effectiveness indicators" of Lewis, Marine, and Van Horn.
2. What are the apparent strengths and weaknesses of each program?
3. How might one or more of these programs be adapted to your school setting?

PARENTS AS ADVERSARIES

In addition to the contributions parents can offer during the educational decision-making process, involving parents can assuage the anger they may harbor toward a system that does not seem to serve their children. This involvement may shift the anger to a more productive focus, that is, determining what needs to change so that the best possible education will be provided for their children (Vosler-Hunter & Hanson, 1992). Fisher and Ury state, "The feeling of participation is perhaps the single most important factor in determining whether . . . a proposal (is accepted). In a sense, the process is the product" (1981, p. 29).

Anger and Conflict

Even in the best of circumstances, special education leaders will inevitably deal with angry parents. To deal effectively with parents in this situation, it is important to understand anger and conflict. Anger can be conceptualized as an intense, hostile emotional response to conflict, which is directed toward someone or something (Margolis & Brannigan, 1990). Conflict involves differences of opinion, but disagreement does not necessarily result in conflict; how disagreement is handled induces either anger or mutual understanding. Conflict begins when individuals become aware that someone has threatened or is about to threaten an interest of theirs. It involves personal perception and subjective constructions of reality, especially when it appears that threats are for selfish or malevolent reasons (Margolis, Shapiro, & Brown, 1987).

Anger may be directed at individuals who are not responsible for the situation. As a matter of fact, anger is frequently aimed at someone who helps most, because people feel safe expressing feelings with that person (Margolis et al., 1987).

Because anger is blinding, people generally lose sight of the total situation. Anger often interferes with getting personal needs met constructively because it is infectious and elicits cycles of escalating hostility, blame, and win-lose struggles. Angered parents become intolerant of strategies and solutions that might hold promise because they attach labels, such as "uncaring" or "incompetent," to individuals offering these solutions. They become focused on the perceived wrongfulness of the people they regard as threatening (Margolis et al., 1987).

There are common mistakes school personnel make that create or exacerbate conflict, such as (a) ignorance of the law, (b) assuming what parents think or feel, (c) being defensive, (d) acting like only they know what is best for the child, and (e) failing to value differences (Margolis & Brannigan, 1990). Parents and school personnel also may attach different values to meetings; if educators misperceive the importance of a conference to a parent, frustration and conflict may naturally ensue. If conflict is not handled properly it can lead to due process proceedings based on rights enumerated in PL 94–142.

It is usually better for school personnel to address rather than ignore parental anger. Benefits of addressing anger include (a) developing a broader understanding of real problems fueling the anger, (b) rejecting inferior ideas without offending parents, (c) using latent resources for developing superior ideas, (d) stimulating healthy interaction, interest, and involvement in the real problem, and (e) establishing better interpersonal relationships as well as heightened feelings of competence and satisfaction.

Methods for Coping with Anger

Fortunately, there are techniques to secure the cooperation of parents and redirect parental energy toward working with school personnel in constructive ways. For school personnel to understand the motivations of angry parents, they must see the situation through the parents' eyes. The quicker personnel empathize with parents, the faster the resolution. Empathy is not agreement, it is the accurate understanding of the parents' difficulties, fears, and proposed solutions from their perspective. You cannot rid people of anger; you can only help people rid themselves of anger and act more rationally and constructively through empathetic listening, trust building, and systematic problem-solving.

Effective listening is the most powerful way to understand accurately another's point of view. Key elements include (a) remaining calm and attentive, (b) encouraging the exploration of critical concerns, (c) using open-ended questions sparingly, (d) exploring concerns until adequate understanding is achieved, (e) summarizing points of agreement and disagreement, and (f) conscientiously adhering to the basics (determine what will meet the parents' needs).

Trust is based on having a cooperative rather than a competitive or dominating mind-set. It requires actively seeking to understand and being honest about your objectives. Subtly demonstrating expertise without being oppressive or signaling superiority is important. Building trust is a process of building reciprocity over time. Behaviors that promote trust are (a) accepting parents as they are, (b) listening carefully and empathetically for both thought *and* feeling, (c) actively helping parents feel comfortable, (d) preparing for meetings, (e) focusing on parents' hopes, aspirations, concerns, and needs, (f) keeping your word, (g) allowing parents' expertise to shine, and (h) being there when parents need someone.

Most **problem-solving** models include at least five basic steps. First, take time to identify the problem, probing issues until everyone agrees. Second, define the problem in terms that are simple and clear, terms that can be used to assess the impact of the solution. Third, explore a range of solution options. Be creative and apply brainstorming techniques. Determine the acceptability of each solution to all members. Fourth, set a timetable to implement the solution which includes scheduling future meetings. Fifth, evaluate the solution. Group members should share in the success or failure. Modify solutions as necessary and continue until goals have been achieved.

Many groups have found interesting formats that facilitate an intuitive approach to problem-solving. For example, when generating alternatives, some groups look for the similarities or differences. Some teams write analogies or metaphors for the problem; others write the definition on index cards and pass them around for each person to add a solution, then copy all cards for the entire group. Other teams form subgroups in which (a) everyone writes down solutions on individual cards, (b) each small group selects the best solution, and (c) groups try to sell their solution to others. This format emphasizes expanding on good ideas and getting increasingly more creative.

Problem-solving is facilitated by the understanding that no solution is perfect—some are better or more acceptable than others. Additionally, problem-solving is facilitated by understanding that when people disagree, they are not necessarily wrong. During tense problem-solving sessions, it is important to remain focused on clearly defined issues rather than on personalities, continue to treat parents with respect, and dispassionately discuss each recommendation and concern.

Managing Conflict

In spite of efforts made by school personnel to address anger and understand parents' concerns, special education leaders will find themselves faced with the need for more systematic procedures to deal with conflict. Maher (1986) has developed a step-by-step process for managing conflict between parents and multidisciplinary teams in such areas as appropriateness of a child's placement, goals, instruction provided, progress, and criteria for evaluation of goals and objectives. Maher trained special education leaders to use this conflict management strategy through a program of instruction and simulation activities. Administrators and observers noted that these conflict management skills generalized to school settings. Parents who participated in meetings chaired by conflict management-trained administrators reacted more positively after training than before.

Phase 1: Conflict Exploration
1. Identify the disputants. Who is involved?
2. Delineate the area of conflict. Is there conflict? Specifically, what is the conflict over?

Phase 2: Discussion and Communication
3. State the purpose of the meeting. Discuss the sources of conflict and work toward conflict resolution.
4. Define authority. School policy and state and federal regulations give the service director the authority to act as mediator.
5. Keep the disputants focused on the disagreement. Refocus discussions when participants forget the purpose of meeting.
6. Maintain impartiality. Accept each disputant's view.
7. Sum up. Periodically review the meeting process and the content of the discussion.
8. Elicit suggestions for the conflict-resolution plan. Request ideas from each disputant about ways to resolve the conflict.
9. Evaluate the plan's suggestions. Request participants to consider the advantages and disadvantages of suggestions.
10. Maintain impartiality on suggestions. Accept the disputants' evaluation of suggestions.
11. Select suggestions. Choose the suggestions that will become part of the conflict resolution plan and state the plan.
12. Reinforce disputants for their meeting participation. Provide social approval and tell them when to expect the plan in writing.
13. Write a conflict resolution plan. Specify goals and objectives, activities, responsibilities, and evaluation criteria.
14. Disseminate the plan to the disputants. Provide team members with written copies.

15. Monitor the plan's implementation. Contact parents and team members to determine whether the plan is being carried out.
16. Assess the plan's outcome. Gather information to determine whether the goals have been attained.

Brock and Shanberg (1990) offer more general guidelines to enhance cooperation during formal conflict resolution. Treat everyone with respect and courtesy. Know the statutes and regulations. Avoid posturing; that is, do not emphasize differences to impress those involved. Divide complex issues into their component parts. Consider provisional or interim solutions. Distinguish people from positions.

Alternative Dispute Resolution

Special education administrators are able to manage many conflict situations. However, if parents are dissatisfied with the results of this conflict resolution, they may request alternative dispute resolution (ADR), in which an outside party attempts to resolve differences.

Vinup (1994) describes seven types of alternative dispute resolution:

1. **Negotiation.** Disputants talk directly with one another to settle their disagreements.
2. **Conciliation.** Parents and administrators are helped to resolve a disagreement by overcoming emotional barriers that keep disputants from communicating with one another.
3. **Mediation.** Mediators help disputants talk to one another in order to reach a mutually acceptable agreement. In mediation, the participants make the final decision on how to resolve their disagreement.
4. **Arbitration.** Parents and school authorities present arguments regarding how to resolve the disagreement. After hearing both sides and reviewing the facts, the arbitrator issues an award.
5. **Neutral Factfinding.** A neutral party collects information to be used by the disputants in finding a resolution. Factfinding can be employed regardless of the resolution procedure used.
6. **Minitrial.** This is a trial in which flexible rules of procedure and evidence accelerate the process. Both parties present their cases to the judge, with or without representation, and a decision is rendered quickly.
7. **Settlement.** With a trial imminent, both parties are encouraged to negotiate an agreement using more informal and flexible procedures than a trial.

Conflicts between school personnel and parents that require a third party to mediate generally involve a request by the parents for additional or more-costly services with which the schools are unwilling to comply. In apparent contrast, other parents of children with severe disabilities have asserted their children would be better served in general education classrooms. Nationwide, parents and schools have gone to ADR or legal hearings to decide what are the most appropriate and least restrictive services and settings.

Fielding (1990) cites many reasons to use alternative dispute resolution rather than litigate. Costs of legal hearings range from $1,000 to $10,000; parents may pay as much as $4,000 in attorney and specialist fees. Most professionals agree that disputes settled through ADR are in the best interest of the child. Legal proceedings, by their very nature, are emotionally draining experiences because parents and schools assume adversarial stances and fight to win. Dobbs, Primm, and Primm (1991) add that alternative resolution can be scheduled quickly and completed faster. Because the rules of evidence do not apply, many forms of ADR offer all parties the opportunity to discuss issues and feelings. In these alternative formats, the role of the outside party is to facilitate understanding and to maximize a working relationship between school and parents.

The following case study presents a description of events and documentation presented to a mediator concerning the appropriate placement of a 9-year-old boy with mild mental retardation and multiple needs for services. In this case, the parents and school personnel have attempted numerous solutions to resolve a conflict over differences of opinion concerning the most appropriate and least restrictive placement.

What Does Brian Need?

Brian was the first child born to Mr. and Mrs. Stallings, a well-educated couple living in the suburbs of a large metropolitan area. It was obvious to his parents that Brian developed slowly and had somewhat unpredictable behavior. Mrs. Stallings left her job to raise Brian; she did an excellent job of stimulating him and coping with his special behavioral needs. When Brian was 18 months old, he was evaluated by an infant development center and found to be in need of services. He was taken to the center for physical and speech therapy twice a week until he was 3. At that time, Brian was found to have significantly delayed speech, language, and motor development, qualifying him for the local school district's preschool program for children with disabilities.

Unfortunately, when Brian was 4, his mother died after giving birth to a second child. Mr. Stallings remarried a woman with two children of her own. With four children in the new family, it was more difficult to attend to Brian's special needs, and his new brother and sister resented the disproportionate amount of time Brian seemed to require.

Brian's parents wanted a thorough evaluation done before he was no longer eligible for his preschool program, so they took him to a developmental evaluation center in a neighboring city. The summary of findings included mild mental retardation, mild cerebral palsy resulting in deficits in fine motor skills, and enuresis. He was described as exhibiting good self-esteem, although he was impulsive at times. It was suggested that Brian would qualify for special education services in the category of "other health impaired" because of the diagnosis of cerebral palsy and his need for other services, including occupational therapy and adaptive PE.

The school personnel and Brian's parents wrote an IEP for daily resource room assistance for a minimum of 1 hour and 15 minutes and weekly occupational therapy. During the fall, the parents were concerned about Brian's apparent lack of growth in speech and requested that speech therapy be added to the IEP in January.

The special education teacher related that Brian made excellent progress during the first grade. His parents, however, were not as impressed and used their personal health insurance to obtain an evaluation at the university medical center. Recommendations from the new evaluation included continued occupational therapy, regular consultation from the speech therapist, consideration of medication for attention-deficit disorder, and increased time with a special education teacher trained to work with students with attention problems. In addition, it was recommended that Mr. and Mrs. Stallings contact parent support groups to learn more about children with disabilities and to have other parents to talk to about the challenges of raising an exceptional child.

CONSIDER THIS

1. From a special education administrator's point of view, what issues have emerged that might predict future challenges?
2. Describe the educational program you might offer to Brian at this time.

The case study continues with no resolution.

No Resolution

Before Brian began second grade, his parents requested a revised IEP to reflect the recommendations of the medical center. The new IEP included continued occupational and speech therapy. Time in the resource room was increased to two hours daily. In October, Brian's parents complained his behavior at home was growing steadily worse, and they blamed this on inadequate educational services. They requested a conference to develop a new IEP for more extensive services. The special education teacher, school psychologist, principal, and parents attended the meeting. The teacher reported she had observed loud talking, difficulty following directions, and poor organization, but progress was evident and the placement seemed appropriate.

After extensive discussion, and in an effort to resolve conflict, the school psychologist suggested a one-month diagnostic placement at an in-patient children's center.

After one month, the children's center diagnostic team suggested placement in an elementary school with resource room services for children with behavior disorders. The parents would not sign an IEP offering only resource services; they said their child needed an institutional placement where his behavioral, academic, and therapeutic needs could be met in an integrated setting.

The school district offered to place Brian in a self-contained program for students with behavior disorders as well as provide additional services for speech and occupational therapy. The parents reluctantly signed the IEP, saying they would be watching closely to determine whether the program was sufficient to meet his needs.

After three months in the BD resource program working on social skills, Brian's special education teacher thought he had made sufficient progress to be ready for mainstreaming. Brian attended a general education classroom for one hour daily; after a successful month, he was increased to two hours daily. The parents, however, kept a daily log of Brian's complaints about school and Brian's poor behavior at home. They also kept the papers he brought home from school which demonstrated difficulty with his class work.

At the end of the second grade, the special education teacher proposed an IEP that split Brian's time equally between BD services and the general education classroom. The parents flatly refused and sought the opinion of a child psychiatrist. The psychiatrist interviewed Brian and his parents and concluded that Brian would most likely fail in mainstream classes without close supervision and individualized, small-group instruction. Further, since Brian needed several therapies to achieve his potential, the psychiatrist recommended a residential setting where he could receive consistent behavior management and a carefully designed educational program.

In August, before Brian entered third grade, his parents requested an IEP meeting. The BD teacher, mainstream teacher, school psychologist, principal, BD coordinator, and special education director met with the parents for the conference. Mr. and Mrs. Stallings presented the recommendations of the child psychiatrist and demanded the district place Brian in a residential program. The principal maintained that, according to all school reports, not only were the BD services appropriate, but Brian appeared ready for further mainstreaming. At this point, the special education director attempted to manage the conflict using Maher's 16 systematic points.

CONSIDER THIS

1. Predict how the school personnel and parents would respond to each step of the conflict resolution procedure.

2. What do you think is the most appropriate placement for this student?
3. What further concessions would you consider before turning this case over to a third-party mediator?

SUMMARY

Parents of exceptional children have been empowered through legislation to be participants in the special education decision-making process. In addition, school personnel are becoming increasingly aware of how involved parents can powerfully affect the outcome of their children's education. For educators and parents to work effectively together, both parties must be willing to change attitudes and learn new skills.

School personnel must accept parents as equal partners and be open to learning from family wisdom. Educators must determine how to accommodate the complexities of social context and parental responsibilities. Through creativity and commitment to the goal of parent involvement, teachers and administrators have established a great variety of successful family-school participation programs.

For parents to succeed as partners or advocates, they need to be educated in their rights and encouraged to feel they are an important part of the system. When parents learn how schools work and how best to communicate with educators, they become effective participants in their children's education.

Conflicts naturally arise between school personnel and parents as they confront different value systems and competing needs. Educators, especially special education administrators, can learn how to deal with angry parents. It is essential that school leaders know how to avoid situations that frequently lead to angry responses and how to develop an atmosphere of mutual trust and respect.

Even under the best of circumstances, conflicts persist, and successful administrators are prepared to mediate when parents' perceptions of their child's needs differ dramatically from the school personnel's assessment of the situation. Many types of alternative dispute resolution procedures offer potential solutions to differences between parents and school authorities. ADR avoids time-consuming, costly, and emotionally draining legal procedures.

REFERENCES

Binkard, B. (1985). A successful handicap awareness program—run by special parents. *Teaching Exceptional Children, 17*(1), 12–16.

Brock, K. A., & Shanberg, R. (1990). Avoiding unnecessary due process hearings. *Reading, Writing, and Learning Disabilities, 6,* 33–39.

Cutler, B. C. (1993). *You, your child, and special education.* Baltimore, MD: Paul H. Brookes.

D'Angelo, D. A., & Adler, C. R. (1991). Chapter I: A catalyst for improving parent involvement. *Phi Delta Kappan,* 350–354.

Dobbs, R. F., Primm, E. B., & Primm, B. (1991). Mediation: A common sense approach for resolving conflicts in education. *Focus on Exceptional Children, 24*(2), 1–12.

Dohrn, B., Bryan, T., & Bryan, J. (1993). Helping parents to help their children. *OSERS News In Print, 5*(4), 10–14.

Fielding, P. S. (1990). Mediation in special education. *Reading, Writing, and Learning Disabilities, 6,* 41–52.

Fisher, R., & Ury, W. (1981). *Getting to yes.* Boston: Houghton Mifflin.

Garfunkel, F. (1986). *Parents and schools: Partnerships or politics.* Boston, MA: Institute for Responsive Education. (ERIC Document Reproduction Service No. ED 280 227)

Hallenbeck, M., & Beernink, M. (1989). A support program for parents of students with mild handicaps. *Teaching Exceptional Children, 21*(3), 44–47.

Harry, B. (1992). Restructuring the participation of African-American parents in special education. *Exceptional Children, 59*(2), 123–131.

Lewis, M., Marine, L., & Van Horn, G. (1991). *Parent involvement in the special education process: A synopsis of exemplary models.* Bloomington, IN: CASE Research Committee.

Maher, C. A. (1986). Evaluation of a program for improving conflict management skills of special education service directors. *Journal of School Psychology, 24*(1), 45–53.

Margolis, H., & Brannigan, G. G. (1990). Strategies for resolving parent-school conflict. *Reading, Writing, and Learning Disabilities, 6,* 1–23.

Margolis, H., Shapiro, A., & Brown, G. (1987). Resolving conflict with parents of handicapped children. *Urban Review, 19,* 209–221.

Obiakor, F. (1995). *The eight-step multicultural approach: Learning and teaching with a smile.* Dubuque, IA: Kendall Hunt.

Salend, S. J. (1990). A migrant education guide for special educators. *Teaching Exceptional Children, 22*(2), 18–21.

Turnbull, A., & Turnbull, R. (1986). *Families, professionals, and exceptionality: A special partnership.* Columbus, OH: Merrill.

Vosler-Hunter, R., & Hanson, S. (1992). Parents as policy makers: Challenges for collaboration. *Focal Point, 6*(1), 1–5.

Vinup, A. (1994). Alternative Dispute Resolution and the ADA. *LDA Newsbriefs, 29*(2), 24.

Winton, P. (1986). Effective strategies for involving families in intervention efforts. *Focus on Exceptional Children, 19*(2), 1–12.

SUGGESTED READINGS

Cegelka, P. T., MacDonald, M., & Gaeta, R. (1987). Bilingual special education. *Teaching Exceptional Children, 19*(1), 48–50.

Exceptional Parent is published nine times a year by Psy-Ed Corporation, 1170 Commonwealth Ave., Boston, MA 02134.

Focal Point is a publication of The Research and Training Center, Regional Research Institute for Humans Services, PO Box 751, Portland, OR 97207-0751.

Innocenti, M. S. (1987). *Helping parents be informed advocates.* Logan, UT: Developmental Center for Handicapped Persons. (ERIC Document Reproduction Service No. ED 298 738)

Lambie, R., & Daniels-Mohring, D. (1993). *Family systems within educational contexts: Understanding students with special needs.* Denver, CO: Love.

Shea, T. M., & Bauer, A. M. (1991). *Parents and teachers of children with exceptionalities.* Boston, MA: Allyn & Bacon.

Steinke, G. L., & Steinke, R. J. (1987). *Public relations for special education.* (ERIC Document Reproduction Service No. ED 345 431)

Chapter 9

COLLABORATIVE TEAMS: SCHOOL-BASED SUPPORT AND INTERAGENCY COOPERATION

Schools and community agencies have spent years developing generic solutions for various categories of disabilities and diagnoses. However, it has become clear that the generic approach cannot provide satisfactory solutions to the unique challenges of exceptional children and their families. In response, schools and community programs have begun a shift toward an ecological model of problem-solving. This approach focuses on the individual nature of problems as they exist in specific environments in order to devise innovative, yet realistic, solutions within the context of the individual's need and the available support systems. Within schools, building-based teams collaborate to solve instructional challenges for students and teachers, and, among schools and agencies, professionals cooperate to create services that wrap around the child, family, and community.

SCHOOL-BASED TEAMS

Most teachers work in relative isolation (York & Vandercook, 1990) and welcome the opportunity for collegial interaction. School-based teams offer many levels of support. They encourage a sense of shared responsibility for the diverse needs of students by pooling knowledge, skills, and resources (LRE Project, 1990). These teams can assist teachers to expand their repertoire of assessment and intervention methods as well as develop better problem-solving strategies (Laycock, Gable, & Korinek, 1991). During group planning, teachers may learn what expertise exists among the staff members and where resources may be located to solve problems (Male, 1991). Additionally, many teachers find it is fun to solve problems collaboratively, while also engaging in stimulating adult dialogue and social interaction (Thousand & Villa, 1990).

Team Formats

A myriad of possible school-based team formats and functions exists. Teams may be designed to empower the general education teacher to succeed with students who might be from diverse cultural backgrounds or who have different learning and behavior needs, but who have not been identified as disabled for educational purposes. Prior to implementation of these teams, teachers felt they had only one alternative when frustrated by students' problems: to request a multidisciplinary team assessment. As the number of referrals for special education services escalated, it became clear to educators that the problem-identification focus of multidisciplinary teams needed to be replaced with a solution-generating process (Saver & Downes, 1991). These solution-oriented teams have been called Peer Intervention Team (PIT Crew) (Saver & Downes, 1991), Student Study Teams (Male, 1991), Teacher Assistance Teams (Chalfant & Van Dusen Pysh, 1989), or Student Program Planning Teams (LRE Project, 1990). Many schools have used already existing teams, such as department or grade-level instructional teams, to empower teachers and generate solutions (Idol & West, 1991).

A second team format, called Child Study Teams (Laycock et al., 1991) and Preassessment or Prereferral Teams (LRE Project, 1990), sometimes appears to the general classroom teacher as the first step in the special education referral process. Despite how these teams have been viewed, their purpose is to work with teachers who have referred students for evaluation in order to generate alternatives to a special education assessment and placement. During the process, teachers learn valuable instructional strategies and identify possible resources for assistance. In addition, these teams ensure that educators have attempted many modes of instruction before referring the student for special education assessment (Chalfant & Van Dusen Pysh, 1989).

A third format for school-based teams is a model for facilitating the mainstreaming of the special education student. The Academic Intervention Model (AIM) proposed by Howell (1991) offers teachers a menu of options to meet diverse student needs. The collaborative teams described by York and Vandercook (1990) for supporting integrated education include the principal, the parents, and special and general educators. These teams plan for change, facilitate communication, find natural support for integrated students, and assist in curriculum development.

Procedures of Successful Teams

For these teams to be successful, their members must first build trust and strengthen their communication skills (LRE Project, 1990). Next, team members negotiate and reach a consensus on their roles, responsibilities, and expectations for the collaboration process (Idol & West, 1991). Collaborative teams use a variety of methods to request help/consultation, ranging from informal contacts with pivotal team members to more formal written requests sent to screening committees (Graden, Casey, & Christenson, 1985).

Once the consultation process begins, most collaborative teams follow a similar problem-solving format (Donaldson & Christiansen, 1990). The first step consists of helping the teacher make sense out of a myriad of concerns in order to identify a specific problem (Saver & Downes, 1991). It is best to write a problem statement in specific, measurable, and observable terms to facilitate the formulation of a clear action plan and evaluation procedure. At this point, many teams assign a member to observe the students and teacher in the classroom (Graden et al., 1985). The observer would identify expectations and environmental factors that affect student performance. Care should be taken to emphasize the gathering of information and not validate the presence of the problem or question the teacher's judgment. All data collected should be openly shared with the teacher (Graden & Bauer, 1992). Following the observation, the observer may be able to offer helpful suggestions to the teacher in a follow-up conference, thereby forgoing the remainder of the collaborative team process. Otherwise, the teacher and observer return to the collaborative team to generate possible solutions to the problem.

Choosing a viable solution has three steps: (a) brainstorming potential interventions, (b) analyzing consequences for each intervention, and (c) selecting the best or most acceptable solution (Idol & West, 1991). During the brainstorming process, team members offer as many solutions to the problem as possible, no matter how outlandish they may seem. Solutions may include different instructional approaches, additional resources, modified expectations, or support from students peers, parents, paraprofessionals, or colleagues. (See Figure 9.1.)

After generating an exhaustive list of alternatives, the team evaluates each solution, taking into account its feasibility and positive or negative consequences (Saver & Downes, 1991). According to this evaluation, the team should prioritize the proposed solutions. However, the teacher's willingness to commit to a solution is more important than the team's opinion that a particular approach is best (Schumm & Vaughn, 1991; Ysseldyke, Thurlow, Wortruba, & Nania, 1990). When teachers agree to use a solution, they accept ownership, and the value of accepting ownership in this process can not be overestimated (Simpson & Myles, 1993).

The next step is the formulation of an action plan. This plan consists of an outline of specific steps for implementation, assignments of team members to implement each step, and a time line for the projected completion of each step (Idol & West, 1991). To guide the evaluation process, the last component of the action plan should be a statement of the expected outcomes. Developing an outline requires team members to be specific, and it provides the teacher with a focus to begin. The time line also offers an impetus to complete each step and indicates a commitment to return to the team for the evaluation of the outcomes.

The final step in the problem-solving process involves monitoring and evaluating the results of the action plan (Saver & Downes, 1991). It is important to use data to assess the team's impact. When the collaborative team convenes to evaluate the outcomes of the action plan, the teacher should bring evidence of the success or shortcomings of the proposed solution. This might include a portfolio of attendance data, test scores, examples of class work, and/or comments made by the student, parents, or peers. As a result of an analysis of the data, team members may decide the intervention was successful. If this is the case, a follow-up meeting could be scheduled for a month later to determine whether the plan has continued to work. If, however, the team is not satisfied with the plan's outcome, a modification or a new plan is proposed (Idol & West, 1991). A new action plan is then drafted.

In the following teaching case, a school-based team attempts to solve a series of problems by attempting to help a teacher accommodate a student with disabling inattention and hyperactivity.

FIGURE 9.1
TEAM PROBLEM-SOLVING MODEL

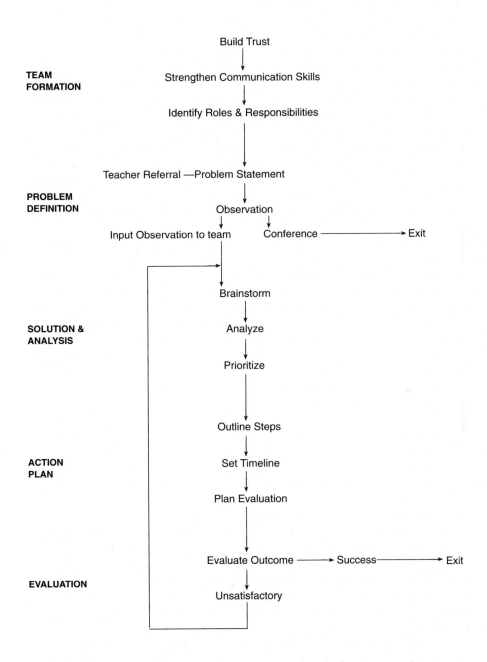

Accommodating a Student with ADHD

Each morning, Lamar Thompson bursts into Mrs. Jones' sixth-grade class chattering incessantly, whacking male peers, and making comments to all the girls. On the playground, Lamar is a gazelle, light on his feet, turning on a dime; he is the first choice of all the team captains for recess sports. In the classroom, however, he doesn't switch off his "playground energy" as most other students do. Luwella Jones has become weary of asking Lamar to settle down and get ready for class. He clearly doesn't attend to directions; he waits until everyone else has begun working and then asks, "What are we supposed to do?" Usually, Lamar is able to distract a peer from class work to talk about something that happened at home or on the bus. There always seems to be chaos around him, including his desk, which is stuffed with months of papers and books that fall out several times a day (McBurnett, Lahey, & Pfiffner, 1993).

Lamar's mother is difficult to reach. She doesn't have a phone, and she works at a restaurant over hectic lunch and dinner hours. Mrs. Jones is sure that no notes make it home, since Lamar can't get a paper from his desk to the teacher's half the time. His grades don't reflect his ability. On tests, he achieves A's and B's, but he so rarely turns in homework and completed class assignments that his report card only shows C's, D's, and F's. At the end of each year, Lamar has been passed to the next teacher with apologies and condolences. Luwella Jones thinks Lamar is capable of better performance, so she contacts a member of the teacher assistance team (TAT) and asks for help.

Team Decision

In this school, the teacher assistance team consists of a primary, intermediate, and special education teacher, as well as the school psychologist. Mrs. Jones met with the TAT to discuss her frustrations with and concerns about Lamar. She explained that Lamar is a student with average to above-average test scores who does poorly in her class, as has been his history throughout school. His group achievement scores are in the 70th to 85th percentile range, yet he has C's, and D's on his report card. Mrs. Jones described the behavior of greatest concern: Lamar begins work only with prompting, then seems to lose interest and starts something else or stirs up the students around him. He frequently distracts other students from their work, and, frankly, she is exhausted from working with him.

After a long discussion, the team suggested that, although Lamar had difficulty with attention and hyperactivity, he would probably not qualify for special education services because he seems, somehow, to be learning what is measured by achievement tests. Instead, what was needed was an intensive campaign to get him on-task and to reinforce his success. The teacher assistance team formulated a behavioral goal for Lamar: He will complete assigned work and turn it in to the teacher. To accomplish this goal, the following strategies were suggested: (a) a contract will be written between Mrs. Jones and Lamar for assignment completion using a response cost format, (b) the teacher will personalize directions for Lamar and remind him of his contract, (c) Lamar will be taught to use a self-monitoring strategy checklist for beginning, completing, checking, and turning in assignments, (d) the teacher will scan every five minutes to check for on-task behavior, (e) the teacher will give feedback every 10–15 minutes as appropriate, (f) the teacher will praise Lamar for completed work and assignments turned in, (g) Lamar will be asked to move to a study carrel if off-task for more than 10 minutes, and (h) the teacher will monitor progress and report back to the team in three weeks (Burcham, Carlson, & Milich, 1993; Fiore, Becker, & Nero, 1993).

Mrs. Jones agreed the suggestions would have a significant effect on Lamar, and if he were her only student, she would be thrilled to implement them. However, all she felt she had the time to do was write a contract, give him a checklist for self-monitoring, and remove him to a study carrel if necessary.

 ## CONSIDER THIS

1. Evaluate the strategies proposed by the teacher assistance team.
2. How would you react to Mrs. Jones' initial response to the team's suggestions?

Section 504

Although it appears Lamar may not qualify for special education services, he may be eligible for modified instruction and support services based on Section 504 of the Rehabilitation Act of 1973. This act requires accommodations and supplementary services for an individual with any physical or mental impairment that substantially limits one or more major life activity. Further, Title II of the Americans With Disabilities Act prohibits the denial of appropriate educational services and classrooms to individuals who are limited by physical or mental conditions. Many educators and legal consultants have argued that attention–deficit disorder is a condition that significantly affects school performance, a major life activity. Services based on Section 504 can be provided in the regular classroom but must be based on an accommodation plan designed to meet individual educational needs through modification of the environment and the use of supplementary aids and services (Aronofsky, 1992).

Based on the requirements of Section 504, the team determined Lamar would benefit from additional help that could be provided by a paraprofessional (Burcham, Carlson, & Milich, 1993). The team requested the principal hire a paraprofessional to assist Mrs. Jones and the other sixth-grade teacher with programs to help Lamar and other students like him. The principal agreed, notified the central office of his intention, and hired someone to start right away.

A New Paraprofessional

A paraprofessional or paraeducator is a member of the instructional team who assists teachers and therapists, enabling them to provide a better education to all children. Paraprofessionals provide (a) increased student learning opportunities, (b) more individualized instruction and attention, (c) additional teacher time for planning, instruction, and evaluation, and (d) better monitoring of student learning (Gerlach, Pickett, & Vasa, 1992). Many school districts are hiring large numbers of paraprofessionals to meet the increasing demands of providing for the individual needs of diverse learners and exceptional students in the general education classroom.

The case continues as a paraprofessional is hired to assist in the sixth-grade classes and the team confronts unexpected challenges.

Paraprofessional for the Sixth Grade

Rita Washington was hired as a paraprofessional by the principal because of her maturity and experience with children. She has three teen-agers who are successful in school, and she has been a church youth leader and a part-time art instructor at the recreation center.

The paraprofessional arrived in Mrs. Luwella Jones' class as the children filed in on Monday morning. Mrs. Jones immediately recognized her from the community and felt comfortable. She introduced Rita to the class as their new helping teacher. Mrs. Washington was given a desk in the back of the room and was told that when the children did seat work, she was to help them stay on-task (especially Lamar, Mrs. Jones indicated with her eyes). After lunch, the paraprofessional went to Ms. Epstein's sixth-grade class. Julie Epstein was a new teacher with bright-eyed enthusiasm and all the latest teaching strategies. When Rita Washington walked into the room, Julie said with all the authority she could muster, "Watch me to see how I run this class."

Over the next few weeks, Rita Washington became like a second teacher in Mrs. Jones' class, helping all the students, giving feedback to off-task students, and grading papers. When a new student arrived, Mrs. Jones wanted to administer reading and math placements tests, so she handed the math book to Rita and asked her to teach the math lesson. Rita didn't want to disagree, but she had never taught math before. When Mrs. Jones left the room, Rita felt lost and confused about her role.

At the same time, in Julie Epstein's class, the paraprofessional was never asked to do anything. After school one day, Rita stopped by Julie's room to offer an observation about a child having trouble with his work. Ms. Epstein replied tersely that she had seen the same thing and was planning a new program for him. Rita felt maybe she had stepped out of line, and she decided she wouldn't share her opinions with Julie Epstein again.

Both Mrs. Jones and Ms. Epstein were asked to attend the next teacher assistance team meeting. A team member asked how Lamar's new program was working and how things were going with the new paraprofessional. Mrs. Jones said everyone in her class was doing better now that there was a second teacher helping with behavior and teaching lessons. Ms. Epstein responded that if it worked so well, Luwella could have Rita all day, as the paraprofessional wasn't any use in her room. The other teachers looked at John Kratovich, the school psychologist, for leadership in this situation, which had become more complex than anyone had anticipated.

CONSIDER THIS

1. What training/preparation might have prepared Rita for her assignment? What training might have prepared the teachers for the appropriate and effective utilization of a paraprofessional?
2. How does the program devised by the teacher assistance team match the actual classroom role of the paraprofessional?
3. What are the sources of conflict between the teachers and the paraprofessional?
4. What should the team do now?

Emerging Roles of School Psychologists

A new role definition for school psychologists is taking shape as a result of school reform efforts toward (a) more site-based management, (b) fewer referrals to special education and less categorical labeling, (c) increased collaboration among general and special educators, and (d) greater emphasis on the outcomes of instructional programs. This redefinition of the role and function of school psychologists de-emphasizes the traditional test-oriented role and focuses more on consultation, prevention, and problem-solving functions. According to Kelly-Vance and Ulman (1993), school psychologists are becoming more involved in classroom interventions, consultation, counseling, systems change, and inservice training.

Previously, when teachers were concerned about students' learning or behavior problems, school psychologists might have responded by administering standardized-test batteries. Now, school psychologists might assist teachers in developing effective interventions that serve students in general classes. They might demonstrate new skills, such as behavior change strategies, cooperative learning techniques, or curriculum-based assessment procedures. School psychologists may also consult with staff members about the stresses of managing difficult-to-teach students in increasingly diverse classes. School psychologists are also becoming more involved with parents in order to include them in a comprehensive approach to helping children. Administrators may rely on school psychologists to facilitate the effective functioning of building-based teams or to resolve problems among personnel.

At the teacher assistance team meeting with Mrs. Jones and Ms. Epstein, the school psychologist delineated three issues of concern: (a) there was obvious staff conflict, probably due to role confusion and lack of preparation for working with another adult, (b) it didn't sound as if the program developed by the TAT was being implemented, indicating a problem of accountability, and (c) there was a need for inservice training in effective management techniques.

 ## CONSIDER THIS

1. What role could school psychologists perform in resolving staff conflicts?
2. What type of issues are the responsibility of the teacher assistance teams? What type of issues should be referred to other decision makers?
3. What elements would you include in an inservice program for this staff?

WRAPAROUND INTERVENTIONS

Many students who have difficulty in school or who qualify for special education services come from families with an array of life challenges. Typically, if these families are not already involved with several agencies, they will eventually associate with many discrete, unconnected community service providers. When several agencies work with an individual or family, there can be overlap and duplication of services on the one hand, or the absence of essential components on the other. For these students and their families to receive the comprehensive programs they require, schools and agencies must communicate and cooperate (Abrams & Frantz, 1991).

The contemporary term for comprehensive programs developed through interagency collaboration is *wraparound intervention*. A wraparound intervention is developed and/or approved by an interdisciplinary services team, based in the community, guaranteed to be unconditional, centered on the strengths of the child and family, and focused on the delivery of coordinated, highly individualized services in several life domain areas of a child and family (Alvis, 1993).

An *interdisciplinary services team* includes (a) the parent and/or surrogate parent, (b) a case manager or services coordinator, (c) a lead teacher and/or vocational counselor and/or special education administrator, (d) an advocate of the child or parent, and—as appropriate—(e) a social worker or probation officer, (f) a mental health worker or therapist, (g) additional professionals such as vision specialist or interpreter, and (h) any other influential person in the child's life, such as a neighbor, relative, or physician.

Community-based wraparound intervention means services are offered in the community where the child and family live. Restrictive or institutional care should be used for brief stabilization only. *Unconditional* means the team agrees never to deny services because of extreme severity of disability or to reject the child or family because of the difficulty of providing specific interventions. *Strengths of the child and family* means that the positive aspects of the child, family, and community must be considered and be part of the individualized services. *Individualized services* are based on specific needs of the child and/or family, and not on a particular categorical intervention model. These individualized services are both traditional (therapy or existing programs) and nontraditional (hiring a friend or bringing staff to live in a family home). Traditional services should be accessed only when they can be tailored to the specific needs of the child and family.

Life domain needs are areas of basic human needs that almost everyone experiences. These are residential, family, social, educational, medical, psychological/emotional, legal, safety, and any other specific life domain areas resulting from cultural/ethnic/language or community needs.

There are two levels of teams in wraparound service delivery. First, there is the community *umbrella* team that assesses the need for wraparound services, appoints specialized teams, and evaluates local systems to determine whether modifications are needed to meet the needs of the community. Second, *specialized* teams form in response to the specific needs of the individuals of concern. These teams can form and re-form, adding new expertise and letting go of unneeded services in response to unique situations or life changes.

Keys to Success

No one agency can meet the complex needs of some individuals and their families. Frequently, there is a wealth of community services, but too often they are loosely related and separate, each focusing on only one life domain. For intervention from multiple, unrelated services to be efficient and comprehensive, a case management approach is utilized. To ensure successful case management and interagency cooperation, training is critical to assist professionals in working collaboratively and to provide information regarding specific problem areas. This new system of providing services has a *family agenda,* that is, the program is family-focused and family-friendly. Finally, funding must be flexible and quickly accessible.

The goal of wraparound intervention is to promote independent, competent, and confident students and families who function well individually and with others. There are eight keys to developing, maintaining, and enhancing successful wraparound services.

1. Develop staff. Use presenters who are employing the approach successfully in order to raise awareness and generate new ideas.
2. Plan. Encourage teams to schedule regular meetings for setting long-range goals and short-term objectives, designating responsibilities, and developing action plans.
3. Communicate regularly. Send newsletters and personal letters, and arrange conferences to share concerns and successes.
4. Identify challenges and obstacles. Anticipate potential challenges or personal resistance and prepare alternative strategies.

5. Schedule proactive time. Observe progress and plan instead of reacting to problems reported secondhand.
6. Evaluate team functioning. Discuss in an honest and straightforward manner the division of labor, channels of communication, and conflicts among team members as they arise.
7. Assess program success. Rather than focus on the child's problems or the family's crises, continually evaluate whether the services are meeting individual needs.
8. Celebrate success. Compliment each other and share the small successes; it helps people (providers) weather what seems at times to be an apparent lack of progress.

The following case study examines the evolution over 3 years of a wraparound intervention developed when a state school for the deaf notified a special education director that one of the district's students was too disturbed to manage in this residential school setting. As you read, look for the elements of a wraparound intervention and the keys to success.

Wraparound Intervention for Linda and Her Family

Basil Kessler
Consultant for Community Transition and Deaf Specialist

Linda is an 11-year-old Hispanic female who has a profound bilateral sensorineural hearing loss. Her preferred mode of communication is American Sign Language (ASL), which she has mastered. She is rather poor at speechreading and does not speak. Linda attended the residential school for the deaf from preschool through the fourth grade. Although her academic performance indicated she had above-average talent, teachers considered her extremely difficult to instruct because of behavior problems.

Early in Linda's fourth-grade year, the principal of the state school contacted the special education director of her local education agency (LEA) to report that Linda's behavior was deteriorating. She was inappropriate and, at times, violent toward classmates as well as noncompliant with teachers and staff, hitting some of her classmates while lashing out in frustration at her teachers.

While attending the school for the deaf, Linda visited her mother and sisters weekly. Her mother, Mrs. Rosa Ortega, reported that Linda's behavior at home had become unmanageable as well. Mrs. Ortega asked that Linda come home less frequently; she feared for the safety of her two younger children as well as for herself. When asked how she handled Linda's uncontrollable outbursts, Mrs. Ortega indicated she would acquiesce to her daughter's demands and allow her to watch R-rated movies, whose themes included fighting and bloodshed.

Linda became so violent she was placed in a psychiatric center for children. After a 2-week evaluation, she was diagnosed with oppositional-defiant disorder. The psychiatric center sent a staff member to train teachers at the school for the deaf to use a behavior management program, and Linda was returned to the residential school. However, after 2 months, Linda was readmitted to the psychiatric center for a 5-week therapeutic intervention program. Hospital staff decided to involve Child Welfare to provide Linda's mother with the support services necessary to help her improve Linda's behavior when Linda returned home. Additionally, Linda received two new diagnoses, ADHD and posttraumatic stress disorder.

By the end of the fourth grade, Linda had been placed at the psychiatric center two more times. During the last stay, the school for the deaf decided not to allow her back for the fifth grade. Linda's LEA was now responsible for her education.

Before returning home, Linda was referred to the local community mental health center for weekly counseling. She was assigned a therapist who had experience with deaf and hard-of-hearing clients. After 2 months of counseling, the therapist reported to Child Welfare that individual counseling was not sufficient and recommended an out-of-state residential treatment program for deaf youngsters. However, Child Welfare was not comfortable with the recommendation and sought guidance from other professionals in Linda's hometown.

CONSIDER THIS

1. What are the major challenges in educating Linda?
2. What impact might cultural and linguistic diversity have on this situation?
3. What do you think is the most appropriate placement for Linda considering her characteristics, behavior, family, and culture?

The case study continues as the community prepares for Linda's return home.

Preparing for Linda in the Community

Linda's caseworker from Child Welfare contacted a university professor who was known to have extensive experience with the deaf community. The caseworker and the professor met to discuss Linda's educational and emotional needs. After this meeting, the professor arranged a conference with Linda, her mother, and her siblings to ascertain a better picture of the problems and concerns, as well as to assess what might be appropriate educational and counseling options. After meeting with the family, the professor recommended Linda's caseworker arrange a meeting of all interested parties to enable them to become acquainted with each other and to familiarize them with all aspects of Linda's strengths, weaknesses, and possibilities.

The resulting conference included the assistant director of special education, a school psychologist, a fifth-grade classroom teacher, a former principal from the school for the deaf, Linda's dorm parent from the residential school, the building principal where Linda might attend public school, Linda's Child Welfare social worker, a school counselor, Linda's mother, the university professor, and the LEA specialist for behavior disorder programs. Participants met for 4 hours, discussing all the possible agencies that could support Linda and her family.

A plan was developed in which Linda would be in the custody of Child Welfare but live with her mother and sisters. To help Mrs. Ortega, Child Welfare hired a child-care worker to spend up to 18 hours a day in the home to teach parenting skills, establish appropriate home rules, model effective discipline techniques, ensure safety, restrain Linda if necessary, and support Mrs. Ortega emotionally.

Child Welfare also became responsible for providing counseling services to Linda and her family. Because the local community mental health center had a waiting list of 136 children and no staff with training or experience in working with deaf clients and sign language, Child Welfare provided psychotherapy through a purchase-of-service contract with a local therapist fluent in ASL.

Before the beginning of school, an IEP meeting was held to discuss Linda's language, academic, and emotional needs. Although a qualified sign language interpreter would have been ideal, the school would most likely hire a paraprofessional who could sign. The proposed educational program included a full-time interpreter/paraprofessional working with Linda in a self-contained classroom for students with behavior disorders.

When the school year began, all those involved were anxious. Initially, the child-care worker brought Linda to school. Because behavior outbursts occurred regularly, it became imperative that the school have a plan to execute when Linda's behavior got out of control. The interpreter was unfamiliar with behavior disorders, so a list of possible support personnel was developed. No. 1 on the list was the child-care worker who had nurtured a trusting relationship with Linda.

Linda's interpreter, teacher, mother, and child-care worker met every two weeks through the first semester to ensure that the educational services Linda needed were being provided. As a result of these biweekly meetings, several additional issues became apparent. Individual counseling was not successful; in its place, a university art therapy student came to Linda's class twice a week.

Linda began to attend a few classes in the general fifth-grade room. Since the hearing students were curious about sign language, a weekly, before-school class was arranged for students interested in learning to sign. This definitely enhanced the mainstreaming effort.

As the second semester began, positive changes in behavior at school and at home were apparent. The team needed only monthly meetings. At the end-of-the-year meeting, another program was developed for the sixth grade. As behavior problems subsided, it became clear Linda truly had above-average academic potential. The proposed program would de-emphasize Linda's behavior and instead address educational issues particular to the deaf learner. A speech pathologist in the school district who had training in deaf education agreed to work with Linda daily.

As the sixth-grade year began, Linda continued to receive the help of a full-time interpreter/paraprofessional. Linda rode her bicycle to school and reported to a general education homeroom, where she received most of her education. In addition, she met with the deaf education teacher, who monitored her academic and behavioral progress. Linda also met with an art therapy student weekly for a program that included both therapy and art skills training.

Child Welfare continued to monitor the family functioning. It was expected that Linda would soon be released to the custody of her mother. Eventually, it is hoped that Child Welfare will not be involved, and if problems arise, the school will be expected to arrange for a new wraparound intervention program.

CONSIDER THIS

1. What elements of wraparound intervention are evident in this case?
2. What variables might have contributed to the success of this comprehensive program?
3. What might have sabotaged the outcome of this wraparound intervention?
4. What perspectives are important for schools to adopt in order to participate successfully in wraparound interventions?

SUMMARY

More than ever before, interdisciplinary school-based teams collaborate and interagency teams cooperate to meet the individual needs of students and their families. School-based teams offer support and assist teachers in expanding their repertoire of assessment and intervention strategies. A variety of team formats exists in schools; some are composed solely of teachers, while others include school psychologists and administrators. Primarily, these teams use a similar problem-solving approach which defines the concern, develops alternative solutions, evaluates and selects desirable strategies, develops an action plan, and monitors and evaluates implementation. These school-based teams seek to enable general educators to help a greater diversity of learners succeed, and they collaborate to provide appropriate programs for students with identified disabilities in the mainstream.

Two members of this team-oriented approach have new emerging roles. Paraprofessionals have been added to classes and programs to provide increased learning opportunities for at-risk as well as identified special education students. The role of the school psychologist is focused on providing more leadership as it evolves away from an assessment orientation toward a consultation, intervention, and problem-solving model.

Many of the students identified as needing help in school come from families with multiple challenges. When several discrete agencies work with an individual or family, a central case management approach reduces duplication and makes it possible to plan for more-comprehensive services. This interdisciplinary approach to community-based, family-focused services has recently been named "wraparound intervention." Wraparound programs are developed by a team that includes the significant service providers and influential family members. These teams form to meet individual needs and re-form as requirements change. The goal of wraparound services is to promote, to the greatest extent possible, independent, competent, and confident students and families within their home community.

REFERENCES

Abrams, P., & Frantz, C. (1991). Best practices of interagency collaboration and implications for training. Paper presentation at "Children on the Edge," The Council for Exceptional Children special topic conference, November 11, New Orleans, LA.

Adams, L., & Cessna, K. (1991). Designing systems to facilitate collaboration: Collective wisdom from Colorado. *Preventing School Failure, 35*(4), 37–42.

Adamson, D. R., Matthews, P., & Schuller, J. (1990). Five ways to bridge the resource room-to-regular classroom gap. *Teaching Exceptional Children, 22*(2), 74–77.

Alvis, L. (1993). *Working towards wraparound.* Presentation at Kansas Federation Council for Exceptional Children, October 14, Salina, KS.

Aronofsky, D. (1992). A brief summary of school district legal obligations and children's educational rights. In *CH.A.D.D. Educators Manual: Attention Deficit Disorders.* (pp. 57–60) Fairfax, VA: CASET Associates.

Ayers, B., & Meyer, L. H. (1992). Helping teachers manage the inclusive classroom. *The School Administrator,* February, 30–37.

Burcham, B., Carlson, L., & Milich, R. (1993). Promising school-based practices for students with attention-deficit disorder. *Exceptional Children, 60*(2), 174–180.

Chalfant, J. C., & Van Dusen Pysh, M. (1989). Teacher assistance teams: Five descriptive studies on 96 teams. *Remedial and Special Education, 10*(6), 49–58.

Cook. L., & Friend, M. (1991). Principles for the practice of collaboration in schools. *Preventing School Failure, 35*(4), 6–9.

Dettmer, P., Thurston, L. P., & Dyck, N. (1993). *Consultation collaboration and teamwork for students with special needs.* Boston: Allyn & Bacon.

Donaldson, R., & Christiansen, J. (1990). Consultation and collaboration: A decision-making model. *Teaching Exceptional Children, 22*(2), 22–25.

Evans, S. B. (1991). A realistic look at the research base for collaboration in special education. *Preventing School Failure, 35*(4), 10–13.

Fiore, T. A., Becker, E. A., & Nero, R. C. (1993). Educational interventions for students with attention-deficit disorder. *Exceptional Children, 60*(2), 163–173.

Fisher, R., & Ury, W. (1981). *Getting to Yes.* Boston: Houghton Mifflin.

Friend, M. (1992, October). *Visionary leadership for today's schools: Professional collaboration.* Paper presentation at the annual meeting of the Council for Learning Disabilities in Kansas City, MO.

Gerber, S. (1991). Supporting the collaborative process. *Preventing School Failure, 35*(4), 48–52.

Gerlach, K., Pickett, A. L., & Vasa, S. F. (1992). *Issues, roles, and responsibilities: A guide for the teacher and para-educator.* Bremerton, WA: Olympic Educational Service District #114.

Graden, J. L., & Bauer, A. M. (1992). Using a collaborative approach to support students and teachers in inclusive classrooms. In S. Stainback & W. Stainback (Eds.), *Curriculum considerations in inclusive classrooms* (pp. 85–99). Baltimore: Brookes.

Graden, J. L., Casey, A., & Christenson, S. L. (1985). Implementing a prereferral intervention system: Part I. The model. *Exceptional Children, 51*, 377–384.

Harris, K. C. (1990). Meeting diverse needs through collaborative consultation. In W. Stainback & S. Stainback (Eds.), *Support networks for inclusive schooling* (pp. 123–137). Baltimore: Brookes.

Howell, P. (1991). Taking AIM to assist middle school students with special needs. *Preventing School Failure, 35*(4), 43–47.

Idol, L., & West, J. F. (1991). Educational collaboration: A catalyst for effective schooling. *Intervention in School and Clinic, 27*(2), 70–78.

Kelly-Vance, L., & Ulman, J. (1993). The changing role of school psychologists in Iowa. *Communique: National Association of School Psychologists, 22*(2), insert.

Laycock, V. K., Gable, R. A., & Korinek, L. (1991). Alternative structures for collaboration in the delivery of special services. *Preventing School Failure, 35*(4), 15–18.

Lowenthal, B. (1992). Collaborative training in the education of early childhood educators. *Teaching Exceptional Children, 24*(4), 25–29.

LRE Project (1990). *Collaborative Teams in Inclusive-Oriented Schools.* Topeka, KS: Kansas State Board of Education.

Male, M. (1991). Effective team participation. *Preventing School Failure, 35*(4), 29–35.

McBurnett, K., Lahey, B. B., & Pfiffner, L. J. (1993). Diagnosis of attention-deficit disorders in DSM-IV: Scientific basis and implications for education. *Exceptional Children, 60*(2), 108–117.

McKinney, J. D., Montague, M., & Hocutt, A. M. (1993). Educational assessment of students with attention-deficit disorder. *Exceptional Children, 60*(2), 125–131.

Phillips, V., & McCullough, L. (1990). Consultation-based programming: Instituting the collaborative ethic in schools. *Exceptional Children, 56*(4), 291–301.

Price, J. P. (1991). Effective communication: A key to successful collaboration. *Preventing School Failure, 35*(4), 25–28.

Pugach, M. C., & Johnson, L. J. (1990). Meeting diverse needs through professional peer collaboration. In W. Stainback & S. Stainback (Eds.), *Support networks for inclusive schooling* (pp. 123–137). Baltimore: Brookes.

Rainforth, B., York, J., & McDonald, C. (1992). *Collaborative teams for students with severe disabilities: Integrating therapy and educational services.* Baltimore, MD: Brookes.

Salisbury, C. L. (1991). Mainstreaming during the early childhood years. *Exceptional Children, 57*, 146–154.

Saver, K., & Downes, B. (1991). PIT crew: A model for teacher collaboration in an elementary school. *Intervention in School and Clinic, 27*(2), 116–122.

Schumm, J. S., & Vaughn, S. (1991). Making adaptations for mainstreamed students: General classroom teachers' perspectives. *Remedial and Special Education, 12*(4), 18–24.

Simpson, R. L., & Myles, B. S. (1993). General education collaboration: A model for successful mainstreaming. In Edward L. Meyen, Glenn A. Vergason, & Richard J. Whelan (Eds.), *Educating students with mild disabilities* (pp. 49–63). Denver, CO: Love Publishing.

Slavin, R. E. (1990). General education under the regular education initiative: How must it change? *Remedial and Special Education, 11*(3), 40–50.

Thousand, J. S., & Villa, R. A. (1990). Sharing expertise and responsibilities through teaching teams. In W. Stainback & S. Stainback (Eds.), *Supportive networks for inclusive schools* (pp. 151–165). Baltimore: Brookes.

Whinnery, K. W., Fuchs, L. S., & Fuchs, D. (1991). General, special, and remedial teachers' acceptance of behavioral and instructional strategies for mainstreaming students with mild handicaps. *Remedial and Special Education, 12*(4), 6–13.

York, J., & Vandercook, T. (1990). Strategies for achieving an integrated education for middle school students with severe disabilities. *Remedial and Special Education, 11*(5), 6–15.

Ysseldyke, J. E., Thurlow, M. L., Wortruba, J. W., & Nania, P. A. (1990). Instructional arrangements: Perceptions from general education. *Teaching Exceptional Children, 22*(4), 4–8.

Zentall, S. S. (1993). Research on the educational implications of attention-deficit hyperactivity disorder. *Exceptional Children, 60*(2), 143–153.

SECTION III

DELIVERING QUALITY SERVICE IN A CHANGING WORLD

Chapter 10

TO INCLUDE OR NOT TO INCLUDE: THAT IS THE QUESTION

Teresa A. Mehring

The concern with what services constitute the most appropriate education and the debate over which educational placement is the least restrictive environment (LRE) for individual students with disabilities began long before the passage of Public Law 94–142 in 1975. In the early days of education in the United States, students with special learning needs were placed in regular classes because that was the only available placement. These students did not receive assistance from trained specialists, and their teachers were left to cope as best they could. Students with severe disabilities were typically excluded from public education.

Significant departures from this system were initiated in the 1950s by parents of children with disabilities when they lobbied policy-makers for more appropriate social and educational services for children with disabilities. The rapid growth of special schools and special education classrooms, especially for students with mental retardation and emotional disturbances, followed. For the most part, these students were educated in environments that isolated them from nondisabled peers. With the growth of special education and other services, the American education system changed. Children and adolescents with severe handicaps who had been denied an education were provided with special schools. Students with learning and/or behavioral problems who had been in regular classes were placed in separate "special" classes. It was thought the learning needs of students with disabilities could best be met by specially trained teachers in "special education" classrooms.

SHIFTING PARADIGMS

As stated by Lewis and Doorlag (1991), "It was soon discovered that full-time special education was not the answer for most handicapped students. Many students did not require full-day services. Many were able to participate in at least some of the activities of the regular class; all could benefit from contact with peers" (p. 8). Additional concerns surrounded special education placements:

1. Leaders in special education began to speak out against special-class abuses. (The 1968 article by Dunn, "Special Education for the Mildly Retarded— Is Much of It Justifiable?" is an example.)

2. The overrepresentation of students of color in special classes was documented through research efforts (e.g., Mercer, 1973).

3. The President's Committee on Mental Retardation (1969) reported that many students were "disabled" only for that portion of the day spent in school.

4. Court cases litigated on behalf of students placed in segregated special education settings provided evidence that discriminatory testing practices had resulted in the inappropriate placement of non–English-speaking students (*Diana v. State Board of Education,* 1970, 1973) and students of color (*Larry P. v. Riles,* 1972, 1979).

5. Disadvantages associated with assigning students labels based on handicapping conditions were identified (Hobbs, 1975, 1976).

6. Normalization, the belief that individuals with disabilities have the right to as normal an existence as possible, became an accepted goal of special services (Nirje, 1969; Wolfensberger, 1972).

The following case study begins the examination of what is the most appropriate educational placement and least restrictive environment.

Too Much of a Good Thing

In kindergarten, Jack had difficulty listening and staying on-task. By the end of first grade, it was clear that his learning was hampered by difficulties with auditory perception, memory, and inattention. Jack had not begun to read and couldn't remember any math facts. He was found to be eligible for special education. At the IEP meeting, his mother pleaded for him to receive full-time special instruction in a self-contained class; otherwise, she said, he might never learn to read or do math.

In the self-contained setting, Jack made excellent academic progress. Because his scores improved so steadily, his mother resisted the special education teacher's efforts to include Jack in any regular classroom instruction. The mother argued that Jack needed the small-group attention and individualized instruction. By the end of sixth grade, reading and math testing revealed grade-level functioning. However, in a discussion at home one evening, Jack's father mentioned he was going on a business trip to Canada. Jack asked where that was. This wasn't the first time his parents had noticed a lack of general knowledge. They were also concerned that no friends ever called to ask Jack to play.

At the end-of-the-year conference, the parents asked whether Jack was ready for middle school. His teacher responded honestly that Jack seemed immature and overly dependent on her. She was concerned about whether he could handle the move to the new school. Jack's mother was quiet. Then she asked, "Have we made a mistake pushing for so much special education at the expense of other experiences?"

CONSIDER THIS

1. What initial concern prompted the request for an intensive level of special education services for Jack?
2. How should the special education teacher respond to the parents' concern about middle school?
3. What would you propose for next year's program?

Once again, the paradigm addressing appropriate education for students with disabilities began to shift. The pendulum swung away from segregated instruction for students with disabilities toward inclusion of these students in the mainstream of instruction. Parents and professionals, as well as state and federal legislation, supported the trend toward inclusive instruction. The landmark legislation that provided an impetus for more inclusive education of students with disabilities was PL 94-142, the Education for All Handicapped Children Act, passed in 1975. Smith and Luckasson (1992) summarized the key points of PL 94-142 as:

- The provision of a free, appropriate education for all handicapped children.
- Nondiscriminatory procedures for testing and evaluating children of all races and cultures.
- The development of individualized education programs (IEPs) for each child with special needs.
- Education in the least restrictive environment, meaning children with disabilities should be educated alongside their nondisabled peers to the greatest extent possible.
- The assurance of due process procedures for the child and his or her parent or guardian (pp. 19–20).

During the past two decades, considerable argument has surrounded the concept of education in the least restrictive environment (LRE). PL 94-142 called for the education of each child with disabilities in the least restrictive appropriate educational setting, removed no further than necessary from the regular public school program. PL 94-142 did *not* require placement of all children with disabilities in regular classes, nor were children with special needs to remain in regular classes without supportive services. It also did not suggest that general education teachers should educate students with disabilities without help from special educators and other specialists. It did, however, call for regular and special educators to cooperate in providing an equal educational opportunity for students with disabilities.

Even though PL 94-142 did not include the term "mainstreaming," it is sometimes known as the "mainstreaming law" because it required that students with disabilities be educated with regular class peers as much as was appropriate. Mainstreaming, as practiced, integrated students with disabilities into general education classes with nondisabled peers. Expanded services beyond special classes in public schools were created. Students with disabilities could remain in the regular classroom for the majority, if not all, of the school day, receiving special education where and when it was needed.

As mainstreaming became a common practice in public schools in the years following the passage of PL 94–142, serious concerns emerged:

1. Regular class placement was viewed as the optimum instructional environment for students with disabilities. Students with disabilities were indiscriminately placed in general education programs without informing or preparing teachers, school personnel, nondisabled students, and parents.

2. Some individuals interpreted the mandate for placement of students in the LRE as synonymous with regular education. Regular education was considered to be the option that educated students with disabilities to the greatest extent possible with nondisabled peers, but it was only *one* option. PL 94–142 provided for a continuum of service alternatives for students with disabilities. Deno's model for a cascade of services (1970) shows options that can be used within the LRE construct.

3. Regular class placement was *not* the appropriate placement for all students with disabilities. Intensive services were needed for some students with various levels of severity and types of exceptionality.

4. Planned transition for students with disabilities from segregated special education classes into general education was, for the most part, nonexistent. Students were "dumped" into general education classes with little preparation academically, socially, or emotionally.

5. Once students with disabilities were placed in general education classes, regular education teachers often did not receive the support needed. Dialogue about methods, materials, and environmental adaptations which would promote success for mainstreamed students often did not occur between regular and special education teachers.

6. Planned and systematic dialogue, communication, and monitoring of the performance and needs of mainstreamed students were frequently overlooked. Factionalism (territoriality) could be observed among the many professionals who had interactions with mainstreamed students (regular and special education teachers, psychologists, administrators, etc.), while parents and students with disabilities were relegated to the role of passive participants in the educational process.

In the last decade, several important factors have begun to influence regular and special education and their collaboration in the mainstreaming of special students. The 1980s witnessed the publication of several reports critical of the quality of education in K–12 schools. *A Nation at Risk: The Imperative for Educational Reform* (National Commission on Excellence in Education, 1983), *Tomorrow's Teachers* (Holmes Group, 1986), and *A Nation Prepared: Teachers for the 21st Century*

(Carnegie Forum on Education and the Economy, 1986) all called for reform throughout the curriculum. Trends in reform have included higher academic standards, increased graduation requirements, more vigorous evaluation of student achievement, and improved discipline (Braaten & Braaten, 1988). One key reform effort has been the outcome-based education (OBE) movement. In many states, OBE has resulted in the specification of one set of standards for *all* students. This has led some to believe there should be *one* educational system for *all* students. Specific outcomes (what students know, what students can *do,* and what we want students to be like) for which mastery must be demonstrated as students progress through the K–12 curriculum have been designed and implemented.

As the decade of the 1990s began, debate continued over the role of mainstreaming in the education of students with disabilities. In the summer of 1990, Congress enacted significant changes in the Education of All Handicapped Children Act, including renaming the law. PL 101-476, the Individuals with Disabilities Education Act (IDEA), expanded the definition of special education to include instruction in such settings as the workplace and training centers, as well as preparation for transition to postschool life. As with PL 94-142, IDEA stipulated that students with disabilities had to receive any *related services* necessary to ensure they benefitted from their educational experience, including special transportation and other support services, such as speech, physical and occupational therapy, and medical services.

IDEA continued the tradition of identifying students as eligible for special education based on categories of disabilities and added two new categories: autism and traumatic brain injury. IDEA reemphasized four specific provisions of PL 94-142: (a) nondiscriminatory and multidisciplinary assessment of educational needs, (b) parental involvement in developing each child's educational program, (c) education in the least restrictive environment, and (d) an individualized educational program.

Hardman, Drew, Egan, and Wolf (1993) summarized the LRE requirements contained in IDEA:

> All students have the right to learn in an environment consistent with their academic, social, and physical needs. Such a setting constitutes the least restrictive environment (LRE). IDEA mandated that students with disabilities receive their education with nondisabled peers to the maximum extent appropriate. In order to meet this mandate, federal regulations required schools to develop a continuum of placements, ranging from regular classrooms with support services to homebound and hospital programs. (p. 26)

The following case study describes a student who was able to move successfully from a state school for the deaf to a less restrictive environment.

A Range of Support Services

Mr. and Mrs. Ashley knew almost immediately that their daughter, Lauren, was born deaf. They sought expert advice and were encouraged to learn sign language to use with their daughter during her critical early language development period. When Lauren was 3, her family moved to a suburb within driving distance of the State School for the Deaf. She attended pre-school and then kindergarten through fourth grade at the state school while living at home.

Lauren showed so much promise academically that her parents felt she should have more opportunity to learn and socialize with her hearing peers than was offered at the state school. Mr. and Mrs. Ashley met with the principal of the neighborhood elementary school to ask what type of program might be available to Lauren if she attended there. The principal arranged a meeting with a counselor from the state school, the assistant special education director from the home district, and Lauren's parents.

A comprehensive program was proposed that included a full-time interpreter, one hour per day of assistance in a resource room, biweekly speech therapy, daily notes home, and quarterly conferences to discuss progress. Lauren began the fifth grade with a full array of instructional and support services, as well as assistance from fellow students taking notes and working cooperatively. Although it was hard work for Lauren, her parents, and her teachers, she excelled.

By her junior year, Lauren was a member of the National Honor Society and was participating in sports. Coaches at the School for the Deaf were aware of Lauren's athletic abilities. They asked her to join the teams at their school, suggesting that it was important for her to maintain contact with peers who are deaf. Lauren initially refused but went to visit. During her senior year, she joined the teams at her old school while continuing to excel academically at her neighborhood high school. Next year, she plans to attend a large junior college that has a support system for students who are deaf.

 CONSIDER THIS

1. What is essential about each of the instructional and support services provided for Lauren so she could succeed in the public school?
2. Read the following descriptions of least restrictive environment alternatives and consider why different levels of services were appropriate at several points during Lauren's education.

A CONTINUUM OF SERVICES

A model for a continuum of educational services is presented in Figure 10.1. The seven levels are summarized as follows:

Level I: At the least restrictive level, the student remains in the **general classroom** and receives no additional support services. Necessary adaptations are handled by

FIGURE 10.1

LEAST RESTRICTIVE ENVIRONMENT PLACEMENT ALTERNATIVES

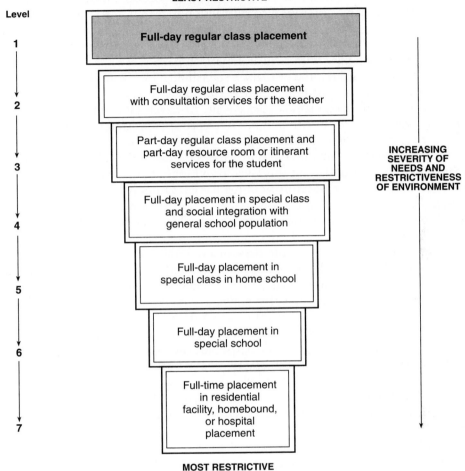

LEAST RESTRICTIVE

Level

1 — Full-day regular class placement

2 — Full-day regular class placement with consultation services for the teacher

3 — Part-day regular class placement and part-day resource room or itinerant services for the student

4 — Full-day placement in special class and social integration with general school population

5 — Full-day placement in special class in home school

6 — Full-day placement in special school

7 — Full-time placement in residential facility, homebound, or hospital placement

INCREASING SEVERITY OF NEEDS AND RESTRICTIVENESS OF ENVIRONMENT

MOST RESTRICTIVE

the classroom teacher. The student's success depends on whether his/her teacher is skillful in developing and adapting programs to meet individual needs.

Level II: A student remains in the **regular classroom**, but **consultative services** are available to both teacher and student. These indirect services may be provided by a variety of professionals, including special educators, speech and language specialists, behavior specialists, physical education specialists, occupational therapists, physical therapists, school psychologists, and social workers. Services may range from assisting a teacher in the use of tests or the modification of curriculum to directing the instruction of students in the classroom setting.

Level III: A student stays in the **regular classroom** for the majority of the school day but also receives **specialized instruction** in deficit areas. Typically, these services are provided in a resource room program under the direction of a qualified special educator. The amount of time a student receives specialized instruction varies according to his/her needs; it may range from as short as 30 minutes to as long as 3 hours a day. Instruction in a resource room is intended to teach requisite learning skills as well as reinforce or supplement the student's work in the regular classroom. Students receive the assistance necessary to ensure that they keep pace with regular education peers.

At Levels I, II, and III, the primary responsibility for the student's education lies with the regular classroom teacher. Consultative services are intended to support the student's regular class placement. At Levels IV and beyond, the primary responsibility for instruction shifts to special education providers.

Level IV: A student's instruction is in a **special education classroom** for the majority of the school day. At this level, provisions are made for students to be **integrated whenever possible** with regular education peers and in accordance with their learning capabilities. For students who are moderately to severely disabled, integration is usually recommended for nonacademic subject areas.

Level V: The student is placed **full-time** in a **special education class**. Although still in a regular school, the student is not integrated with regular education students for formalized instructional activities. However, some level of social integration may take place during recess, lunch, assemblies, field trips, and tutoring.

Level VI: A student is placed in a separate facility designed for students with disabilities. This type of facility includes **special day schools**, where the educational program is one aspect of a comprehensive treatment program.

Level VII: At the most restrictive level, a student with severe disabilities unable to attend any school program receives services through a **homebound** or **hospital program**.

INCREASED INTEGRATION INTO GENERAL EDUCATION

One suggestion for providing increased integration of students with disabilities into general education classrooms has been advanced by the Regular Education Initiative (REI). REI advocates criticize the dual system of special and regular education. Instead, they propose a commitment to serve all students with learning problems, not just those identified for special education, within the regular classroom. In the article considered the position statement for the REI, *Educating Children With Learning Problems: A Shared Responsibility,* Will (1986) called the current service delivery system, which emphasizes mainstreaming, a "flawed vision of education for our children" (p. 412).

Proponents of the REI endorse full-time integration for students with mild levels of disability into general education classrooms, although they do not advocate the abolition of special education services (Reynolds, Wang, & Walberg, 1987; Wang & Birch, 1984; Wang & Walberg, 1988; Will, 1986). According to Lewis (1989), in REI, "the placement of choice would be the regular classroom, albeit an *enhanced regular classroom* in which powerful instructional technologies such as cooperative learning and peer tutoring are routinely employed to increase the probability of academic and social success of low-achieving students" (p. 49). REI critics point to the need for a range of service options. Braaten, Kauffman, Braaten, Polsgrove, and Nelson (1988) comment, "Research clearly does not support the assertion that all students can be managed and taught effectively in regular classrooms" (p. 23). According to Wiederholt (1989), "A range of services from programs of total segregation to full-time integration appears as appropriate for the 1990s as it has been for past decades" (p. 189).

Another criticism of the REI movement is that it is based in part on research regarding the Adaptive Learning Environments Model (ALEM). Although REI supporters point to the ALEM as a "successful, large-scale, full-time mainstreaming program" (Reynolds et al., 1987, p. 115), critics state that research concerning ALEM was methodologically weak and lacked clarity in describing the characteristics of students studied (Fuchs & Fuchs, 1991). The Council for Children with Behavioral Disorders (1989), the Council for Learning Disabilities (1993), and other professional associations support the inclusion of students with disabilities in general education classrooms, but only when *deemed appropriate and only when necessary support services are provided*.

One of the major fears of special educators who oppose the REI is that students with disabilities will be placed in regular classrooms on a full-time basis without adequate support. Although provision of special services within the regular class is a viable model for some students, others require more intensive intervention. For example, full-time mainstreaming faces many barriers at the secondary level (Schumaker & Deshler, 1988). In junior and senior high schools, there are large gaps between the skills of students with mild disabilities and the demands of the instructional setting; instruction tends to be teacher-centered rather than student-centered. Making the systemic changes necessary to implement the REI in secondary schools may be a difficult and lengthy process for most school districts.

Another consideration is the already difficult task facing general education teachers as they attempt to meet the needs of the diverse learners who make up regular classes. The general classroom of the 1990s includes an increasing number of students at risk for school failure, and "more variability than now exists in most regular classrooms is not a reasonable option without additional protected resources for the teacher" (Kauffman, Gerber, & Semmel, 1988, p. 10).

Many school districts have taken the integration of students with mild disabilities into general education classrooms very seriously. This case study illustrates the planning and responsible decision-making employed by one suburban district, which has resulted in the successful integration of students with mild disabilities into general education classrooms.

USD 123

Faced with mandated inclusion of students with disabilities into general education over a 3-year period, USD 123, a suburban school district in the Midwest, planned a series of yearlong staff development activities designed to increase awareness and understanding about disabilities. Faculty and administrators participated in monthly inservice sessions within each elementary and secondary building. Teams of special and general education teachers and administrators used a case study approach to collaboratively brainstorm appropriate adaptations in instructional methods, classroom materials, and the physical arrangement of the classroom.

Parents and students were also prepared throughout the planning year for the integration process. PTO meetings and parent conferences provided opportunities for parents to be educated about the district's plan for including students with disabilities in general education. School and classroom newsletters served as additional vehicles for increasing awareness. Students were informed through classroom instruction that focused on individual differences and experimental activities that provided simulations of varied disabilities. Social integration activities were also planned and conducted in both general and special education settings.

A class-within-a-class instructional model was phased in over several months within K–6 classrooms. Within this instructional model, regular and special education teachers served as coteachers. Everyone was responsible for providing unit planning, delivering instruction to all students (including those with disabilities) in the general education classroom, and monitoring student progress once guided and independent practice were initiated.

Students with mild disabilities (learning disabilities, mental retardation, and behavioral disorders) were gradually integrated into elementary general education classrooms in all content areas in which their skills and abilities ensured success. Some students with disabilities received all of their instruction within the general education setting. Others spent the majority of the day in general education but worked one to three class periods each day in a resource room with the special education teacher on individualized lessons tailored to specific needs.

Team meetings involving regular and special education teachers, the school counselor, the school psychologist, and other personnel as needed (principal, parent, speech pathologist, etc.) were held weekly. A case study approach was also used at team meetings to review *any* student (with or without a disability) experiencing difficulty—social, academic, or behavioral. A specific plan of action was drawn up for any student needing extra assistance. Team members monitored student performance in targeted areas until improvement was noted.

The year of planning had helped provide for a smooth first year of integration. One fifth-grade teacher reported he was "none too happy when

he learned that his class would have to include special education students."
He dreaded the paperwork and extra planning burden, when his planning time was already limited. "I didn't want to get involved," he said. Something exciting happened, however, when three students with disabilities joined his class. Most of the regular students rose to the occasion, befriending the students with disabilities. The fifth-grade teacher said he and his students learned as much from the newcomers as the newcomers learned from being in regular classes. Other teachers within USD 123 agreed that, when done properly, integration benefits special and regular education children.

CONSIDER THIS

1. How did this district prepare for the shift toward more inclusive programming?
2. What part do teams play in meeting students' and teachers' needs?
3. What changes in the school environment must be made to support greater inclusion of students with disabilities in general education?

FULL INCLUSION

While REI focuses on students with mild disabilities, a similar movement calls for increased integration of students with severe disabilities (Falvey, Grenot-Scheyer, & Bishop, 1989; OSERS, 1986; Pumpian, 1988; Brown, Long, Udvari-Solner, Davis, VanDeventer, Ahlgren, Johnson, Gruenwald, & Jorgensen, 1989; Sailor, Anderson, Halvorsen, Doering, Filler, & Goetz, 1989). Leaders such as Stainback and Stainback (1985) call for the full inclusion of all students with disabilities, including those with severe handicaps, not only in neighborhood schools but also in regular classrooms.

Brown et al. (1989) made a strong case for why students with severe handicaps should attend their "home school" (the school a student would attend if he or she were not disabled):

> The environments in which students with severe intellectual disabilities receive instructional services have critical effects on where and how they spend their postschool lives. Segregation begets segregation. We believe that when children with intellectual disabilities attend segregated schools, they are denied opportunities to demonstrate to the rest of the community that they can function in integrated environments and activities; their nondisabled peers do not know or understand them and too often think negatively of them; their parents become afraid to risk allowing them opportunities to learn to function in integrated environments later in life; and taxpayers assume they need to be sequestered in segregated group homes, enclaves, work crews, activity centers, sheltered workshops, institutions, and nursing homes. (p. 1)

Brown and his colleagues offer four reasons why home schools should replace segregated schools. First, when students without disabilities go to an integrated school with peers who are disabled, they are more likely to function responsibly as adults in a pluralistic society. Second, various sources of information demonstrate that instruction in integrated schools offers more meaningful IEP objectives for students with severe handicaps than education at segregated schools in terms of age–appropriateness, functionality, and the potential for generalization of learning to other environments. Third, parents and families have greater access to school activities when children are attending their home schools. Fourth, and perhaps most convincing, is the argument there are greater opportunities to develop in one's home school.

The full inclusion of students with severe disabilities into regular classrooms has generated significant debate among general and special educators. At one end of the continuum, some professionals (Gartner & Lipsky, 1987; Stainback & Stainback, 1989) maintain that even students with severe disabilities should be placed and educated in regular classrooms. These and other professionals (Will, 1986) have argued that labels are not beneficial to children with disabilities. The labeling process may lead to placing students in programs outside of the regular classroom, thereby stigmatizing them and resulting in negative perceptions by peers, parents, and teachers. The proponents of full inclusion maintain that the current system of educating students with disabilities in segregated classrooms simply does not work because it fails to serve the unique needs of each student. Such programs result in a fragmented approach to the delivery of a total educational program.

The proponents of full inclusion have also argued that placement in regular education classrooms with a partnership between regular and special educators results in a learning environment that is diverse and rich, rather than just a collection of discrete programming slots and funding pots. A partnership between regular and special education may personalize each student's instructional program and implement it in the least restrictive environment. Additionally, special educators are more effective in a partnership because they can use their knowledge and resources to assist regular educators in developing intervention strategies that meet student needs in the natural classroom setting.

Opponents of full inclusion (Braaten et al., 1988; Fuchs & Fuchs, 1991; Kauffman, 1991) have argued that regular educators have little expertise in assisting students with severe learning and behavioral problems and are already overburdened with large class sizes and inadequate support services. Special educators have been trained to develop instructional strategies and use teaching techniques, such as individualized instruction, that are not part of the training of most regular education teachers. More specialized academic and social instruction can be provided in special education classrooms. Specialized settings also allow for the centralization of both human and material resources.

Examine the following case study in light of key elements associated with the debate surrounding full inclusion.

Jose

Jose is an 11-year-old male who has a full-scale WISC-III score of 47. He has severe behavior outbursts which generally involve kicking, screaming, and tantrums. These outbursts occur from 15 to 20 times daily and usually last from 3 to 5 minutes each. Jose's speech is characterized by several articulation errors. He can be understood when he speaks slowly, but when excited, he is almost unintelligible. Academically, Jose reads at the first-grade level (comprehends at the primer level), can add and subtract (when no regrouping is required), and can write simple sentences and some words in isolation (although inventive spelling is a frequent occurrence). When his behavior is regulated, Jose relates well with other students. He enjoys talking about baseball and football and knows statistics for most major league players in both sports. Jose's physical skills are quite good. During recess he enjoys playing kickball and tag football.

Jose and his family lived in an urban setting in California. For the first 4 years of his formal education, he was placed in a self-contained classroom for students with moderate mental retardation. When he was 9, Jose's parents asked the school to change his placement from full-time, self-contained special education to a full-time, general education classroom. When the school district refused full-time regular education, offering instead a resource room/regular classroom option, Jose's parents successfully argued their case in a California court. The court ordered full inclusion, stating that the local school district failed to show why full inclusion within a regular classroom was not an appropriate placement.

Midyear, Jose and his parents moved from California to a rural school district in the Midwest. Jose's parents met with the special education director, informing her that while Jose had "some special learning needs," he was to be placed in a general education classroom with same-age peers. The parents also informed the school district that if Jose was placed in any setting other than a regular sixth-grade class 100% of the day, they were ready to go to court. They were determined that Jose would receive instruction in the least restrictive environment, and cited the California court case and ruling.

Consequently, Jose was enrolled in a sixth-grade class with 27 students. His new teacher had taught learning-disabled students for 5 years before returning to general education at the beginning of the school year. By the end of the first week of Jose's inclusion, she had documented spending an average of 30 minutes each hour working individually with Jose. A paraprofessional was brought into the classroom to assist Jose. Jose's teacher resigned 3 weeks after Jose transferred into her class. By the end of the year (3½ months later) four teachers were hired—and each resigned. Several parents of sixth-grade students complained to school and district administrators, stating that their children were being denied adequate instruction because the teacher was required to spend an inordinate amount of time with Jose. Jose's parents could not be encouraged to consider any placement other than full inclusion. The school district is contemplating a due process hearing to review Jose's placement in the least restrictive environment.

 CONSIDER THIS

1. The parents assumed that the program developed for Jose in California would naturally be offered anywhere they moved. Is this justifiable?
2. What factors may have contributed to problems in the new placement?

RESPONSIBLE INCLUSION

There is no simple answer when faced with the dilemma raised by the title of this chapter: "To include or not to include—that is the question." One principle is clear, however: The practice of integrating students with disabilities into general education must be done *responsibly*. Educators should examine several questions when considering responsible inclusion for individual students with disabilities into general education classrooms.

1. To what extent do classroom teachers accept responsibilities for (a) educating all students assigned to them, (b) making and monitoring major instructional decisions for all students in their class, (c) providing instruction that follows a normal developmental curriculum in the basic skills area that is designed to bring students to a level of adult competence, (d) managing instruction for diverse populations, and (e) seeking, using, and coordinating assistance for students who require more intense service than those provided to their peers?
2. To what extent do principals have sufficient knowledge about instruction and learning to distribute resources across classrooms so that students with special needs can be accommodated and served effectively?
3. To what extent are specialists able to collaborate and communicate with classroom teachers and relinquish to them final authority regarding instructional decision-making?
4. To what extent are multidisciplinary teams prepared to require hard evidence that students have received high-quality, direct instruction from classroom teachers and support staff?
5. Are multidisciplinary teams prepared to decide students may not develop competency in basic skills during their school career, and recommend the students be segregated from their regular classroom peers? (Jenkins, Pious, & Jewell, 1990, pp. 481–482, 489)

The placement of students with disabilities (regardless of severity) into a regular classroom should be considered only when these questions can be answered yes. In addition, inclusion should occur within a systematically planned and well-conceived organizational structure that has included preparation for parents, teachers (both general and special education), and administrators. Preservice and inservice training must prepare special educators for consultative and collaborative roles in addition to the current emphasis on specialized instruction. Educators also need to expand their repertoire of effective instruction techniques so that students work in more flexible learning environments. Schrag (1993) states that successful inclusive classrooms typically include cooperative learning, multiage grouping, peer-mediated learning, and coteaching. Teachers must be able to adapt curriculum, particularly to accommodate students who require more functional, developmentally appropriate instruction. General and special educators also need to be facile in using varied behavior management strategies and student self-management techniques.

Students (general and special education) should be informed and prepared for inclusionary practices. It is essential for the school environment to reflect an attitude that celebrates diversity and values individuals of all abilities and limitations, thus promoting a sense of self-worth, concern, and respect for others (Schrag, 1993). Responsible inclusion should not be implemented until essential support systems are in place within the general education setting. Lewis and Doorlag (1991) listed reading specialists, psychologists, speech-language pathologists, occupational therapists, and physical therapists as members of support systems critical to successful integration. Support systems also include assistance teams in which specialists, teachers, and parents collaborate to solve problems. In addition, an array of community of services may be necessary to support students in their home school.

PL 94–142 and IDEA stipulate that students with disabilities have the right to be educated within the least restrictive environment. IDEA specifically states:

1. To the maximum extent appropriate, children with disabilities, including children in public or private institutions or other care facilities, are educated with children who are not disabled.
2. Special classes with separate schooling, or other removal of children with disabilities from the general educational environment, is to occur only when the nature or severity of the disability is such that education in general education classes with the use of supplementary aids and services cannot be achieved satisfactorily. (Public Law 101–476, Individuals with Disabilities Education Act, 20 U.S.C., 1412[5][B]; 1414[a][1][C][iv])

Least restrictive environment is a relative concept; the ideal environment for one child may be too restrictive for another. Even though some educators, parents, and lawyers consider any decision to place a student with a disability in a special class or school to be overly restrictive, most recognize that a regular class placement can be restrictive and inappropriate if the child's instructional and social needs are not adequately met. It is also generally accepted that there are wide individual differences among children and there can be more than one "best" way to provide appropriate educational services to an exceptional child. As stated by

Heward and Orlansky (1992), "A child's educational program should be based on consideration of that child's needs. Not all children with the same disability should be placed in the same setting; the goal, instead, is to find an appropriate LRE for each child" (p. 59).

The question: to include or not to include.

The answer: responsible inclusion.

SUMMARY

For decades, there have been debates over what is an appropriate educational program in a least restrictive environment for students with disabilities. After the passage of PL 94-142, many segregated special education services were provided. However, researchers concluded that the pendulum had swung too far and students with special needs would benefit from greater participation in the general classroom with nondisabled peers. In the past decade, special and general educators have begun to work collaboratively to create more effective instructional programs.

As schools respond to public criticism and the call for reform, concern has been raised about the impact of changes on students with special needs. The rights of individuals with disabilities were reaffirmed with the passage of IDEA in 1990. IDEA states that students with disabilities have the right to education in the least restrictive environment and to placement in the most appropriate program among a continuum of services.

Proponents of more inclusive programming advocate that students with even the most severe disabilities should be educated in a regular classroom in their neighborhood schools. Other educators argue that schools and teachers are not prepared to provide the necessary quality services to meet individual needs. All would agree there are many significant questions to ask concerning what is the most appropriate educational program and which is the least restrictive environment for each student with disabilities. Responsible inclusion is founded on the analysis of an individual student's needs, systematic planning, ongoing communication, support structures, and continuous program evaluation. The question is not whether to include but rather how to include responsibly.

REFERENCES

Braaten, S., Kauffman, J., Braaten, B., Polsgrove, L., & Nelson, C. M. (1988). The regular education initiative: Patent medicine for behavioral disorders. *Exceptional Children, 55*(1), 21–27.

Braaten, B., & Braaten, S. (1988). Reform: For everyone? *Teaching Exceptional Children, 21*(1), 46–47.

Brown, L., Long, E., Udvari-Solner, A., Davis, L., VanDeventer, P., Ahlgren, C., Johnson, F., Gruenwald, L., & Jorgensen, J. (1989). The home school: Why students with severe disabilities must attend the school of their brothers, sisters, friends, and neighbors. *The Journal of the Association for Persons With Severe Handicaps, 14,* 1–7.

Carnegie Forum on Education and the Economy. (1986). *A nation prepared: Teachers for the 21st century.* Washington, DC: Author.

Council for Children with Behavioral Disorders. (1989). Position statement on the regular education initiative. *Behavior Disorders, 14,* 201–207.

Council for Learning Disabilities. (1993). *Position statement on the regular education initiative.* Austin, TX: Author.

Davis, W. E. (1989). The regular education initiative debate: Its promises and problems. *Exceptional Children, 55,* 440–446.

Deno, E. (1970). Special education as developmental capital. *Exceptional Children, 37,* 236.

Diana v. State Board of Education. (1970, 1973). C–70, 37RFP (N.D. Cal., 1970, 1973).

Dunn, L. M. (1968). Special education for the mildly retarded—Is much of it justifiable? *Exceptional Children, 35,* 5–22.

Falvey, M. A., Grenot-Scheyer, M., & Bishop, K. (1989). Integrating students with severe handicaps. *California State Federation/CEC Journal, 35*(3), 8–10.

Fuchs, D., & Fuchs, L. (1991). Framing the REI debate: Abolitionists versus conservationists. In J. W. Lloyd, N. N. Singh, & A. C. Repp (Eds.), *The regular education initiative: Alternative perspectives on concepts, issues, and models* (pp. 241–255). Sycamore, IL: Sycamore.

Gartner, A., & Lipsky, D. K. (1987). Beyond special education: Toward a quality system for all students. *Harvard Educational Review, 57*(4), 367–395.

Hardman, M. L., Drew, C. J., Egan, M. W., & Wolf, B. (1993). *Human exceptionality: Society, school, and family.* Needham Heights, MA: Allyn & Bacon.

Heward, W. L., & Orlansky, M. D. (1992). *Exceptional Children* (4th ed.). New York: Merrill.

Hobbs, N. (1975). *The futures of children.* San Francisco, CA: Jossey-Bass.

Hobbs, N. (1976). *Issues in the classification of children.* San Francisco, CA: Jossey-Bass.

Holmes Group. (1986). *Tomorrow's teachers: A report of the Holmes Group.* East Lansing, MI: Author.

Hunt, P., Goetz, L., & Anderson, J. (1986). The quality of IEP objectives associated with placement on integrated versus segregated school sites. *The Journal of the Association for Persons with Severe Handicaps, 11,* 125–130.

Individuals With Disabilities Education Act of 1990, PL 101-476, 602[a][19].

Jenkins, J. R., Pious, C. G., & Jewell, M. (1990). Special education and the regular education initiative: Basic assumptions. *Exceptional Children, 56*(6), 479–491.

Kauffman, J. M. (1991), Restructuring in sociopolitical context: Reservations about the effects of current reform proposals on students with disabilities. In J. W. Lloyd, N. N. Singh, & A. C. Repp (Eds.), *The regular education initiative: Alternative perspectives on concepts, issues, and models.* (pp. 57–66). Sycamore, IL: Sycamore.

Kauffman, J. M., Gerber, M. M., & Semmel, M. I. (1988). Arguable assumptions underlying the regular education initiative. *Journal of Learning Disabilities, 21*(1), 6–11.

Larry P. v. Riles. (1972). C–71–2270 U.S.C., 353 F. Supp. 1306 (N.D. Cal. 1972).

Larry P. v. Riles. (1979). 343 F. Supp. 1306, 502 F. 2d 963 (N.D. Cal. 1979).

Lewis, R. B. (1989). Educational assessment of learning disabilities: a new generation of achievement measures. *Learning Disabilities: A Multidisciplinary Journal, 1,* 49–55.

Lewis, R. B., & Doorlag, D. H. (1991). *Teaching special students in the mainstream.* New York: Merrill.

Mercer, J. R. (1973). *Labeling the mentally retarded.* Berkeley, CA: University of California Press.

National Commission on Excellence in Education. (1983). *A nation at risk: The imperative for educational reform.* Washington, DC: Author.

Nirje, B. (1969). The normalization principle and its human management implications. In R. B. Kugel & W. Wolfensberger (Eds.), *Changing patterns in residential services for the mentally retarded* (pp. 231–240). Washington, DC: U.S. Government Printing Office.

OSERS answers questions about LRE. (1986). *OSERS News in Print, 1*(2), 6–7.

The President's Committee on Mental Retardation. (1969). *The six-hour retarded child.* Washington, DC: U.S. Government Printing Office.

Pumpian, I. (1988). Severe multiple handicaps. In E. W. Lynch & R. B. Lewis (Eds.), *Exceptional children and adults* (pp. 180–226). Glenview, IL: Scott-Foresman.

Reynolds, M. L., Wang, M. L., and Walberg, H. J. (1987). The necessary restructuring of special and regular education. *Exceptional Children, 53,* 391–398.

Sailor, W., Anderson, J. L., Halvorsen, A., Doering, K., Filler, J., & Goetz, L. (1989). *The comprehensive local school: Regular education for all students with disabilities.* Baltimore, MD: Paul H. Brookes.

Schrag, J. (1993). *Features of inclusive schools.* Personal communication.

Schumaker, J., & Deshler, D. (1988). Implementing the regular education initiative in secondary schools: A different ball game. *Journal of Learning Disabilities, 21,* 43–52.

Smith, D. D., & Luckasson, R. (1992). *Introduction to special education: Teaching in an age of challenge.* Boston, MA: Allyn & Bacon.

Stainback, S., & Stainback, W. (Eds.). (1985). *Integrating students with severe handicaps into regular schools.* Reston, VA: The Council for Exceptional Children.

Stainback, W., & Stainback, S. (1989). Practical organizational strategies. In S. Stainback, W. Stainback, & M. Forrest (Eds.), *Educating all students in the mainstream of education* (pp. 71–87). Baltimore, MD: Paul H. Brookes.

Wang, M. C., & Birch, J. W. (1984). Effective special education in regular classes. *Exceptional Children, 50,* 391–399.

Wang, M. C., & Walberg, H. J. (1988). Four fallacies of segregationalism. *Exceptional Children, 55,* 391–399.

Wiederholt, J. L. (1989). Restructuring special education services: The past, the present, the future. *Learning Disability Quarterly, 12,* 181–191.

Will, M. (1986). Educating children with learning problems: A shared responsibility. *Exceptional Children, 52,* 411–415.

Wolfensberger, W. (1972). *Normalization: The principle of normalization in human services.* Toronto: National Institute of Mental Retardation.

Chapter 11

CHILDREN WITH SPECIAL HEALTH CONDITIONS IN SCHOOL

Janice Rutledge Janz, Terry Heintz Caldwell, and Jacqueline Harrison

The day is long past when school administrators are simply expected to provide academic leadership. Administrators of today must also be concerned with the multiple complexities that threaten the welfare of children in our society. Administrators must deal with issues concerning children who are abused, neglected, impoverished, and homeless, as well as with a rapidly increasing number of children with special health-care needs.

As a result of advances in medical technology and treatment, improved response to medical emergencies and the survival of premature infants, many more children with chronic conditions are living well into adulthood. In fact, Newacheck and Taylor (1992), reporting the results of a 1988 study, concluded that an estimated 20% of children in the United States experience mild chronic conditions, 9% experience chronic conditions of moderate severity, and 2% experience severe chronic conditions. Evidence also suggests that more people born with a chronic illness or disability will survive beyond their 20th birthday (National Center for Youth with Disabilities, 1991).

Concurrently, the increase in the number of students with special health conditions seeking school services is affected by deinstitutionalization, dehospitalization, parents' knowledge of children's rights, and inclusionary educational practices. In addition, children's rights have been affected by civil rights legislation, such as Section 504 of the Rehabilitation Act of 1973, and entitlement legislation, such as the Individuals With Disabilities Education Act (IDEA).

Who are these students whose numbers are growing and who are increasingly seeking services in their neighborhood schools? Students with special health conditions include children with:

- **Chronic conditions** such as asthma, diabetes and sickle cell disease.
- Conditions that require **technology assistance and treatment**, including ventilation, catheterization, and gastrostomy feedings.
- Conditions that cause **body and skin deformities**, such as burns and craniofacial abnormalities.
- **Infectious** conditions such as HIV and hepatitis B.

- Conditions that cause **neurological changes**, such as severe seizure disorders and traumatic brain injury.
- Conditions that compromise the child's health status, causing the child to be **medically fragile**, such as the end stage of AIDS and renal disease. (Caldwell, Todaro, & Gates, 1990)

These children pose complex issues to school administrators. Several case studies will be presented in this chapter to illustrate relevant issues such as liability, the need for health care and emergency plans, and the need for collaboration between health and education personnel. Each case study includes questions to consider. This chapter uses a slightly different format from previous chapters in that these questions are addressed in a section titled "Administrative Strategies and Organizational Tools" that follows each case study and offers suggestions to facilitate the administration of programs for such children.

Issues of Confidentiality

Rhonda is a 10-year-old female who is in the fifth grade. She is popular among her peers. She is particularly close to Melissa, Amy, and Kelly, three other girls in her class. One day she confided to her friends the biggest secret of her life and swore them to secrecy. She told them she was HIV-positive and that one day she may die from AIDS.

Her friends had heard of AIDS but didn't know much about it. Kelly went home and asked her mother what HIV-positive was and could people really die from it. Kelly's mother asked where she had heard about HIV, and after some prodding Kelly confessed that Rhonda had told her friends that she was HIV-positive. Kelly's mother immediately telephoned the principal, asking whether she knew Rhonda had AIDS. The principal replied that she had never been informed of the matter and assured the parent there was no need to be alarmed as there had been no cases of HIV spread through casual contact. Kelly's mother was not satisfied with this answer and called the parents of Amy and Melissa to learn whether their daughters had shared this information and what they were planning to do about it.

The next morning, the principal was greeted by 10 parents wanting to know whether Rhonda was really HIV-positive and, if so, "when was she going to be asked to leave the school?"

CONSIDER THIS

1. How can administrators address concerns/fears of parents, students, faculty, and staff?
2. How do you balance issues of confidentiality with the "right to know"?

3. What policies and procedures regarding HIV and AIDS must be developed?

4. What training should be provided regarding "universal precautions"?

ADMINISTRATIVE STRATEGIES AND ORGANIZATIONAL TOOLS

Addressing Concerns/Fears of Parents, Students, Faculty, and Staff

Fear can be reduced if the school community (including parents) is provided with legal mandates as well as current and accurate information regarding the disease (Harvey, Seidel, & Crocker, 1992). The school community should also receive assurances that this information will be updated and disseminated on a regular basis. Opportunities for staff, students, and families to share their fears about the disease may also help dispel myths. Harvey et al. (1992) recommend the development of a committee to assist the administrator in implementing suggestions as concerns arise. The importance of ongoing education, as well as updates, cannot be underestimated, and a flow of information appears to be more effective than a one-time discussion that occurs as the result of an incident.

Managing Issues Involving Confidentiality and the "Right to Know"

The privacy of children with HIV infection must be preserved in the school system. Rosen and Granger (1992) have argued that since HIV infection is not transmitted through casual contact, staff members need not be informed of the diagnosis of a child who is HIV-positive. Many school systems have adopted policies that involve "right to know" and appropriate confidentiality protection. School personnel who have the "right to know" may include the principal, the child's teacher, and/or the school nurse. School personnel, if informed, may not share this diagnosis with anyone unless they have the written consent of the parent. The constraints regarding confidentiality are numerous and technical. Information about confidentiality is included in two publications by the American Bar Association (1989, 1991). Administrators should consult the district's legal counsel in developing policies regarding this issue.

Developing Policies and Procedures

Policies and procedures should address the issues of confidentiality, disclosure, and universal precautions. Most local districts will have a policy developed by their central office or the state department of education. The board of directors of the National Education Association has adopted *Someone at School Has AIDS* (Fraser, 1989) as NEA's policy guidelines on HIV and AIDS. Other sources of information about the development of policy include *The Medically Fragile Child in the School Setting,* published by the American Federation of Teachers (1992), and *HIV Infection and Developmental Disabilities: A Resource for Service Providers,* edited by Crocker, Cohen, and Kastner (1992).

Providing Training Regarding Universal Precautions

The major approach used to protect all children and staff members from infectious diseases is known as universal precautions. If one looks at the population of any one school, there may be children who are HIV-positive and have been identified to the principal, children who are HIV-positive but who have not been identified to the principal, and still other children who are HIV-positive but have not been diagnosed. Thus, treating everyone as if they are potentially infectious and using universal precautions consistently is the safest practice.

Universal precautions are methods to create barriers between one individual and the blood and body fluids of another. The American Federation of Teachers (1992, p. 21) says universal precautions call for the following:

1. *Protective equipment.* Staff members who may come in contact with blood and body fluid should wear gloves (preferably latex). When there is potential for splashes of large amounts of blood or body fluid, staff should have gowns, goggles/face shields/masks, and any other effective barriers.
2. *Puncture-proof containers.* Any school staff member who administers injections should have puncture-proof containers to dispose of contaminated needles. Contaminated needles transmit HIV and the hepatitis viruses.
3. *Disinfectants to kill the viruses.* To clean up spills, staff members should have disinfectants readily available, including common household bleach diluted with water (1 part bleach to 10 parts water), which has been effective in killing HIV and hepatitis viruses.
4. *Special receptacles in which to discard items and articles contaminated with blood.*
5. *Adequate facilities and opportunities for staff members to wash their hands immediately after an exposure.*

The school nurse may be able to train school staff members and students in universal precautions. If this is not possible, administrators may want to contact the infection control unit of a local hospital or the public health department to locate someone to conduct this training.

Planning for Health Procedures

Mary, a 9-year-old with insulin-dependent diabetes, attended school in a rural area. Mary would come to school in the morning ready to work, but within 2 hours would many times be lethargic and unable to concentrate. Frequently, she would have to go home before lunch. On the days she ate lunch at school, there was always confusion about what she could eat and how much she needed. One day, during a field day at school, she complained of a headache. The teacher told her to sit in the shade. After about 15 minutes, she began vomiting, had severe abdominal pains, and was taking shallow and rapid breaths. The teacher sent a child to the office to tell the secretary to call an ambulance. When Mary arrived at the hospital, it was determined that her blood glucose level was critically high. She was in diabetic ketoacidosis. The school nurse, who was assigned to Mary's school as well as two other schools, was not aware that Mary had diabetes.

 CONSIDER THIS

1. What procedures should be developed for gathering and disseminating relevant health information?
2. How could students be encouraged to be involved in their own health care?
3. How should special health procedures be delegated?
4. What planning is necessary for emergencies?

Gathering and Disseminating Relevant Health Information

Serving children with special health needs requires planning if they are to function safely in school. It is not enough to simply communicate the diagnosis of the child's condition. There is also a need for frank discussions about the educational implications of the condition. Project School Care of Boston Children's Hospital recommends that a health-care coordinator, preferably a school nurse, be selected to develop the plan with the family. Planning should include procedures for delineating lines of communication. For instance, to whom does the parent communicate health needs? How does the information get to the teacher and other personnel who work directly with the child? What is the school nurse's ongoing role?

Planning will also provide the opportunity for the school nurse and the school committee to prepare for the child's education. Preparation will include the development of:

- A nursing assessment.
- A written individualized health care plan.
- A written individualized health services plan.

A nursing assessment includes at least a review of the written medical records (including physician's orders if applicable) and the educational records of the student, an interview with the family, child, and physician (when indicated), and a physical assessment of the child. This provides the nurse with the opportunity to assess the need for health procedures and to determine whether those procedures can be delegated to the student or to nonlicensed caregivers such as classroom assistants. Decisions regarding delegation are an important part of the assessment. Delegation is regulated by the state's Nurse Practice Act and by school district policies and procedures (Todaro, Failla, & Caldwell, 1993).

Table 11.1 includes guidelines from the state of Louisiana to be addressed by the school nurse when developing an individualized health care plan. Information

TABLE 11.1
Guidelines for Developing an Individualized Health Care Plan

The school nurse shall write an Individualized Health Care Plan (IHCP) which includes the following: (The list is not complete and all areas listed may not be appropriate for each student.)

(1) Health needs
- (a) Diagnosis and description of the condition
- (b) Procedures and equipment needed
- (c) Treatment and side effects
- (d) Maintenance of skin integrity
- (e) Infection control
- (f) Safety issues
- (g) Nutrition and fluid requirement
- (h) Level of activity
- (i) Precautions and/or restrictions

(2) Emergency plan
- (a) Warning signs and symptoms of problems/distress
- (b) Parameters, intervention, emergency reaction time
- (c) Emergency contacts: Family, friends, agencies, physicians, etc.
- (d) Natural disaster plan

(3) Communication: ongoing exchange of health information
- (a) Multidisciplinary evaluation team
- (b) Student's family and caregiver
- (c) School personnel and consultants
- (d) Community resources, workplace

(4) Student/family concerns and consideration
- (a) Present level of functioning and potential
- (b) Attitudes and preferences

(5) School absence
- (a) Reduce vitality
- (b) Time factors influencing absence
- (c) Program accommodations

(6) Environment
- (a) Accessibility
- (b) Temperature control
- (c) Allergens
- (d) Environmental hazards
- (e) Availability of hot and cold running water
- (f) Electrical needs and hazards

TABLE 11.1 *(Continued)*

   (g) Storage areas
   (h) Privacy needs/area
   (i) Infection control routine

(7) Personnel/student considerations
   (a) Need for supplemental support services
   (b) Need for consultation with other certified/licensed health professionals
   (c) Immunizations

(8) Orientation and technical assistance
   (a) Direct care personnel
   (b) Supplemental support service personnel
   (c) Administrators and school faculty
   (d) Classmates and schoolmates
   (e) PTA, community, job site

(9) Consideration for entry or change in setting
   (a) Safety and comfort
   (b) Hygiene
   (c) Equipment operation maintenance, etc.
   (d) All items included under environment

(10) Transportation
   (a) Accessibility
   (b) Security of the student
   (c) Security of the equipment
   (d) Temperature control
   (e) Trained personnel
   (f) Emergency plan

(11) Information for documentation and monitoring of the noncomplex health procedures
   (a) Date and time, length and time for procedure
   (b) Student-specific typical patterns or responses to health care procedures
   (c) Student toleration of procedure
   (d) Student-specific warning signs and symptoms
   (e) Condition of skin
   (f) Body position and associated activity
   (g) Other
   (h) Signature of the caregiver, appropriate staff
   (i) Requirement of the Health Services Plan
   (j) Student's highest level of independence in performance of procedure

Source: From *Guidelines for Training: Noncomplex Health Procedures* by Louisiana Department of Education, 1993, *Bulletin 1909.*

gathered by the nurse can then be used by a team to develop the required individualized health services plan (IHSP). Figure 11.1 is the form that Louisiana has developed to document the individualized health services plan. The state guidelines recommend that all children with a health need in the school have an IHSP developed by a team consisting of the school nurse, school or system administrator, teacher, parents, and student, when appropriate, as well as other related personnel. The authors recommend that goals and objectives leading to independence in self-care be developed and included in this document. If a child also qualifies for special education, pertinent information, including the goals and objectives for self-care, can be incorporated into the IEP.

Encouraging Improved Student Involvement in Health Care

The ability of students to provide for their own health care can allow them greater freedom in school and the community. It can also make the difference between whether they can live independently as adults or will need to be placed in a restrictive setting such as a nursing care facility. In Mary's case, self-awareness about her condition could have prevented an emergency.

Objectives for achieving maximum independence in self-care can be developed whether or not a student will eventually be independent. Three tiers of student involvement are (a) improved tolerance of care, (b) direction of care, and (c) independence in care (Caldwell, Todaro, & Gates, 1989).

Some children may never be able to participate in their own care due to the extent of their cognitive and/or physical disabilities. Improvement for these children will be based on determining ways to increase their tolerance of care. For instance, a student who does not tolerate his gastrostomy feeding may require an alternative position for feeding (e.g., elevating or lowering the head of the chair) or an adjustment of the flow rate for the feeding.

Other students have physical limitations that prevent them from completing procedures. These students can often assist with and verbally direct the caregiver in performing the procedure. For instance, a student with quadraplegia and limited use of his arms can let caregivers know when it is time for catheterization and can verbally direct the procedure.

Still other students can learn to perform the procedure independently. Their need for supervision will depend on their age and maturity. This hierarchy of skill levels is essential to keep in mind when developing goals and objectives for the child. Table 11.2 includes information about promoting student involvement in health care. At any level, involvement can contribute to the child's feelings of competency and control.

Delegating Health Procedures

The role of the school nurse can be critical to the ability of children to access adequate health services in school. Each state has its own Nurse Practice Act which determines whether a procedure can be delegated to unlicensed persons. Familiarity with the Nurse Practice Act and school board policy regarding delegation is important in decision-making. Administrators are cautioned about delegating a health procedure, even the administration of medication, without consulting their

FIGURE 11.1
FORM USED IN LOUISIANA TO DOCUMENT THE INDIVIDUALIZED HEALTH SERVICES PLAN

LOUISIANA DEPARTMENT OF EDUCATION
INDIVIDUALIZED HEALTH SERVICES PLAN
for
STUDENTS WITH SPECIAL HEALTH CARE NEEDS

(Please attach forms if room is insufficient)

STUDENT IDENTIFICATION

Student Name _____   Date of Birth _____
School _____   Grade _____

BACKGROUND INFORMATION/NURSING ASSESSMENT   (complete all applicable sections)

Brief Medical History/Specific Health Care   __ (additional information is attached)

Psychosocial Concerns   __ (additional information is attached)   Family Concerns/Strengths   __ (additional information is attached)

GOALS AND ACTIONS

Attach physician's order and other standards for care.
1) Procedures and Interventions (student specific)

Procedure	Administered By	Equipment	Maintained By	Authorized/trained By
(a)				
(b)				
(c)				

2) Medications   __ Attach medication guideline and administration log.   3) Diet   __ (additional information attached)

4) Transportation Needs   __(additional information is attached)   5) Class/School Modifications   __ (additional information is attached)

6) Equipment and Supplies: __Parent __ School System __None   7) Safety Measures   __(additional information is attached

8) Student Participation in Procedures   __No   __Yes (if yes, attach description of participation level)
___(check if student is enrolled in special education)

CONTINGENCIES   Emergency Plan   __Attached   Possible Alerts
Training Plan   __Attached

AUTHORIZATIONS   *I have participated in the development of the Health Services Plan and agree with the contents.*

	Date			Date
Parent(s) _____	_/_/_	Teacher(s) _____		_/_/_
School Nurse _____	_/_/_	Other _____		_/_/_
School Administrator _____	_/_/_	Other _____		_/_/_

Effective Beginning Date _____   Next Review Date _____

Source: From *Guidelines for Training: Noncomplex Health Procedures* by Louisiana Department of Education, 1993, *Bulletin 1909.*

TABLE 11.2
INDIVIDUALIZED EDUCATION PROGRAM (IEP) DEVELOPMENT

I. Tolerance
1. Tolerate position
2. Tolerate procedure

II. Assistance/Direction
1. Position
   a. Maintain position
   b. Assume/describe position
2. Awareness of need schedule
   a. Respond to verbal or physical cues related to physical signs of need or according to schedule
   b. Respond independently to physical signs of need or according to schedule
3. Equipment
   a. Recognize equipment
   b. Name equipment
   c. Hand equipment during procedure
   d. Gather equipment
   e. Maintain equipment
4. Procedure
   a. Identify area to be dealt with
   b. Assist with preparing (cleaning) area
   c. Increase assistance with procedure, e.g., holding container, disposing of urine, hand-over-hand insertion
   d. Supervise/outline procedure
   Note: Objectives 1 through 4 may be dealt with concurrently.

III. Independence
1. With supervision
2. Without supervision

Source: From *Community Provider's Guide: An Information Outline for Working with Children with Special Health Care Needs* (p. 172) by T. H. Caldwell, A. W. Todaro, and A. J. Gates, 1989, New Orleans, LA: Children's Hospital. Reprinted by permission.

school nurse and representatives from the State Board of Nursing who interpret the state's Nurse Practice Act. ("In the state of Connecticut, individuals may be jailed for up to five years and fined up to $500, or both, for practicing without a license the following health professions: medicine, nursing, . . ." [State of Connecticut Department of Education, 1992, p. 22]).

It is also recommended that administrators inquire into the extent of the responsibility assigned to the school nurse. In many cases, the school nurse will have the responsibility for the health procedures of all children in assigned schools whether she is aware of a student's health need or not. This makes school nurse involvement imperative in the early stages of identification of a student with a health need.

Developing Emergency Plans

Mary weathered this emergency relatively well. There were no obvious long-term effects, but there was also no reason that Mary or the school staff should have gone through this emergency. Through planning and training, Mary and the school staff could have prevented this emergency from occurring. The next section will address emergency planning in greater detail.

Flood of '91: Disaster Management

On October 24, 1991, torrential rains fell on a low-lying coastal area and flooding occurred during school hours. The pumping station was unable to manage the swift water and predicted it would be at least 8 hours before floodwaters would subside enough so that certain areas could be reached. The school superintendent advised the principal of an elementary school to keep her students at school and to make plans for them to stay overnight. The principal immediately convened a meeting of a committee to oversee the preparation, which included arrangements for recreation activities, dinner, and sleeping accommodations. School board personnel notified parents that their children would be kept at school until the water subsided.

The water receded sooner than had been anticipated, and students did not have to spend the night at school. The next day the principal learned that the school system had been inundated with calls from parents whose children needed medication and other health treatments during their delay at school.

 CONSIDER THIS

1. How can administrators prepare for the emergency needs of students with special health conditions?
2. What should a school nurse do during emergencies?
3. What preparation is necessary to provide systematic access to health information?

Preparing to Provide Specialized Emergency Care
for Students with Special Health Conditions

Although many school systems do not have to contend with floods, each region has indigenous emergencies for which it is important to plan. Figure 11.2

FIGURE 11.2

SAMPLE NOTIFICATION LETTER FOR PUBLIC SERVICE OFFICES

(Date)

(Name and Address of Vendor)*

_____

_____

_____

RE:
Guardian:
Home Address:
City, State, ZIP:
Home Telephone:
School:
School Address:
City, State, ZIP:
School Telephone:
Principal:

To Whom It May Concern:

_____is a student with a diagnosis of_____who has a tracheostomy and requires ventilatory support _____hours per day. _____'s health and medical status are monitored by Dr. _____, Pediatrician (___ -___-____) at Children's Hospital (504-999-9999).

_____is currently attending _____grade at _____school with an LP6 ventilator. He/she is receiving ventilator support _____at school and is assisted by an aide who has been trained in suctioning, ventilator maintenance, tracheostomy care and emergency signs, symptoms and procedures. _____also requires a wheelchair for mobility. School hours are_____a.m. until_____p.m.

When the ventilator is fully charged, it has a forty (40) minute internal battery with an eight (8) hour back-up battery (marine battery). While he/she is attending school and at home, the equipment is plugged into a wall current so that the batteries are preserved for transporting and/or emergencies.

We wanted to notify you of this child's chronic health condition and the assistive equipment which provides support for him/her at home and at school in the event your services are needed during an emergency.

Sincerely,

*Telephone Company, Electric Company, Gas Company, Fire Department, Red Cross/Civil Defense, Local Emergency Room, Ambulance or Emergency Transport Company

Source: From the Ventilator Assisted Care Program, New Orleans, LA: Children's Hospital. Reprinted by permission.

includes a sample notification letter to be sent to pertinent community public service offices. Figure 11.3 provides a sample form to be used to document the emergency numbers of community providers who are contacted when a child requires technology in school. Not all children with special health needs will require this extent of planning, but each requires individual consideration when the school's emergency plan is being written.

When interviewed, school personnel consistently reported that their greatest fear about providing school services to children with health conditions is having an emergency they cannot handle. School personnel can overreact or underreact unless they know the parameters of an emergency and appropriate intervention (Caldwell, Sirvis, Todaro, & Alcouloumre, 1991). What does it mean if a child is hypoglycemic? Does a child need to go to the emergency room after a seizure? These are significant questions that must be answered before a child experiences a health problem at school. A sample form for individualizing emergency interaction is provided in Figure 11.4. Emergency forms for specific conditions are available through the National MCH Resource Center, which is listed under Resources at the end of this chapter. At a minimum, the form should include the signs and symptoms of the emergency and the appropriate response to the situation.

Coordinating with School Nurses

The school nurse plays a pivotal role in coordinating and caring for the needs of children with health conditions. This role can include (a) ensuring that teachers are trained in CPR, (b) developing individualized emergency protocol for students, as well as assisting in the planning of step-by-step interventions for each emergency situation, and (c) developing systems to periodically review emergency plans. It is obvious from the list of these responsibilities that the nurse does not work alone. Planning for the health needs of students requires a team effort.

Developing Methods for Systematic Access to Health Information

Once the floodwaters subsided, one of the first things the principal realized was that she had no information about the special health needs of her students. The school nurse, who had that information, was not in the building on the day of the flood, and no one was familiar enough with her records to find the information the principal needed. The principal selected a teacher to work with the school nurse to develop a chart that included each student's name, health condition, need for medication, and need for treatment. A separate chart outlining potential emergencies and interventions was also completed. The nurse recommended quarterly updates of these charts. In addition, the school nurse recommended that copies of these charts be maintained in the confidential files in the principal's office and in the coordinating teacher's files. These efforts would ensure access to information to assist administrators in responding appropriately to emergency situations.

FIGURE 11.3
FORM FOR DOCUMENTING EMERGENCY TELEPHONE NUMBERS

HOME INSTRUCTIONS

TELEPHONE LIST FOR EMERGENCIES:		<u>Name</u>	<u>Telephone No.</u>
Ambulance*:	Home:	_____	_____
	School:	_____	_____
Hospital*:	Home:	_____	_____
	School:	_____	_____
	Primary:	_____	_____

- -

	Name	Telephone No.
Physicians	_____	_____
	_____	_____
Home Health Care	_____	_____
	_____	_____
Home Case Manager	_____	_____
	_____	_____
Home Equipment	_____	_____
	_____	_____
Drug Store	_____	_____
	_____	_____
Telephone Company*	_____	_____
Electric Company*	_____	_____
Gas Company*	_____	_____
Fire Department*	_____	_____
School	_____	_____
Parent Group	_____	_____
Red Cross/Civil Defense*	_____	_____
Funder's	_____	_____
Other (Transportation, Parent work #s, etc.)	_____	_____

*If electrically operated life-sustaining equipment is to be used at home, a letter from your physician can be requested for emergency and/or priority restoration services.

Nursing/115
3/89

Source: From *Home Instruction Manual,* (Form # 115 dated 3/89), Division of Nursing Administration, Department of Nursing Education, New Orleans, LA: Children's Hospital. Reprinted by permission.

FIGURE 11.4
EMERGENCY FORM FOR SPECIFIC CONDITIONS

DIABETES: (TYPE 1: INSULIN DEPENDENT)

EMERGENCY PROCEDURES

WARNING SIGNS & SYMPTOMS – HYPOGLYCEMIA

COMMON SYMPTOMS   CHILD'S NORMAL SYMPTOMS

1. Headache   _____

2. Nausea/Vomiting   _____

3. Irritability/Crying/Confusion   _____

4. Tremors/Shaky Body Parts   _____

5. Cold/Moist Skin   _____

TREATMENT

1. Administer a Food or Beverage that Contains a Sugar *immediately* (e.g., 1/2 cup juice or soda). Child may need coaxing.
2. Do Not Leave Child Alone until Symptoms Disappear
3. Additional Foods May Need to be Eaten to Prevent Reoccurrence of the Reaction
4. Contact Parent
5. Contact Emergency Room if Symptoms Do Not Disappear within_____minutes

WARNING SIGNS & SYMPTOMS – HYPERGLYCEMIA (Slow Onset)

COMMON SYMPTOMS   CHILD'S NORMAL SYMPTOMS

1. Tired/Drowsy/Weak   _____

2. Increased Thirst   _____

3. Increased Need to Go to the Bathroom   _____

4. Warm/Dry Skin or Flushed Skin   _____

5. Abdominal Pain   _____

TREATMENT

1. Contact Parent

IMMEDIATE DANGER: KETOACIDOSIS (Medical Emergency)

SYMPTOMS   CHILD'S NORMAL SYMPTOMS

1. High Blood Sugar Level
   (Blood Glucose Greater Than_____)   _____

2. Severe Nausea and Vomiting   _____

3. Severe Abdominal Pain   _____

4. Rapid Shallow Breathing   _____

TREATMENT

1. Contact Parent
2. Contact Emergency Room

Form was individualized by:

_____   _____   _____

Parent's signature   Provider's signature   Date

FIGURE 11.4 *(Continued)*

EMERGENCY INFORMATION

AMBULANCE SERVICE_____ _____
                              name   number

EMERGENCY ROOM _____ _____
                              name   number

PHYSICIAN_____ _____
                           name   number

PARENT OR GUARDIAN_____
                                          name

_____   _____
           home num-   work num-

ALTERNATE CONTACT_____
                                          name

_____   _____
           home num-   work num-

I am aware that if my child has an emergency in school and I am not available, the school principal or alternate will have my child transported to the emergency room.

_____   _____
Signature   Date

Original: School Nursing   Copy: Principal, Teacher   Chronic Illness Program at Children's Hospital
                                                            New Orleans, Louisiana
                                                            2/89

Source: From *Community Provider's Guide: An Information Outline for Working with Children with Special Health Care Needs* (p. 31) by T. H. Caldwell, A. W. Todaro, and A. J. Gates, 1989, New Orleans, LA: Children's Hospital. Reprinted by permission.

Orientation for School Personnel and Peers Regarding Steve and Chris

Steve

Steve has spina bifida; as a result, he is mobile in a wheelchair, requires catheterization, and has some fine motor disabilities. When he was tested before the third grade, he was functioning on grade level but needed assistance with setting up his work because of fine motor movement limitations. Although Steve was usually an independent, motivated worker, the special education teacher reported he was shy and not likely to ask for assistance.

Steve spent the first 3 years of his education in a separate school for students with physical disabilities. When he was in third grade, he was moved to a regular class on a regular school campus. Neither Steve, the school faculty, nor the other students were prepared for his participation. After a 6-month period, Steve was no longer attending school consistently. A consultant was engaged to assess his needs. She reported Steve's daily assignments consisted of art projects, mostly coloring, while the other students were involved in the regular academic program. In addition, Steve's desk was located in the back corner of the room. Steve was not allowed to participate in activities in the auditorium (which was not accessible) or go on field trips. The educational consultant did not note any interaction between Steve and other students.

Steve was now exhibiting school phobia. The consultant recommended individual counseling for Steve and training for his teacher and classmates. These interventions were not successful, and Steve continued to be absent frequently for his remaining 8 years at school. Steve formally withdrew from school on his 16th birthday.

Chris

Chris is a 6-year-old with a seizure disorder. Chris was referred to a private consultant because his mother was concerned he was no longer excited about going to school and was, in fact, complaining of stomach aches. The private consultant interviewed Chris and completed a school observation. She noted that when Chris had a seizure in school, he appeared to be sleeping and sometimes urinated on himself. The other children in the classroom would tease him and call him a baby. "Kids on the Block," a puppet troupe, was used to explain to Chris' classmates about seizure disorders. During this orientation, Chris then told his classmates why he looked like he was sleeping and why he sometimes had accidents. His mother reported there was an immediate, positive change in Chris' attitude toward going to school.

CONSIDER THIS

1. When should an orientation presentation be conducted for faculty and students?
2. How can administrators plan for support services and continuity in the regular class?

Conducting Timely Orientation for Faculty and Students

Orientation for faculty and students can assist in alleviating fears. Ideally, it should occur before the child's entry/reentry to school. Orientation presentations should be considered for school personnel (secretary, custodian, related service personnel, volunteers, teachers, bus drivers, etc.), faculty and staff members directly involved with the student, the entire student body, and the student's classmates.

The orientation presentation should be tailored to the group seeing it and should address important issues about the child's health condition. For school personnel, the orientation should include information about the student's condition, potential emergencies, teacher intervention, and how the condition affects the student's participation and ability to learn. The detail and depth of the presentation will depend on such issues as the child's condition and the potential interaction of the faculty with the student.

Orientation for peers should be developmentally appropriate. Younger children typically are curious about concrete details, such as how the child goes to the bathroom, gets out of the wheelchair, etc. Older children are more concerned with the ramifications of the condition, such as the potential for childbearing, dating, living until old age, etc. Table 11.3 provides useful guidelines for the orientation of peers.

Administrators are not expected to know everything about a student's condition. They can request the assistance of school nurses, parents, the medical community, the state department of education, and organizations specific to

TABLE 11.3
ORIENTATION OF PEERS

There are a few standard guidelines that can be helpful to consider when designing student-orientation plans.

1. Involve the child with special health needs in decision-making and planning.
2. Allow the child to decide whether he/she will participate or whether he/she wants to be identified as the child with the condition being discussed.
3. Keep in mind the age of the child and child's peers when designing interventions. The complexity and type of materials used will vary depending on the age of the child.
4. Use pictures, drawings, and audiovisuals. Whenever possible, provide the opportunity for hands-on experiences.
5. Compare "normal" anatomy so they can compare special functioning to their functioning, e.g., compare a tracheostomy to a nose.
6. Prepare the child with special health needs ahead of time. Some questions may be difficult to answer. Make sure to include some of the more difficult questions in your preparation, e.g., will you die soon? Let the child know that he/she may choose to answer or not answer difficult questions.
7. Prepare classmates for the presentation by providing background information and encouraging open communication regarding the health condition.
8. Training plans should include the opportunity for children to gain specific information, to relate the disability to their own experiences (e.g., "My grandmother has arthritis"), and to discuss their experiences and feelings about the topic being discussed.
9. Answer questions simply and without a lot of detail. Give simple answers and ask if more clarification is needed.
10. Treat the child and peers with respect, and answer questions as openly as possible.

Source: From *Community Provider's Guide: An Information Outline for Working with Children with Special Health Care Needs, 1991 Addendum* (p. 24) by T. H. Caldwell, A. W. Todaro, A. J. Gates, S. Failla, and K. Kirkhart, 1991, New Orleans, LA: Children's Hospital. Reprinted by permission.

particular health conditions to assist in the planning and the presentation to faculty and students.

Planning for Support Services and Continuity in the Regular Class

Many children with special health-care needs are now beginning school with their peers and may require support services in the regular classroom. Teachers and students may require special education services on a consultative basis. These questions will help in determining what services are needed:

- Do the child's physical disabilities interfere with the ability to access materials, write, and communicate orally?
- Does the child need special health procedures, such as catheterization, which may take him/her out of class and interfere with academic activities?
- How can these procedures be scheduled in order to limit disruption to the daily routine and classroom instruction?
- Will the regular education teacher know how to include the student?
- Will the teacher need training, ongoing assistance, or resources so that effective inclusionary practices occur?

These questions are important to ask on an ongoing basis to ensure quality programming for children in the least restrictive setting.

A Focus on Adjustment

In the beginning of Ralph's senior year, he was involved in a motor vehicle accident and sustained a closed head injury. He was hospitalized for 3 months. As a result of the injury, he now walks with short steps. His speech is slow and he talks softly, though he can generally be understood. He has difficulty with new learning. He appears stubborn and may even refuse to participate in activities, although the frequency of refusal is decreasing. Many of his responses are impulsive, and perseveration on certain topics occasionally occurs. While he needs to have information repeated and manifests a mild receptive aphasia, hearing acuity appears to be intact. Ralph's therapists and physician believe he has made good progress, but expect he will have long-term problems with new learning and in managing aspects of his life that require abstract reasoning and judgment.

Ralph's parents report that he is "not the same person he was before his accident." Ralph and his parents had planned for him to attend college after graduation. Despite the significance of his deficits, and the number of school days he has missed, Ralph's parents still believe he can graduate if he attends summer school. They believe he will be able to start college with his classmates.

CONSIDER THIS

1. What issues may be involved in adjusting to the survivor's present condition?
2. What should be considered in determining the most appropriate educational placement?

Adjusting to Ralph's Present Condition

The National Head Injury Foundation (1988) reports that more than 2 million head injuries occur each year, including 1 million involving persons younger than 19. Equally alarming are the statistics which show that within this age category, the highest incidence of head injury occurs between the ages of 15–19. This is not surprising, considering the activities usually pursued by young adults. Typically, they spend more time in automobiles, experiment with alcohol and drugs, and/or find themselves in other risky situations. The U.S. Department of Education has recognized the unique needs of children with head injuries and has included a separate category for traumatic brain injury in the special education classifications described by IDEA. "Traumatic brain injury" means an acquired injury to the brain caused by an external physical force, resulting in total or partial disability or psychosocial impairment, or both, that adversely affects a child's educational performance. The term does not apply to brain injuries that are congenital or degenerative, or brain injuries induced by birth trauma (*Federal Register,* 1992, p. 44, 842).

One of the greatest difficulties for children with head injuries is the adjustment others must make in accepting how the person has changed. There are many degrees of severity within this population. In some instances, the head injury has altered the individual's life so significantly that differences are obvious. In other instances, the characteristics are more subtle, and people associating with the child may be unsure as to whether the differences are the result of the injury or a former characteristic that has been intensified due to the injury (e.g., difficulty initiating a task). For many survivors of head injury, the knowledge of who they "were" before is a great cause for frustration. Family and friends, who initially are patient with the survivor, may become frustrated and angry as time goes on and the survivor continues to have major problems. This is particularly true when the adolescent can no longer function on his own, can no longer be trusted to make decisions, or has behaviors that are embarrassing to the family. The family continues to hope for changes that may not occur.

In the same way, teachers and students who have known the survivor expect him to behave and operate as he had in the past. They expect him to do things independently, to remember instructions, to be a friend, and to have the skills necessary to handle all situations. They are confused because there are still some things he can do, but there are "simple" things he has difficulty managing. Teachers and friends will need opportunities to grieve for the person they formerly knew and to find ways to relate to the survivor.

Most school personnel have limited information about traumatic brain injury. There are a number of excellent resources being published throughout the country. The National Head Injury Foundation (listed in the Resources section at the end of this chapter) offers valuable support for families, friends, and professionals working with survivors. Most states have local chapters that have a list of persons or professionals who can be of assistance during the transition back to school. Other resources include state departments of education, the hospital where the young adult was treated, Veterans Administration hospitals, or rehabilitation centers. These organizations may have personnel available who can serve as a resource for additional information and technical assistance.

Determining the Most Appropriate Educational Placement

Ralph was a senior in high school. He had four credits to complete before graduation. Ralph could easily be allowed to graduate with his class because his past performance had been adequate and he could make up work during summer school. What would be best for Ralph?

The decision about whether or not to let a student graduate is an important one. Because his age group has the highest incidence of injury, secondary administrators frequently have to face complex issues of this nature. Many of these students do not have the skills they had before their injury. Important questions must be answered.

- What options exist for Ralph?
- Would it be more beneficial for him to graduate and be eligible for vocational rehabilitation services?
- Are there job opportunities for him in the community?
- Could he handle the work of college courses and all that college life involves?
- Does the student feel he is really prepared to make the transition to the adult world?
- Will a diploma help him move on with his life or will it keep him and his family from being realistic about his skills and his vocational needs?
- What would the emotional toll of graduating or not graduating be?
- Would it be possible for him to participate in graduation exercises and not receive a diploma?
- What educational options exist if he does not complete his senior year?
- Would repeating his senior year be beneficial?
- Is there a special education program that could build on the student's strengths and address social skills that may have been affected?
- Would a special education program focusing on job training meet his needs?

There are no easy answers to these questions. Decisions are difficult and require an understanding of the student's recovery, prognosis, interests, resources in the school, other resources in the community (such as vocational rehabilitation), and what the family and student want. It is important to keep in mind the student's future and to involve the student in all decision-making from the beginning. As in most instances, it is important to explore all possibilities, creating new ones in the process, before reaching a decision. Everyone should keep in mind that students are eligible for special educational services until their 22nd birthday, and other support services may be nonexistent once the student has graduated.

Training and Technical Assistance

At age 12, Brian was involved in a bicycle accident. He sustained a high-level spinal cord injury and as a result cannot move his arms and legs. He is dependent on mechanical ventilation to substitute for the muscles that draw air into his lungs.

Brian was hospitalized for 4 months. His major care needs in school include (a) gastrostomy feedings once during the school day as a supplement to the nutrition he takes in orally, (b) catheterization twice during the school day to assist in the elimination of urine, (c) ventilator maintenance, to assure that settings are correct and circuits are intact, (d) suctioning as needed to manually remove secretions from his tracheostomy airway, and (e) pressure relief every 2 hours to promote circulation and prevent pressure sores.

Brian is mobile in an electric wheelchair, which he operates using a chin switch. He uses a computer for all written work. He requires assistance in order to complete all academic activities and all tasks of daily living.

Brian was an average student before his accident. However, it was decided that he would be retained in the sixth grade. This decision was based on the fact that he had missed 4 months of school, with only limited school intervention, while in the hospital. School personnel and his parents also felt he would require an adjustment period when he returned to school and feared that seventh grade might be too demanding.

Brian's school system is rural; his school is reached by a dirt road. The superintendent was not initially supportive of Brian's return to school.

CONSIDER THIS

1. What risk management and safety concerns must be addressed?
2. What transition issues should be considered?
3. How can administrators secure resources and funding?
4. What training and technical assistance must be provided?
5. What transportation issues must be considered?

Addressing Risk Management Concerns

School inclusion of a child dependent on mechanical ventilation may cause anxiety. It is critical for school personnel to visit the child and family in the hospital and participate in discharge planning. Still, the reality of the actual move of the child from the hospital to home and subsequently to school may be frightening. School personnel are concerned about the safety of the student and their own liability. Are school personnel liable for the health care provided during the school day? Table 11.4, "Reducing the Risk of Liability," addresses risk management strategies. The better prepared education systems are to provide health care, the less likely they will be regarded as negligent.

Planning Transitions

One significant aspect of safety management is appropriate transition to school. It is critical for staff to receive orientation and training before the child

TABLE 11.4
CHILDREN WITH HEALTH IMPAIRMENTS: REDUCING THE RISK OF LIABILITY IN THE CLASSROOM/COMMUNITY

1. Obtain individualized prescriptions and protocols for procedures to be performed.
2. Review protocols approved by the physician with parents, and have them sign form indicating their agreement with the procedures outlined in the protocol.
3. Document that appropriate training, based on protocols, has occurred. Include persons' names, specific procedures demonstrated, and date of scheduled rechecks.
4. Train anyone who will be involved in the child's care, i.e., bus driver, etc.
5. Establish contingency plans. Train other personnel who will take over when the major caretakers are not available and who will be available to assist major caretaker in any emergency situation.
6. Include maintenance and emergency procedures in your training.
7. Develop and document plans with physicians and parents for transport and provision of service in local emergency room.
8. Provide information to agencies providing services to the school/agency (i.e., electric and telephone companies) to advise them of the need for priority service reinstatement.
9. Provide information to agencies interacting with the school/agency during natural disasters (i.e., fire department, Red Cross) to acquaint them with the child's participation in a particular school/agency and the needs that child will have during an emergency.
10. Effectively document needs and how they will be met in the IEP or the school Health Care Plan.

Source: From *Community Provider's Guide: An Information Outline for Working with Children with Special Health Care Needs* (p. 167) by T. H. Caldwell, A. W. Todaro, A. J. Gates, S. Failla, and K. Kirkhart, 1991, New Orleans, LA: Children's Hospital. Reprinted by permission.

begins school. It is also important that staff receive backup assistance in care until they are not only competent but also comfortable in providing care on their own. The process of transition to school is often delayed because of the fear of including these children in school. Caldwell, Sirvis, Todaro, and Alcouloumre (1991) recommend that transition planning involve specific objectives with time limits (e.g., the direct caregiver will be trained by a school nurse by a particular date, the parent will attend school for two weeks or until the parent and caregiver are confident that a particular procedure is performed correctly). Transition plans can focus on issues including modification of the physical plant, setting up transportation, and preparing direct caregivers and school personnel.

Securing Resources and Funding

Brian's participation in school required extra resources. His need for care was ongoing, and emergency situations required immediate attention. Questions such as "What personnel are needed to attend to Brian's health needs?" and "Who will provide the funding for this service?" must be considered. School health services can be considered as related services for students who qualify under IDEA (CFR. Sec. 300.16[b] 11, 1992). Special education and related services "are to be provided at public expense, under public supervision and direction, and without charge" (CFR. 300.8[a], 1992). Much controversy still exists over the extent of the school system's obligation to provide these services (*Irving Independent School District v. Tatro,* 1984; *Bevin H. v. Wright,* 1987; *Detsel v. Board of Education,* 1987).

Funding for school health services can at times present an enormous fiscal obligation to school systems. One way to address the problem is to seek alternative funding to add to the money already provided through IDEA. The National Information Center for Children and Youth with Disabilities (NICHCY) (1991) mentions several funding sources for these services. The Medicare Catastrophic Coverage Act authorizes reimbursements for Medicaid-covered related services in the IEPs of Medicare-eligible students. In addition, the Omnibus Budget Reconciliation Act (1989) provides for the treatment needs recommended through Medicaid's Early and Periodic Screening, Diagnosis, and Treatment process (EPSDT). Third-party billing is another avenue worth pursuing. However, this is controversial, as the use of private insurance could pose a financial loss to parents, such as decreasing available coverage and paying the deductibles. School systems have generated funds for school health services through millage increases, by blending state and local funding, and through local organizations such as the Muscular Dystrophy Association or other foundations. Each school system has its own way to secure money for necessary services.

Training and Technical Assistance

One of the most difficult administrative aspects of preparing for the inclusion of children who require technology is staff training, support, and supervision. Todaro, Failla, and Caldwell (in press) recommend that training include everyone who will deal with the child. Teachers and students will require orientation, while direct caregivers will require student-specific training. Table 11.5 gives information about training levels and recommendations for training in community

TABLE 11.5
STAFF TRAINING, SUPPORT, AND SUPERVISION GUIDELINES

Training Levels:

Orientation:
Introduce current practice/technology and affect attitudes;

Diagnostic Specific Training:
Provide detailed information about a specific condition or procedure and associated care;

Child-Specific Training:
Assess and teach daily and emergency care and implications of the child's function in the community;

Trainer's Training:
Teach licensed professionals how to train other care providers.

Recommendations for Training in Community Settings:
1. Secure individualized prescriptions and protocols, including warning signs and symptoms. Develop these in collaboration with parents and health care providers.
2. Begin training before the child's return to his/her community. Have parent observe and/or participate in the training.
3. Train at least two people so that backup is available. Delivery of care by a consistent provider(s) is important to the child's health.
4. Train all personnel who will work with the child to deal with emergency situations (i.e., bus driver, adapted physical education teacher, or anyone else who will be teaching the child). Recommend that the program administrator and/or secretary learn emergency procedures.
5. Provide backup for a designated period; an expert (i.e., qualified professional, trained parent caregiver) should be present for continued training and on-site backup. Length of backup is determined by care provider's competency and comfort. It is recommended that at least five trials of procedures and emergencies with 100% accuracy be documented before care provider works independently.
6. Document training using an individualized checklist. The trainer and parent sign the checklist after training is completed.
7. Provide supervision. Rechecks are recommended by the trainer, with time lines based on complexity of procedures and competency of care provider.
8. Include recognition and implementation of emergency procedures as part of training and rechecks.

Barriers and Solutions:
The following is a list of major barriers encountered by program staff and the approaches that have been successful in overcoming these barriers.

TABLE 11.5 (*Continued*)

Barrier:

Lack of communication

Approaches:

- Develop linkage committee (multiagency systems planning including hospital, school, and community providers)
- Facilitate multiagency staffings
- Clarify and interpret information from multiple disciplines
- Use protocols and other tools for communication
- Include educators in discharge planning

Barrier:

Attitudes including fear, uncertainty, and resistance to change among professionals, providers, and parents

Approaches:

- Assess individual and community needs and orientation
- Focus on child, transition plans, support, and individual training

Barrier:

Territorial issues

Approaches:

- Exemplify a model of interdisciplinary collaboration and network through interactions of program personnel
- Encourage collaboration among disciplines, agencies, and individuals (consumers, educators, social and health services personnel, and funding agents)
- Provide forums to discuss issues

Barrier:

Liability issues

Approaches:

- Involve families in planning, implementation, and evaluation
- Document training of routine and emergency care
- Promote systematic monitoring and evaluation

Barrier:

Interpretation of professionals' roles and regulations

Approaches:

- Work closely with the governing body of each profession to provide information and education
- Advocate for professional involvement and growth

Source: From *Community Provider's Guide: An Information Outline for Working with Children with Special Health Care Needs* (p. 94) by T. H. Caldwell, A. W. Todaro, A. J. Gates, S. Failla, and K. Kirkhart, 1991, New Orleans, LA: Children's Hospital. Reprinted by permission.

settings, along with a list of typical barriers and solutions. "Training is a collaborative effort involving families, professionals, and community providers. Each child, family, community, and care provider is unique and requires special considerations. Continued communication among all is the key component to a successful training model" (Caldwell, Todaro, & Gates, 1989, p. 94).

Providing Transportation

Another crucial consideration is the transportation of the student to school. Students who are ventilator-dependent need a trained caregiver to be on the bus. Expensive equipment must be transported safely, and plans must be made in case of medical emergencies. Long distances can be tiring for the child, so enrollment in a neighborhood school can preserve the student's energy. Transportation for students who are technology-assisted should be evaluated in terms of "accessibility, security for student, security for equipment, temperature control, need for the availability of a trained caregiver, and the need for an emergency plan" (Caldwell, Todaro, & Gates, 1989, p. 169). An emergency plan should answer these questions:

- Who will care for the child during an emergency?
- What is the driver's role?
- Does the driver have a means of communication?
- Where is the closest emergency room on the school bus route equipped to provide pediatric care?

SUMMARY

The case studies in this chapter illustrate some of the issues facing administrators, such as liability, emergency planning, and collaboration between health and education personnel. As the authors have followed the progress of these cases, some of the students have exceeded expectations, while others have not. Some have grown and begun to confront the challenge of adult issues; others still have a long road ahead of them.

Rhonda, who is HIV-positive, has experienced many ups and downs in the last two years. She continues to struggle with the knowledge of her diagnosis. However, Rhonda's friends have become a major support in her life. Mary, who has diabetes, is now in the sixth grade. The school system provided many resources to help her, and school personnel learned about her disorder. She is now able to independently provide her own care. She even explains her condition to her new teachers and classmates at the beginning of each year. The school in the "low-lying coastal area" has experienced several other floods, and the staff is now better prepared to care for the health needs of the students. The relationship that developed between the school nurse and the teacher liaison has been productive. Teachers often seek out the school nurse to discuss possible classroom modifications for children with health needs. Unfortunately, Steve, who has spina bifida, dropped out of school and spends most of his time at home alone watching TV. Whereas Chris, who has a seizure disorder, is in the fourth grade and doing well both academically and socially. He continues to be teased but realizes all kids get teased. Ralph, the survivor of a head injury, is still struggling. Ralph, his parents, and school personnel decided to delay graduation in hopes of working on socialization and study skills. He is making progress, but like many persons who have experienced a traumatic head injury, his recovery will take years. Brian, who is dependent on the ventilator, graduated from high school. He is having trouble deciding what he wants to study in college. He did not begin planning early enough, and will probably have to delay college for a semester until he makes living arrangements, secures vocational rehabilitation services, and hires attendants to provide care.

Many children with special health-care needs present enormous challenges to administrators. However, the well-being of each child demands they be addressed. As these case studies have shown, each relevant issue can be addressed in a systematic and thoughtful way. Collaboration between administrators and all parties involved will yield strategies and organizational tools that will help the system provide the quality education to which all children are entitled.

RESOURCES

American Diabetes Association
    Diabetes Information Service Center
    1660 Duke St., Alexandria, VA 22314
    (800) 485-9950
National Head Injury Foundation, Inc.
    333 Turnpike Road, Southborough, MA 01772
    (508) 485-9950
National Information Center for Children and Youth With Disabilities (NICHCY)
    PO Box 1492, Washington, DC 20013-1492
    (800) 695-0285
National MCH Resource Center for Ensuring Adequate Preparation of Care Providers
    Children's Hospital
    200 Henry Clay Ave., New Orleans, LA 70118
    (504) 896-9287
National Organization for Rare Disorders
    PO Box 8923, New Fairfield, CT 06812
    (800) 999-6673

REFERENCES

American Academy of Pediatrics Task Force on Pediatric AIDS. (1989). Infants and children with acquired immunodeficiency syndrome: Placement in adoption and foster care. *Pediatrics, 83,* 609–612.

American Bar Association. (1991). *AIDS/HIV and confidentiality: Model policy and procedures.* Washington, DC: Author.

American Bar Association. (1989). *AIDS and persons with developmental disabilities: The legal perspective.* Washington, DC: Author.

American Federation of Teachers. (1992). *The medically fragile child in the school setting.* Washington, DC: Author.

Bevin H. v. Wright, 666 F. Supp. 71 (W.D. Pa. 1987).

Caldwell, T. H., Sirvis, B., Todaro, A. W., & Alcouloumre, D. (1991). *Special health care in the school.* Reston, VA: The Council for Exceptional Children.

Caldwell, T. H., Todaro, A. W., Gates, A. J., Failla, S., & Kirkhart, K. (1991). *Community provider's guide: An information outline for working with children with special health care needs (1991 Addendum).* New Orleans, LA: Children's Hospital.

Caldwell, T. H., Todaro, A. W., & Gates, A. J. (1989). *Community provider's guide: An information outline for working with children with special health care needs in the community.* New Orleans, LA: Children's Hospital.

Caldwell, T. H., Todaro, A. W., & Gates, A. J. (1991). Special health care needs. In J. Bigge (Ed.), *Teaching individuals with physical and multiple disabilities* (3rd ed., pp. 50–74). New York: Macmillan.

Crocker, A., Cohen, H. J., & Kastner, T. A. (1992). *HIV infection and developmental disabilities: A resource for service providers.* Baltimore, MD: Paul H. Brookes.

Detsel v. Board of Education of the Enlarged Auburn School District, 820 F.2d 587 (2nd Cir. 1987).

Fraser, K. (1989). *Someone at school has AIDS: A guide to developing policies for students and school staff members who are infected with HIV.* Alexandria, VA: National Association of State Boards of Education.

Harvey, D., Seidel, J., & Crocker, A. (1992). Public opinion, discrimination, and integration. In A. Crocker, H. Cohen, & T. Kastner. *HIV infection and developmental disabilities: A resource for service providers.* Baltimore, MD: Paul H. Brookes.

Haynie, M., Porter, S., & Palfrey, J. (1989). *Children assisted by medical technology in education settings: Guidelines for care.* Boston, MA: Children's Hospital, Project School Care.

Individuals With Disabilities Education Act (1992). Traumatic brain injury. *Federal Register, 44,* 842.

Irving Independent School District v. Tatro, 468 U.S. 883 (1984).

Louisiana Department of Education. (1993). *Guidelines for training: Noncomplex health procedures (Bulletin 1909).* Baton Rouge, LA: Author.

National Center for Youth With Disabilities. (1991). Living through childhood. *FYI Bulletin, 1*(1), University of Minnesota.

National Association of State Boards of Education. (1989). *Someone at school has AIDS. A guide to developing policies for students and school staff members who are infected with HIV.* Alexandria, VA: Author.

National Head Injury Foundation Task Force on Special Education. (1988). *An educator's manual: What educators need to know about students with traumatic brain injury.* Southborough, MA: National Head Injury Foundation Inc.

National Information Center for Children and Youth with Disabilities (NICHCY). (1991). Related services for school-aged children with disabilities. *News Digest, 1*(2).

Newacheck, P., & Taylor, W. (1992). Childhood chronic illness: Prevalence, severity, and impact. *American Journal of Public Health, 82*(3), 364–371.

Rosen, S., & Granger, M. (1992). Early intervention and school programs. In Crocker, Cohen, & Kastner, (Eds.), *HIV infection and developmental disabilities* (pp. 75–84). Baltimore, MD: Paul H. Brookes.

State of Connecticut Department of Education (1992). *Serving students with special health care needs.* Middletown, CT: Author.

Todaro, A. W., Failla, S., & Caldwell, T. H. (in press). A model for training community-based providers for children with special health care needs.

Utah State Office of Education. (1992). *Guidelines for serving students with special health care needs.* Salt Lake City, UT: Author.

Walker, P. (1991). Where there is a way, there is not always a will: Technology, public policy, and the school integration of children who are technology-assisted. *Children's Health Care, 20*(2), 68–74.

ACKNOWLEDGMENTS

The authors wish to express appreciation to the following persons who served as consultants to the writing of this chapter: Joanne Gates, M.D., M.B.A.; Michael Kaiser, M.D.; Kathryn Kirkhart, Ph.D.; Carole McCutcheon-Goodwin, B.S.; Terry Compton, R.N., M.S., C.D.E.; Debbie Alcouloumre, M.A., C.T.R.S.

Preparation of this chapter is supported in part by Project #MCJ-225047 from the Maternal & Child Health Program (Title V Social Security Act), Health Resources and Services Administration, Department of Health and Human Services.

Chapter 12

CHALLENGES OF SPECIAL EDUCATION IN RURAL AND URBAN SCHOOLS

The population density of a community and its school district creates unique challenges for special education service delivery. Both rural and urban settings have attributes that define the activities and predicaments administrators typically will face on a daily basis, as well as determine the way students receive or do not receive appropriate education. Specifically, these communities face educational challenges due to inherent characteristics such as geography, personal values, family constellations, availability of resources and personnel, poverty, funding, bureaucracy, complexity, and cultural diversity.

RURAL SPECIAL EDUCATION

A school district is considered rural when the number of inhabitants is fewer than 150 per square mile or when located in counties where 60% or more of the population live in communities with no more than 5,000 inhabitants. Districts with more than 10,000 students and those within a Standard Metropolitan Statistical Area, as determined by the U.S. Census Bureau, are not considered rural (Helge, 1984a). City dwellers might imagine these conditions describe relatively few districts; however, 25% of the school districts in the United States enroll fewer than 300 students (Helge, 1984b).

Rural school districts have unique structural and cultural characteristics. Structurally, they are small and isolated. This reduces layers of bureaucracy while requiring that individuals be responsible for a variety of roles. Communication is typically less formal than in other settings. The ability to facilitate change more expediently without the complex layers of administrative hierarchy generally found in city schools may be an advantage rural administrators have over their urban counterparts. Because personnel are responsible for so many roles, they share expertise and skills in the regular course of business (Capper, 1990). Rural administrators may be able to participate in more building-level team decision-making.

Small size facilitates sharing decision-making and implementing pilot projects. Lack of bureaucratic layers and the presence of informal communication among staff allow quick responses and more efficient transfer of information, which may result in implementation of innovations faster than in an urban setting.

Rural Culture

Culturally, there is often a greater homogeneity than in larger communities, resulting in dichotomies between locals and "outsiders" (Capper & Larkin, 1992). These communities are often viewed as rich in cultural history and family integrity but poor in resources (William & Cross, 1985). So, although there are limited police and social services, as well as fewer entertainment and socialization options (Swift, 1984), the close-knit nature of rural communities results in fewer and less-severe discipline problems (Bell, 1991).

Although there is often a greater homogeneity in rural environments, another cultural dynamic exists. In many rural environments there are subcultures that exist outside of the main community, such as migrant workers, Native Americans on reservations, or minorities who relocated to provide labor for a certain industry. Children and families from these subpopulations may have significantly different needs for services. School personnel and administrators are challenged to accurately assess needs, communicate effectively, and operate within the groups' cultural contexts.

Some rural communities value the educational system and view the school as an extension of their families. These rural citizens participate more in school activities (Bell et al., 1991), feel more a part of the decision-making process, and have greater control over budgets than urban parents (Grippin et al., 1984). Schools in these communities experience support from parents and good relationships among parents, staff, and administrators (Collins, 1992). At the same time, there may be a complacency or satisfaction with the status quo that results in suspicion of new programs and resistance toward outside agencies, fearing their district will lose control (Ellzey & Karnes, 1991).

Other rural residents may perceive the school as an unwelcome influence on their children (Howley, Pendarvis, & Howley, 1988). These communities seek to preserve the traditions of previous generations and resist diverse ideas. These parents may consider the school curriculum to be irrelevant and antithetical to their values (Kleinsasser, 1986); education may be viewed as a way for the larger society to lure their children away from the rural community (Nachtigal, 1982).

The first case study introduces some of the challenges of hiring qualified personnel and begins to examine unique characteristics of rural environments.

Recruit from Chicago

Floyd Sauder, the special education director of a rural Montana cooperative, was excited. After two years of advertising for a qualified speech pathologist with no response, an application had arrived in the mail from an ASHA-certified speech pathologist recently graduated from a university in the Chicago area.

Mr. Sauder wasted no time in calling the applicant, Eileen Reardon, to encourage her to interview for the position. He described the opportunities and advantages. The job would offer endless variety, with the opportunity to work with children in medium-sized buildings to one-room schools. The students are wonderful kids from nice farm families. There is diversity, too, working with Native-American children, children who live on remote ranches, and the children of migrant families. A therapist could custom-design the speech program. Teachers are receptive to assistance, and parents want to be involved. Plus, money goes far here; a home can be purchased for less than $50,000 or rented for less than $250 a month.

Eileen was impressed. She arranged to drive out for an interview two weeks later. Floyd made reservations for her at a motel about 20 miles away. At the interview, the special education director, school psychologist, and a local principal met with Eileen for two hours. The team was impressed with her knowledge, ideas, and attitude toward children and education. Eileen seemed a little assertive and high strung, but the interviewers believed the open spaces and rural community would calm her down.

Eileen liked these folks. They were relaxed, and it seemed that people and children were more important to them than theory and paperwork. How refreshing! Indeed, everything the special education director had said on the telephone was corroborated by the other interviewers. Eileen said she didn't think she'd mind driving 2 or 3 hours to schools on some days (no one mentioned the few times she'd have to stay overnight in order to reach certain remote locations); it was a relief to be out of the smog and traffic.

As Eileen became more relaxed with her new potential colleagues, she asked them what they did for fun. She was not prepared for their answers. The principal said most people spend time with their families, hunt, fish, ski, and attend church gatherings. The director added that Eileen could meet a lot of singles if she went two-stepping at the cowboy bars. The school psychologist noticed the worried look on Eileen's face and offered to include Eileen when she and her friends drive into the city to see a movie. Because it's 120 miles each way, she said, they plan the trip pretty far ahead, but it's fun shopping and going to real restaurants.

Everyone began to feel the tension build. Eileen asked where she would be able to find a condominium with a pool. Thinking she was joking, the director laughed uproariously, but then he realized Eileen was not kidding. Floyd replied, "We told the bank president you might be coming, and he's already agreed to offer you a mortgage on one of two homes the Realtor is ready to show this afternoon. Anyway, no one puts pools in the ground here; we have 8 months of winter." Eileen replied that she had not realized what she would be getting into. The job might offer a great opportunity, but she was pretty sure she'd never get used to the life-style.

CONSIDER THIS

1. What realities of rural education did Eileen learn from this interview process?

2. What else might have been discussed on the telephone before the interview?

3. This administrator desperately wanted to hire a badly needed professional. What are the ethical considerations of "sugarcoating" a situation or leaving out essential details in order to entice a professional to work with you?

Challenges of Special Education in Rural Environments

The rural teacher must be adaptive and resourceful, stretching available materials and services across many areas of exceptionality (Grippin et al., 1984). Helge (1987) cites the shortage of qualified personnel as the most significant obstacle to serving students with disabilities in rural schools. Teacher training institutions are not preparing future special educators for the realities of teaching and living in rural areas (Miller & Sidebottom, 1987; Reetz, 1988; Rydell, Gage, & Colnes, 1986; Smith & Burke, 1983). Generally, preservice teachers are educated in urban or suburban university settings and are unprepared for the culture shock of living and working in rural environments (Helge, 1981). Teachers in these settings experience social, cultural, and geographic isolation (Helge & Marrs, 1982), lack of support services (Adelman, 1986), and limited career mobility (Helge, 1983). Often public awareness of the need for specialized services, such as speech or physical therapy, is lower in rural areas (Chezik, Pratt, Stewart, & Dear, 1989). Consequently, a high percentage of new rural special education teachers leave their jobs, creating an endless cycle of openings (Davis, 1989; Helge, 1992). This shortage results in the necessity of offering emergency certification to teachers with limited experience and minimal training in special education (Schofer & Duncan, 1986). Students in rural areas, therefore, have a high probability of being educated by overextended or poorly trained teachers.

Students in rural areas are particularly vulnerable to leaving school before graduating (Bull, 1991; Helge, 1989). Those with unidentified learning disabilities experience high frustration in high school and tend to drop out (Bull, Salyer, & Montgomery, 1990). Students from migrant or other subcultures in rural settings are especially vulnerable (Harrington, 1987; Morse, 1987). Those requiring medical intervention frequently leave to find necessary services (Helge, 1990). Finally, there is a lack of available career and vocational education services that might offer guidance or provide relevant training after high school (Maddux & Arvig, 1988).

Providing services for gifted and talented students is also problematic. The few students who qualify may be spread out over the vast expanse of the district, resulting in insufficient enrollment to justify a special class or additional staff (Gear, 1984; Spicker, Southern, & Davis, 1987). Parents of these students may not have the awareness of the potential for special school programming. Many rural schools are located in low-income areas and are unable to afford high-quality academic programs or technology (Ellzey & Karnes, 1991).

Because of the great distances between home and school, a large percentage of students in rural settings depends on school buses for transportation. The experiences students have on the bus affect their performance in the classroom (Raper, 1990). Many rural students ride more than an hour each way to school over poorly maintained roads, impassable during bad weather, arriving at the school tired and unprepared for a full day's work. Even though transportation is a special education related service mandated by law (Raper, 1990), exceptional students in remote areas who require special transportation may have to be accommodated in personal cars or on poorly equipped buses.

The following case material is a letter describing working conditions in a remote rural area.

Letter to the New School Psychologist

Ann accepted a position as school psychologist for a regional service center in northern Arizona. On her first day, there was a letter waiting on her desk from the former psychologist.

Dear Ann,

Welcome to the new job and best of luck. I thought you might appreciate some suggestions and words of wisdom about the roles and tasks you are about to embark upon. I wish I could say I did a great job over the 5 years I worked for the service center, but, more honestly, I did my best as I learned each lesson the hard way.

You have an important role and can make a difference for many students and a few teachers, but there will be surprises and challenges. First, I want to prepare you for the condition of some of the schools and the children's homes. The farther you go from the city, the more you can expect the schools to be in poor repair with limited play areas and equipment. At first, I was shocked to see the conditions in which these children had to learn. Although I never got used to it, after a while I was able to do my job without being distracted by the sadness of it. In addition, there are not enough materials, and what is available is outdated. When you go to visit teachers, you may want to bring curriculum materials from the resource center that might be useful for teaching the students you are testing. Then, be prepared to help the teacher learn how to use those materials.

Teachers will be excited to see you, and some will go all out to make you feel welcome, bringing food and wanting to talk. You may be their lifeline to developments in the field as well as a major source of emotional support. Tell them you appreciate their efforts and offer them something new to try. On the other hand, you may meet a lot of teachers and allied professionals who are burnt out. Listen to their concerns but don't listen to their pessimism; they would like to snare you into their hopelessness.

You may feel a camaraderie with the new teachers who have moved in from elsewhere because they seem to have enthusiasm and energy. However, although some of our best teachers may not appear at first to have that ambition, they've stood the test of time. The young teachers may give up after a few years and leave, but those who have grown up around here understand their community and have made a commitment to make a difference.

Take time to get prepared for whatever you plan to do. Once you leave the service center, you've left your source of materials. By the way, do you have a mobile phone? I'd suggest it. And pack an emergency box for your car with a sleeping bag, water, and snacks. There will be times when you're driving across nowhere at meal time; plan to bring meals with you.

You'll be asked to do a wide variety of tasks. Be prepared to be in charge of kindergarten screenings as well as hearing and vision testing for other grades. You'll be in constant contact with social service and government agencies. Remember, you're there for the students and their families. It's easy to forget that when you get enmeshed in those bureaucratic systems.

Testing is a challenge. Clearly, we do not have culturally appropriate assessment instruments for many of the ethnic and linguistic groups you'll work with. Gather narrative data and work samples to help make sense out of the tests you use. It may be hard to communicate with some of the parents. They really do care about their children, but the school intimidates them, differences in language and culture are an obstacle to communication, and many do not have telephones.

Also, when you do find students eligible for special education services, don't be too surprised by the few options that are available. For children with severe disabilities, the choice is the regular classroom or a residential school. Despite all the challenges, though, I learned to love the job and to take pride in what I was able to do for children in these schools. I hope you'll love it, too!

Sincerely,
Jessica Marshall

 ## CONSIDER THIS

1. What challenges of this setting do you think might be hardest to deal with?
2. How can an administrator help the school psychologist to do her job well?

Further Administrative Challenges

Most rural communities experience limited funding and services, difficulty recruiting trained personnel, and geographic isolation (Helge, 1981). Rural areas typically receive less federal and state money than do urban and suburban areas (Helge, 1990). Because there are fewer staff members, grant writing is an extra burden. Consequently, rural schools are poorly represented in grant competitions (Sher, 1988). Limited funding is often coupled with higher costs for delivery of services due to higher transportation cost, difficulty in obtaining services of specialists or technical equipment, a wide diversity of disabilities spread over great distances (ACRES, 1988), and the extra time it takes to convene trans-disciplinary teams (Helge, 1984b).

Having fewer administrators may sound like an advantage, but special education administrators in rural settings are responsible for an incredible range of roles and functions for which they do not always have adequate preparation or readily available expert consultants. These administrators may supervise a great range of personnel; complete state and federal reports that require an understanding of law, policy, and practice; collect data and evaluate programs; and respond to complex due process procedures (Hutto & Page, 1990).

The following case study presents a picture of the challenges and joys of one rural special education administrator.

Making a Difference in Western Kentucky

Ten years ago, the superintendent of a rural school district in western Kentucky needed someone to take responsibility for special education programs, but he was unable to justify a full-time position. He created a job description by combining responsibilities for coordinating Chapter I programs, coordinating district inservice training, overseeing the revision of district policy and course descriptions, writing grants, and supervising the special education programs. Albert Hunsinger was hired for this position and was called "program coordinator."

He was a natural for the job because of his "people skills" and understanding of the nature of a rural school system. Principals raved about how much help he was. When asked what his formula for success was, Albert replied, "I communicate face to face with everyone. I only use the telephone to make appointments, and I never send memos. I visit every school every week. When I get there, I talk with the secretary, catch up with the principal, and stop into every special and remedial education teacher's room. I eat in the cafeteria and compliment the cook. And, before I leave, I make sure to chat with the custodian and check up on bus drivers."

At first it had been difficult for Albert. Because he came from about 80 miles away and wasn't considered a "local," it took more than a year, and in some cases three years, for him to be accepted. Initially, Albert would see a need for a specific change and suggest an innovative approach. Teachers and principals typically responded, "That's not the way we do it here." Albert spent a lot of time feeling frustrated. He got the insight he needed when a teacher suggested that if Albert was going to be at the high school basketball game, they could talk there. Ever since, Albert has learned to hint and plant seeds with local educators at every possible community supper, sports event, or festival and then watch the fruits of his effort take hold over time.

Albert still gets frustrated that principals defer to him for leadership in all special education matters. He has built preassessment teams in every school to encourage site-based decision-making, but he finds he frequently has to attend these meetings. When teachers don't feel competent to test students who have been referred for a special education evaluation, Albert does the assessment and trains the teacher to use the tests in the hope that next time he won't be needed. He attends most eligibility committee meetings and ensures there is an administrative representative at all IEP meetings (which sometimes means he must attend). Some weeks, Albert spends half his time involved in preassessment, assessment, eligibility, and IEP activities.

The remainder of the week is spent in planned and spontaneous meetings. There's the weekly conference with the superintendent and the weekly gathering of principals. Some days, there is time after everyone goes home to fill out reports, prepare for meetings or inservice programs, and write grants.

Parents call or stop by both home and office to complain about how their child is being treated or not getting what is needed. Albert has learned this is the way of the community. The parents see themselves as the primary teachers of their children and expect the schools to support them in that role. Some days he dreams of a simpler, more anonymous job, but most days he revels in the feeling of being so important to so many people he really loves.

 CONSIDER THIS

1. What are some of the administrative realities of Albert's role as a special education leader in a small school district?
2. What has Albert learned that works in his setting?

Suggestions

The following are suggestions relevant to rural settings:

1. Increase funding and staffing creatively; both are necessary to improving special education services (DeYoung, 1991).
2. Develop a vast telecommunication network to expedite the delivery of information to teachers working in rural schools (Kendall, 1992). Technology, such as computers, public television, videotapes, interactive television, and satellite programming, can be used to deliver both teacher training and student curriculum (Ellzey & Karnes, 1991).
3. Encourage cooperation among several districts in sharing personnel and financial resources (Ellzey & Karnes, 1991).
4. Attract and retain personnel by offering competitive salaries and benefits, providing teacher support in pleasant working environments, and making

provisions for readily available professional growth (Matthes & Carlson, 1986).

5. Supplement salaries for intensive or extra duty with money from local educational foundations or corporate endowments. Salary supplements may be useful both for recruiting and for motivating existing personnel to retrain in shortage areas (Smith-Davis, 1989).

6. Rotate from special areas to general education to reduce burnout and provide insights from experiences on the "other side" (Smith-Davis, 1989).

7. Increase use of paraprofessionals to support teachers and extend services to exceptional students. Extended day, week, or year programs may provide more options for serving students (Smith-Davis, 1989).

8. Use retired teachers as part-time employees to provide services for isolated students or for extra duties (Smith-Davis, 1989).

9. Develop internship programs for student teachers in rural areas where students are paired with mentor teachers and meet regularly with other students in similar environments to discuss experiences (Smith-Davis, 1989). This provides extra help for teachers and better prepares student teachers.

10. Develop teaching training programs specifically for the realities of rural education (Bell et al., 1991).

11. Add a strong vocational track to rural education to reduce the dropout problem (Bull, Salyer, & Montgomery, 1990). The focus should be on matching individual needs of youth with disabilities to the employment opportunities of the community (Spruill, 1989).

12. Advocate for better special transportation and collaborate with transportation providers to ensure students' needs are being addressed before and after school while on the bus (Raper, 1990).

13. Channel state and federal monies toward collaborative relationships between universities and state and local education agencies to provide access to expert personnel and examples of positive service strategies that can increase expectations for student potential (Capper, 1990).

14. Utilize computers to individualize curriculum for small but diverse student populations (Lazzari & Wilds, 1989).

15. Develop site-based collaborative teams of teachers and administrators to share expertise and support each other through difficult situations (Hutto & Page, 1990).

16. Create a central data-collecting agency for rural schools to research and evaluate the current salient issues and successful programs in rural settings (Helge, 1984a).

URBAN SPECIAL EDUCATION

An urban area is defined as a city that has at least 50,000 inhabitants or that includes an outlying county with close economic and social relationships to a city (Kanny & Crowe, 1991). Urban environments are densely populated and generally characterized by racial, ethnic, and linguistic diversity (Gollnick &

Chinn, 1990). School systems in urban areas are large, complex, and compart-mentalized (Berkeley & Lipinski, 1991).

The student population of today's urban classrooms is more racially and eth-nically diverse than in any previous generation in American history, a trend that is expected to continue (Gollnick & Chinn, 1990; Peng, Wang, & Walberg, 1992). Of the 25 largest systems in the nation, 23 are primarily composed of eth-nic minority students, 75% of whom are African American (Obiakor, Algozzine, & Ford, 1993).

A significant portion of the urban population comes from low- to low-middle-income families (Bay & Bryan, 1992). Low socioeconomic status brings con-comitant problems of poor nutrition, lack of medical care, and fewer early educational opportunities. These children are more likely to be exposed to vio-lence and family instability (Ellsworth, 1993). In addition, child abuse and ne-glect, as well as prenatal exposure to drugs, result in a significantly higher risk for educational disabilities (Chinn & Hughes, 1987).

At-Risk and Special Education Students

Cities have higher concentrations of at-risk and special education students than rural or suburban settings (McIntyre, 1992). There are several reasons. First, minority, bilingual, and low-income students are almost three times more likely to be referred for special education and related services than students from upper socioeconomic levels (Fleischner & Van Acker, 1990). Second, urban classes are typically larger and more diverse than rural or suburban classes (McIntyre, 1992). Teachers have less time to individualize instruction and, consequently, will refer a student more readily. Rural or suburban educators may be more likely or bet-ter able to accommodate students with special needs in the general classroom. When administrators realize special education funding is more stable than inno-vative programs for at-risk students, they encourage the referral and placement of these students in an attempt to meet the needs of those who are at risk for school failure.

Third, traditional teaching methods fail to take into account the life experi-ences of these students (Cuban, 1989). Minority students do not feel they belong to the schools; they find more satisfying social and financial rewards outside of the school environment (Grant, 1989). Teachers are ill-prepared to instruct this population. They lower expectations, offer less challenging material, and reward and punish behavior differentially by class as well as by race (Fleischner & Van Acker, 1990). Bay and Bryan (1992) found that teachers offer less corrective feed-back to minority students.

Although educators recognize the importance of parent involvement, city schools are characterized by fewer parent-school partnerships than other settings. Obiakor, Algozzine, and Ford (1993) state teachers traditionally view African-American parents as deficient and dysfunctional. Therefore, they provide fewer opportunities for parent involvement, and the parents feel less valued and un-necessary in the decision-making process. Teachers may lack the skills and un-derstanding to create bridges between the community, family, and school life (Hughes, Ruhl, & Gorman, 1987).

Teachers of Urban Special Education Students

Teachers with special education training are especially needed in metropolitan areas (Peng, Wang, & Walberg, 1992). Teaching in urban environments is extremely demanding and stressful, resulting in high attrition (McNergney & Haberman, 1989), especially for special educators. The number of teachers leaving the profession in urban environments is higher than in other settings, creating a more unstable environment (Obiakor et al., 1993). Darling-Hammond (1988) noted that teacher vacancies are three times greater in central cities than in suburban and rural districts. Beginning teachers say that job prospects in urban schools are less appealing because of the stress of working with large classes and diverse populations and because there is less potential for support (Bell et al., 1991). Because the need for special educators is so great in cities, and new teachers are less likely to choose employment in these environments, city districts may employ more special education teachers who hold emergency certification than other districts (Colorado Department of Education, 1991).

One complaint of teachers in urban schools is the lack of support to maintain students in mainstream environments. Compared with suburban districts, city schools are less likely to have prereferral procedures, such as teacher assistance teams, where teachers might turn for assistance (Bay & Bryan, 1992).

The following case offers a glimpse of the frustration of one urban special education administrator.

The Offer

The phone call was unexpected: "We're looking for a strong leader for special programs in our growing suburban district, and you're the type of professional we have in mind." Ned felt flattered. The salary was attractive and the working conditions would be a delightful change.

For 20 years, Ned had been a leader and fighter for special education programs in his city. He had been proud of the exemplary services offered, but now he felt as if special education was a runaway locomotive heading for disaster. It seemed everyone complained that Ned's budget soaked up 25% of the city school total, yet these same people wanted to know what he intended to provide to help every group that didn't succeed. Ned's job seemed to be endlessly responding to crises, appeasing people, and answering questions about medical, behavioral, and legal issues he'd never dealt with before.

Poverty, drugs, and violence touched the lives of every child in the city. Nurses asked what special education label to assign to teen-agers with gunshot wounds to the head and how to get more medical intervention for the burgeoning number of drug-exposed preschoolers. Preschool teachers wanted to know what services Ned would recommend for this growing population of demanding and perplexing children.

Half the high school administrators were angry with Ned for defending the rights of BD students who were involved in gang activity. He wasn't sure how he really felt about this himself. Today a principal told Ned to hire a teacher for the Teen Moms program because more than half of the students had special ed labels.

On a recent visit to a middle school, Ned was shocked to find that after years of inservice training concerning cultural/linguistic diversity, LD programs still served only Anglo students, MR programs served primarily African-American students, and the BD program was composed of almost all minority students. The final straw was the inability to staff special classes in certain schools. Currently, Ned has 17 "permanent substitutes" whom he moves from school to school every month, because their emergency waiver from the state expires every 20 days.

After two decades of dedication, Ned asks himself if accepting the recent job offer would be abandoning his district in its greatest hour of need or if it would be the reward he richly deserves for his 20 years in the trenches.

CONSIDER THIS

1. Why do some educators continue to work in seemingly hopeless conditions?
2. What advice would you give Ned?

Reform

The impetus for national reform may have its heart in the concern for the plight of urban students. Unfortunately, reformers are attempting to solve socioeconomic and multicultural issues of the city using a suburban, middle-class mentality (McIntyre, 1992). One proposal for reform involves parental choice, which means schools offer alternatives, and parents choose among the best or most appropriate. Proponents of choice assert students would be able to escape inadequate urban schools if their parents had a choice (Wells, 1989). Ironically, those who would benefit most from school choice are talented students with well-informed parents. Few parents from middle-class environments will choose to send their children to schools in urban settings which seem to be filled with violent, low-achieving students. McDonnell (1989) stresses that urban parents, especially from low-socioeconomic backgrounds, are ill-informed about how the system works and are often too burdened with daily survival to research educational options. Therefore, school choice offers little potential help to students of inner cities.

Other reformers focus on goals, such as the federal government's guidelines for improved education for all, called America 2000. Even though the administration claims its testing program for America 2000 will be voluntary, experience with this type of reform suggests that lower-achieving students will be tracked into "drill and kill" instruction, designed to raise test scores (McIntyre, 1992). Additionally, goal-oriented programs too often result in standardized curriculum which hinders individualization. Instead of improving the circumstances for students with special needs in cities, goal-oriented programs will likely result in more feedback to the schools that their students are doing poorly. One administrative solution that further sabotages efforts to improve schools in an achievement-oriented atmosphere is for the administrator to encourage low-achieving students to be identified for special education programs and then exempted from taking the tests.

Reformers concerned with low graduation rates of urban students have responded with plans to raise expectations, proposing more demanding standards that will motivate students to try harder. However, the administration might be better advised to address the precursors to dropping out, such as poverty, limited English proficiency, lack of family-school partnerships (National Education Goals Panel, 1991), cultural pressures not to succeed in a "white" institution (McIntyre, 1992), and peer violence, which keeps many students away from school (Perales, 1988).

Of all the proposed reforms, the one that seems most appropriate is the National Urban Schools Program proposal in which the federal government would allocate funding for urban schools targeted for teacher renewal and programmatic innovation. Additionally, low-interest loans or matching grants are also necessary for the much-needed renovation of buildings and acquisition of technology (McIntyre, 1992).

Early Childhood Special Education

One response to confronting the devastating long-term effects of social, health, and environmental challenges of the inner city is to develop comprehensive infant, toddler, and preschool programs (Milian-Perrone & Ferrell, 1993). Current efforts have been largely unsuccessful because of funding limitations. Head Start programs reach only 20% of the children poor enough to qualify (McIntyre, 1992). Cities are reluctant to raise tax bases to pay for early intervention programs, and social services continue to experience cutbacks. Federal plans do not include programs for strengthening early-intervention programs (Miller & Sidebottom, 1987).

The following case material summarizes an interview with a special education leader from one of the nation's largest school systems.

Special Education in Los Angeles

Steven Mark

**Administrative Coordinator of Special Education,
Los Angeles Unified School District**

Los Angeles is a giant, sprawling metropolis with more than 600 schools. Of the 639,000 students, 65,000 have active individualized education programs. Los Angeles schools offer a full range of services, unimaginable to residents of smaller communities. For example, students with a hearing loss may receive their complete education in a general education inclusive classroom (interpreters are available), or they might attend a nearby neighborhood school that provides supplementary instruction in resource rooms for students with hearing impairment (both oral and total communication programs are offered). Or, these students might attend a special school in the city for students who are deaf and hearing-impaired. This special school is one of 18 such building programs provided by the Los Angeles Unified School District that focuses on specific populations of more severely involved students.

A newcomer to Los Angeles schools might be awestruck by the sheer numbers of programs and complex issues addressed by a district of this magnitude. As many as 60 languages are spoken at schools in the district; bilingual instruction is a major curriculum consideration. The socioeconomic status of its students ranges from the rich and famous to the destitute and homeless. There is a task force for every imaginable major problem faced by schools and society today. As a result, innovative programs address issues such as meeting the needs of children from impoverished families, parental neglect and drug abuse, and transient life-styles.

The district is divided into six regions: four elementary school, one middle school, and one high school. Each area has its own regional special education director who reports to the administrative coordinator. This central office coordinator is also responsible for the special schools. The district's multilayered system of administration and bureaucracy has caused some discontent among educators and parents. Teachers might work for the school district their entire lives and never meet the superintendent, much less feel like an important part of the system.

The district responded to this feeling of anonymity with a restructuring program. Announcements were made in newspapers and newsletters that 10 grass-roots committees were forming to be composed of parents, educational professionals, and community members. These committees were to address general issues, such as methods to meet the needs of students and families of Los Angeles, and ways to promote site-based management in schools. One committee focused on special education, and one dealt with support services. After meeting, the committees reported to the superintendent.

The consequent restructuring plan calls for the development of K–12 administrative clusters of catchment areas consisting of one high school and the elementary and middle schools that feed into it. In addition, California has mandated the development of "charter schools," which are neighborhood schools given waivers from traditional, mandated services so that local educators can provide innovative programs to serve the needs of their students. Los Angeles has 10 of the state's 100 proposed charter schools.

The big concern for central office special education administrators during this restructuring is how to continue to provide necessary continuum of quality special education services to smaller administrative units and locally controlled schools. Will principals in crowded administrative clusters be receptive to housing centralized programs for low-incidence students from outside of their cluster? At a time when the courts appear to be supporting increasingly more complex and specific services, can smaller units provide the necessary range of options?

Funding is a challenging issue for all special education administrators. Federal and state dollars are shrinking while federal and state litigation and local due process actions demand more comprehensive services for ever-increasing populations of students with multiple disabilities. Parents want their severely involved children to receive education in inclusive environments, but they also want the students to receive speech therapy, counseling, OT/PT, and paraprofessional support. Every time special education has to pay for an additional program that was not in the budget, we have to go to the general education budget. Administrators in general education, who are strapped for funds, are angry about our encroachment on their money.

Speaking of inclusion, we have been including students for as long as anyone can remember. As a matter of fact, we have parents move into our district because they have heard we support special students in the general classroom. Recently, a parent who moved from Los Angeles to another state called to express her frustration with the new school district and to ask for suggestions in dealing with the principal and special education director. She had expected the same level of service and similar attitudes about inclusion but instead found disbelief and an unwillingness to accommodate her child. Urban schools get criticized for everything, but we provide a fantastic range of services. Only when parents leave do they realize what they had here.

It's hard to tell whether it's sheer numbers or a unique litigious environment, but our district has numerous hearings each week. At this moment, I have four or five on my desk to handle. There are attorneys in Los Angeles who specialize in special education litigation. We regularly receive calls from lawyers demanding services for their clients and threatening legal action. Yesterday, a parent called to say that we must provide home-to-school transportation for her child because it is unsafe to walk to the school where the child receives special education services.

Even though most students in Los Angeles attend neighborhood schools, we provide a great deal of special bus transportation. All students with severe disabilities are bused from home to school. Most special education students are bused to school from preschool through third grade. After that, if children attend a special program outside the neighborhood, they walk to their home school and are transported to the program. Los Angeles is hilly, and some children live at the end of roads that are difficult to access. Students with low-incidence disabilities who attend special schools and live in remote areas may be on the bus for more than an hour; rural educators may have thought they were in the only districts where students spend hours on buses.

Actually, my job consists almost entirely of solving problems and mediating between people. At least half of my day is spent on the telephone listening, counseling, and advocating. I spent the first hour today talking with principals. One discovered asbestos in his old school and has to evacuate a hall which includes special education classrooms. Another is a new principal meeting with Spanish-speaking parents. It seems the Spanish interpreter previously was told to translate only what the former principal told her to, but not everything that was said; the new principal realized this was unethical and wasn't sure how to handle the situation. A third principal reported the parents of a student with autism were told the child had destroyed his seat on the bus and would be excluded from the special transportation. Many parents call me directly, bypassing the principal and area administrators, hoping for greater clout. I am involved in all phases of due process, from informal conferences to mediation to legal hearings.

We used to have an entire administrative division for staff development and another for curriculum development. With administrative downsizing those are gone. Their functions have been absorbed by staff in my office. So, I also deal with these two areas.

The other half of my day is spent sitting in committee meetings. We do everything here by committee. Currently, I'm on a committee that addresses special transportation issues and another that examines procedures for dealing with students with behavioral problems. Last night, I was at a restructuring program meeting until 7:15. It was a long day.

Because our operation is so large, we have compartmentalized administrative operations. Other administrators specialize in areas such as managing the budget, writing grants, and writing policy and procedures.

Los Angeles is involved in Total Quality Management. At every level, we are assessing the outcomes of our work, such as the impact of teachers on students and the effect of administrators on schools. Districtwide curriculum committees are developing suggested outcomes for each grade level. Administrators are asked to do a self-analysis, listing the expected outcomes of their efforts. The upper-level administrators submitted their proposal outcomes to the school board for approval. Everyone is accountable.

The enormity of Los Angeles, its schools, and its challenges is probably mind-boggling for most administrators. But we offer quality services for every conceivable student need. Also, because there is so much available, as well as so many people doing similar jobs and working with similar students, there seems to be more camaraderie here than in other systems. Although individuals may not feel they have a major impact on the system, educators in Los Angeles may feel less alone and more supported than those in smaller school districts.

CONSIDER THIS

1. Compare the roles and tasks of the urban administrator, as presented in this case study, with those of the rural administrator in the case study from western Kentucky.
2. What challenges are unique to the job of an urban special educator?
3. How is the job of the special education administrator similar across environments?

Suggestions

The following are suggestions relevant to urban settings:

1. Confront a negative school climate and the poor quality of instruction provided by educators who possess attitudes that devalue or limit students from minority backgrounds. Assessment of the environment, inservice training, and teacher renewal is essential (Obiakor et al., 1993).
2. Stress greater involvement of inner-city parents and communities (Obiakor et al., 1993). Parent involvement programs could instruct parents in how to support literacy and social competence at home (Kozleski, Sands, & French, 1993).
3. Emphasize a team approach to education services, with administrators and classroom teachers collaborating (Obiakor et al., 1993).
4. Establish a school climate in which minority students feel they belong and are part of the decision-making (Obiakor et al., 1993).
5. Develop early intervention programs that address the children's intellectual, social, and health needs (McIntyre, 1992).
6. Provide preservice teacher training programs that assist educators to teach effectively in inner-city environments. Specially trained teachers should be recruited and encouraged to establish a career in urban education (Kozleski et al., 1993).
7. Prepare teachers in urban environments to teach students to use prosocial approaches to conflict resolution, deescalate potentially violent students, and intervene in crisis situations, providing safety for all.
8. Prepare early childhood educators with information about child-rearing practices, perceptions of HIV and AIDS by community members, views of death and dying based on cultural and religious views, the role and responsibilities of extended family members and nontraditional families, perceptions of disabilities, and procedures to locate help within the community (Milian-Perrone & Ferrell, 1993).
9. Focus teacher education reform on changes in school organization that facilitate teaching in an inner city, preparation to teach students from diverse

backgrounds, differentiated jobs for teachers with appropriate incentives and rewards, and partnerships between schools and universities (Fager, Andrews, Shepherd, & Quinn, 1993).

SUMMARY

Characteristics of rural and urban environments, such as geography, culture, community values, and availability of resources, affect the job of the special education leader. Rural schools are small and relatively isolated. Special education administrators in rural schools must perform a wide range of responsibilities, including active involvement in each school. Rural communities are typically more homogeneous than are urban settings, although in many rural environments, there are small subcultures of different socioeconomic, ethnic, or linguistic populations. Rural parents are often involved with their schools to ensure the values of the school are consistent with those of the home. New teachers who did not grow up in rural environments have a difficult time adjusting to the isolation and lack of resources, and consequently leave more often than new teachers in suburban schools. Educators in rural environments must be resourceful because funds and materials are often limited. It is also difficult to provide a full continuum of services in rural schools because the small number of students in low-incidence categories often is spread over a large area. Transportation is definitely a challenge over long distances and difficult terrain. Few special education administrators are prepared for the many responsibilities of managing special services in a rural system.

Urban environments are densely populated and characterized by diverse populations as well as the challenges of low-socioeconomic families. The school systems are large, complex, and compartmentalized. Cities have higher concentrations of at-risk and special education students than do rural or suburban settings. Traditional approaches to education do not seem to match the unique needs of urban children. Larger classes may mean teachers have less time for individualizing programs. Parents are less likely to be involved with urban schools than they are in rural and suburban systems. Many reform measures have been proposed to address the plight of inner-city schools but, unfortunately, they do not seem to deal with the true issues that lead to student failure.

REFERENCES

Adelman, H. A. (1986). Staffing the field for the future. *Journal of Learning Disabilities, 19,* 477–479.

American Council on Rural Special Education (ACRES). (1988). Response to PL 99-457, Title I and II: Issues concerning families residing in rural and remote areas of the United States. *Rural Special Education Quarterly, 9*(1), 24–28.

Bay, M., & Bryan, T. (1992). Differentiating children who are at risk for referral from others on critical classroom factors. *Remedial and Special Education, 13*(4), 27–33.

Bell, T. L. (1991). *Perceptions of future special education teachers concerning rural teaching environments.* (ERIC Document Reproduction Service No. ED 342 542)

Berkeley, T. R., & Lipinski, T. A. (1991). An inquiry into rural special education: A discussion with Judy Schrag, director, Office of Special Education Programs, U.S. Department of Education. *Rural Special Education Quarterly, 10*(4), 18–20.

Bull, L. S. (1991). *Administrators' perceptions of special education dropouts: A comparison of priorities by school location.* (ERIC Document Reproduction Service No. ED 342 550)

Bull, K. S., Salyer, B. K., & Montgomery, D. (1990). *ACRES at-risk task force: Dropout survey.* Paper presented at the 10th annual conference of the American Council for Rural Special Education, Tucson, AZ.

Capper, C. A. (1990). Students with low-incidence disabilities in disadvantaged, rural settings. *Exceptional Children, 56*(4), 338–344.

Capper, C. A., & Larkin, J. (1992). The regular education initiative: Educational reorganization for rural school districts. *Journal of School Leadership, 2*(2), 232–245.

Chezik, K. H., Pratt, J. E., Stewart, J. L., & Dear, V. (1989). Addressing services delivery in remote/rural areas. *ASHA, 31,* 52–55.

Chinn, P. C., & Hughes, S. (1987). Representation of minority students in special education classes. *Remedial and Special Education, 8*(4), 41–46.

Collins, B. C. (1992). Identification of the advantages and disadvantages of special education service delivery in rural Kentucky as a basis for generating solutions to problems. *Rural Special Education Quarterly, 11*(3), 30–34.

Colorado Department of Education (1991). *The state plan for Colorado.* Denver, CO: Colorado Department of Education.

Cuban, L. (1989). The "at-risk" label and the problem of urban school reform. *Phi Delta Kappan, 70,* 780–784.

Darling-Hammond, L. (1988). Teacher quality and educational equality. *College Board Review,* pp. 16–33, 39–41.

Davis, J. S. (1989). Recruiting and retaining special educators in rural areas: Strategies from the field. *Educational Considerations, 17*(1), 33–35.

DeYoung, A. (1987). The status of American rural education research: An integrated review and commentary. *Review of Educational Research, 57*(2), 123–148.

Ellsworth, N. J. (1993). Trainees' perceptions of types of instructional practices modeled in an urban teacher education program. *Teacher Education and Special Education, 16*(1), 34–41.

Ellzey, J. T., & Karnes, F. A. (1991). Gifted education and rural youths: What parents and educators should know. *The Gifted Child Today, 14*(3), 56–57.

Fager, P., Andrews, T., Shepherd, M. J., & Quinn, E. (1993). Teamed to teach: Integrating teacher training through cooperative teaching at an urban professional development school. *Teacher Education and Special Education, 16*(1), 51–59.

Fleischner, J., & Van Acker, R. (1990). Changes in the urban school population: Challenges in meeting the need for special education leadership and teacher preparation personnel. In L. M. Bullock & R. L. Simpson (Eds.), *Critical issues in special education: Implications for personnel preparation* (73–92). Denton, TX: University of North Texas.

Gear, G. H. (1984). Providing services for rural gifted children. *Exceptional Children, 50*(4), 326–331.

Gollnick, D. M., & Chinn, P. C. (1990). *Multicultural education in a pluralistic society.* Columbus, OH: Merrill.

Grant, C. A. (1989). Urban teachers: Their new colleagues and curriculum. *Phi Delta Kappan,* 764–770.

Grippin, P. (1984). *Improving service for handicapped students in rural areas: A program.* (ERIC Document Reproduction Service No. ED 243 624)

Harrington, S. (1987). Children of the road. *Instructor, 97*(4), 36–39.

Helge, D. I. (1981). Problems in implementing comprehensive special education programming in rural areas. *Exceptional Children, 47,* 514–520.

Helge, D. I. (1983). *Images: Issues and trends in rural special education.* Bellingham, WA: Western Washington University.

Helge, D. I. (1984a). Models for serving rural children with low-incidence handicapping conditions. *Exceptional Children, 50*(4), 313–324.

Helge, D. I. (1984b). The state of the art of rural special education. *Exceptional Children, 50*(4), 294–305.

Helge, D. I. (1987). Strategies for improving rural special education program evaluation. *Remedial and Special Education, 8*(4), 52–60.

Helge, D. I. (1989). Rural "at-risk" students: Directions for policy and intervention. *Rural Special Education Quarterly, 10*(1), 3–16.

Helge, D. I. (1990). *A national study regarding at-risk students.* (ERIC Document Reproduction Service No. ED 342 521)

Helge, D. I. (1992). Solving special education reform problems in rural areas. *Preventing School Failure, 36*(4), 11–15.

Helge, D. I., & Marrs, L. W. (1982). Personnel recruitment and retention in rural America: A growing problem. *The Pointer, 26*(2), 28–33.

Howley, A. A., Pendarvis, E. D., & Howley, C. B. (1988). Gifted students in rural environments: Implications for school programs. *Rural Special Education Quarterly, 8*(4), 43–50.

Hughes, J., Ruhl, K., & Gorman, J. (1987). Preparation of special educators to work with parents. *Teacher Education and Special Education, 10,* 81–87.

Hutto, N., & Page, B. (1990). Special education: An administrative dilemma. *Journal of Rural and Small Schools, 4*(3), 43–46.

Kanny, E. M., & Crowe, T. K. (1991). A comparison of occupational therapy practice in rural and urban school systems. *Rural Special Education Quarterly, 10*(4), 10–17.

Kendall, R. M. (1992). Evaluating the benefits of a computer based telecommunication network: Telementoring and teletraining for educators in rural areas. *Journal of Research in Rural Education, 8*(1), 41–46.

Kleinsasser, A. M. (1986). *Exploration of an ambiguous culture: Conflicts facing gifted females in rural environments.* Paper presented at the annual conference of the National Rural and Small Schools Consortium, Bellingham, WA. (ERIC Document Reproduction Service No. ED 278 522)

Kozleski, E. B., Sands, D. J., & French, N. (1993). Preparing special education teachers for urban settings. *Teacher Education and Special Education, 16*(1), 14–22.

Lazzari, A. M., & Wilds, M. (1989). Technology in early childhood special education access for rural programs. *Rural Special Education Quarterly, 9*(4), 21–24.

Maddux, C. D., & Arvig, S. (1988). Special teacher perceptions of vocational education for mildly handicapped students in rural, urban, and suburban high schools. *Rural Special Education Quarterly, 8*(3), 33–39.

Matthes, W. A., & Carlson, R. V. (1986). Conditions for practice: Why teachers select rural schools. *Journal of Rural and Small Schools, 1,* 25–28.

McDonnell, L. (1989). *Restructuring American schools: The promise and the pitfalls.* ERIC Clearinghouse on Urban Education Digest #57. New York: Columbia University Teachers College.

McIntyre, T. (1992). The impact of reform recommendations on urban special education. *Preventing School Failure, 36*(4), 6–10.

McNergney, R., & Haberman, M. (1989). Factors contributing to the shortage of teachers in America's 100 largest urban districts. *NEA Today,* p. 14.

Milian-Perrone, M., & Ferrell, K. A. (1993). Preparing early childhood special educators for urban settings. *Teacher Education and Special Education, 16*(1), 83–90.

Miller, J. (1991, May). Bush plan: The closer some look, the less they see. *Education Week,* 1, 24.

Miller, J., & Sidebottom, D. (1987). *Teachers: Finding and keeping the best in small and rural districts.* Arlington, VA: American Association of School Administrators.

Morse, S. C. (1987). *Focus dropouts.* Summary report on an interstate forum on the migrant dropout. San Diego, CA: Interstate Migrant Secondary Team Project. (ERIC Document Reproduction Service No. ED 281 688)

Nachtigal, P. (1982). *Rural education: In search of a better way.* Boulder, CO: Westview Press.

National Education Goals Panel. (1991). *Measuring progress toward the national education goals.* Des Moines, IA: Governor's Office.

Obiakor, F. E., Algozzine, B., & Ford, B. A. (1993). Urban education, the general education initiative, and service delivery to African-American students. *Urban Education, 28*(3), 313–327.

Peng, S. S., Wang, M. C., & Walberg, H. J. (1992). Demographic disparities of inner-city eighth graders. *Urban Education, 26,* 441–459.

Perales, C. A. (1988). Black and Hispanic children: Their future is ours. *Journal of State Government, 61*(2), 45–48.

Raper, T. L. (1990). Two roads diverged in the woods and I . . . took the bus: Rural transportation for exceptional students. *Rural Special Education Quarterly, 10*(2), 11–14.

Reetz, L. (1988). Conflict and stress among rural special educators. *Rural Special Education Quarterly, 8*(3), 22–26.

Rydell, L., Gage, B., & Colnes, A. (1986). Teacher recruitment and retention in Maine: An overview. *Rural Special Education Quarterly, 7*(2), 22–23.

Schofer, R. C., & Duncan, J. R. (1986). A study of certain personnel preparation factors in special education. *Journal of Special Education, 20,* 61–68.

Sher, J. (1988). Why rural education has not received its "fair share" of funding—and what to do about it. *Journal of Rural and Small Schools, 2*(2), 31–37.

Smith-Davis, J. (1989). Recruiting and retaining special educators in rural areas: Strategies from the field. *Educational Considerations, 17*(1), 33–35.

Smith, J., & Burke, P. J. (1983). *A national survey of manpower supply and demand in special education.* College Park, MD: University of Maryland Institute for the Study of Handicapped Children and Youth.

Spicker, H. H., Southern, W. T., & Davis, B. I. (1987). The rural gifted child. *Gifted Child Quarterly, 3*(4), 155–157.

Spruill, J. A. (1989). *The transition of secondary age students in Maine from high school to the community.* (ERIC Document Reproduction Service No. ED 315 232)

Swift, D. (1984). *Finding and keeping teachers: Strategies for small schools.* Las Cruces, NM: ERIC Digest (ERIC Document Reproduction Service No. ED 259 875)

Wells, A. (1989). *Public school choice: Issues and concerns for urban educators.* ERIC Clearinghouse on Urban Education Digest No. 63. New York: Columbia University Teachers College.

William, N., & Cross, W. K. (1985). *Early field experience: A recipe for rural teacher retention.* Paper presented at the Annual National Rural and Small Schools Conference, Bellingham, WA.

Chapter 13

ADVANCING TECHNOLOGY: THE ON-LINE ADMINISTRATOR

Diana Larson and James R. Wheeler

Ten years ago, it would have been difficult to predict that special education administrators in the 1990s would:

- Be more prone to carpal tunnel syndrome than pencil calluses.
- Use the modem and fax machine more than the U.S. Postal Service.
- Conduct business from their car or an airplane.

Most current administrators and teachers were educated in an era of emerging technology. Some even used a slide rule in their statistics classes and remember when computers were room-sized machines clacking away in syncopation. Yet now these administrators work in an era of advanced technology. "Advancing" may be a more appropriate term, since innovations in hardware and software, as well as in technological capability, are moving forward at ever-increasing speed.

Through robotics, the bionic limbs of science fiction in the 1970s are now reality. People without voices are speaking, and people without hands are typing (Luttner, 1981; Howe, 1981). In the not-so-distant future, "virtual reality" may be a commonplace instructional and staff development tool, and artificial intelligence may be used to diagnose learning disabilities (Hofmeister & Ferrara, 1986). Technology has the potential to address the problems of professional isolation and long distances between services and students, thereby aiding rural administrators in retaining and utilizing limited staff effectively (Helge, 1984).

After considerable media coverage concerning the role of computers as instructional aids and as prosthetic devices for students with sensory or physical disabilities, the practicality of management may seem to pale in comparison. However, management responsibilities of administrators are paramount, as regulations and accountability require accurate and current monitoring of the individual programs for the nearly 5 million students with disabilities being served by special education (The Council for Exceptional Children, 1994). Microcomputers are vital tools for special education administrators.

Current special education leaders must be prepared to use microcomputer technology in their program administration. However, there are issues involving the use of computers that administrators should consider before the implementation of new technology will be successful. The authors will provide information special education administrators need to successfully implement a comprehensive microcomputer system and recommend procedures for facilitation.

CURRENT STATUS OF MICROCOMPUTERS IN SPECIAL EDUCATION ADMINISTRATION

Applications

A primary challenge for special education administrators today is to provide an increasing number of services and remain accountable in the face of budgetary constraints and changing school environments. In facing this challenge, many administrators have turned to the microcomputer. By the early 1980s, some administrators were using microcomputers for preparing timetables, keeping records, evaluating programs, managing personnel and budgets (accounting and payroll), collecting data, planning curriculum, surveying research, locating information in the library, preparing proposals, developing individualized education programs, and analyzing data on student performance (Roecks, 1981; Seyfried & Lowe, 1980; Taber, 1981). Wilson (1981) added tracking students from screening through assessment, placement, and review. Case, Heiman, and Williams (1988) reviewed the use of the microcomputer in the administration of a large urban district's special education program. These authors expanded this list with: applying desktop publishing, scheduling classes, forecasting the impact of budget cuts, developing and maintaining materials and equipment inventories, writing reports and correspondence, assessing students, accessing electronic bulletin boards, providing and evaluating staff development, and networking. In 1989, Robey reported that two-thirds of special education administrators surveyed had purchased computers for administrative use. The four most common professional applications were (a) preparing correspondence and reports, (b) managing staff or student records, (c) developing individualized education programs (IEPs) for students, and (d) preparing and managing budgets.

Because applications are numerous and increasing continuously and technology is becoming an integral component of school systems, administrators must address several issues in formulating successful technology programs.

Issues

Rationale Technological advances will become a more integral part of education and administration each year and will affect nearly every facet of life in the very near future. Education cannot risk getting behind at this stage. Access to computers is now a requirement for anyone who stores, retrieves, and organizes information on a daily basis (Johnson, 1993).

Knowledge Computer literacy is essential for special education administrators today. Thomas (1980) defines computer literacy as understanding the history, operations, and applications of computers, as well as the social, psychological, and vocational impact of computer-based technology. Dickerson and Pritchard (1981) stress the need for computer literacy courses within training programs.

Inservice and continuing education programs are alternatives (Taber, 1981). Many manufacturers provide classes or have self-teaching programs available, although these alternatives may not address the specific needs of a special education administrator.

Financial responsibility The cost of computer systems is decreasing and quality is increasing. How could this, then, remain an issue? Any major outlay in a school district's budget is an issue. Wilson (1981) reminds administrators there are many hidden costs in developing microcomputer systems. Equally important is the question of quality. Administrators must ask the right questions to know when they are getting the best buy. Taber (1981) suggested that the potential for expansion, the availability of maintenance service, and an evaluation of the software should be considered before purchasing a system. Other considerations include compatibility with current systems; installation, training, and ongoing support; timely and expert maintenance of software; ease of use; reduced training time; extended capabilities and versatility; and cost (Perez, 1988). Wilson (1981) simplified the decision with three questions: How easy is the computer to use? What can it do for me? How much does it cost?

Expert advice Administrators should not overlook previous developments when designing management systems. Implementing a new system or even buying off-the-shelf software should be preceded by some understanding of existing management systems (Wilson, 1981). Yet it is also wise to be wary when buying extensions of existing systems. Continued technical assistance and maintenance as well as the availability and frequency of updates should be questioned.

IMPLEMENTING A COMPREHENSIVE MICROCOMPUTER SYSTEM

In 1992, the Office of Special Education and Rehabilitative Services (OSERS) funded eight projects to study the administrative aspects of technology implementation in special education. Administrative practices were categorized as (a) performing administrative functions, (b) promoting communication and collaboration, and (c) developing human resources. Using these job role descriptive categories, an outline can be developed for systematically implementing a comprehensive microcomputer system for administering special education programs.

Performing Administrative Functions

Planning The districtwide mission and vision statements should support the incorporation of technology into the educational structure. The special education administrator may be given the responsibility for the development of a long-range plan for a comprehensive computer system. In a 1992 study, OSERS found the involvement and commitment of top-level administrators were necessary for the successful implementation of computers in special education administration. This involvement increased the availability of resources and supports that ultimately led to increased student use of computers. They caution, however, that long-range goals need to be tempered with an understanding of the more immediate concerns.

For successful integration of technology, administrators must have a vision of the value and potential of computers and understand that integration implies change. Involving all stakeholders, such as teachers, community representatives, and building-level administrators, in the planning will facilitate support and participation throughout this change. The planning process begins with determining the overall needs and commitment of the organization and the expectations of prospective users of the system (Johnson, 1993). An individualized technology plan (ITP) could be developed based on a thorough evaluation of the present degree of implementation and the goals identified in the long-range plan. This could be a one-year, multiyear, or continuing plan based on the unique circumstances of the school system involved. These factors would include the present degree of integration, readiness and interest, staff comfort with computers, administrative support, and staff and monetary resources. It is recommended that if the level of use is low, the plan should focus on knowledge and skill development; if moderate or high, the plan should address developing management systems and writing long-range plans for integrating technology into the curriculum (Office of Special Education and Rehabilitative Services, 1992).

Accountability Comprehensive program evaluation necessitates the collection of data. Piles of paper or a data base full of numbers are worthless if an organizational plan for analysis has not been developed. This is true for both instructional and organizational accountability. If all records are maintained on the computer, they can be merged or arranged in unlimited ways, providing the necessary information to evaluate program effectiveness and efficiency.

A management information system (MIS) has been developed by the Northeast Kansas Education Service Center, which collects information required for compliance with all state and federal regulations related to the provision of special education services to students with disabilities or giftedness. An MIS is simply a comprehensive data base (here, of special education students) that is updated frequently to reflect the current status of the program. Figure 13.1 is a screen from the MIS that shows the services a student is receiving and the number of minutes per day, days per week, and weeks per year. The MIS, if kept current and accurate, provides administrators with a virtual "window" on their special education programs. It provides the basis for all required state and federal reports and can be used in creative ways for program evaluation and needs assessments.

In addition to assuring compliance, the MIS can be used to gather information about the students being served in special education. For example, lists can be electronically compiled of all boys at the middle school level receiving services for emotional/behavioral disorders or of all students in a specific school district receiving transportation as a related service. The applications are unlimited.

Record keeping Some administrators have the goal of a "paper-free" office. Instead of buying another file cabinet, they may purchase additional electronic storage and backup space on additional hard drives or even reusable optical disks. Records that can be maintained on a computer include:

- personnel and payroll records
- purchase orders
- student demographic information
- teacher class lists
- transportation schedules
- mailing lists of parents
- state and federal regulations
- equipment and materials inventories
- all outgoing correspondence and reports
- Special Olympics team data bases

In addition to maintaining records, the computer can be used to monitor and update their status so that all information is current. The importance of maintaining up-to-date and accurate records cannot be overemphasized. It takes only one due process procedure that identifies a weak record-keeping system to convince even the most skeptical of the importance of up-to-date central records.

Budget records are of critical concern to all administrators. Having the most current status of all accounts at your fingertips is essential. The microcomputer spreadsheet makes it possible to project budget plans based on various proposed increases or decreases in salaries or revenue. Figure 13.2 is a spreadsheet screen that shows a state grant form that has been formatted and reproduced on the computer. The individual figures and line items are dynamically linked so that

FIGURE 13.1
MANAGEMENT INFORMATION SYSTEM

SERVICES NEEDED AND SPECIAL CONSIDERATIONS:

MILLIE   L   JONES   Preferred AMANDA   JONES

SSN   dob 06/14/89   sex F   Ethnic W   Lang E

Grade PH   Status R   Attends 9990 : 608   Enrollment 9990 : 377   Fund 1   decision maker 1

	Serv	Plcmt	Type	Min	Days	Wks	Init	End	Teacher-First	Last	Teacher - SSN
1	EC	A		25	1	36	11/01/93	11/01/94	Dena	Debank	598541846
2	PI	A		25	1	36	11/01/93	11/01/94	Debra	Smith	415486085
3	PI	A		25	1	36	11/01/93	11/01/94	Martha	Jackson	413528321
4	SL	A		25	1	36	11/01/93	11/01/94	Gail	Rebank	415788778
5	HI	A		45	1	36	11/01/93	11/01/94	Dianne	Day	598404269
6	VI	X		10	1	36	11/01/93	11/01/94	Janet	Tyler	455802707
7	SL	X		10	1	36	11/01/93	11/01/94	Nancy	Fernburn	412427846

SPECIAL CONSIDERATIONS:

JANET TYLER, VISION CONSULTANT, WILL PROVIDE SERVICES AS

REQUESTED BY PARENTS AND STAFF. MILLIE HAS PERIODIC SEIZURES.

MOTHER SHOULD BE CONTACTED IF SEIZURE LASTS MORE THAN 2

MINUTES. MILLIE IS IN AN INTEGRATED PRESCHOOL CLASSROOM.

FIGURE 13.2
Budget Spreadsheet Screen

	A	B	C	D	E
1		**PROGRAM IMPROVEMENT BUDGET SHEET - FISCAL YEAR 1995**			
2		**Description of Instructions - Page 6**			
3					
4		*Northeast Kansas Education Service Center*			*608*
5		Institution Name			Institution No.
6					
7		**1. ADMINISTRATION (Maximum of 5% of the total grant)**			$2,425
8		**2. Salaries (Instructional/Professional)**			
9		Itemize salaries below:			
10		Personnel Title	Salary	Fixed	
11			Amount	Charges	
12		2a. Consortium Staff Development Coordinator .16 FTE	$9,166	$680	
13		2b. Secretarial/Clerical .25 FTE	$3,000	$255	
14		2c.			
15		2d.			
16		Total	$13,101	$13,101	
17		**3. GUIDANCE AND COUNSELING SERVICES**			
18		Salaries	Salary	Fixed	
19			Amount	Charges	
20		3a.			
21		Description of Purchase	Amount		
22		3b.			
23		3c.			
24		3d.			
25		Total		$0	
26		**4. SPECIAL POPULATIONS SERVICES**			
27		Salaries	Salary	Fixed	
28			Amount	Charges	
29		4a. Special Populations Counselor (Contracted Services)	$500	$40	

a change in any one line item figure will cause the spreadsheet to automatically recalculate new subtotals and totals. When the budget is completed, it simply is printed out. There is no need to type the figures into the state's paper form. Using the computer in this way reduces the chance for errors and speeds up the process of budgeting.

Reports By recording the information and data needed for government reports throughout the year, personnel and end-of-year reports are easily compiled. The format for the reports can be stored in the computer and the information updated on a periodic basis. The same holds true for reports on the status of state or federally funded projects. In addition, preparing proposals for available projects is facilitated by maintaining a current computer file of organizational data and demographics. By maintaining a format for instructional and managerial procedures on the computer, changes can be easily made.

Time management The special education administrator must be a model of efficiency (or have a secretary who is). Software is available that has calendars and daily schedule planners to remind the administrator of important dates and meetings. Organizational outlines for planning and conducting meetings efficiently, monitoring the outcomes, and planning follow-up activities are also available.

Many administrators are now able to actually leave the office while it is still light outside. They can take their work home or on the road by using a laptop computer to finish the board of education agenda, grant proposal, or budget revision.

Promoting Communication and Collaboration

Accessibility Access to technology is a significant factor in its implementation. Technology acquisition, allocation, and application should be appropriate to the current level of usage, identified needs, curricular goals, and staff experience and expertise (Office of Special Education and Rehabilitative Services, 1992).

An electronic mail system can connect computers districtwide to provide instant communication between individual schools and the central office (Roecks, 1981). The benefits of electronic communication to provide special services to districts in rural areas are numerous, especially those covering vast geographic areas. Special education administrators can stay in contact with district and building-level administrators and with special educators electronically instead of playing "phone tag." Policies, procedures, memoranda, and reports can be exchanged directly through the computer network. It may take more than a week to deliver this same information through an interoffice mail system or the U.S. mail.

All instructional and assessment materials can be catalogued on a data base. If teachers need specific materials, they can locate all available copies while sitting at a keyboard.

Correspondence Merging word-processing documents and data base mailing lists saves hours of secretarial time and personalizes correspondence. Instead of a "Dear Parent" or "Dear Teacher" letter, individuals can receive personalized correspondence, which enhances the image of the organization. Additionally, people may be more likely to read a letter addressed to them by name rather than as a member of a group.

Desktop publishing is another computer application that can save valuable time and money for a school system. Graphics capability enlivens any published document. Newsletters are effective ways to communicate with staff members and parents. Policy and procedure manuals; the local comprehensive plan; handbooks for parents, staff, and building administrators; and crisis plans are examples of materials that could be prepared with desktop publishing. By publishing in-house, the organization can send this information in a cost-effective and timely manner.

Networking Electronic bulletin boards, such as SpecialNet and SpecialLaw, provide the latest on federal and state regulatory and legislative action. With a computer, an administrator can keep current on litigation, legislation, decisions by the U.S. Office of Civil Rights, and interpretations of state or federal requirements.

The most recent information on grant availability is immediately accessible on electronic networks. Bulletin boards and electronic mail also facilitate communication between local, state, and federal education agencies.

Through the modem, access can be made to computerized data bases and information services such as ERIC. By entering keywords of interest, these data bases generate lists of articles and abstracts. Administrators find these services useful when preparing project proposals or conducting research on best practices.

Another telecommunications service, InterNet, provides administrators and teachers with global access to information and software. Referred to as the backbone of the information superhighway, InterNet access can provide an international perspective to special educators, allowing for the global exchange of information. Lesson plans, a growing number of electronic journals, special education news groups, and access to worldwide electronic mail are all available.

Developing Human Resources

Recruitment   The recruitment of new personnel can be facilitated through the microcomputer. A data base of positions available and applicants for the positions can be used to track the procedure from initial contact through employment.

Caseload   Teacher caseload recommendations have historically been based on head count only. However, a student with behavioral disorders receiving 5 minutes of consultation time daily for monitoring a point sheet counts the same as a student placed in a self-contained behavioral disorders classroom for 6 to 7 hours a day. An additive, weighted formula (Northeast Kansas Education Service Center, 1990) has been developed to provide a more equitable method of determining teacher caseload in rural areas. Information collected on each teacher includes the number of different disabilities served, the full time equivalency (FTE) of paraprofessionals assigned, the average number of miles driven daily, the number of buildings served, the primary and secondary student FTE, and the actual head count. All of this data, with the exception of the number of paraprofessionals and miles driven, are electronically collected through the management information system. Each teacher's data are combined through an additive formula into a single number which is then converted to a standard score with a mean of 5 and a standard deviation of 1. Administrators can review teachers with the highest and lowest scores and make decisions regarding their workload and possible need for paraprofessional help or decreased student load. These kinds of administrative decisions are made more objectively and accurately with the use of the weighted formula. Figure 13.3 shows a spreadsheet that has been developed to automatically calculate the formula when any of the variables are entered or changed.

Teachers' caseloads can be compared by reviewing graphs of their standard scores. Figure 13.4 is a three-dimensional graph comparing the caseload standard scores of all teachers of the behavior-disordered in a special education cooperative.

Training   For an administrator to be most effective in the use of technology, the total organization must be supportive. Teachers must have access to and must use computers, not only for instructional purposes, but for management as well.

FIGURE 13.3
WORKLOAD SPREADSHEET

														CSCL Jan 31st.EXCEL
	A	D	E	F	G	H	I	J	K	L	M	N	O	P	Q
631			Prime	Prime	Age	2dary	Indirect	2dary	# of Diff	Bldgs	AveMiles	Para	CSCL	Local	State
632	Batch Name	Excep	Count	FTE	Range	Head	FTE	FTE	Disabil	Served	Per Day	FTE	Formula	Stand S.	Stand S.
633	NEKESC	BD	4	1.42	4	2	0	0.34	2	1	0	2	72.2	3.65	3.86
634	NEKESC	BD	4	0.53	4	4	0	0.23	1	3	5	0.6	73.54	3.67	3.87
635	NEKESC	BD	5	0.62	3	10	0.11	0.3	2	3	8	0	110.1	4.20	4.24
636	NEKESC	BD	9	2.72	2	2	0	0.41	2	3	11	1	143.1	4.67	4.57
637	NEKESC	BD	5	1.39	8	3	0.03	0.07	1	6	36	0.5	152.8	4.81	4.67
638	NEKESC	BD	7	0.89	6	11	0.1	1.03	3	3	18	0.5	156.4	4.86	4.7
639	NEKESC	DD	3	0	5	1	0	0.41	2	2	0	1	47.7	3.30	3.61
640	NEKESC	DD	2	0.4	1	22	0.3	0.76	3	8	31	1	169.2	5.04	4.83
641	NEKESC	EC	6	0.12	2	3	0	0.23	1	3	33	0	118.5	4.32	4.32
642	NEKESC	EC	10	3.4	2	9	0	0	1	1	10	2.8	153.56	4.82	4.68
643	NEKESC	EM	5	1.42	4	0	0	0	3	1	0	0.7	76.16	3.71	3.9

The 1992 OSERS study found teacher training was essential for implementation of technology. The following factors were identified as contributing to teacher participation and effective use of technology:

- Controlled introduction of content to avoid overwhelming staff and to allow teachers time to acquire and integrate knowledge about students, technology, curriculum, instructional, and assessment.
- Teacher reflection with others about their instructional use of technology.
- Training in the use of teacher-modifiable software to increase the use of computer-assisted instruction and curriculum correspondence.
- Relevance of training and teacher participation in planning of training.

Inservice training can now be provided utilizing the microcomputer. Not only can a staff member receive individualized training on the computer keyboard, but the technology of the liquid crystal display panels (LCD), which can be positioned on a standard overhead projector, opens up the computer demonstration to large audiences by projecting it onto a screen.

FIGURE 13.4
WORKLOAD STANDARD SCORES

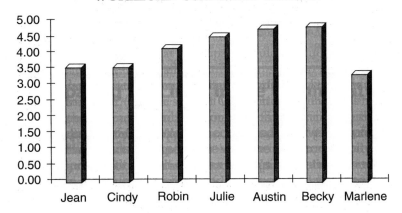

Evaluation of inservice training can also be accomplished through the computer. A computerized workshop evaluation question bank (Case, Heiman, & Williams, 1988) utilizes a data base to evaluate workshops and give feedback to presenters and staff development committee members. Bubble sheet-style evaluation forms (see Figure 13.5) developed on the computer can be "read" by a batch scanner, sending the information into a data base. The data can then be analyzed and a statistical summary printed.

Technical assistance and support for teachers using computers are also critical as a follow-up to the training. In addition, paraprofessionals can be trained to record information in a data base. This relieves teachers of some of the time-consuming aspects of computer use.

Participation Staff members can be given choices as to the degree of implementation they want to use after the basic requirements for record keeping are met. These expectations will vary based on individual need, interest, and ability. Staff members could be encouraged to develop personal goals for improving their use of technology as part of the evaluation process. Innovation and creativity should be encouraged and supported.

FIGURE 13.5
EVALUATION FORM FOR SCANNER

INCLUSION SURVEY

Grade	USD	Level:	Have you ever had a student(s) with:

Grade: (0)(0) (1)(1) (2)(2) (3)(3) (4)(4) (5)(5) (6)(6) (7)(7) (8)(8) (9)(9)

USD: (0)(0)(0) (1)(1)(1) (2)(2)(2) (3)(3)(3) (4)(4)(4) (5)(5)(5) (6)(6)(6) (7)(7)(7) (8)(8)(8) (9)(9)(9)

Level:
○ Elementary
○ Middle School
○ Secondary

Have you ever had a student(s) with:
(Bubble all that apply):
○ Behavior Disorders (BD)
○ Learning Disabilities (LD)
○ Educable Mental Retardation (EMR)
○ Trainable Mental Retardation (TMR)
○ Severe Multiple Disabilities (SMD)
○ I have never had a student in my class with a disability.

1=Strongly Disagree 2=Disagree 3=Undecided 4=Agree 5=Strongly Agree

(1)(2)(3)(4)(5) 1. I feel qualified to teach students with special needs.

(1)(2)(3)(4)(5) 2. I am able to adapt instructional materials for teaching students with special needs.

(1)(2)(3)(4)(5) 3. Adequate support services are readily available to help me with students with special needs.

(1)(2)(3)(4)(5) 4. I have enough time to prepare assignments for the regular class and for the student with special needs.

(1)(2)(3)(4)(5) 5. I am able to meet the instructional needs of the other students and the students with special needs.

(1)(2)(3)(4)(5) 6. I am able to manage the behavior of students with special needs.

(1)(2)(3)(4)(5) 7. Adequate instructional materials are available to me for teaching students with special needs.

Monitoring Students from Referral to IEP Review

The following case study exemplifies how one special education cooperative uses microcomputers in the identification, placement, and communication process of special education.

Tracking Students with a Microcomputer

Patty is an 8-year-old girl in the second grade. She was first referred to her school assistance team by her second-grade teacher due to her difficulty learning math. Mrs. Williams was an experienced classroom teacher and had used a variety of different techniques and materials in an attempt to keep Patty on the same level with her peers. Patty continued to experience difficulty even with the modifications.

The progress of all the students in Patty's school is monitored continually through the use of curriculum-based measurement (CBM) (Shinn, 1989). By assessing the students on their own curriculum, local norms have been developed that more realistically demonstrate individual students' performances compared to their peers. The teacher assistance team recommended Patty be referred to special education for a comprehensive evaluation based on her performance on the curriculum-based measurement math probes, classroom observations, and product analysis. To analyze Patty's performance on the CBM local norms, her teacher referred to a box plot (see Figure 13.6) that allowed her to compare Patty's math basic tool skill performance with all other second graders. This graph was produced with statistical analysis software allowing the special education administrator and staff to maintain their own local norms and graphically display the results for teachers and parents.

The psychologist assigned to Patty's school used diagnostic instruments with accompanying software that had one or more of the following capabilities: (a) diagnostic, (b) interpretation of test results, (c) information management of test results and data, (d) report writing, and (e) informational strategies corresponding to areas of weakness identified through assessment (Johnson, 1993). The Key Math-Revised has a computerized software program for scoring and printing test results called "Assist." The Wechsler Intelligence Scale for Children-Revised (WISC-R) has software called "WISC-R Compilation," which provides diagnostic and interpretive statements for each subtest and lists short-term objectives related to the diagnosed weakness.

These computer programs for diagnostic instruments provided a report format, but the school psychologist chose to enter Patty's data into a school psychologist report-writer format. A computerized report-writer saves valuable time for both school psychologists and the secretarial staff. More important, the time between testing and the final report is shortened considerably, enabling eligible students to be placed in needed services sooner (Case et al., 1988).

FIGURE 13.6
CURRICULUM-BASED MEASUREMENT:
PATTY COMPARED WITH NORMS

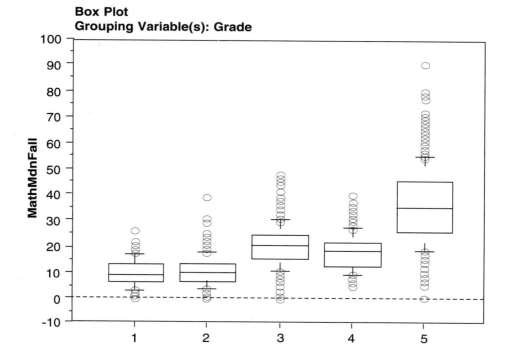

Box Plot
Grouping Variable(s): Grade

As a result of the comprehensive evaluation, the eligibility team determined Patty had a learning disability in mathematics. The individualized educational program (IEP) team then met to develop goals and determine the services needed to meet the goals. Patty's IEP was generated on a computer program called "NETworkingIEP" (developed at the Northeast Kansas Education Service Center), which was adopted by the majority of school districts in Kansas (Dellegrotto, Gelatt, & Novakovich, 1990).

This program meets all of the requirements for an individualized education program. In addition, objective banks are available to assist in writing appropriate short-term objectives. Patty's teacher had the option of adopting the objectives as written, modifying the objectives, or writing customized objectives. Once Patty was placed in a program for students with learning disabilities, her progress on the goals and objectives was monitored on a regular basis. After updating her progress on the computer disk, Patty's teacher provided a copy to her parents. Through the management system, mailing labels are provided to facilitate this process.

The NETworkingIEP format provides all of the information required for state reports. When Patty's special education teacher turns in a copy of the disk, all the data are entered into the MIS, which, in Kansas, can be sent directly to the state Department of Education by computer.

The management information system will be used to send reminders of upcoming time lines, such as the annual review and triennial reevaluation. Letters to remind both Patty's teacher and her parents will be generated. Lists will be provided to the school psychologist of upcoming time lines. Figure 13.7 is an example of a letter generated by a data base that can be printed

FIGURE 13.7
PARENT NOTIFICATION FORM

NORTHEAST KANSAS EDUCATION
SERVICE CENTER

Oskaloosa Office
404 Park, P.O. Box
Oskaloosa, KS 66066
(913) 863-2919

Lecompton Office
601 Woodson
Lecompton, KS 66050
(913) 887-6711

<<Parent>>
<<Addr>>
<<City>>, <<St>> <<zip>>

Dear <<Parent>>,

I am writing to let you know that it is time to review <<Stu LFirst>>'s Individualized Education Program (IEP). The current IEP which was developed <<IEP>> will need to be reviewed and possibly changed to meet any new needs that we can identify as a "team" by the annual review date of <<IEP Due>>. Our procedures require that we update <<Stu LFirst>>'s IEP on or before this annual review due date. We have scheduled this meeting for (Date:_____ Time:_____) at <<Attend Schl Name>>. The following people are expected to be participating in the meeting:

Teacher - <<Tch 1 first>> <<Tch 1 last>>

Regular Education Teacher -_____
Principal -_____
Other -_____
Other -_____

Please complete and return the bottom portion of this letter with your date and time preferences for this upcoming meeting. If you have any questions call me at _____anytime during the day.

Sincerely,

for all students whose last evaluation was completed 3 years ago. The data base software will place the student's name, parents' name and address, and teacher in the appropriate "place holders."

Other forms, like Figure 13.8, can be used both to notify (remind) teachers and inform parents of an upcoming IEP review.

FIGURE 13.8
IEP REVIEW LETTER

NORTHEAST KANSAS EDUCATION SERVICE CENTER

Oskaloosa Office
404 Park, P.O. Box
Oskaloosa, KS 66066
(913) 863-2919

Lecompton Office
601 Woodson
Lecompton, KS 66050
(913) 887-6711

Bob and Susan Smith
1606 Holly Lane
Atchison, KS 66002

Dear Bob and Susan Smith,

I am writing to let you know that it is time to review Jane's Individualized Education Program (IEP). The current IEP which was developed 01/20/93 will need to be reviewed and possibly changed to meet any new needs that we can identify as a "team" by the annual review date of <<IEP Due>>. Our procedures require that we update Jane's IEP on or before this annual review due date. We have scheduled this meeting for (Date:_____
Time:_____) at Highland Park School. The following people are expected to be participating in the meeting:

Teacher - Paul Bloom

Regular Education Teacher -_____
Principal -_____
Other -_____
Other -_____

Please complete and return the bottom portion of this letter with your date and time preferences for this upcoming meeting. If you have any questions call me at _____anytime during the day.

Sincerely,

CONSIDER THIS

1. How can administrators support teachers in using microcomputers?
2. What issues of record management might be affected by the new technology (e.g., confidentiality)?
3. What advantages and disadvantages are inherent in computerized IEPs?
4. How might computer-generated letters and notices decrease the "individualization" of the process?

ASSISTIVE TECHNOLOGY: ISSUES, ROLES, AND RESPONSIBILITIES OF SPECIAL EDUCATION ADMINISTRATORS

Special education administration must be prepared to initiate and manage assistive technology because it clearly benefits individuals with disabilities, and it is mandated by law. The National Council on Disabilities (1993) asserts that assistive technology for individuals with disabilities makes education in regular school settings possible, reduces dependence on family members and teachers, saves money, enables individuals to sustain and improve employment, and generally improves the quality of life. IDEA clearly defines devices and services and mandates schools to provide them as a necessary part of a free, appropriate public education. The Office of Special Education Programs (OSEP) has clarified this, stating that school districts must determine the need for assistive technology on a case-by-case basis. If the IEP team decides assistive technology is a necessary part of a student's education, the devices and services must be provided to the district at no cost to the parents (Mittler, 1994). Parents of children who do not qualify for special education but who require assistive technology to be successful in schools may invoke Section 504 of the Rehabilitation Act of 1973 and the Americans With Disabilities Act to obtain the necessary accommodations.

Definitions

The Technology-Related Assistance for Individuals with Disabilities Act (PL 100-407) and the Individuals With Disabilities Education Act (IDEA, PL 101-476) define an assistive technology device as "any item, piece of equipment, or product system, whether acquired commercially off the shelf, modified, or customized, that is used to increase, maintain, or improve functional capabilities of individuals with disabilities" (Lewis, 1993, p. 4).

Some assistive technologies are adaptations of generic devices, such as the talking calculator. Other devices are designed to be used on conjunction with such technologies as a special keyboard or breath-controlled mouse for computers. Technology is often classified as either high or low. "High" refers to sophisticated devices such as Kurzweil readers for the blind. Low technology devices are simpler. For example, switches operated with gross motor movements enable individuals with physical disabilities to control tape recorders, and small pillows position wrists for typing on a keyboard (Lewis, 1993).

According to IDEA, an assistive technology service is "any service that directly assists an individual with a disability in the selection, acquisition, or use of an assistive technology device" (Lewis, 1993, p. 11). These services include:

- Evaluating the need, including a functional evaluation of the individual in the individual's customary environment.
- Purchasing, leasing, or otherwise providing for the acquisition of assistive technology devices.
- Selecting, designing, fitting, customizing, adapting, applying, maintaining, repairing, or replacing assistive technology devices.
- Coordinating and using other therapies, interventions, or services with assistive technology devices, such as those associated with existing education and rehabilitation plans and programs.
- Training or technical assistance for an individual with disabilities, or, where appropriate, his/her family.
- Training or technical assistance for professionals, including individuals who provide services to, employ, or are otherwise substantially involved in the major life functions of individuals with disabilities.

Local Policies, Procedures, and Funding

The law is clear that schools must provide technology to students, but few schools are currently prepared to do so. Local administrators should begin by developing policies to address such issues as (a) who will become the designated "expert" on teams or in districts; (b) what criteria will be used to determine students' needs; and (c) who is responsible for monitoring the use of devices (Scherer, 1991).

Multidisciplinary evaluation teams must receive training in (a) understanding assistive technology devices and services, (b) assessing students to determine the need for technology, (c) evaluating what technologies are best, (d) matching technologies with student needs, and (e) including technology in the development of IEPs and individualized family service plans.

Assistive devices can be inexpensive or they can be large-budget items. Ultimately the school district is responsible for providing technology to students, but with stagnant budgets and escalating demands, administrators must begin to identify additional sources of funding to assist in purchasing devices (Church & Glennen, 1992). States may offer grants to develop libraries of devices for educators to check out on a trial basis to determine which may be most appropriate or to lend to students on an annual basis. Administrators may apply for Medicare coverage where appropriate. Community vocational rehabilitation services may be able to purchase devices for clients. Additionally, school districts may seek partnerships with universities in applying for OSEP-funded grants in personnel preparation or the implementation of innovative technology services.

The following case study describes a student who uses basic assistive technology to communicate and who might benefit from more-elaborate devices.

Appropriate or Ideal?

Mike is a 13-year-old with severe cerebral palsy. His muscle tone is variable, and he has involuntary movements that require him to use a motorized wheelchair. Mike is unable to use speech to communicate except for a few basic words. On his wheelchair is a communication device which has been programmed to say 24 phrases and sentences in response to the push of a button.

A full-time paraprofessional has been assigned to Mike to enable him to attend some general education classes. She takes notes for him and has developed systems to test his subject knowledge. Mike's parents want him to participate more in scholastic activities and encourage his independence. Specifically, they have requested a meeting with his IEP team to discuss devices that would allow Mike to communicate in writing.

The special education teacher asked her coordinator to attend the meeting to help with what might be a challenging decision. Mike's parents brought a catalogue of assistive technology devices to the meeting and showed the IEP team a word-processing program for a computer with touch-screen capabilities, and several supportive programs that would expand on abbreviated words and provide alternative sentence structures.

Although the technology looked impressive, the coordinator said the district had hired a paraprofessional to provide Mike with an appropriate education. These new programs might be ideal, but the additional expense seemed excessive considering Mike's academic potential.

 CONSIDER THIS

1. What are the major issues this IEP team must address?
2. Comment on the position the coordinator has taken.

SUMMARY

Special education administrators require powerful systems to manage the overwhelming data generated when monitoring services for the nearly 5 million students with disabilities in schools today (The Council for Exceptional Children, 1994). These administrators are challenged to provide an increasing number of services and remain accountable in the face of budgetary constraints and changing school environments. In response, many administrators have turned to the use of microcomputers.

There are some issues that should be considered by school systems as they develop a technology program based on microcomputers. These include defining a clear purpose, acquiring the necessary knowledge and skill, assuring financial responsibility, and seeking expert advice.

The applications for microcomputers are numerous and continually increasing. Administrative use of technology in special education can be categorized as performing administrative functions, promoting communication and collaboration, and developing human resources.

Administrative leadership requires comprehensive planning, development or adoption of a management system for accountability, accurate record keeping and reports, and efficient time management. The administrator's use of technology sets a model for the entire staff. For successful integration of technology, administrators must have a vision of the value and potential of computers and understand that integration implies change.

Communication and collaboration are greatly enhanced by the immediate accessibility provided through technology. Correspondence becomes far less time-consuming and more personal. By publishing in-house, the organization can get information out in a cost-effective, timely manner. National data bases can be accessed to aid in conducting research, identifying best practices, and staying abreast of current legal actions.

The computer can be used for tracking the process of recruiting, employing, and retaining personnel. New programs allow the monitoring of teachers' caseloads to ensure equity and quality services. Staff development and evaluation can now be conducted utilizing the microcomputer. Providing training for teachers increases the likelihood of their implementation and effective use of technology for both instructional and administrative purposes. Technical assistance and support for staff utilization of computers is critical as a follow-up to training. Expectations of staff participation will vary on the basis of individual need, interest, and ability. Administrators should encourage and support staff to use microcomputers in innovative and creative ways.

The full potential for the use of technology in special education administration will not be realized until computers are as familiar as telephones and typewriters. Computers must be perceived by administrators as routine and powerful tools, rather than as inaccessible and sophisticated high technology. Special education management technology must be considered an investment, not an expense.

REFERENCES

Case, E. J., Heiman, B., & Williams, R. (1988, March). *What can computer technology offer special education administrators?* Washington, DC: The Council for Exceptional Children. (ERIC Document Reproduction Service No. ED 316 988)

Church, G., & Glennen, S. (1992). *The handbook of assistive technology.* San Diego, CA: Singular Publishing Group.

Council for Exceptional Children (1994). Statistical profile of special education in the United States, 1994. *Teaching Exceptional Children, 26*(3), (Suppl.), 1–4.

Dellegrotto, J., Gelatt, J., & Novakovich, H. (1990). *Computerizing administrative tasks in schools.* Rockville, MD: American Speech and Hearing Association.

Dickerson, L., & Pritchard, W. H. (1981). Microcomputers and education: Planning for the coming revolution in the classroom. *Educational Technology, 1,* 7–12.

Helge, D. (1984). Technologies as rural special education problem-solvers. *Exceptional Children, 51*(1), 351–359.

Hofmeister, A. M., & Ferrara, J. M. (1986). Expert systems and special education. *Exceptional Children, 53*(3), 235–239.

Howe, C. E. (1981). *Administration of special education.* Denver: Love Publishing.

Johnson, J. E. (1993). Administrative data management for special education. In J. D. Lindsey (Ed.), *Computers and exceptional individuals* (pp. 251–269). Austin, TX: Pro-Ed.

Lewis, R. B. (1993). *Special education technology: Classroom applications.* Pacific Grove, CA: Brookes/Cole.

Luttner, S. (1981). Computers for the handicapped. *Apple, 2*(1), 26–29.

Mittler, J. E. (1994). *Assistive technology: A historical perspective on research and development and policy development.* A paper presented at the annual convention of the International Council for Exceptional Children, April 7, Denver, CO.

National Council on Disabilities. (1993). *Study on the financing of assistive technology devices and services for individuals with disabilities.* A report to the President and Congress of the United States, Washington, DC: Author.

Northeast Kansas Education Service Center. (1990). *Getting a handle on your M.I.S.* Lecompton, KS: Author.

Office of Special Education and Rehabilitative Services. (1992). *Administrative aspects of technology implementation in special education: A synthesis of information.* Washington, DC: Author.

Perez, R. E. (1988). Apple Macintosh–IBM System 36 connectivity for administrative applications. In *Technology across the curriculum.* Proceedings of the annual conference of the Texas Computer Education Association. Lubbock, TX: Texas Computer Education Association.

Robey, E. (1989, February). *Studies of special education administrative involvement in computer implementation.* Silver Spring, MD: Macro Systems, Inc. (ERIC Document Reproduction Service No. ED 324 837)

Roecks, A. L. (1981). How many ways can the computer be used in education? A baker's dozen. *Educational Technology, 16.*

Scherer, M. (1991). *The development of two instruments assessing the predispositions people have toward technology use: The value of integrating quantitative and qualitative methods.* (ERIC Document Reproduction Service No. ED 334 206)

Seyfried, D., & Lowe, D. (1980). Microcomputers in teaching handicapped students. *Monitor,* 14–15.

Shinn, M. R. (1989). *Curriculum-based measurement: Assessing special children.* New York: Guilford Press.

Taber, F. M. (1981). The microcomputer—Its applicability to special education. *Focus on Exceptional Children, 14*(2), 1–14.

Thomas, R. (1980). Our computer skills are lacking. *Counterpoint, 1*(2), 1–4.

Wilson, K. (1981, November). Computers for special education management: Progress, potential, and pitfalls. *Counterpoint,* 17–18.

Chapter 14

PROGRAM EVALUATION FOR SPECIAL EDUCATION IN OUTCOME-BASED SCHOOLS

David E. Kingsley

Not everything that can be counted counts; and not everything that counts can be counted.

Albert Einstein

Professionals have become discouraged with the data-collection process of traditional program evaluation. For example, conventional measures used to determine whether special education is serving the needs of students include counting the number of students eligible for special programming and calculating the percentage of special education teachers with full certification. Although counting the number of students served or the percentage of teachers certified is a necessary component of accountability, it does not result in information useful for program improvement. In contrast, a more relevant measure of the success of special education programs would be to determine the number of students who are literate and gainfully employed after graduating (Ysseldyke, 1993). Assessing authentic outcomes demonstrated by students who have participated in special programs provides more meaningful data to assess program effectiveness and thereby modify or create excellent services.

OUTCOME-BASED EDUCATION

Outcome-based education (OBE) promotes the identification of student-achievement indicators that enable schools to make informed decisions, which may result in higher and more meaningful student achievement (Ysseldyke, 1993). An outcome-oriented approach attempts to provide (a) a process for program improvement and policy analysis, (b) a system for accountability, and (c) a mechanism for communicating the impact of programs to concerned parties.

The inception of outcome-based education was a response to government policy-makers and new paradigms in business (Spady, 1992). Policy-makers have attempted to set new standards for education with a goal of higher student achievement, expecting subsequently greater productivity of the workforce. Further, many school districts modeled their outcome-based systems after Total Quality Management approaches of industry in which employees identified desired products and collaborated in teams to create those products as well as to monitor the quality of their efforts.

Throughout school districts in North America, there is a rapidly growing movement to restructure schools using an outcome-based education model (Spady, 1992). As conceptualized in education, an "outcome" is a demonstration of learning that occurs at the end of a learning experience. It is an observable demonstration of knowledge, competence, and orientation (attitude, affect, or motivation) within an authentic context. For example, in a traditional setting, students learn about the functions of various levels of government, then they take a paper-and-pen exam in which they demonstrate what they remember and can apply. In comparison, in an outcome-based system, students in a class learning about the functions of government might be assessed through a project in which students determine a community need, ascertain which government office is responsible for that arena, propose a solution, and follow through with implementation using correct procedures. "Based" in this context means to define and direct curriculum, instructional planning, service delivery, and assessment to achieve the desired outcomes. In outcome-based systems, educators and community members determine intended outcomes, then organize and design learning environments to achieve those outcomes.

Over 20 years, the outcome-based movement has gone through three phases, from a micro to a macro conceptualization of outcomes, and has explored what this might mean for educating students (Spady, 1992). In the first phase, outcomes were instructional objectives for students toward which teachers focused their efforts. This became the **traditional** concept of outcomes; it was essentially a mastery approach in which the goals were to improve teacher effectiveness and to increase the number of students doing well according to standard measures. The context was the classroom and the school calendar.

The second phase was **transitional,** examining outcomes in a larger perspective. During this phase, educators reflected on outcomes across disciplines and in the context of higher order competencies. To make outcomes more relevant, educators began to examine "exit outcomes," that is, ultimate goals for students leaving the system. New outcomes included critical thinking, problem-solving, and communication skills. Additionally, this phase introduced the concept of authentic assessment.

The third and current phase is **transformational.** Recent implementers of transformational OBE are questioning the purpose of the educational system, the preparation students need for postschool life, and the restructuring of schools to facilitate the accomplishment of broader life goals. These educators want to examine (a) the conditions current students are likely to find when leaving school, (b) the roles that will be required of them in those conditions, and (c) the learning experiences, processes, and contexts necessary for students to learn to perform those roles.

Traditional OBE necessitates the least change; it requires only that teachers become more efficient and students become better test-takers. Transitional OBE stretches educators to work with each other more effectively and to redesign curriculum to prepare students for leaving the educational system and entering postschool environments. Transformational OBE implies a fundamental redefinition of education. This most recent conceptualization demands that educators understand the purpose of education and the type of experiences in and outside of school buildings that will prepare students for their adult roles in a global society and rapidly changing technological environment.

Clearly, essential components of outcome-based education are the determination of meaningful outcomes and the assessment of whether students are achieving those goals. Programs are successful if students demonstrate the desired knowledge, competence, and orientation. Evaluation of the success of programs is integrally linked with transformation of schools to more effective learning environments.

PROGRAM EVALUATION: SHIFTING PARADIGMS

Program evaluation has been defined as the collection of data for the purpose of making decisions (Cronbach, 1982). Special education leaders are continually involved in making program decisions that should be based on meaningful data resulting from program evaluation activities. Special education administrators are regular participants in program evaluation because (a) it is required by federal, state, and local government, (b) programs should be continually assessed to determine whether they are effective, (c) an individual or a group may be seeking specific information, and (d) evaluation is a critical component of the evolution of education toward a more meaningful experience.

Traditionally, evaluation has been **summative.** That is, at the end of a program, expert evaluators from outside of the program designed evaluation procedures, collected data, and interpreted the results for their clients (McLaughlin, 1990). This type of evaluation has been associated with judgmental behavior by either evaluators or higher-level management. Although summative evaluation is necessary to evaluate the impact of programs and ultimately determine whether programs are viable and should continue, it is critical to collect data while a program is in operation in order to improve services. This type of evaluation is labeled **formative,** as it guides the formation of programs as they are implemented. Unfortunately, although formative evaluation is critical, it is a neglected enterprise in education in general, and in special education in particular (Wolf, 1990).

Stufflebeam (1983) describes the concept of formative evaluation as the context, process, and input aspects of a program rather than the assessment of final program products. Along with this emphasis on formative evaluation, a new paradigm has emerged in which program evaluation is perceived as a support system. In this new paradigm, evaluators are team members who inform others, facilitate the process of examination and change, and interpret data in the context of the situation (McLaughlin, 1990).

The new paradigm of formative evaluation is a process, rather than a product, that continually measures outcomes and their impact on the system. It is typically characterized by four key elements:

1. **Team formation.** A team of stakeholders using whatever technical assistance it chooses to utilize has ultimate responsibility for allocating resources and deciding the focus of evaluation projects.
2. **Focus of the study.** The team must decide what questions need to be answered; specifically it must clarify what its members want to learn and what is important to the stakeholders (Stufflebeam, 1983).
3. **Data collection.** The team determines the potential sources of information, which may include already existing documentation or may involve controlled research. Methodologies are eclectic and may include experimental, quasiexperimental, and nonexperimental quantitative analyses as well as a variety of qualitative approaches such as observation, interviews, and surveys. State-of-the art data management techniques are utilized and made more accessible through microprocessor capability.
4. **Interpretation.** To interpret the data, the team selects standards or expectations and evaluates the information according to these established standards, making decisions regarding both the standards and the program (McLaughlin, 1990). Data are analyzed and interpreted within the context of the program in a manner that stakeholders can utilize.

TEAM FORMATION

The concept of team evaluation implies that no one individual is responsible for or has the authority over all aspects of the program evaluation. The team process involves exchanges among stakeholders to brainstorm and set priorities. Most important, team evaluation means professionals solve problems and make decisions as part of a collaborative process. These interactions require communication skills that professionals in the United States generally do not feel comfortable with or competent to perform. Further, organizations are not typically structured to foster collaboration and teamwork (Thousand & Villa, 1992). The irony of the new age of technology is that instead of requiring less interaction among employees, more is necessary; leaders of organizations have found they have a greater need for the development of human relations skills among staff members than before (Kolodny & Van Beinum, 1983; Toffler, 1990).

Professionals involved in program evaluation must be as adept at facilitating healthy group processes as they are at the technical aspects of data collection and analyses. In fact, as soon as the decision is made to evaluate a program, the staff or consultant should begin the process of assembling an evaluation team.

Patton (1980) suggests a team should have no fewer than three members and no more than 10. Tradition and management style will generally guide team formation. The team should be composed of individuals who can make an important contribution to the process. Teams consist of "decision-makers" (staff and administrators), "influencers" (board members and parents), and "evaluators" (skilled staff and consultants) (McLaughlin, 1990). It has been suggested that teams include stakeholders with some political clout because they might increase the likelihood of dissemination and utilization of evaluation results and recommendations (Patton, 1980). However, committed professionals who desire to improve educational opportunities will be effective, with or without political clout, while politically powerful individuals who operate from agendas that are not in the best interest of students, teachers, and schools may misuse the process and undermine the efforts of the team.

Generally in a special education agency, the director, school psychologist, principal, special education teacher, and professional evaluation consultant will constitute the entire team or will form a core around which a team can be built. If a university or college is near the program, a faculty member with expertise in the special education program area might be invited to participate and contribute to the evaluation team. In some cases, school board members have been invited to join the team in order to garner support or provide input when evaluation results may have a significant impact on the needs of the local education agency. Additionally, it is essential to include parents on a program evaluation team. Their input can facilitate focusing on relevant outcomes and commonsense data-collection procedures.

This new evaluation model does not preclude outside experts, but the framework leads to an internal or "in-house" capability that vests control in local education agencies who need data for management decision-making. Initial efforts at evaluation may not prove to be sophisticated or appear to be as helpful to the district or program as one might wish them to be, but this is a developmental paradigm that stresses progress rather than perfection. The role of experts is to assist the team in generating an evaluation design, facilitating administration of the evaluation plan, and developing decision-making capabilities, rather than taking control and dominating the process by proposing sophisticated procedures and overwhelming the team with technical jargon.

The following teaching case describes a team evaluation of a secondary gifted/talented education program. It has been divided into sections to explore each of the four elements: (a) team formation, (b) focus of the study, (c) data collection, and (d) data interpretation.

Evaluating a Secondary Gifted/Talented Education Program: Team Formation

A special education director in a large, suburban district with six high schools was interested in evaluating its secondary gifted and talented education program. He believed in the team approach to evaluation and therefore developed a list of stakeholders of this program. It included gifted/talented teachers, the coordinator of the gifted/talented program, graduates of the program, parents, high school administrators, and college faculty concerned with gifted education. The director contacted a representative of each of these stakeholder groups and invited them to participate in a program evaluation process.

CONSIDER THIS

List the stakeholders of a special education program in your area of expertise who might be invited to participate on a program evaluation team.

FOCUS OF THE STUDY

Programs have intricately interwoven components that are difficult to separate in order to evaluate areas of strengths and weaknesses. George and George have designed a conceptual scheme to describe and evaluate programs for students with behavioral disorders (Grosenick, George, & George, 1990), which has wide applicability for all special education program evaluation. Their model identifies eight program components that should be considered during evaluation: (a) philosophy, (b) student needs and identification, (c) goals, (d) instructional methods and curriculum, (e) community involvement, (f) program design and operation, (g) exit procedures, and (h) evaluation.

Philosophy The philosophy of an educational program is a statement of its purpose and assumptions about what is important to provide to students, and how best to provide it. It is an operational statement of the values and beliefs that guide the program.

Student needs and identification The needs and identification component describes who qualifies for the program and what process is used to determine qualification. Criteria should be delineated with clear examples and guidelines for evaluating students, including who will be involved in the assessment.

Goals Goals are generally established for all students in special education programs, but, too often, educators do not set goals for the entire program. Goals should be an outgrowth of philosophy, communicating the purpose of the program and the mission of the staff. These goals provide planners and evaluators with standards to measure the success of the program.

Instructional methods and curriculum Daily practices, including subject matter and intervention strategies, are outlined in this component. Methods and content should be consistent with the program's philosophy and goals. Educational practices must reflect current research, substantiating their effectiveness.

Community involvement When programs foster community involvement, they recognize the importance of support from parents, businesses, and social agencies. Formal mechanisms should be established for increasing awareness of the program, developing lines of communication, and facilitating collaboration with parents and community members.

Program design and operation Taking into consideration the philosophy and goals of the program, program design describes the way services are delivered, such as site, type of service, age range, and mechanism for transition to and from the program. It also includes policies and procedures that may have an impact on the quality of services and effective use of resources.

Exit procedures Exit procedures state what behaviors, competencies, and attitudes students will exhibit to demonstrate readiness to leave the program. Determining exit procedures may assist in formulating goals. Further, they describe the process for leaving and who will be involved in the exit procedure. Interestingly, the establishment of exit procedures creates an expectation that students will achieve the stated outcomes of the program.

Evaluation This component describes an ongoing process of data gathering and appraisal of the program by staff, students, and other concerned individuals. The evaluation should address all eight components. Purpose and objectives are established for the program evaluation. All programs can be improved, and one of the primary functions of program evaluation is to gather information to make decisions about improvement. Plans must also be made to assess the effectiveness of the program evaluation.

During program evaluation, each of these eight components is assessed through the use of four questions:

1. Is the component available in written form?
2. Who participates in the development and implementation of this aspect of the program?
3. How effectively is the component communicated to groups associated with the program?
4. How satisfied are participants with the component?

The teaching case continues as the team focuses its evaluation on some of the program components.

Evaluating a Secondary Gifted/Talented Education Program: Focus of the Study

The evaluation team consisted of the gifted education coordinator, a gifted education teacher, general education teacher, a principal, a parent, a graduate of the program, university faculty member, and an evaluation consultant. The coordinator explained to the evaluation team that the school district was interested in evaluating its senior high school gifted education program. The district planned to implement a new "life-skills" program for gifted senior students in the next academic year. The coordinator hoped to build an evaluation process into the implementation of this new program. Team members decided to gather some preliminary data before developing an evaluation plan. They reviewed available documents and interviewed stakeholders such as teachers, students, and parents.

After collecting data from a variety of sources, including consultation with college faculty members and experts in the field, team members decided the first step was to establish program outcomes with which to measure program success. They concluded that the most relevant indicator of the impact of the program was determining what happens to the gifted students after high school graduation, particularly in college, career, and social life.

The question of how to measure the impact of the new life-skills program was addressed. Team members thought it would be unethical to assign some students to the new program while denying others in order to have a "control group." Instead, the evaluation team decided to collect data on current seniors for use in baseline measures against which to compare measures of subsequent graduates who would participate in the life-skills program.

 CONSIDER THIS

1. Spady (1992) described three phases of OBE as traditional, transitional, and transformative. In which phase does this program evaluation appear to be operating?
2. Which of the eight components of the George and George conceptual design for evaluating programs (Grosenick et al., 1990) are addressed by this evaluation team?

DATA COLLECTION

After focusing the study, the team decides what measures would assess the expected outcomes and how this information would be obtained, as well as how the information is to be managed, analyzed, interpreted, and reported. Data is the *sine qua non* of program evaluation. Without data, there is no evaluation. However, the evaluation is only as good as the data collected, and the usefulness of an evaluation depends on the effectiveness of the analysis, interpretation, and reporting.

Many books and articles on program evaluation emphasize complex methodologies involving experimental designs and advanced statistical analyses. More advanced statistics such as correlation, partial correlation, and multiple regression can be helpful but are generally beyond the capability of most local educational agency staff. The evaluation team can request assistance from a local university or other educational agency if more complicated analysis is desired.

There is much to be said for descriptive statistics such as means, medians, modes, and standard deviations. However, the reality of program evaluation in a field setting renders strict control over internal validity impractical at best and unethical at worst. It is unfortunate that graduate programs in educational research and statistics have placed so much emphasis on testing the null hypotheses (i.e., confirmatory data analysis) and so little emphasis on using data to discern patterns and to guide further data collection and analyses (i.e., exploratory data analysis). This is especially true in the case of curriculum-based measurement and criterion-referenced testing (Tindal & Marston, 1990).

There are effective ways to organize complex data that are quite powerful and easily understood by individuals who have not had statistics courses or have forgotten the statistics they reluctantly completed as a prerequisite to a degree. The reader could refer to several good books related to exploratory data analyses for assistance in organizing the massive amount of quantitative information collected by school districts. (See Erickson & Nosanchuk, 1992; Tukey, 1977.) In addition, qualitative techniques such as interviewing, observation, and content analysis can provide potent evidence for decision-making. Among the most helpful and readable works on these methodologies are Eisner and Peshkin (1990), Lincoln and Guba (1985), Merriam (1988), and Patton (1980).

No matter what research methodologies are employed, the program evaluation process must be guided by common sense and relevance to the local education agency, providing a basis for decision-making. Although it has become easier to conduct advanced statistical analyses with user-friendly statistical software, if the data generated by computer programs provide no help to individuals charged with responsibility for program decisions and resource distribution, it is a waste of time. Special education administrators need practical, easily understood data to make decisions about how valuable instructional time, as well as federal, state, and local funds, will be allocated.

The data function is essentially the collecting, managing, analyzing, interpreting, and reporting of data that measure outcomes or success. The ability to utilize data is the "weak link" in education systems, not only in program evaluation but in most aspects of day-to-day management of educational systems. There are several reasons why data utilization has been so poorly developed in the educational establishment. Perhaps math phobia explains some of the problem. However, complicated statistics aside, there are valuable accountability systems that require simple addition, subtraction, and multiplication but are rarely used. The most likely explanation for this phenomenon is the failure to understand and appreciate the viability, feasibility, and utility of collecting data for the purpose of decision-making.

If a school district were to build a new high school that included state-of-the-art vocational education facilities, the program would be designed, constructed, and operated with the tools needed to do the job. Further, the facility would be modern as well as appropriate for teaching sheet metal, carpentry, printing, and other such crafts. To design and construct buildings and programs without full attention to proper tools, including high-tech machines, would be not only ludicrous, it would be malfeasance. Similarly, an athletic program, such as football, also requires tools and equipment such as footballs, helmets, and pads. It would be unthinkable to field a team that was lacking the necessary equipment and, in fact, would probably lead to someone's dismissal.

Yet, school systems rarely have the necessary tools for good data collection, management, and analyses, or if they have them, they do not use them. It is rare to find an educational organization that understands or uses state-of-the-art tools for meeting its data needs. It is more common to find a program evaluation team without expertise in microprocessing evaluation data and with little access to software that would be essential to a professional data system. Although one would hope there are team members with expertise in data processing and analyses, if there are not, it is the responsibility of the team to find the technical assistance necessary.

Data must be well managed; the most economical and efficient management is through effective utilization of microprocessors and software programs. Figure 14.1 represents a model for entering, interpreting, and reporting data. This model suggests the use of certain proprietary software such as EXCEL 4.0, Lotus 1-2-3, FoxPro, and SPSS. Although it is likely some individuals in schools are adept at using one or all of these, many others feel intimidated by spreadsheets, data base programs, and statistical software. However, with few exceptions, statistical packages listed in the model are not difficult to learn. In fact, the entering of data into a data base or spreadsheet should be a secretarial responsibility. Secretaries and paraprofessionals can enter data as well as generate graphs, tables, and other report formats.

FIGURE 14.1
ENTERING, INTERPRETING, AND REPORTING DATA

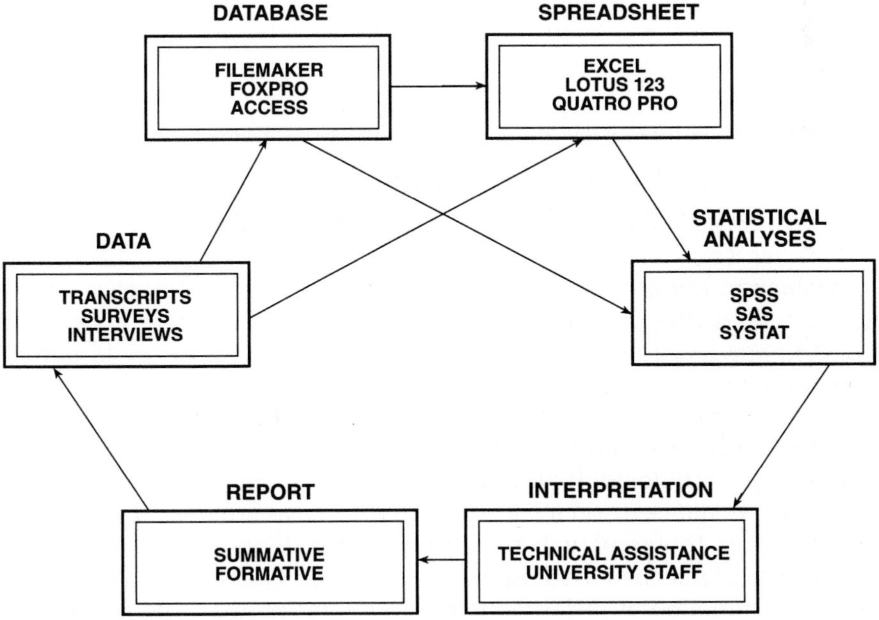

The evaluation team is responsible for reviewing the data management capability of the organization before data collection efforts. The absolute minimum capability that must be available to the team is a data base management system (DBMS). The DBMS could be established with a desktop computer that has 4 MB of RAM and 80 MB hard drive and software programs. The current generation of Macintosh and IBM-compatible desktops is more than adequate to handle the evaluation needs of a very large special education program.

It is critical for an evaluation team to consult with a person knowledgeable about both computers and the construction of data bases. The consultant should be competent to construct a relational data base and know the available hardware and software that would support the needs of the school system.

There is an abundance of easy-to-understand books about data base software packages as well as helpful publications that explain spreadsheet software such as EXCEL 4.0, Lotus 1-2-3, and Quattro Pro. There are times when it is convenient to export data from a data base to a spreadsheet. A spreadsheet arranges data in rows and columns for ease of organization and manipulation. There are other situations when data should be entered directly onto a spreadsheet. It is not always necessary to utilize both spreadsheets and data bases. Data can be exported directly from some data base programs to a statistical package. For instance, there is considerable connectivity between SPSS for Windows and most of the spreadsheet and data base programs mentioned.

A data base related to program evaluation will, at the very least, allow the evaluators to establish some statistical control and set appropriate parameters. In the evaluation of the gifted education program, this means the baseline information from the first cohort is a measure against which subsequent cohorts can be compared.

The teaching case continues as the team turns its attention to the data collection process.

Evaluating a Secondary Gifted/Talented Education Program: Data Collection

The evaluation team decided to focus the study on the impact of the proposed life-skills program on graduates of the gifted/talented program. Because the new program was designed to teach skills that would enhance gifted students' chances of success in postschool life, the team decided to assess outcomes using measures of self-esteem and life skills.

The consultant explained to the group there might be differences in cohorts (groups of students) that would confound the study. That is, the current seniors who would be used for a baseline may have critically different characteristics from the seniors in the new program. Significant differences on any measure of success studied, such as college grade point average, may simply be a function of differences in groups rather than the result of any particular treatment (life-skills program). Therefore, the team decided to collect data from the high school transcripts (IQ, class rank, achievement tests, grade point averages, and number of years in gifted education) to identify variables that could be considered as possible causes of differences between cohorts. With the assistance of a competent researcher, a multivariate analysis could control for or hold constant these variables. Hence, it could be determined whether there were a relationship between the life-skills program and college success apart from influential variables. The team decided it would be valuable to collect this data and conduct these analyses with the researcher's assistance.

Although this seems straightforward, rarely does this type of evaluation take place. Generally, the data requirements are a formidable obstacle. In this large gifted program, there were 120 seniors whose transcripts revealed grade point average, class ranking, memberships in various honor societies, and test scores on achievement tests (some may be taken several times and some include several batteries), all of which may be important in the analyses. Each of these pieces of data (e.g., PSAT Verbal, PSAT Math, class standing) is a separate variable. When these variables were added to measures of both self-esteem and various life-skills instruments, the total number of variables eventually reached 50.

These data were entered onto a spreadsheet by a secretary. In this case, the spreadsheet program utilized was EXCEL 4.0, which is a versatile and powerful software program for arranging data in rows and columns. The technical consultant to the team suggested this program because it was available for the Macintosh computer and also has good connectivity with SPSS, a statistical package commonly used in education. The university faculty member on the evaluation team was adept at conducting statistical analyses with SPSS and was assigned the responsibility for conducting statistical analyses or supervising graduate students in this activity.

Before graduation, team members met with the 120 seniors to explain they would be part of an evaluation project. Students were provided with a packet of information that included questionnaires to be returned to the evaluation team at the end of their first, second, third, fourth, and fifth years following graduation.

These questionnaires included items that indicated levels of success in school and career, as well as a measure of mental well-being and satisfaction with life in general. Addressed and stamped envelopes were included for the students so they would be more likely to return the surveys. Because a 100% return rate was highly improbable, 10 teachers of gifted students from throughout the district volunteered to take responsibility for 12 students each. The students who failed to return their surveys were "tracked down" by the volunteers.

This evaluation design provided a wealth of "rich" data, which was quickly and easily analyzed utilizing computers. It is important to note that the analysis was quick and easy only because the members of the evaluation team were willing to enter data on microprocessor programs.

CONSIDER THIS

1. Evaluate the data collection process the team utilized for this program evaluation.
2. Why did the team select the data on self-esteem, life skills, high school grade point average, and IQ?

DATA INTERPRETATION

Interpretation of results involves a comparison of the collected data to some standard or statement of expectation. Sources of standards include legislation, research, and experience. Analysis may be based on simple descriptive information, or more extensive analysis may involve complex methodologies to produce the desired result. However, even if high–powered analysis is used to determine program effectiveness, the results still must be considered in relation to all other relevant variables before decisions can be made. The comparison of performance to standards is the essence of the evaluation.

It is important to note that both the standards and the program are scrutinized by the team. If the team decides the standards are good but the program does not meet the standards, the decision might be to (a) continue the program until standards are met, (b) modify the program to reduce the discrepancy between the standards and the outcomes of the program, or (c) discontinue the program. If it is decided that standards are inappropriate or unreasonable, the team can revise the standards. Finally, the team could decide the program meets the prescribed standards. At this point, results of the evaluation should be disseminated for others to utilize.

The results of an evaluation procedure must then be organized into a reporting format that best suits the needs of the intended audience. Data may be presented in written or oral form, and may be either formal or informal, depending on the situation. However, the results should be conveyed in some form to everyone involved in order to verify the value of their participation in the process.

Evaluating a Senior Gifted/Talented Education Program: Data Interpretation

The evaluation team researched the computer processing capabilities of the school district for statistical evaluations and made recommendations for the purchase of software. In addition, the team recommended a secretary be trained to enter data into data base and spreadsheet programs. So, not only did the team members prepare for their own statistical needs, they propelled the school district in the direction of better evaluation capabilities.

One year following the graduation of the 120 seniors, 80%, or 96 students, had returned their questionnaires without needing to be contacted. Of the remaining 24, 20 were located. Hence "one year out," a remarkable 97% remained in the follow-up study.

Most of the items on the questionnaire were directly amenable to quantification. For instance, the life satisfaction portion of the survey consisted of several items with which a respondent could agree or disagree on a scale of 1 to 5 (a Likert scale). In addition, there were some "open-ended" questions which yielded qualitative data.

One open-ended question asked respondents to discuss how the gifted program was helpful to their current and recent efforts in college. Another open-ended question was worded: "What suggestions do you have for improvements in the gifted education program, that is, how could it have been more helpful to you?" This was analyzed by a doctoral student with an interest in the use of qualitative data for evaluating educational programs. She codified the responses and organized the resulting data. This student was adept at utilizing computer software designed to assist with the organization of responses to open-ended questions, interview data, and other forms of qualitative data.

Using multiple methods of collecting data to determine causal relationships between phenomena is known as triangulation (Lincoln & Guba, 1985). The team was creative in designing a variety of methods for obtaining and comparing data. It was able to rely on documents (e.g., transcripts), responses to items on a Likert scale, and open-ended questions.

The team's analyses included multivariate statistics such as multiple regression analyses, and more simple statistics such as means and standard deviations. Graphs and charts were created by the computer software (data base, spreadsheet, and statistical).

Analyses indicated that the number of years a student participated in the gifted program was related to most of the indicators of success in college. However, self-esteem and life satisfaction measures seemed to be the true predictors of success in college.

CONSIDER THIS

1. Based on the results of this program evaluation, what might the team recommend to the special education director?
2. What information would be important for all stakeholders to learn from this evaluation?

PROGRAM EVALUATION AS PROCESS

The efforts of the team evaluating the senior high gifted education program were focused on the effectiveness of the overall program rather than on one particular component. Team members did not intend to pass judgment on the gifted program, nor were they charged with the duty of determining whether or not to maintain it. Instead, the purpose of the evaluation was to collect data in order to improve the program. There was a clear understanding this was a formative or "process" evaluation, and the team's intention was to determine what modifications and improvements might be indicated.

Perhaps some component or a smaller program nested within the gifted program (e.g., instruction addressing life skills) might be determined to be of no value and discontinued. In this sense, the evaluation would include a summative dimension. If innovations do not appear to contribute to the overall objective of the program, a decision could be made to discontinue that component. The formative team program evaluation process does not preclude continuance or discontinuance decisions.

There can be no doubt that special education is characterized by legally mandated programs that cannot be summarily discontinued, and state as well as federal law requires compliance monitoring of these programs. Some educators consider process evaluation in special education to be primarily monitoring for compliance (Borich & Nance, 1987). However, this view is too restrictive and does not allow for a continual flow of information for adjusting and correcting a system or program. Compliance monitoring is only one function of process evaluation. Although the collection of data and the flow of information may to some degree be controlled by legislation, evaluation teams can create systems tailored for collecting meaningful information and managing data to make both summative and formative program decisions.

SUMMARY

Educators and policy-makers have begun to reconceptualize education in terms of the outcomes they expect for students to demonstrate. Over two decades, the concept of outcomes has evolved from the idea of students mastering specific learning objectives to a broader understanding of preparing students for post-school life. An integral part of an outcome-based educational system is effective evaluation of programs.

Program evaluation is the purposeful collection of data to make informed decisions. Because of legal mandates and a desire to improve services, special education leaders are continually involved with evaluating programs. A new paradigm of program evaluation emphasizes process or formative evaluation in which there are four key elements: (a) team formation and collaboration, (b) identification of program elements and selection of a focus for the study, (c) development of an effective data-management program with flexibility in utilizing methodologies for collecting and analyzing data, and (d) evaluation of the results with the goal of improving programs rather than making judgments regarding the continuation of programs. Process evaluation is ongoing, providing continual feedback for program improvement and for compliance monitoring.

Teams are composed of stakeholders or individuals concerned with the outcomes of programs. Team evaluation relies primarily on the insights and expertise of individuals within the school district. In addition, outside consultants may provide advice on team process and data collection, management, interpretation, and reporting. Evaluations are most useful when they are relevant to the audience and specific enough to use, when communication is tailored to the stakeholders and ongoing, and when data are interpreted meaningfully and are connected with users' beliefs.

The purpose of the team is to collaborate in identifying the goals of the program and the focus of the investigation. Team members consider all aspects of the program, deciding what evaluation procedures and instruments will answer their questions. They must assess the school district's capabilities for collecting and managing statistical data. New computers and statistical software are more user-friendly than ever and facilitate powerful program evaluations. There is a variety of procedures available, from quantitative multivariate analyses to qualitative tools such as surveys and interviews. Generally, consultants provide technical assistance and train district staff members to utilize computer programs.

The evaluation of the senior high gifted/talented education program demonstrates that a group of educators can work collaboratively to improve a program and the school district. The program benefitted from the data gathered and interpreted by the team. The school district profited from the team's suggestions for increasing the capability for program evaluation by training staff members and purchasing computer hardware and software.

REFERENCES

Borich, G., & Nance, D. (1987). Evaluating special education programs: Shifting the professional mandate from process to outcome. *Remedial and Special Education, 8*(3), 7–15.

Cronbach, L. J. (1982). *Designing evaluations of educational and social programs.* San Francisco: Jossey-Bass.

Eisner, E. W., & Peshkin, A. (1990). *Qualitative inquiry in education: The continuing debate.* New York: Teachers College Press.

Erickson, B. H., & Nosanchuk, T. A. (1992). *Understanding Data.* Toronto: University of Toronto Press.

Grosenick, J., George, M., & George, N. (1990). A conceptual scheme for describing and evaluating programs in behavioral disorders. *Behavioral Disorders, 16*(1), 66–73.

Kolodny, H., & Van Beinum, H. (1983). *The quality of working life and the 1980s.* New York: Praeger.

Lincoln, Y., & Guba, E. (1985). *Naturalistic inquiry.* Newbury Park, CA: Sage Publications.

McLaughlin, J. (1990). *Special education program evaluation: A planning guide.* Richmond, VA: Virginia Department of Education, Special Education Programs.

Merriam, S. B. (1988). *Case study research in education: A qualitative approach.* San Francisco, CA: Jossey-Bass.

Patton, M. Q. (1980). *Qualitative Evaluation Methods.* Newbury Park, CA: Sage Publications.

Rouse, W. H. D. (1956). *Great Dialogues of Plato.* New York: New American Library.

Spady, W. G. (1992). It's time to take a close look at outcome-based education. *Outcomes,* Summer, 6–13.

Stufflebeam, D. (1983). The CIPP model for program evaluation. In Madaus, Scriven, & Stufflebeam (Eds.), *Evaluation models* (pp. 117–141). Boston, MA: Kluwer-Nijhoff.

Thousand, J., & Villa, R. (1992). Collaborative teams: A powerful tool in school restructuring. In Richard Villa, Jacqueline Thousand, William Stainback, & Susan Stainback, (Eds.), *Restructuring for caring and effective education,* (pp. 73–108). Baltimore, MD: Paul H. Brookes.

Tindal, G., & Marston, D. (1990). *Classroom-based assessment.* Columbus, OH: Merrill.

Toffler, A. (1990). *Power shift.* New York: Bantam Books.

Tukey, J. (1977). *Exploratory data analysis.* Reading, MA: Addison-Westly Publishing Co.

Wolf, R. (1990). *Evaluation in education.* New York: Praeger.

Ysseldyke, J. (1993). *Outcome-Based Education: Education and Accountability.* Presentation at the International Council for Exceptional Children, San Antonio, TX, April, 1993.

INDEX